500

LOW CHOLESTEROL

RECIPES

500
LOW CHOLESTEROL
RECIPES

FLAVORFUL HEART-HEALTHY DISHES YOUR
WHOLE FAMILY WILL LOVE

Dick Logue

FAIR WINDS
PRESS
BEVERLY, MASSACHUSETTS

Brimming with creative inspiration, how-to projects, and useful information to enrich your everyday life, Quarto Knows is a favorite destination for those pursuing their interests and passions. Visit our site and dig deeper with our books into your area of interest: Quarto Creates, Quarto Cooks, Quarto Homes, Quarto Lives, Quarto Drives, Quarto Explores, Quarto Gifts, or Quarto Kids.

First published in 2009 by Fair Winds Press,
an imprint of The Quarto Group, 100 Cummings Center,
Suite 265-D, Beverly, MA 01915, USA.
T (978) 282-9590 F (978) 283-2742
www.QuartoKnows.com

Fair Winds titles are also available at discount for retail, wholesale, promotional, and bulk purchase. For details, contact the Special Sales Manager by email at specialsales@quarto.com or by mail at The Quarto Group, Attn: Special Sales Manager, 100 Cummings Center, Suite 265-D, Beverly, MA 01915, USA.

21   9

ISBN-13: 978-1-59233-396-7
ISBN-10: 1-59233-396-6

Library of Congress Cataloging-in-Publication Data
Logue, Dick.
   500 low-cholesterol recipes : flavorful dishes your family will love / Dick Logue.
      p. cm.
   Includes index.
   ISBN-13: 978-1-59233-396-7
   ISBN-10: 1-59233-396-6
   1. Low-cholesterol diet--Recipes. 2. Heart--Diseases--Diet therapy--Recipes. I. Title.
RM237.75.L64 2009
641.5'638--dc22

                          2009012613

Printed in the U.S.A.

Dedication

*To my wife, Ginger DeMarco, who has supported me
through the good recipes and the failures.*

Contents

What Is This Cholesterol Thing Anyway?

These days it seems like the topic of lowering your cholesterol is on everyone's lips. You see articles about it in your local newspaper and ads for medications on TV, and it's become a common topic of conversation. Perhaps you are looking at this book because your doctor told you your cholesterol was "high" or "borderline." It seems that terms like these are thrown out all the time. Perhaps you already have other heart or vascular problems that can be aggravated by elevated cholesterol. Or perhaps you're just trying to eat a heart-healthy diet.

Whatever the reason, you probably have questions like:

- What is cholesterol, and how high does it have to be to be a problem?
- What's all this talk about good and bad cholesterol?
- What kind of changes do I need to make to my diet and lifestyle to lower my cholesterol?
- Who are you and why are you writing this book?

In this introduction, we're going to try to answer some of those questions. We'll look at lowering your cholesterol primarily from a dietary standpoint because, after all, this is a cookbook. But I'll also mention some of the other things that can also help. What I'm not going to do is give you medical advice. You should always talk to your doctor or other health care provider if you have medical questions.

A Quick Basic Course in Cholesterol

To start, let's see if we can come up with a simple explanation of what cholesterol is and how it affects our health. Cholesterol is a fatty substance that exists in all of our bodies. Some of our organs, like the brain and the heart, actually need cholesterol to perform their functions. It travels through the body in the bloodstream and is processed by the liver. So far, that's not a problem. The problem comes when we have excess cholesterol. It can attach itself to the walls of our blood vessels, forming a substance called plaque, which is really just cholesterol that the body stores in a blood vessel and is covered over with a protective coating. But there are several problems with that. One is that the plaque can build up to the point where it can block a blood vessel. This can cause a restriction of blood flow to important organs like the heart and the brain. The other problem occurs if the coating gets broken and the cholesterol gets released back into the bloodstream. This causes the body to send chemicals that help the blood to clot to try and get the cholesterol back under cover and can cause a blood clot. If that clot blocks an artery in the heart, that's what we call a heart attack. If it happens in the brain, that's a stroke.

The next question is what causes us to have high cholesterol. As you've probably heard in the advertisements on television, cholesterol is caused both by genetic factors and your diet. If your parents or grandparents had high cholesterol, the chances increase that you will too. The one thing doctors don't know at this point is whether that elevated risk is caused entirely by genetics or whether people whose parents had bad eating habits tend to eat the same way, meaning that even the hereditary risk may still be caused partly by diet. What we do know is that diet plays a major part in determining cholesterol levels. And the biggest culprit in our diets is saturated fats. Unfortunately, a lot of the things that we like to eat are high in saturated fats, such as fatty meats; fried foods; high-fat dairy products like whole milk, cream, and cheese made from whole milk; and commercial baked products. As we get into the recipes in this book, we'll look at some alternatives that are lower in saturated fats, but still taste good.

What about This Good and Bad Cholesterol?

When your doctor does a blood test to check your cholesterol levels, he's looking for a couple of different things. These are subcomponents of cholesterol, and they are not at all the same in terms of your health. The three primary ones most often tested for are low-density lipo-proteins (LDL), high-density lipoproteins (HDL), and triglycerides. The levels of these cholesterol components are measured in mg/dl, the number of milligrams of the substance in a deciliter of blood. Let take a quick look at each of them.

LDL is commonly referred to as bad cholesterol. It is the part of your total cholesterol that plays the biggest role in blocking your arteries. When LDL attaches to an artery wall, it causes an inflammation that encourages more cholesterol to be deposited there, increasing the risk of a blockage or blood clot. Eating foods high in saturated fats is a major cause of an increase in LDL. The level of LDL that poses a risk is still a subject of discussion, but everyone agrees that anything over 200 mg/dl is dangerous. Some doctors believe that, depending on the source and on what other risk factors (like smoking and being overweight) you may have, even levels over 100 mg/dl may increase your risk of heart attack and stroke.

HDL is usually called the good cholesterol. HDL helps the body rid itself of the cholesterol deposits in the arteries. A high HDL level indicates that you probably have a low risk of heart attack. It has been recommended that men have an HDL of at least 40 mg/dl and women at least 50 mg/dl. The good news is that doing the things that lower your LDL tend to raise your HDL levels. And adding good fat to your diet helps to raise HDL. Some sources are fatty fish like tuna and salmon, olive and canola oil, and the oils found in nuts and soybeans. Some studies even suggest that a moderate amount of alcohol will raise your HDL.

The third major component of a typical cholesterol screening is triglycerides. Like LDL, triglycerides can contribute to a buildup of deposits in the arteries. And like LDL, they are raised by a diet high in saturated fats. It's recommended that triglyceride levels be less than 150 mg/dl.

It should probably be noted that a number of doctors believe that the ratio between HDL and LDL is even more important than the individual numbers. So anything we do to lower our LDL or raise our HDL has a positive effect on that ratio.

How Do I Lower My Cholesterol?

As we've seen, there are a number of factors that contribute to your cholesterol and overall heart health. Some of them, like genetics and age, we have no control over. But others we do. When it comes down to it, there are three main things we can do to lower cholesterol. One is medication, and that is something to take up with your doctor. Another is exercise. Studies have shown that regular exercise can lower cholesterol and reduce the risk of heart disease and stroke. My cardiologist recommends 30 minutes of walking a day as a minimum. It isn't all that difficult, but it does take a commitment.

The final factor is diet. And that is the reason for this book. There are a couple of things we can do from a dietary standpoint that will help. The first thing, which goes hand in hand with exercise, is to maintain your proper body weight. Being overweight is a known risk factor for heart disease.

The second, as mentioned earlier, is to limit the amount of saturated fat in your diet. The good news is that nutrition labels are now required to list the amount of saturated fat, so it's fairly easy to keep track of. But saturated fat isn't the only bad fat. There are also trans fatty acids, or trans fats, which are produced by hydrogenating liquid fat to make it solid at room temperature, like in making margarine. Trans fats are now also listed on the nutrition labels of packaged foods, making them easier to track. If trans fats are not given in the nutritional information, such as in a recipe, you can easily calculate them by taking the total fat and subtracting the saturated fat, monounsaturated fat, and polyunsaturated fat that are listed. That is also true of the nutrition information in this book. In general, any solid fat is bad fat. Also bad are tropical oils like coconut and palm oil. One rule of thumb is that that you should consume no more than 10 percent of your calories per day from saturated fats and trans fats. Since each gram of fat contains about 100 calories, that makes the calculation fairly easy. If you are eating 2,000 calories a day (the number used as a reference on nutrition labels), then 200 of those calories, at the most, should come from saturated fats and trans fat. That would be 20 grams of bad fats per day maximum.

There are also positive diet changes that you can make. Let's take a quick look at some of them here. We'll go into a more detail in Chapter 1 about how to get them into your diet.

Olive and Canola Oils

While we want to limit the amount of fats in our diet to help us maintain our ideal weight, oils like olive and canola can actually help lower cholesterol. They contain polyunsaturated fat, which is the most healthful kind. All of the recipes in this book that contain oil specify either olive or canola.

Fish

The oils in fish contain a compound called omega-3 fatty acids that help reduce blood vessel blockages and clots. Medical experts often recommend that you eat fish at least twice a week.

Soy

Soy protein, such as that found in tofu, soybeans, and soy-based dairy substitutes, contains compounds that encourage blood vessels to dilate effectively so they can supply the blood needed by the body. It also contains antioxidants, which have been shown to help lower the incidence of cancer and heart disease.

Nuts

Like fish, nuts contain omega-3 fatty acids. They are high in calories, though, so you should eat them in moderation.

Oats and Other Whole Grains

Oats and whole grains contain a number of nutrients that are removed from refined grain products like white flour. Oats also contains water-soluble fiber, which has been proven in a number of studies to reduce LDL cholesterol levels without also lowering the HDL levels. Other foods containing significant soluble fiber include beans, barley, and wheat bran.

How This Book Came About

Perhaps the best way to start in telling you who I am is by telling you who I'm not. I'm not a doctor. I'm not a dietician. I'm not a professional chef. What I *am* is an ordinary person just like you who has some special dietary needs. What I am going to do is give you 500 recipes that I have made for myself and my family that I think will put you on the right track to beating high cholesterol through diet. Many of them are the kind of things people cook in their own kitchens all the time, but modified to make them healthier without losing the flavor.

I've enjoyed cooking most of my life. I guess I started seriously about the time my mother went back to work when I was 12 or so. In those days, it was simple stuff like burgers and hot dogs and spaghetti. But the interest stayed. After I married my wife, we got pretty involved in some food-related stuff like growing vegetables in our garden, making bread and other baked goods, canning and jelly making, that kind of thing. She always said that my "mad chemist" cooking was an outgrowth of the time I spent in college as a chemistry major, and she might be right.

Some of you may already know me from my Low Sodium Cooking website and newsletter, or from my *500 Low Sodium Recipes* book. I started thinking about low sodium cooking after being diagnosed with congestive heart failure in 1999. One of the first, and biggest, things I had to deal with was the doctor's insistence that I follow a low sodium diet: 1,200 mg a day or less. At first, I found it easiest just to avoid the things that had a lot of sodium in them. But I was bored. I was convinced that there had to be a way to create low sodium versions of the foods I missed. I researched where to get low sodium substitutes for the things that I couldn't have any more, bought cookbooks, and basically re-did my whole diet.

Along the way, I learned some things. So I decided to try to share this information with others who may in the same position I had been in. I started a website, www.lowsodiumcooking .com, to share recipes and information. I sent out an email newsletter with recipes that now has over 17,000 subscribers. And I wrote my first book.

Everything was going along well. Then the doctor mentioned that my cholesterol had been creeping up and was now at a level where I should start to make some dietary modifications. All of a sudden, the recipes I had weren't what I needed anymore. I'd been using unsalted butter because it was easy to find and tasty. No more, too much saturated fat. The same with eggs and all the fried food and red meat we'd come to love. So it was back to the kitchen to create more recipes, ones that would be low cholesterol as well as low sodium. This book is the result.

How Is the Nutritional Information Calculated?

The nutritional information included with these recipes was calculated using the AccuChef program. It calculates the values using the latest U.S. Department of Agriculture Standard reference nutritional database. I've been using this program since I first started trying to figure out how much sodium was in the recipes I've created. It's inexpensive, easy to use, and has a number of really handy features. AccuChef is available online from www.accuchef.com. They offer a free trial version if you want to try it out, and the full version costs less than $20 USD.

Of course, that implies that these figures are estimates. Every brand of canned tomatoes, or any other product, is a little different in nutritional content. These figures were calculated using products that I buy where I live in southern Maryland. If you use a different brand, your nutrition figures may be different. Use the nutritional analysis as a guideline in determining whether a recipe is right for your diet.

1

What Should I Be Eating?

I would imagine that the title of this chapter is really the key question on the minds of people who pick up this book. If you're looking at a book of low cholesterol recipes, it stands to reason that what you are looking for is information on dietary changes that can help you reduce your cholesterol. We talked very quickly about some of these things in the introduction. Now let's get into details. We're going to cover the areas in the following outline. For each of them, we'll look at how the recipes in this book reflect the recommendations and what you should look for in other foods and recipes.

Foods that tend to raise your cholesterol:

- Saturated fats
- Trans fats
- Foods containing cholesterol

Foods that tend to lower your cholesterol:

- Healthy oils
- Foods containing omega-3 fatty acids
- Foods containing whole grains and soluble fiber

Saturated Fats

Saturated fats are a primary culprit in raising your cholesterol level. In general, saturated fats are fats that are solid at room temperature. There are several categories of saturated fats, and the amount of saturated fat is listed on the U.S. nutrition facts label on packaged foods. This means that *you* are in control of how much saturated fat you eat. A general recommendation from the American Heart Association and others is to limit yourself to no more than 20 grams of saturated fat a day. The recipes in this book will point the way to the cuts of meat and the cooking techniques that will let you meet that goal.

Red Meats

Beef, pork, and lamb are often considered the worst in terms of saturated fat. It's true that they tend to have more than fish or poultry. But how much they have is very dependent on which cut you choose. Some high-fat cuts of beef may contain five times the amount of saturated fat as a lean cut.

Poultry Skin

While not containing as much saturated fat as red meat, poultry skin does have a significant amount. A chicken thigh with the skin has more than 2 grams additional saturated fat compared to the meat only. And this is a case where eliminating that fat is really easy—just don't eat the skin.

Whole-Milk Dairy

Dairy products are another area where making smart choices can significantly reduce the amount of saturated fat. Avoid using products made from whole milk or cream. Choose skim milk, reduced-fat cheeses, and fat-free versions of sour cream and cream cheese. Use fat-free evaporated milk in place of cream.

Tropical Oils

Some plant oils in this category also contain saturated fats. These include palm, palm kernel, and coconut oils, and cocoa butter. They are generally easy to avoid, but be aware that some commercial baked goods and processed foods may contain them.

Trans Fats

Trans fats are also called trans-fatty acids. They are produced by adding hydrogen to vegetable oil through a process called hydrogenation. This makes the fat more solid and less likely to spoil. Although increased awareness of their health risks have started to reduce their use, trans fats are still a common ingredient in commercial baked goods and fried foods. Food manufacturers are required to list trans fat content on nutrition labels. Amounts less than 0.5 grams per serving can be listed as 0 grams trans fat on the food label.

Margarine and Other Hydrogenated Oils

Avoid margarine and solid shortening containing hydrogenated or partially hydrogenated oils. You will see a few recipes in this book that call for margarine where the texture of the food requires solid fat, but in general use liquid or soft margarines whenever possible. We have come to use butter spray bottles, such as I Can't Believe It's Not Butter! Original Buttery Spray, almost exclusively for "buttering" bread and vegetables.

Commercial Baked Goods and Fried Foods

Read ingredient labels and be aware that hydrogenated oils are a common ingredient in commercial baked goods. Even though awareness has increased and many restaurants now fry in oils without trans fats, make sure that you know what you are eating.

Foods Containing Cholesterol

Your body makes all of the cholesterol it needs, but you also get cholesterol from animal products, such as meat, seafood, eggs, and dairy products. While some experts now believe that the amount of cholesterol you eat is less a factor in raised cholesterol levels than was once thought, they still recommend that adults limit their cholesterol intake to 300 mg per day.

Egg Yolks

An egg yolk contains 214 mg of cholesterol, more than two-thirds of the daily maximum recommendation. The good news is that, other than deviled eggs and eggs fried over-easy, I've not found anywhere that you can't use the egg substitute made primarily from egg whites instead of whole eggs. I've even made egg salad by microwaving some, chopping it up, and adding mayonnaise and mustard.

Organ Meats

Beef liver contains over 300 mg of cholesterol per serving; other kinds of liver and organ meats contain similar amounts. I admit I was one of those people who liked liver, but I don't eat it any more.

Shellfish

Shrimp contains over 130 mg of cholesterol per 3-ounce serving. Other shellfish also tends to be higher than meats and fish. I love shellfish, but we now only have it about once a month.

Healthy Oils

When choosing fats, the best choices are monounsaturated and polyunsaturated fats. These fats have been shown to lower your risk of heart disease by reducing the total and LDL (bad) cholesterol levels in your blood.

Monounsaturated Oils

Monounsaturated fats are the healthiest kind. Replace other fats in your diet with them as often as possible. They are usually liquid at room temperature and begin to solidify when refrigerated. Examples are olive, canola, and peanut oils, and the fat found in avocados. The recipes in this book generally use olive oil for cooking and canola oil for baking.

Polyunsaturated Oils

While not having quite the benefits of monounsaturated oils, polyunsaturated oils are still a much better choice than saturated fats and trans fats. They are usually liquid at both room temperature and in the refrigerator and tend to become rancid if stored too long unrefrigerated. Examples are safflower, sesame, soy, corn, and sunflower-seed oils, and the oils in nuts and seeds.

Foods Containing Omega-3 Fatty Acids

One particular kind of polyunsaturated fat, omega-3 fatty acids, may be especially good for your heart. Omega-3 fatty acids appear to decrease the risk of coronary artery disease.

Fish

Recent dietary recommendations usually call for one or two servings of fish a week. Fortunately, fish lends itself to many kinds of recipes. You'll find a number of fish recipes in this book to get you started. Some are specific to one kind of fish, like tuna steaks, but many can be adapted to use whatever you have on hand or find at a good price.

Nuts

Nuts can be added to many foods to give a little extra boost of omega-3s. While they don't contain as much as fish, they are still a healthy addition. Consider using them as salad toppings rather than bacon bits, stir them into baked goods, or add them to your breakfast cereal.

Flaxseed and Soybeans

I have to admit that I've not tried adding flaxseed to recipes. It does contain omega-3 fatty acids, but not the same levels as fish and nuts. We *have* added more soy to our diet, though, finding not only that tofu is good stir-fried, but also that it works great as a substitute for cheese in things like lasagna and enchiladas. You'll find some good tofu recipes scattered throughout this book.

Foods Containing Whole Grains and Soluble Fiber

Soluble fiber has been shown to lower total cholesterol and LDL without affecting the good cholesterol (HDL).

Oats

Oats have certainly gotten the most notice for their cholesterol-fighting abilities. The U.S. Food and Drug Administration was convinced enough to allow medical claims of cholesterol reduction on packages of oatmeal and oat bran. You can easily add oat bran to many foods, such as breading mixes for meat, as well as the more common baked goods. I've included a number of recipes here that include oat bran. The manufacturers of oatmeal and oat bran also provide lots of information on how to include more of their products in your diet.

Beans and Barley

Dried beans and peas contain a significant amount of soluble fiber. So do grains like barley. These products can also help you cut back on saturated fats by being the basis of meals containing little or no meat. Often they are used in soups and stews, and you'll find a variety of recipes here that include them.

Whole Grains

Experts knew that whole grains are healthier than refined grains long before the benefits of soluble fiber were understood. In many cases, it's an easy switch to choose whole-grain products like bread, rice, and pasta rather than their refined counterparts. The great news is that some people find they also taste better.

Fruits and Vegetables

Some fruits and vegetables contain enough soluble fiber to provide benefits. The most common are apples, strawberries, oranges, bananas, carrots, corn, cauliflower, and sweet potatoes.

How Can We Make Our Diets Healthier?

So what did I really do to make my diet healthier than the way I used to eat? In general, here are the guidelines I followed:

- Reduce saturated fats as much as possible by making healthy ingredient choices. Limit the number of servings of red meat each week, and choose lean cuts when it is on the menu. Choose fat-free or reduced-fat dairy products whenever available. Avoiding using tropical oils that contain saturated fat.
- Avoid using trans fats as much as possible. Use olive oil for cooking and canola oil for baking in place of other fats.
- Reduce your total fat intake. While some fats are healthier than others and do provide benefits, it is still recommended that less than 10 percent of your total calories come from fat. Reduce consumption of fried foods and high-fat baked goods. Replace some or all of the fat in baked goods with fruit.
- Avoid whole eggs. Use egg substitute in place of whole eggs wherever possible.

- Reduce consumption of other foods with high cholesterol levels, particularly organ meats and shellfish.
- Increase consumption of omega-3 fatty acids. Eat more fish. Adds nuts to baked goods and salads for an extra omega-3 boost.
- Add more whole grains to your diet. Eat whole-grain breads and other baked goods. Replace white rice with brown. Choose whole-grain pastas over regular.
- Increase the amount of other soluble fiber in your diet. Eat more oat bran, beans, and barley.

Where's the Salt?

One question that may occur to some people looking over the recipes in this book is, "Why is there no salt in any of the ingredient lists?" That's a fair question and deserves an answer. As I said in the Introduction, I first got involved with heart-healthy cooking because my doctor put me on a low sodium diet. It took some time and lots of experimentation, but I learned how to cook things that taste good, are easy to prepare, and are still low in sodium. Along the way, we literally threw away our saltshaker. There's one shaker full of light salt (half salt and half salt substitute) on the table. My wife uses that occasionally. Two of my children have given up salt completely, not because they need to for medical reasons, but because they are convinced like I am that it's the healthy thing to do. When I started looking at creating low cholesterol recipes, going back to using salt wasn't even something I considered.

Most Americans get far more than the 2,400 mg of sodium a day recommended for a healthy adult. This happens without our even thinking about it. In creating these recipes, I was not as strict about the amount of sodium as I usually am. I didn't plan on people buying special sodium-free baking powder that is difficult to find except online. I didn't eliminate most cheeses except Swiss. But I also didn't add any salt. I think if you try the recipes, you'll find that they taste good without it. If you are tempted to add some salt because you think it's needed, I'd suggest you check with your cardiologist or other doctor first. I believe that most of them will agree that in the interest of total heart healthiness, you are better off without the salt.

2

Sauces, Condiments, Mixes, and Spice Blends

When you are trying to reduce the amount of fat in your diet, particularly saturated fat, sauces and condiments can be a problem. White sauce? Let's see, that contains 2 tablespoons (28 g) of butter per cup (235 ml) of sauce, right? Not anymore. This chapter contains some tasty, low fat sauces that you can use in your everyday dishes. It also includes a smattering of other things. There are a couple of low fat baking mixes to use in place of commercial mixes and some condiments that are heart-healthier than anything you can find in the store. And, finally, there are a few spice blends for grilling. While these aren't exactly cholesterol-reducing themselves, perhaps they'll encourage you to try some of the grilling and smoking recipes. These methods of cooking are good for reducing the amount of fat in your final dish, since it's allowed to drip away during the cooking process.

Low Fat White Sauce

Use this recipe to help cut the calories in a variety of dishes calling for a white sauce, such as pastas, rice, casseroles, etc.

6 tablespoons (48 g) flour

3 cups (710 ml) skim milk, divided

¼ teaspoon (0.6 g) ground nutmeg

¼ cup (60 ml) egg substitute

In a heavy medium saucepan, whisk flour to remove any lumps. Gradually add 1 cup (235 ml) milk, whisking until smooth. Add remaining 2 cups (475 ml) of milk and nutmeg. Cook over medium heat, whisking constantly, about 10 minutes, until mixture thickens and boils. Remove from heat. Whisk a little of the mixture into the egg substitute. Then add the egg substitute mixture to the rest of the white sauce mixture, whisking constantly. Season to taste.

Yield: 6 servings

Per serving: 88 calories (8% from fat, 32% from protein, 60% from carbohydrate); 7 g protein; 1 g total fat; 0 g saturated fat; 0 g monounsaturated fat; 0 g polyunsaturated fat; 13 g carbohydrate; 0 g fiber; 0 g sugar; 159 mg phosphorus; 183 mg calcium; 1 mg iron; 91 mg sodium; 267 mg potassium; 287 IU vitamin A; 75 mg ATE vitamin E; 1 mg vitamin C; 3 mg cholesterol; 120 g water

TIP *Can be made ahead, covered, and refrigerated. Reheat before using.*

Low Fat Cheese Sauce

A low fat, full-flavored cheese sauce you can use over vegetables or for macaroni and cheese. The cream cheese gives it an extra richness.

2 cups (475 ml) skim milk

2 tablespoons (16 g) cornstarch

1 cup (120 g) low fat cheddar cheese, shredded

8 ounces (225 g) fat free cream cheese, cubed

Combine the milk and the cornstarch in a saucepan. Bring slowly to almost the boiling point, stirring constantly. Cook at this temperature until the milk begins to thicken. Remove from heat and stir in the cheeses. Let stand until the cheese melts, then stir or whisk until smooth.

Yield: 4 servings

Per serving: 123 calories (20% from fat, 43% from protein, 37% from carbohydrate); 13 g protein; 3 g total fat; 2 g saturated fat; 1 g monounsaturated fat; 0 g polyunsaturated fat; 11 g carbohydrate; 0 g fiber; 0 g sugar; 298 mg phosphorus; 313 mg calcium; 0 mg iron; 275 mg sodium; 246 mg potassium; 318 IU vitamin a; 95 mg ATE vitamin e; 1 mg vitamin c; 9 mg cholesterol; 131 g water

Tofu Mayonnaise

This recipe makes a low fat, almost sodium-free, egg-free mayo—or mayo substitute, I suppose, is more accurate. At any rate, it works well for dishes like potato or tuna salads where there tend to be other flavors that predominate, because it isn't quite the same flavor as real mayonnaise.

½ pound (225 g) firm tofu

½ teaspoon (1.5 g) dry mustard

⅛ teaspoon (0.3 g) cayenne pepper

2 tablespoons (30 ml) fresh lemon juice

2 tablespoons (30 ml) olive oil

2 tablespoons (30 ml) water

In a food processor or blender, process tofu, mustard, cayenne pepper, and lemon juice until mixed. With machine still running add oil very slowly and then add water. Blend until smooth. Stop the machine a few times during processing and scrape the sides. Keeps up to 3 months when refrigerated in an airtight container.

Yield: 12 servings

Per serving: 32 calories (76% from fat, 16% from protein, 8% from carbohydrate); 1 g protein; 3 g total fat; 0 g saturated fat; 2 g monounsaturated fat; 1 g polyunsaturated fat; 1 g carbohydrate; 0 g fiber; 0 g sugar; 17 mg phosphorus; 6 mg calcium; 0 mg iron; 7 mg sodium; 41 mg potassium; 8 IU vitamin A; 0 mg ATE vitamin E; 1 mg vitamin C; 0 mg cholesterol; 21 g water

Creamy Lemon Sauce

Another fat-free sauce, this one is great heated over fish or broccoli or as a topping for fruit.

1 cup (230 g) fat-free sour cream

1 teaspoon (1.7 g) grated lemon peel

2 tablespoons (30 ml) lemon juice

½ teaspoon (2 g) sugar

In a medium bowl, combine sour cream, lemon peel, lemon juice, and sugar; mix until well blended.

Yield: 6 servings

Per serving: 57 calories (0% from fat, 32% from protein, 68% from carbohydrate); 1 g protein; 0 g total fat; 0 g saturated fat; 0 g monounsaturated fat; 0 g polyunsaturated fat; 3 g carbohydrate; 0 g fiber; 1 g sugar; 39 mg phosphorus; 43 mg calcium; 0 mg iron; 17 mg sodium; 59 mg potassium; 151 IU vitamin A; 40 mg ATE vitamin E; 3 mg vitamin C; 16 mg cholesterol; 37 g water

Reduced-Fat Creamy Chicken Sauce

An easy white sauce recipe. The chicken broth and onion give it additional flavor.

2 tablespoons (20 g) onion, minced

½ cup (120 ml) low sodium chicken broth

⅓ cup (40 g) flour

2 cups (475 ml) skim milk

½ cup (120 ml) dry white wine

1 teaspoon (2 g) chicken bouillon

TIP *This makes a good base for an Italian sauce, with the addition of some Italian seasoning and Parmesan cheese.*

Cook onion and broth in a 1-quart (946-ml) saucepan until liquid is almost all cooked away. In a small bowl, whisk flour with the milk. Add to the onion mixture in the saucepan and continue to cook, whisking, until sauce begins to thicken. Add wine and bouillon and whisk to combine.

Yield: 4 servings

Per serving: 120 calories (6% from fat, 27% from protein, 67% from carbohydrate); 7 g protein; 1 g total fat; 0 g saturated fat; 0 g monounsaturated fat; 0 g polyunsaturated fat; 16 g carbohydrate; 0 g fiber; 1 g sugar; 165 mg phosphorus; 183 mg calcium; 1 mg iron; 91 mg sodium; 289 mg potassium; 250 IU vitamin A; 75 mg ATE vitamin E; 2 mg vitamin C; 2 mg cholesterol; 170 g water

Cottage Cheese Sauce

This sounds a little strange, but it makes a nice creamy sauce with just a little cheese flavor, and it's fat-free.

1 cup (226 g) nonfat cottage cheese

1 cup (235 ml) skim milk

2 tablespoons (30 ml) water

2 tablespoons (16 g) cornstarch

In blender, blend cottage cheese and milk. Pour into a saucepan and heat almost to a boil. Set aside. Add the water to the cornstarch and mix to a paste. Add to cottage cheese mixture in saucepan and stir well. Cook 10 minutes, stirring constantly until thickened.

Yield: 4 servings

Per serving: 71 calories (4% from fat, 51% from protein, 45% from carbohydrate); 9 g protein; 0 g total fat; 0 g saturated fat; 0 g monounsaturated fat; 0 g polyunsaturated fat; 8 g carbohydrate; 0 g fiber; 1 g sugar; 107 mg phosphorus; 100 mg calcium; 0 mg iron; 42 mg sodium; 124 mg potassium; 136 IU vitamin A; 41 mg ATE vitamin E; 1 mg vitamin C; 4 mg cholesterol; 92 g water

Cabernet Sauce

This sauce is great served over steak. If you pan-fry the steak, you could use the same pan for the sauce, adding extra flavor.

¼ cup (40 g) onion, chopped

¾ cup (53 g) mushrooms, sliced

1 tablespoon (8 g) flour

½ cup (120 ml) cabernet sauvignon

¼ cup (60 ml) low sodium chicken broth

1 tablespoon (2.7 g) dried thyme

Spray a medium-sized nonstick skillet with olive oil spray. Over medium heat, sauté onions and mushrooms until softened, about 4 to 5 minutes. Add flour to the skillet and mix with vegetables until dissolved. Raise the heat and add the wine. Cook 1 minute. Add the broth and thyme. Cook 4 minutes to reduce liquid and thicken. Add pepper to taste. Spoon sauce over steak.

Yield: 2 servings

Per serving: 87 calories (8% from fat, 19% from protein, 73% from carbohydrate); 2 g protein; 0 g total fat; 0 g saturated fat; 0 g monounsaturated fat; 0 g polyunsaturated fat; 9 g carbohydrate; 1 g fiber; 2 g sugar; 58 mg phosphorus; 40 mg calcium; 3 mg iron; 14 mg sodium; 230 mg potassium; 57 IU vitamin A; 0 mg ATE vitamin E; 3 mg vitamin C; 0 mg cholesterol; 122 g water

Roasted Red Pepper Sauce

I developed this sauce when I had a good crop of red Italian peppers in the garden. It's a simple sauce that is great over pasta or chicken.

4 red bell peppers

½ cup (115 g) fat-free sour cream

¼ teaspoon (0.5 g) black pepper

½ teaspoon (1.6 g) garlic powder

Preheat broiler. Place peppers on a baking sheet and broil until the skin blackens and blisters, turning frequently. Place in a paper bag and seal until cooled to loosen skin. Remove skin and place peppers in a blender or food processor and process until smooth. Add remaining ingredients; blend well. May be heated or used cold over meat or pasta.

Yield: 6 servings

Per serving: 48 calories (7% from fat, 18% from protein, 75% from carbohydrate); 1 g protein; 0 g total fat; 0 g saturated fat; 0 g monounsaturated fat; 0 g polyunsaturated fat; 6 g carbohydrate; 2 g fiber; 3 g sugar; 40 mg phosphorus; 27 mg calcium; 0 mg iron; 11 mg sodium; 187 mg potassium; 2408 IU vitamin A; 20 mg ATE vitamin E; 95 mg vitamin C; 8 mg cholesterol; 85 g water.

Fat-Free Fajita Marinade

Marinate chicken or beef in this, then grill and slice thinly for easy fajitas. You won't miss the fat that is in most marinades at all.

¼ cup (60 ml) red wine vinegar

2 tablespoons (30 ml) Worcestershire sauce

2 tablespoons (30 ml) lemon juice

2 tablespoons (30 ml) lime juice

½ teaspoon (1 g) black pepper

1 tablespoon (4 g) cilantro

1 tablespoon (7 g) cumin

1 teaspoon (3 g) garlic powder

1 teaspoon (1 g) dried oregano

Mix ingredients together and use to marinate beef or chicken at least 6 hours or overnight.

Yield: 8 servings

Per serving: 11 calories (15% from fat, 12% from protein, 73% from carbohydrate); 0 g protein; 0 g total fat; 0 g saturated fat; 0 g monounsaturated fat; 0 g polyunsaturated fat; 2 g carbohydrate; 0 g fiber; 0 g sugar; 11 mg phosphorus; 11 mg calcium; 1 mg iron; 39 mg sodium; 65 mg potassium; 47 IU vitamin A; 0 mg ATE vitamin E; 10 mg vitamin C; 0 mg cholesterol; 15 g water

Enchilada Sauce

You can make your own enchilada sauce that not only tastes better, but also is healthier than any you can buy in a can or jar. Plus, you can make it as mild or hot as you like. Dried chili peppers are available in the fresh food section of larger grocery stores. There are usually several varieties of varying heat levels. The most common are labeled New Mexico (spicy) or California (mild) chilis. The ones I get are 3 ounces (85 g) per bag, and I usually use one bag of each, giving a fairly mild sauce.

6 ounces (170 g) dried chilis
2 quarts (1.9 L) water
1 teaspoon (3 g) garlic, minced

Wash and remove the stems from the chilis, but do not remove the seeds. Placed washed chilis in a pot with just enough water to cover. If the chilis float, just push them down with a wooden spoon. Cook over medium heat for 45 minutes or until softened, adding water if necessary. Allow them to cool to a warm temperature. Remove chilis from the liquid and reserve liquid. Put chilis in a blender, and add a cup of liquid and the garlic. Start the blender on low and increase speed to high. Run the blender on high until the mixture is a smooth consistency (this may take 5 to 10 minutes). When the chilis are completely blended you should not see seeds. If the sauce is too thick, add water for a smoother consistency.

Yield: 32 servings

Per serving: 17 calories (14% from fat, 11% from protein, 75% from carbohydrate); 1 g protein; 0 g total fat; 0 g saturated fat; 0 g monounsaturated fat; 0 g polyunsaturated fat; 4 g carbohydrate; 2 g fiber; 2 g sugar; 9 mg phosphorus; 4 mg calcium; 0 mg iron; 7 mg sodium; 100 mg potassium; 1408 IU vitamin A; 0 mg ATE vitamin E; 2 mg vitamin C; 0 mg cholesterol; 60 g water

Tomato and Avocado Salsa

Can't make up your mind if you want salsa or guacamole? Then have both together!

5 plum tomatoes

¼ cup (40 g) red onion, diced

1 jalapeño, seeded and chopped

1 avocado, diced

2 tablespoons (30 ml) lime juice

1 tablespoon (4 g) cilantro

Halve the tomatoes and remove the seeds, then chop finely. Put into a bowl with other ingredients. Stir to mix.

Yield: 8 servings

Per serving: 34 calories (65% from fat, 6% from protein, 30% from carbohydrate); 1 g protein; 3 g total fat; 0 g saturated fat; 2 g monounsaturated fat; 0 g polyunsaturated fat; 3 g carbohydrate; 1 g fiber; 1 g sugar; 14 mg phosphorus; 5 mg calcium; 0 mg iron; 2 mg sodium; 125 mg potassium; 140 IU vitamin A; 0 mg ATE vitamin E; 5 mg vitamin C; 0 mg cholesterol; 31 g water

Dick's Reduced-Sodium Soy Sauce

Even though sodium is not directly tied to cholesterol, it is definitely connected to heart health. Soy sauce, even the reduced-sodium kinds, contains more sodium than many people's diets can stand. A teaspoonful often contains at least a quarter of the daily amount of sodium that is recommended for a healthy adult. If you have heart disease or are African American, the recommendation is even less. This sauce gives you real soy sauce flavor while holding the sodium to a level that should fit in most people's diets.

4 tablespoons (24 g) sodium-free beef bouillon

¼ cup (60 ml) cider vinegar

2 tablespoons (30 ml) molasses

1½ cups (355 ml) boiling water

⅛ teaspoon (0.3 g) black pepper

⅛ teaspoon (0.2 g) ground ginger

¼ teaspoon (0.8 g) garlic powder

¼ cup (60 ml) reduced-sodium soy sauce

Combine ingredients, stirring to blend thoroughly. Pour into jars. Cover and seal tightly. Keeps indefinitely if refrigerated.

Yield: 48 servings

Per serving: 6 calories (13% from fat, 11% from protein, 76% from carbohydrate); 0 g protein; 0 g total fat; 0 g saturated fat; 0 g monounsaturated fat; 0 g polyunsaturated fat; 1 g carbohydrate; 0 g fiber; 1 g sugar; 3 mg phosphorus; 4 mg calcium; 0 mg iron; 52 mg sodium; 19 mg potassium; 3 IU vitamin A; 0 mg ATE vitamin E; 0 mg vitamin C; 0 mg cholesterol; 10 g water

Dick's Reduced-Sodium Teriyaki Sauce

The story on this recipe is the same as the soy sauce. In this case, you can sometimes find commercial teriyaki sauces that aren't too high in sodium, but this one is much lower and, to my mind, tastes just as good, if not better.

1 cup (235 ml) Dick's Reduced-Sodium Soy Sauce
(see recipe page 30)

1 tablespoon (15 ml) sesame oil

2 tablespoons (30 ml) mirin wine

½ cup (100 g) sugar

2 cloves garlic, crushed

Two ⅛-inch (31-mm) slices ginger root

Dash black pepper

TIP *Mirin is a sweet Japanese rice wine; you can substitute sherry or sake.*

Combine all ingredients in a saucepan and heat until the sugar is dissolved. Store in the refrigerator.

Yield: 20 servings

(continued on page 32)

Per serving: 37 calories (2% from fat, 0% from protein, 98% from carbohydrate); 0 g protein; 1 g total fat; 0 g saturated fat; 0 g monounsaturated fat; 2 g polyunsaturated fat; 84 g carbohydrate; 0 g fiber; 7 g sugar; 10 mg phosphorus; 7 mg calcium; 0 mg iron; 83 mg sodium; 32 mg potassium; 5 IU vitamin A; 0 mg ATE vitamin E; 0 mg vitamin C; 0 mg cholesterol; 17 g water

Chipotle Marinade

Depending on the peppers you use, this can be hot or not. The ancho chilis are less hot than some. A serving is one tablespoon.

2 ounces (55 g) dried ancho chilis

1 teaspoon (2 g) black pepper

2 teaspoons (4.7 g) cumin

2 tablespoons (8 g) fresh oregano, chopped

1 small red onion, quartered

½ cup (120 ml) lime juice

½ cup (120 ml) cider vinegar

3 cloves garlic, peeled

1 cup (60 g) fresh cilantro

½ cup (120 ml) olive oil

Soak dry chilis in water overnight, or until soft. Remove seeds. Place chilis and remaining ingredients in a food processor or blender and process until smooth.

Yield: 32 servings

Per serving: 39 calories (79% from fat, 3% from protein, 18% from carbohydrate); 0 g protein; 4 g total fat; 0 g saturated fat; 2 g monounsaturated fat; 0 g polyunsaturated fat; 2 g carbohydrate; 1 g fiber; 0 g sugar; 7 mg phosphorus; 8 mg calcium; 0 mg iron; 2 mg sodium; 67 mg potassium; 467 IU vitamin A; 0 mg ATE vitamin E; 2 mg vitamin C; 0 mg cholesterol; 11 g water

Chipotle Sauce

This creamy sauce can be used in a number of dishes and is traditional for fish tacos.

½ cup (115 g) low fat mayonnaise

½ cup (115 g) fat-free sour cream

¼ cup (60 ml) Chipotle Marinade (see recipe page 32)

Mix ingredients and chill.

Yield: 10 servings

Per serving: 56 calories (82% from fat, 4% from protein, 14% from carbohydrate); 0 g protein; 4 g total fat; 1 g saturated fat; 0 g monounsaturated fat; 0 g polyunsaturated fat; 2 g carbohydrate; 0 g fiber; 1 g sugar; 18 mg phosphorus; 13 mg calcium; 0 mg iron; 101 mg sodium; 22 mg potassium; 67 IU vitamin A; 12 mg ATE vitamin E; 0 mg vitamin C; 9 mg cholesterol; 16 g water

Bread and Butter Onions

Okay, I admit there isn't really anything about this recipe that is, by itself, good for your cholesterol. But I made a batch of these this summer after seeing them at an Amish stand at the local farmer's market, and I've become fond of them as a condiment with a number of things. They just add a nice little extra bit of flavor.

4 onions

1¼ cups (300 ml) cider vinegar

1¼ cups (250 g) sugar

½ teaspoon (1.1 g) turmeric

½ teaspoon (1.8 g) mustard seed

¼ teaspoon (0.5 g) celery seed

(continued on page 34)

Thinly slice onions and separate into rings. In a saucepan, combine vinegar, sugar, turmeric, mustard seed, and celery seed. Heat to boiling. Add onions. Heat 2 to 3 minutes. Chill and serve. May be stored in the refrigerator for one month. For longer storage, sterilize two pint (475 ml) jars. Pack hot pickles to within ½ inch (1.3 cm) of the top. Wipe off the rim, screw on the lid, and place in a Dutch oven or other deep pan. Cover with hot water, bring to a boil, and cook 5 minutes.

Yield: 32 servings

Per serving: 41 calories (1% from fat, 2% from protein, 97% from carbohydrate); 0 g protein; 0 g total fat; 0 g saturated fat; 0 g monounsaturated fat; 0 g polyunsaturated fat; 10 g carbohydrate; 0 g fiber; 9 g sugar; 7 mg phosphorus; 6 mg calcium; 0 mg iron; 1 mg sodium; 38 mg potassium; 0 IU vitamin A; 0 mg ATE vitamin E; 1 mg vitamin C; 0 mg cholesterol; 27 g water

Reduced-Fat Biscuit Mix

This makes a mix similar to Reduced Fat Bisquick, but mine is even lower in fat. Use it in any recipes that call for baking mix.

6 cups (750 g) flour

3 tablespoons (41.5 g) **baking powder**

⅓ cup (75 g) unsalted **margarine**

Stir flour and baking powder together. Cut in margarine with pastry blender or two knives until mixture resembles coarse crumbs. Store in a container with a tight-fitting lid.

Yield: 12 servings

Per serving: 274 calories (19% from fat, 10% from protein, 72% from carbohydrate); 7 g protein; 6 g total fat; 1 g saturated fat; 3 g monounsaturated fat; 1 g polyunsaturated fat; 49 g carbohydrate; 2 g fiber; 0 g sugar; 146 mg phosphorus; 216 mg calcium; 3 mg iron; 422 mg sodium; 73 mg potassium; 267 IU vitamin A; 61 mg ATE vitamin E; 0 mg vitamin C; 0 mg cholesterol; 9 g water

Reduced-Fat Whole Wheat Biscuit Mix

I use this mix almost all the time in place of the white flour one.

4 cups (500 g) flour

2 cups (250 g) whole wheat flour

3 tablespoons (41.5 g) baking powder

⅓ cup (75 g) unsalted margarine

Stir flours and baking powder together. Cut in margarine with pastry blender or two knives until mixture resembles coarse crumbs. Store in a container with a tight-fitting lid.

Yield: 12 servings

Per serving: 266 calories (19% from fat, 11% from protein, 70% from carbohydrate); 7 g protein; 6 g total fat; 1 g saturated fat; 3 g monounsaturated fat; 1 g polyunsaturated fat; 47 g carbohydrate; 4 g fiber; 0 g sugar; 193 mg phosphorus; 220 mg calcium; 3 mg iron; 422 mg sodium; 132 mg potassium; 268 IU vitamin A; 61 mg ATE vitamin E; 0 mg vitamin C; 0 mg cholesterol; 8 g water

Beer Mop

You can use this on any grilled or smoked meat, but it is particularly good on pork.

12 ounces (355 ml) beer

½ cup (120 ml) cider vinegar

¼ cup (60 ml) olive oil

½ teaspoon (1.5 g) minced garlic

1 tablespoon (9 g) onion powder

1 tablespoon (15 ml) Worcestershire sauce

1 tablespoon (8 g) The Wild Rub or The Mild Rub (see recipes pages 37–38)

Combine ingredients in a saucepan and heat. Use warm on grilling or smoking meat.

Yield: 24 servings

(continued on page 36)

Per serving: 29 calories (83% from fat, 2% from protein, 15% from carbohydrate); 0 g protein; 2 g total fat; 0 g saturated fat; 2 g monounsaturated fat; 0 g polyunsaturated fat; 1 g carbohydrate; 0 g fiber; 0 g sugar; 4 mg phosphorus; 2 mg calcium; 0 mg iron; 7 mg sodium; 15 mg potassium; 1 IU vitamin A; 0 mg ATE vitamin E; 1 mg vitamin C; 0 mg cholesterol; 18 g water

Smoky Chicken Rub

I recently discovered smoked paprika. It is wonderful to add a smoky flavor to food even if you aren't going to grill it. You should be able to find it in your local grocery store. This rub adds a great flavor to chicken, whether you grill it, smoke it, cook it on a rotisserie, or just oven roast it.

3 tablespoons (21 g) smoked paprika

1 tablespoon (6.4 g) freshly ground black pepper

1 tablespoon (6.5 g) celery seed

1 tablespoon (13 g) sugar

1 tablespoon (9 g) dry mustard

1 tablespoon (9 g) onion powder

1½ teaspoons (4 g) poultry seasoning

1 tablespoon (2.7 g) dried thyme

Combine all ingredients, mixing well. Store in an airtight container. Makes enough for one large roasting chicken or two small chickens.

Yield: 8 servings

Per serving: 32 calories (21% from fat, 11% from protein, 68% from carbohydrate); 1 g protein; 1 g total fat; 0 g saturated fat; 0 g monounsaturated fat; 0 g polyunsaturated fat; 6 g carbohydrate; 2 g fiber; 2 g sugar; 23 mg phosphorus; 58 mg calcium; 3 mg iron; 4 mg sodium; 113 mg potassium; 1446 IU vitamin A; 0 mg ATE vitamin E; 3 mg vitamin C; 0 mg cholesterol; 1 g water

The Wild Rub

A traditional southern dry rub for barbecue, typically rubbed into the meat and allowed to flavor it overnight in the refrigerator before long, low heat cooking. The main ingredient is paprika, so if you plan to do a lot of grilling or smoking, you may want to get a big bottle at one of the warehouse clubs like Sam's or BJ's. The rub tends to be a bit on the spicy side, so if you don't like your food hot, you may want to try The Mild Rub (see page 38).

½ cup (56 g) paprika

3 tablespoons (19 g) freshly ground black pepper

¼ cup (60 g) brown sugar

2 tablespoons (15 g) chili powder

2 tablespoons (18 g) onion powder

2 tablespoons (18 g) garlic powder

2 teaspoons (3.6 g) cayenne pepper

Mix well, and store in a cool, dark place.

Yield: 22 servings

Per serving: 26 calories (15% from fat, 10% from protein, 76% from carbohydrate); 1 g protein; 1 g total fat; 0 g saturated fat; 0 g monounsaturated fat; 0 g polyunsaturated fat; 6 g carbohydrate; 2 g fiber; 3 g sugar; 15 mg calcium; 1 mg iron; 10 mg sodium; 109 mg potassium; 1595 IU vitamin A; 0 mg ATE vitamin E; 3 mg vitamin C; 0 mg cholesterol; 1 g water

The Mild Rub

A sweeter, less spicy rub for grilling and smoking.

½ cup (56 g) paprika

2 tablespoons (13 g) freshly ground black pepper

⅓ cup (75 g) brown sugar

2 tablespoons (15 g) chili powder

2 tablespoons (18 g) onion powder

2 tablespoons (18 g) garlic powder

Mix well, and store in a cool, dark place.

Yield: 22 servings

Per serving: 28 calories (13% from fat, 9% from protein, 78% from carbohydrate); 1 g protein; 0 g total fat; 0 g saturated fat; 0 g monounsaturated fat; 0 g polyunsaturated fat; 6 g carbohydrate; 1 g fiber; 4 g sugar; 15 mg calcium; 1 mg iron; 10 mg sodium; 105 mg potassium; 1527 IU vitamin A; 0 mg ATE vitamin E; 3 mg vitamin C; 0 mg cholesterol

3

Appetizers and Snacks

Appetizers and snacks can be a real problem for people trying to watch their fat intake. Don't believe me? Chili's Awesome Blossom contains over 200 grams of fat, the equivalent of 67 slices of bacon. But it doesn't have to be so. Only one of the recipes in this chapter has as much as 2 grams of saturated fat per serving. These are the kind of snacks you can serve your family or your guests and feel good that they are healthy as well as tasty.

Reduced-Fat Pesto

This makes a fairly typical pesto, but lower in fat and sodium than commercial ones.

TIP

Serve over pasta or on toasted bread.

2 cups (80 g) packed fresh basil

3 tablespoons (27 g) pine nuts

1 teaspoon (3 g) finely minced garlic

¼ cup (25 g) grated Parmesan cheese

¼ cup (60 ml) olive oil

Place basil leaves in small batches in food processor and process until well chopped (do about ¾ cup (30 g) at a time). Add one-third of the pine nuts and garlic and blend again. Add one-third of the Parmesan cheese; blend while slowly adding one-third of the olive oil, stopping to scrape down the sides of the container. Process until it forms a thick, smooth paste. Repeat until all ingredients are used; mix all batches together well. Pesto keeps in the refrigerator one week, or a few months in the freezer.

Yield: 12 servings

Per serving: 77 calories (73% from fat, 9% from protein, 18% from carbohydrate); 2 g protein; 7 g total fat; 1 g saturated fat; 4 g monounsaturated fat; 1 g polyunsaturated fat; 4 g carbohydrate; 2 g fiber; 0 g sugar; 55 mg phosphorus; 142 mg calcium; 3 mg iron; 34 mg sodium; 208 mg potassium; 535 IU vitamin A; 2 mg ATE vitamin E; 4 mg vitamin C; 2 mg cholesterol; 1 g water

Reduced-Fat Sun-Dried Tomato Pesto

¼ cup (40 g) walnuts

½ cup (55 g) oil-packed sun-dried tomatoes

¼ cup (25 g) grated Parmesan cheese

½ teaspoon (1.5 g) minced garlic

2 tablespoons (30 ml) olive oil

¼ teaspoon (0.5 g) pepper

Preheat oven to 375°F (190°C, or gas mark 5). Toast the nuts for 7 to 8 minutes; let cool. Drain the oil from the tomatoes. In a food processor, combine all ingredients. Process until smooth.

Yield: 8 servings

Per serving: 82 calories (78% from fat, 12% from protein, 10% from carbohydrate); 3 g protein; 8 g total fat; 1 g saturated fat; 4 g monounsaturated fat; 2 g polyunsaturated fat; 2 g carbohydrate; 1 g fiber; 0 g sugar; 53 mg phosphorus; 41 mg calcium; 0 mg iron; 66 mg sodium; 133 mg potassium; 107 IU vitamin A; 4 mg ATE vitamin E; 7 mg vitamin C; 3 mg cholesterol; 5 g water

TIP *Serve this as a spread for Italian bread, on a sandwich, or (my particular favorite) mixed with warm pasta.*

Crostini with Mushrooms

Another appetizer that's fancy enough to serve to company, but still easy to make.

2 cups (140 g) mushrooms, whole

1 tablespoon (15 ml) olive oil

¼ teaspoon (0.8 g) crushed garlic

1 tablespoon (4 g) fresh parsley, chopped

12 slices Italian bread, sliced ¼-inch (0.64 cm) thick

Clean and cut the mushrooms into very thin little pieces. In a large saucepan, heat oil with crushed garlic. Cook over medium heat until the garlic turns light brown, and then add the mushrooms. Cook the mushrooms for 10 minutes, or until the liquid from the mushrooms dries. Turn off the heat and allow to cool. Add parsley and stir. Toast the bread and spread the mushroom mixture on top. Serve at once.

Yield: 6 servings

Per serving: 188 calories (21% from fat, 13% from protein, 66% from carbohydrate); 6 g protein; 4 g total fat; 1 g saturated fat; 2 g monounsaturated fat; 1 g polyunsaturated fat; 31 g carbohydrate; 2 g fiber; 1 g sugar; 82 mg phosphorus; 49 mg calcium; 2 mg iron; 352 mg sodium; 144 mg potassium; 53 IU vitamin a; 0 mg ATE vitamin e; 1 mg vitamin c; 0 mg cholesterol; 44 g water

Tuscan Bruschetta

The simplest form of bruschetta, with just enough garlic to taste and a little olive oil.

4 slices low sodium Italian bread, sliced no more than ½-inch (1.3 cm) thick

1 small clove garlic

2 tablespoons (30 ml) extra-virgin olive oil

Toast bread until light brown. Take off the garlic skin and rub garlic firmly across the face of the toast. Drizzle with just enough olive oil to cover the entire surface of the bread.

Yield: 4 servings

Per serving: 143 calories (49% from fat, 8% from protein, 43% from carbohydrate); 3 g protein; 8 g total fat; 1 g saturated fat; 5 g monounsaturated fat; 1 g polyunsaturated fat; 15 g carbohydrate; 1 g fiber; 0 g sugar; 26 mg calcium; 1 mg iron; 16 mg sodium; 39 mg potassium; 0 IU vitamin A; 0 mg vitamin C; 0 mg cholesterol; exchanges = 1 starch−1½ fat; 12 g water

Boneless Buffalo Wings

Chicken wings tend to be high in saturated fat, since it isn't easy to avoid eating the skin, where most of it is. Instead, make boneless wings from chicken breasts, cooking them in the oven instead of frying them.

6 boneless, skinless chicken breasts

3 tablespoons (45 ml) hot pepper sauce

2 tablespoons (30 ml) white vinegar

Preheat oven to 350°F (180°C, or gas mark 4). Cut the breasts into strips, about eight per breast. Place in roasting pan sprayed with nonstick vegetable oil spray and roast for 20 minutes, or until done. Mix hot pepper sauce and white vinegar. Place chicken pieces in a large bowl with a tight-sealing cover. Pour vinegar mixture over the pieces and shake to coat. Remove, allowing extra sauce to drain.

Yield: 16 servings

Per serving: 30 calories (11% from fat, 88% from protein, 1% from carbohydrate); 6 g protein; 0 g total fat; 0 g saturated fat; 0 g monounsaturated fat; 0 g polyunsaturated fat; 0 g carbohydrate; 0 g fiber; 0 g sugar; 53 mg phosphorus; 3 mg calcium; 0 mg iron; 34 mg sodium; 73 mg potassium; 49 IU vitamin A; 2 mg ATE vitamin E; 0 mg vitamin C; 15 mg cholesterol; 24 g water

Chicken Wings Nibblers

These can be used as an appetizer or the basis of a meal.

20 chicken wings

½ cup (120 ml) egg substitute

2 tablespoons (30 ml) skim milk

1½ cups (190 g) Reduced-Fat Biscuit Mix (see recipe page 34)

½ cup (60 g) sesame seeds

2 teaspoons (5 g) paprika

1½ teaspoons (4.5 g) dry mustard

Preheat oven to 425°F (220°C, or gas mark 7). Separate chicken wings at joints; discard tips. Spray two rectangular 9 × 13-inch (23 × 33-cm) pans with nonstick vegetable oil spray. Beat egg substitute and milk with fork in bowl. Mix biscuit mix, sesame seeds, paprika, and mustard in a second bowl. Soak chicken in egg mixture and then coat with sesame seed mixture. Arrange close together in baking pans. Bake uncovered for 35 to 40 minutes, or until brown and crisp.

Yield: 10 servings

Per serving: 139 calories (23% from fat, 33% from protein, 44% from carbohydrate); 11 g protein; 4 g total fat; 1 g saturated fat; 1 g monounsaturated fat; 1 g polyunsaturated fat; 15 g carbohydrate; 1 g fiber; 0 g sugar; 171 mg phosphorus; 70 mg calcium; 2 mg iron; 69 mg sodium; 260 mg potassium; 395 IU vitamin A; 26 mg ATE vitamin E; 1 mg vitamin C; 20 mg cholesterol; 41 g water

Taco Chicken Wings

You can use these taco-flavored wings either as appetizers or the main dish. This particular dish seems to be very popular with young people.

12 chicken wings

½ cup (62 g) flour

2 tablespoons (15 g) chili powder

1 teaspoon (2.5 g) cumin

1 teaspoon (1 g) dried oregano

½ teaspoon (1.5 g) onion powder

¼ teaspoon (0.8 g) garlic powder

⅛ teaspoon (0.3 g) cayenne pepper

¼ cup (60 ml) egg substitute

1 cup (28 g) corn chips, crushed

Preheat oven to 350°F (180°C, or gas mark 4). Cut wings into sections, discarding the tips. Combine flour and next 6 ingredients (through cayenne pepper) in a plastic bag. Pour egg substitute into a shallow dish. Spread crushed corn chips in another shallow dish. Shake a few wing sections at a time in the flour mixture, then roll in the egg substitute, then the corn chips. Place in a 9 × 13-inch (23 × 33-cm) pan. Bake for 45 minutes, or until done.

Yield: 6 servings

Per serving: 198 calories (34% from fat, 23% from protein, 43% from carbohydrate); 11 g protein; 8 g total fat; 1 g saturated fat; 2 g monounsaturated fat; 3 g polyunsaturated fat; 22 g carbohydrate; 2 g fiber; 1 g sugar; 117 mg phosphorus; 56 mg calcium; 2 mg iron; 189 mg sodium; 198 mg potassium; 830 IU vitamin A; 6 mg ATE vitamin E; 2 mg vitamin C; 19 mg cholesterol; 36 g water

Steak Bites

These little steak bites will please the toughest one in your party crowd.

½ cup (120 ml) Dick's Reduced-Sodium Soy Sauce (see recipe page 30)

6 tablespoons (78 g) sugar

3 tablespoons (45 ml) sesame oil

2 pounds (1 kg) round steak, cubed

½ cup (50 g) chopped scallions

2 tablespoons (30 ml) white wine

Combine soy sauce, sugar, and sesame oil in a shallow dish. Add steak, and refrigerate for 4 hours. Remove steak from marinade, reserving marinade. Place a large skillet over medium-high heat, and cook steak to desired doneness. Pour the reserved marinade into a medium saucepan and place over medium-high heat. Bring to a boil and cook for 5 minutes. Add cooked steak, scallions, and wine to the boiling marinade. Transfer the entire contents of the saucepan to a large bowl, and serve hot.

Yield: 16 servings

Per serving: 141 calories (14% from fat, 20% from protein, 66% from carbohydrate); 16 g protein; 5 g total fat; 1 g saturated fat; 2 g monounsaturated fat; 2 g polyunsaturated fat; 54 g carbohydrate; 0 g fiber; 6 g sugar; 111 mg phosphorus; 10 mg calcium; 1 mg iron; 74 mg sodium; 163 mg potassium; 34 IU vitamin A; 0 mg ATE vitamin E; 1 mg vitamin C; 33 mg cholesterol, 52 g water

Turkey Cocktail Meatballs

These tasty little meatballs can also be used as the basis of a dinner, served over rice with a vegetable. When we've made them for a get-together, they are always one of the first items to disappear.

1 pound (455 g) ground turkey breast

¼ cup (60 ml) egg substitute

¾ cup (50 g) saltine crackers, crushed

4 ounces part-skim shredded mozzarella

¼ cup (40 g) chopped onion

½ teaspoon (0.9 g) ground ginger

6 tablespoons (90 g) Dijon mustard, divided

1¼ cups (295 ml) unsweetened pineapple juice

¼ cup (37 g) chopped green bell pepper

2 tablespoons (30 ml) honey

1 tablespoon (8 g) cornstarch

¼ teaspoon (0.7 g) onion powder

Preheat oven to 350°F (180°C, or gas mark 4). In a bowl, combine turkey, egg substitute, cracker crumbs, mozzarella, onion, ginger and 3 tablespoons (45 g) mustard. Form into 30 balls, 1 inch (2.5 cm) each. Spray a 9 × 13-inch (23 × 33-cm) baking dish with nonstick vegetable oil spray. Place meatballs in dish. Bake, uncovered, for 20 to 25 minutes, or until cooked through. In a saucepan, combine pineapple juice, green pepper, honey, cornstarch, onion powder, and remaining mustard. Bring to a boil, stirring constantly. Cook and stir until thickened. Brush meatballs with about ¼ cup (60 ml) sauce and return to the oven for 10 minutes. Serve remaining sauce as a dip for meatballs.

Yield: 15 servings

Per serving: 100 calories (23% from fat, 41% from protein, 36% from carbohydrate); 10 g protein; 2 g total fat; 1 g saturated fat; 1 g monounsaturated fat; 0 g polyunsaturated fat; 9 g carbohydrate; 0 g fiber; 5 g sugar; 116 mg phosphorus; 75 mg calcium; 1 mg iron; 181 mg sodium; 167 mg potassium; 66 IU vitamin A; 9 mg ATE vitamin E; 4 mg vitamin C; 24 mg cholesterol; 58 g water

Texas Caviar

A traditional southern dip made with black-eyed peas. Serve with corn chips or toasted pita bread.

⅓ cup (55 g) onion, chopped

½ cup (75 g) green bell pepper, chopped

½ cup (50 g) scallions, chopped

¼ cup (36 g) jalapeño peppers, chopped

1 tablespoon (10 g) minced garlic

20 cherry tomatoes, quartered

8 ounces (235 ml) reduced-fat Italian dressing

2 cups (450 g) canned black eyed peas, drained

½ teaspoon (1 g) ground coriander

¼ cup (15 g) fresh cilantro, chopped

In a large bowl, mix together onion, green bell pepper, scallions, jalapeño peppers, garlic, cherry tomatoes, Italian dressing, black-eyed peas, and coriander. Cover and chill in the refrigerator approximately 2 hours. Toss with fresh cilantro just before serving.

Yield: 16 servings

Per serving: 78 calories (47% from fat, 11% from protein, 42% from carbohydrate); 2 g protein; 4 g total fat; 1 g saturated fat; 1 g monounsaturated fat; 2 g polyunsaturated fat; 9 g carbohydrate; 2 g fiber; 3 g sugar; 32 mg phosphorus; 12 mg calcium; 1 mg iron; 237 mg sodium; 165 mg potassium; 258 IU vitamin A; 0 mg ATE vitamin E; 10 mg vitamin C; 0 mg cholesterol; 34 g water

Fat-Free Potato Chips

These potato chips are very easy to make in the microwave. Also, they are healthier for you since they are not cooked in any oils. They can be made plain or with your choice of herbs and spices. They need to be sliced fairly thin to get crisp, but not paper thin. The original recipe called for a covered microwave bacon rack, but I found that putting them between two plates worked great. You may need to spray the plates with a little nonstick vegetable oil spray before the first batch to keep them from sticking.

4 medium potatoes
Your choice of spices or herbs

If the potatoes are old, peel them before slicing. If the potatoes are new or have good skins, do not peel, just scrub well. Slice potatoes $\frac{1}{16}$ inch (1.5 mm) in thickness, slicing across the potato. Sprinkle with your choice of spices or herbs, if desired. If you have a microwave bacon tray, place the sliced potatoes flat on the tray in a single layer. Cover with a microwavable, round, heavy plastic cover. If you do not have a bacon tray, place potatoes between two microwave-safe plates. Microwave on high (full power) for 7 to 8 minutes. Cooking time could vary slightly, depending on the wattage of your microwave. You do not have to turn the sliced potatoes over. Plates will be hot by the time potatoes are done. Continue to microwave the remainder of sliced potatoes as directed above.

Yield: 8 servings

Per serving: 129 calories (2% from fat, 10% from protein, 88% from carbohydrate); 3 g protein; 0 g total fat; 0 g saturated fat; 0 g monounsaturated fat; 0 g polyunsaturated fat; 29 g carbohydrate; 3 g fiber; 2 g sugar; 113 mg phosphorus; 18 mg calcium; 1 mg iron; 11 mg sodium; 839 mg potassium; 13 IU vitamin A; 0 mg ATE vitamin E; 16 mg vitamin C; 0 mg cholesterol; 149 g water

Low Fat Tortilla Chips

Just like you used to get at your favorite Mexican restaurant. I like these sprinkled with a little salt-free taco seasoning.

1 corn tortilla

Nonstick vegetable oil spray

Preheat oven to 350°F (180°C, or gas mark 4). Cut tortilla into 6 wedges. Place tortilla pieces on a baking sheet. Spray with nonstick vegetable oil spray. Turn tortillas over and spray the other side. Bake for 10 minutes, or until crispy and browned on the edges.

Yield: 1 serving

Per serving: 58 calories (10% from fat, 10% from protein, 80% from carbohydrate); 1 g protein; 1 g total fat; 0 g saturated fat; 0 g monounsaturated fat; 0 g polyunsaturated fat; 12 g carbohydrate; 1 g fiber; 0 g sugar; 82 mg phosphorus; 46 mg calcium; 0 mg iron; 3 mg sodium; 40 mg potassium; 0 IU vitamin A; 0 mg ATE vitamin E; 0 mg vitamin C; 0 mg cholesterol; 11 g water

Low Fat Scallion Dip

Not at all like the packaged mixes, it's still very tasty, and it has a little more tang.

1 cup (225 g) low fat cottage cheese

¼ cup (25 g) scallions, chopped

2 teaspoons (10 ml) lemon juice

Combine all ingredients in a blender or food processor and process until smooth. Refrigerate for at least an hour to give the flavors time to develop.

Yield: 8 servings

Per serving: 27 calories (19% from fat, 60% from protein, 21% from carbohydrate); 4 g protein; 1 g total fat; 0 g saturated fat; 0 g monounsaturated fat; 0 g polyunsaturated fat; 1 g carbohydrate; 0 g fiber; 0 g sugar; 44 mg phosphorus; 22 mg calcium; 0 mg iron; 115 mg sodium; 37 mg potassium; 53 IU vitamin A; 6 mg ATE vitamin E; 1 mg vitamin C; 2 mg cholesterol; 26 g water

Garbanzo Dip

A tasty garbanzo dip topped with crunchy vegetables.

2 cups (450 g) canned garbanzo beans, drained and rinsed

1 cup (230 g) plain fat-free yogurt

2 tablespoons (30 ml) lemon juice

2 tablespoons (30 ml) olive oil

Dash of hot pepper sauce

1 cup (135 g) cucumber, peeled and diced

¼ cup (40 g) red onion, chopped

¼ cup (30 g) carrots, grated

½ cup (90 g) roma tomatoes, chopped

TIP

Serve with toasted pita bread or flatbread.

Blend the garbanzos, yogurt, lemon juice, olive oil, and
hot pepper sauce in a blender or food processor until smooth. Transfer the dip to a shallow
serving bowl. Mix the remaining ingredients together and spread over the dip.

Yield: 16 servings

Per serving: 63 calories (29% from fat, 15% from protein, 56% from carbohydrate); 2 g protein; 2 g total fat;
0 g saturated fat; 1 g monounsaturated fat; 0 g polyunsaturated fat; 9 g carbohydrate; 2 g fiber; 2 g sugar;
55 mg phosphorus; 43 mg calcium; 0 mg iron; 103 mg sodium; 124 mg potassium; 391 IU vitamin A;
0 mg ATE vitamin E; 3 mg vitamin C; 0 mg cholesterol; 50 g water

Hummus

A traditional Middle Eastern dip. You should be able to find dried garbanzo beans, or chickpeas, with the other dried beans in most large grocery stores. Tahini, a sesame-seed paste, should also be available in large grocery stores or natural food stores. Feel free to adjust the spices or use different herbs to suit your own taste.

1 cup (240 g) cooked garbanzo beans

¾ teaspoon (0.2 g) minced garlic

3 tablespoons (45 ml) lemon juice

¼ cup (60 ml) water

¼ cup (60 g) tahini

1 teaspoon (2.5 g) cumin

½ teaspoon (1.3 g) paprika

1 tablespoon (15 ml) olive oil

In a food processor combine the cooked garbanzo beans, garlic, lemon juice, and water. Process for 1 minute, or until smooth. If the mixture is too thick, add more water to reach the desired consistency. Add the tahini, cumin, and paprika; stir until well combined. If desired, add more lemon juice, tahini, cumin, or paprika to taste. Spread into a shallow bowl and drizzle with olive oil. Serve chilled.

Yield: 8 servings

Per serving: 98 calories (53% from fat, 11% from protein, 35% from carbohydrate); 3 g protein; 6 g total fat; 1 g saturated fat; 3 g monounsaturated fat; 2 g polyunsaturated fat; 9 g carbohydrate; 2 g fiber; 0 g sugar; 84 mg phosphorus; 45 mg calcium; 1 mg iron; 99 mg sodium; 99 mg potassium; 92 IU vitamin A; 0 mg ATE vitamin E; 4 mg vitamin C; 0 mg cholesterol; 34 g water

Spinach and Artichoke Dip

This makes a nice dip for entertaining. It's similar to the dip served at a number of restaurants but lower in fat.

6 ounces (170 g) frozen chopped spinach, thawed and drained

7 ounces (210 g) artichoke hearts

2 ounces (55 g) fat-free cream cheese

½ cup (115 g) fat-free sour cream

¼ teaspoon (0.8 g) garlic powder

2 tablespoons (10 g) grated Parmesan

¼ cup (30 g) shredded low fat Monterey jack cheese

TIP

Serve with tortilla chips or French bread slices.

Preheat broiler. Combine all ingredients in the bowl of a food processor. Process until smooth. Place in an oven-proof dish and broil until the top begins to brown.

Yield: 8 servings

Per serving: 69 calories (35% from fat, 31% from protein, 33% from carbohydrate); 4 g protein; 2 g total fat; 1 g saturated fat; 1 g monounsaturated fat; 0 3g polyunsaturated fat; 5 g carbohydrate; 2 g fiber; 0 g sugar; 82 mg phosphorus; 96 mg calcium; 1 mg iron; 110 mg sodium; 167 mg potassium; 2725 IU vitamin A; 32 mg ATE vitamin E; 2 mg vitamin C; 12 mg cholesterol; 60 g water

Broccoli Dip

Yes, that's what it says: broccoli dip. It's sort of like guacamole with a southwestern flavor, but made with broccoli.

1½ cups (105 g) broccoli, cooked

1½ tablespoons (22 ml) lemon juice

¼ teaspoon (0.6 g) cumin

⅛ teaspoon (0.4 g) garlic powder

½ cup (90 g) diced tomato

2 tablespoons (12 g) sliced scallions

1 tablespoon (7.5 g) canned jalapeño peppers

In a food processor, blend the broccoli with the lemon juice, cumin, and garlic powder until completely smooth. Add the remaining ingredients and mix well by hand. Chill before serving for best flavor.

Yield: 12 servings

Per serving: 6 calories (8% from fat, 22% from protein, 69% from carbohydrate); 0 g protein; 0 g total fat; 0 g saturated fat; 0 g monounsaturated fat; 0 g polyunsaturated fat; 1 g carbohydrate; 0 g fiber; 0 g sugar; 10 mg phosphorus; 7 mg calcium; 0 mg iron; 4 mg sodium; 58 mg potassium; 138 IU vitamin A; 0 mg ATE vitamin E; 12 mg vitamin C; 0 mg cholesterol; 19 g water

Seven-Layer Dip

Just like you'd find at your favorite Mexican restaurant, except this one you're allowed to eat.

½ cup (115 g) refried beans

½ cup (112 g) guacamole

¼ cup (60 g) fat-free sour cream

1 cup (180 g) chopped tomato

¼ cup (30 g) shredded low fat cheddar cheese

¼ cup (25 g) chopped scallions

¼ cup (56 g) salsa

In a serving dish, layer the ingredients in the order shown.

Yield: 8 servings

Per serving: 54 calories (36% from fat, 22% from protein, 42% from carbohydrate); 3 g protein; 2 g total fat; 0 g saturated fat; 1 g monounsaturated fat; 0 g polyunsaturated fat; 5 g carbohydrate; 2 g fiber; 1 g sugar; 54 mg phosphorus; 38 mg calcium; 0 mg iron; 126 mg sodium; 177 mg potassium; 260 IU vitamin A; 10 mg ATE vitamin E; 5 mg vitamin C; 5 mg cholesterol; 55 g water

Salmon Appetizer Ball

Pretty and delicious, this makes a great party food that guests can eat without guilt.

16 ounces (455 g) canned salmon

8 ounces (225 g) fat-free cream cheese, softened

2 teaspoons (6 g) grated onion

1 tablespoon (15 ml) fresh lemon juice

2 teaspoons (10 g) prepared horseradish

¼ teaspoon (1.2 ml) liquid smoke

½ cup (60 g) chopped pecans

3 tablespoons (12 g) fresh parsley

Drain and flake salmon. Combine salmon, cream cheese, onion, lemon juice, horseradish, and liquid smoke. Mix thoroughly. Chill for several hours. Combine pecans and parsley on a sheet of waxed paper. Shape salmon mixture into ball and roll in nut mixture. Chill well. Serve with assorted crackers.

Yield: 16 Servings

Per serving: 97 calories (60% from fat, 33% from protein, 7% from carbohydrate); 8 g protein; 7 g total fat; 2 g saturated fat; 3 g monounsaturated fat; 1 g polyunsaturated fat; 2 g carbohydrate; 0 g fiber; 0 g sugar; 131 mg phosphorus; 90 mg calcium; 1 mg iron; 66 mg sodium; 130 mg potassium; 175 IU vitamin A; 31 mg ATE vitamin E; 2 mg vitamin C; 19 mg cholesterol; 32 g water

Black Bean Spread

A good-for-you dip that tastes good too.

½ cup (125 g) dried black beans

2 teaspoons (10 ml) olive oil

¼ cup (40 g) onion, finely chopped

½ teaspoon (1.5 g) minced garlic

4 ounces (115 g) fresh mushrooms, sliced

½ cup (75 g) walnuts

¼ teaspoon (0.3 g) dried thyme

¼ teaspoon (0.5 g) pepper

TIP

Serve with chips or crackers.

Soak the beans in 2 cups (470 ml) of water overnight or combine them with 2 cups (470 ml) of water in a saucepan, boil for 2 minutes, and let stand 1 hour. Cook in soaking water over medium heat for 1 hour, or until very tender, then drain and purée in a food processor. Heat the oil in a skillet over medium heat and sauté the onion for 3 minutes, or until soft. Add the garlic and cook 1 minute. Add the mushrooms, cover, and cook 5 minutes. Remove from heat. Place the walnuts in a blender or food processor and grind to the consistency of cornmeal. Combine the sautéed vegetables, ground walnuts, thyme, and pepper in a blender or food processor until fairly smooth but not creamy. Spoon into a serving dish and chill.

Yield: 16 Servings

Per serving: 39 calories (63% from fat, 16% from protein, 21% from carbohydrate); 2 g protein; 3 g total fat; 0 g saturated fat; 1 g monounsaturated fat; 1 g polyunsaturated fat; 2 g carbohydrate; 1 g fiber; 0 g sugar; 35 mg phosphorus; 5 mg calcium; 0 mg iron; 1 mg sodium; 66 mg potassium; 4 IU vitamin A; 0 mg ATE vitamin E; 0 mg vitamin C; 0 mg cholesterol; 13 g water

Chicken and Mushroom Quesadillas .

If you have an indoor grill like the George Foreman models, it is perfect for making these quesadillas. Otherwise, place them on a baking sheet and bake at 350°F (180°C, or gas mark 4) until crisp.

1 tablespoon (15 ml) olive oil

2½ teaspoons (6.5 g) chili powder

½ teaspoon (1.5 g) minced garlic

1 teaspoon (1 g) dried oregano

8 ounces (225 g) mushrooms, sliced

1 cup (110 g) chicken breast, cooked and shredded

⅔ cup (110 g) onion, finely chopped

½ cup (30 g) fresh cilantro, chopped

1½ cups (170 g) shredded low fat Monterey jack cheese

16 5½-inch (13.75-cm) corn tortillas

TIP

Serve with salsa and fat-free sour cream.

Heat olive oil in a large skillet over medium-high heat. Add chili powder, garlic, and oregano and sauté for 1 minute. Add mushrooms and sauté for 10 minutes, or until tender. Remove from heat and stir in the chicken, onion, and cilantro. Cool for 10 minutes, then mix in the cheese. Spray olive oil spray on one side of 8 of the tortillas and place them oiled-side down on a baking sheet. Divide chicken mixture among tortillas, spreading to an even thickness. Top with the remaining tortillas and spray the tops with olive oil spray. Grill quesadillas for 3 minutes per side, or until heated through and golden brown. Cut into wedges to serve.

Yield: 12 servings

Per serving: 122 calories (26% from fat, 32% from protein, 43% from carbohydrate); 10 g protein; 4 g total fat; 1 g saturated fat; 2 g monounsaturated fat; 1 g polyunsaturated fat; 13 g carbohydrate; 2 g fiber; 1 g sugar; 206 mg phosphorus; 97 mg calcium; 1 mg iron; 128 mg sodium; 181 mg potassium; 315 IU vitamin A; 11 mg ATE vitamin E; 2 mg vitamin C; 13 mg cholesterol; 57 g water

Fat-Free Potato Skins

Because they're baked instead of fried, these tasty potato skins contain no fat.

4 potatoes

1½ teaspoons (3 g) ground coriander

½ teaspoon (1 g) black pepper

1½ teaspoons (4 g) chili powder

1½ teaspoons (3 g) curry powder

Preheat the oven to 400°F (200°C, or gas mark 6). Bake the potatoes for 1 hour. Remove the potatoes from the oven, but keep the oven on. Slice the potatoes in half lengthwise, and let them cool for 10 minutes Scoop out most of the potato flesh, leaving about ¼ inch (0.6 cm) of flesh against the potato skin (you can save the potato flesh for another use, like mashed potatoes). Cut each potato half crosswise into 3 pieces. Spray with olive oil spray. Combine the spices and sprinkle the mixture over the potatoes. Bake the potato skins for 15 minutes or until they are crispy and brown.

Yield: 24 servings

Per serving: 44 calories (3% from fat, 11% from protein, 87% from carbohydrate); 1 g protein; 0 g total fat; 0 g saturated fat; 0 g monounsaturated fat; 0 g polyunsaturated fat; 10 g carbohydrate; 1 g fiber; 1 g sugar; 39 mg phosphorus; 8 mg calcium; 1 mg iron; 5 mg sodium; 287 mg potassium; 54 IU vitamin A; 0 mg ATE vitamin E; 6 mg vitamin C; 0 mg cholesterol; 50 g water

Potstickers

A fairly traditional recipe for Chinese dumplings.

For Filling:

4 ounces (115 g) napa cabbage, shredded

½ pound (225 g) ground pork loin

2 tablespoons (12 g) scallions, chopped

½ tablespoon (7.5 ml) white wine

½ teaspoon (1.3 g) cornstarch

½ teaspoon (2.5 ml) sesame oil

Dash white pepper

For Dough:

1 cup (125 g) flour

½ cup (120 ml) boiling water

1 tablespoon (15 ml) olive oil

To make the filling: In a large bowl, mix the cabbage, pork, scallions, wine, cornstarch, sesame oil, and pepper. Set aside.

To make the dough: In a bowl, mix the flour and boiling water until a soft dough forms. Knead the dough on a lightly floured surface for 5 minutes, or until smooth. Shape into a roll 12 inches (30 cm) long and cut into ½-inch (1.3-cm) slices.

To assemble, roll 1 slice of dough into a 3-inch (7.5-cm) circle and place 1 tablespoon (13 g) pork mixture in the center of the circle. Lift up the edges of the circle and pinch 5 pleats to create a sealed pouch to encase the mixture. Repeat with the remaining dough and filling. Heat a wok or nonstick skillet until very hot. Add 1 tablespoon (15 ml) olive oil, tilting the wok to coat the sides. Place 12 dumplings in a single layer in the wok and fry 2 minutes, or until the bottoms are golden brown. Add ½ cup (120 ml) water. Cover and cook 6 to 7 minutes, or until the water is absorbed. Repeat with the remaining dumplings.

Yield: 24 servings

Per serving: 46 calories (33% from fat, 29% from protein, 37% from carbohydrate); 3 g protein; 2 g total fat; 0 g saturated fat; 1 g monounsaturated fat; 0 g polyunsaturated fat; 4 g carbohydrate; 0 g fiber; 0 g sugar; 28 mg phosphorus; 3 mg calcium; 0 mg iron; 6 mg sodium; 46 mg potassium; 18 IU vitamin A; 0 mg ATE vitamin E; 0 mg vitamin C; 8 mg cholesterol; 17 g water

Quiche Nibblers

Low fat, crustless quiche bites that are sure to be a hit, whether they're just for your family or for guests. No one will ever know that we've taken out the fat, the cholesterol, and the calories.

1 tablespoon (15 ml) olive oil

½ cup (75 g) red bell pepper, finely chopped

¼ cup (25 g) scallions, finely chopped

¾ cup (180 ml) egg substitute

2 tablespoons (30 ml) skim milk

2 ounces (55 g) low fat cheddar cheese, shredded

⅛ teaspoon (0.3 g) ground black pepper

Preheat oven to 425°F (220°C, or gas mark 7). Grease 24 mini-muffin cups with nonstick vegetable oil spray. In a small saucepan, heat olive oil over moderate heat. Add red bell pepper and scallions; sauté for 5 minutes, or until soft. Remove the pan from the heat and let the mixture cool slightly. In a medium bowl, combine egg substitute, milk, cheese, and pepper. Stir in the bell pepper mixture. Spoon about 1 tablespoon of the mixture into each muffin cup. Bake for 8 to 10 minutes, or until the centers are set. Let cool for 1 minute. Using a knife, loosen the quiches around the edges and remove.

Yield: 12 servings

Per serving: 35 calories (52% from fat, 38% from protein, 10% from carbohydrate); 3 g protein; 2 g total fat; 0 g saturated fat; 1 g monounsaturated fat; 0 g polyunsaturated fat; 1 g carbohydrate; 0 g fiber; 0 g sugar; 47 mg phosphorus; 34 mg calcium; 0 mg iron; 59 mg sodium; 79 mg potassium; 287 IU vitamin A; 4 mg ATE vitamin E; 8 mg vitamin C; 1 mg cholesterol; 26 g water

Spicy Snack Mix

Marti, a subscriber to my email newsletter, sent me this recipe for a snack mix. It makes a nice alternative to Chex Mix.

1 egg white

2 teaspoons (10 ml) water

3 tablespoons (39 g) sugar

¾ teaspoon (1.7 g) cinnamon

⅛ teaspoon (0.3 g) nutmeg

⅛ teaspoon (0.2 g) ground ginger

5 cups (250 g) spoon-sized shredded wheat squares

1½ cups (220 g) unsalted dry roasted peanuts

Preheat oven to 250°F (120°C, or gas mark ½). Combine egg white and water; stir in sugar, cinnamon, nutmeg, and ginger. Beat until frothy. Mix cereal and nuts in a 9 × 13-inch (23 × 33-cm) baking pan. Add egg white mixture; toss to coat. Bake for 15 minutes. Cool 5 minutes. Remove from pan; cool completely. Store in tightly covered container.

Yield: 14 servings

Per serving: 169 calories (40% from fat, 12% from protein, 48% from carbohydrate); 5 g protein; 8 g total fat; 1 g saturated fat; 4 g monounsaturated fat; 2 g polyunsaturated fat; 22 g carbohydrate; 3 g fiber; 8 g sugar; 108 mg phosphorus; 13 mg calcium; 1 mg iron; 8 mg sodium; 169 mg potassium; 0 IU vitamin A; 0 mg ATE vitamin E; 0 mg vitamin C; 0 mg cholesterol; 4 g water

Hot Spiced Nuts

These make a great snack during the game (whatever game happens to be on). Make sure you have plenty of drinks available. Nuts contain the good kind of fat, so you can feel good about this snack.

1 egg white

1 cup (145 g) unsalted peanuts

1 cup (150 g) unsalted cashews

1 cup (100 g) unsalted pecans

1 teaspoon (2 g) curry powder

1 teaspoon (2.3 g) cinnamon

1 teaspoon (2.5 g) cumin

¼ teaspoon (0.5 g) cayenne pepper

3 tablespoons (35 g) brown sugar

Preheat oven to 250°F (120°C, or gas mark ½). Beat egg white until foamy. Add peanuts, cashews, and pecans, tossing to coat. Combine remaining ingredients in a medium bowl; toss with nuts to coat. Spread nuts on a greased baking sheet in a single layer. Bake for 1 hour, stirring once. Cool slightly and break apart. Cool completely and store in an airtight container for up to two weeks.

Yield: 15 servings

Per serving: 129 calories (69% from fat, 9% from protein, 23% from carbohydrate); 3 g protein; 10 g total fat; 1 g saturated fat; 6 g monounsaturated fat; 3 g polyunsaturated fat; 8 g carbohydrate; 1 g fiber; 4 g sugar; 76 mg phosphorus; 18 mg calcium; 1 mg iron; 38 mg sodium; 108 mg potassium; 20 IU vitamin a; 0 mg ATE vitamin e; 0 mg vitamin c; 0 mg cholesterol; 4 g water

Sweet Spiced Nuts

I've been trying for several years to come up with a recipe that is similar to the cinnamon nuts they sell at Nissan Pavilion in Virginia. This isn't it. The ones there have a hard sugar and spice coating and are made in a machine that spins them around, similar to a cotton candy machine. These have a flavor I like, though, so I'm including them here.

1 egg white

1 teaspoon (5 ml) water

2 cups (300 g) unsalted cashews

2 cups (300 g) unsalted almonds

½ cup (100 g) sugar

½ teaspoon (1.2 g) cinnamon

⅛ teaspoon (0.2 g) ground ginger

⅛ teaspoon (0.3 g) nutmeg

Preheat oven to 250°F (120°C, or gas mark ½). Beat the egg white and water until frothy, but not stiff. Add the cashews and almonds, and stir to coat. Combine the remaining ingredients and pour over the nuts. Stir until the sugar is dissolved. Place on a greased baking sheet and bake for 1 hour, stirring occasionally. Cool on waxed paper. Store in an airtight container.

Yield: 16 servings

Per serving: 229 calories (63% from fat, 11% from protein, 26% from carbohydrate); 7 g protein; 17 g total fat; 2 g saturated fat; 11 g monounsaturated fat; 4 g polyunsaturated fat; 16 g carbohydrate; 2 g fiber; 8 g sugar; 171 mg phosphorus; 48 mg calcium; 2 mg iron; 11 mg sodium; 225 mg potassium; 2 IU vitamin a; 0 mg ATE vitamin e; 0 mg vitamin c; 0 mg cholesterol; 3 g water

4

Breakfasts

Breakfast can be another problem time for those of us trying to eat in a cholesterol-friendly way. First, there's the saturated fat in traditional breakfast meats. Then there's the amount of cholesterol in eggs. For those who don't really fancy the idea of granola every day, we have some options. You can easily make sausage that is lower in fat than any you can buy at the store. And egg substitutes, made from egg whites, work fine for omelets, scrambled eggs, and other dishes. As an alternative, there are smoothies, packed with things that are good for you, as well as healthier versions of things like pancakes and French toast. And don't forget to check out the breakfast recipes in Chapters 18 and 19.

Turkey Breakfast Sausage

I've been back at the chemistry table—I mean, kitchen counter—trying various recipes for sausage again. This is my favorite so far. It contains about one twentieth of the sodium, one tenth of the fat, and one third of the calories of the average store-bought sausage.

1 pound (455 g) ground turkey

¼ teaspoon (0.5 g) black pepper

¼ teaspoon (0.5 g) white pepper

¾ teaspoon (0.6 g) dried sage

¼ teaspoon (0.4 g) ground mace

½ teaspoon (1.5 g) garlic powder

¼ teaspoon (0.8 g) onion powder

¼ teaspoon (0.5 g) ground allspice

1 teaspoon (5 ml) olive oil

Combine all ingredients, mixing well. Fry, grill, or preheat oven to 325°F (170°C, or gas mark 3) and cook on a greased baking sheet to desired doneness.

Yield: 8 servings

Per serving: 69 calories (20% from fat, 77% from protein, 2% from carbohydrate); 13 g protein; 1 g total fat; 0 g saturated fat; 1 g monounsaturated fat; 0 g polyunsaturated fat; 0 g carbohydrate; 0 g fiber; 0 g sugar; 106 mg phosphorus; 9 mg calcium; 1 mg iron; 35 mg sodium; 153 mg potassium; 5 IU vitamin A; 0 mg ATE vitamin E; 0 mg vitamin C; 41 mg cholesterol; 43 g water

Snowy Day Breakfast Casserole

My wife came up with this one winter when we were snowed in. It has since become a standard in our house, just the sort of thing you need when sitting in front of the fire.

2 slices low sodium bacon

3 potatoes, shredded

½ cup (80 g) onion, chopped

¼ cup (37 g) green bell pepper, chopped

1 cup (235 ml) egg substitute

¼ cup (30 g) low fat cheddar cheese, shredded

Preheat oven to 350°F (180°C, or gas mark 4). Fry bacon in a large skillet. Remove bacon to a paper towel–covered plate to drain. Add potatoes, onion, and green pepper to skillet and sauté until potatoes are crispy and onion soft. Stir in crumbled bacon. Transfer to greased 8-inch (20-cm) square baking dish. Pour egg substitute over. Sprinkle with cheese. Bake until eggs are set, about 20 minutes.

Yield: 4 servings

Per serving: 292 calories (14% from fat, 22% from protein, 63% from carbohydrate); 17 g protein; 5 g total fat; 1 g saturated fat; 1 g monounsaturated fat; 1 g polyunsaturated fat; 47 g carbohydrate; 5 g fiber; 4 g sugar; 314 mg phosphorus; 101 mg calcium; 4 mg iron; 221 mg sodium; 1540 mg potassium; 299 IU vitamin A; 5 mg ATE vitamin E; 33 mg vitamin C; 7 mg cholesterol; 308 g water

Breakfast Skillet

This was originally a Sunday-morning breakfast in late summer. At that time of year, I usually have extra tomatoes and peppers from the garden, and this recipe used up a few of them.

1 tablespoon (15 ml) olive oil

¼ cup (40 g) onion, finely chopped

¼ cup (38 g) red bell pepper, finely chopped

½ cup (105 g) frozen hash brown potatoes, thawed

¾ cup (180 ml) egg substitute

Heat oil in a large skillet over medium heat. Sauté onion and red bell pepper until tender. Add hash browns and cook until potatoes are softened and beginning to brown, stirring occasionally. Pour egg substitute over vegetables and continue to cook for 5 minutes, or until set, stirring occasionally.

Yield: 2 servings

Per serving: 195 calories (47% from fat, 26% from protein, 26% from carbohydrate); 13 g protein; 10 g total fat; 2 g saturated fat; 6 g monounsaturated fat; 2 g polyunsaturated fat; 13 g carbohydrate; 1 g fiber; 2 g sugar; 149 mg phosphorus; 61 mg calcium; 3 mg iron; 180 mg sodium; 529 mg potassium; 922 IU vitamin A; 0 mg ATE vitamin E; 30 mg vitamin C; 1 mg cholesterol; 154 g water

Breakfast Wraps

Similar to the breakfast burritos served at several fast food restaurants, but with a lot less fat.

1 medium potato

½ pound (225 g) Turkey Breakfast Sausage (see recipe page 64)

½ cup (80 g) onion, chopped

1 teaspoon (2.6 g) chili powder

¼ teaspoon (0.5 g) cayenne pepper

½ cup (120 ml) egg substitute

6 flour tortillas

½ cup (58 g) low fat cheddar cheese, shredded

Boil or microwave potato until tender. Peel and cut into cubes. Brown sausage in a frying pan. Add chopped onion, chili powder, and cayenne pepper and cook for 10 minutes. Drain and discard any fat. Add potato and eggs. Stir until eggs are set. Divide mixture evenly among warmed tortillas, top with shredded cheese, and roll up tortillas to enclose mixture.

Yield: 6 servings

Per serving: 269 calories (36% from fat, 22% from protein, 42% from carbohydrate); 15 g protein; 11 g total fat; 4 g saturated fat; 3 g monounsaturated fat; 2 g polyunsaturated fat; 28 g carbohydrate; 2 g fiber; 2 g sugar; 211 mg phosphorus; 116 mg calcium; 2 mg iron; 524 mg sodium; 390 mg potassium; 254 IU vitamin A; 7 mg ATE vitamin E; 16 mg vitamin C; 25 mg cholesterol; 108 g water

Breakfast Quesadilla

These are easy to make if you have a portable contact grill like the George Foreman models. If not, you can also grill them in a dry skillet, turning once.

1 cup (240 ml) egg substitute

¼ cup (56 g) salsa

¼ cup (30 g) low fat cheddar cheese, shredded

8 corn tortillas

Scramble egg substitute, stirring in salsa and cheese when it is almost set. Lightly spray one side of the tortillas in nonstick olive oil spray and place 4 of them oiled-side down on a baking sheet. Divide egg mixture among tortillas, spreading to even thickness. Top with the remaining tortillas, oiled-side up. Grill quesadillas for 3 minutes per side, or until heated through and golden brown. Cut into quarters to serve.

Yield: 4 servings

Per serving: 152 calories (22% from fat, 31% from protein, 47% from carbohydrate); 12 g protein; 4 g total fat; 1 g saturated fat; 1 g monounsaturated fat; 2 g polyunsaturated fat; 18 g carbohydrate; 3 g fiber; 1 g sugar; 237 mg phosphorus; 102 mg calcium; 2 mg iron; 275 mg sodium; 330 mg potassium; 291 IU vitamin A; 5 mg ATE vitamin E; 0 mg vitamin C; 2 mg cholesterol; 89 g water

Vegetable Omelet

This can be either a breakfast or the main part of an evening meal.

1 tablespoon (15 ml) olive oil

2 ounces (55 g) mushrooms, sliced

¼ cup (40 g) onion, diced

¼ cup (37 g) green bell peppers, diced

¼ cup (28 g) zucchini, sliced

½ cup (90 g) tomato, diced

1 cup (240 ml) egg substitute

2 tablespoons (30 g) fat-free sour cream

2 tablespoons (30 ml) water

2 ounces (55 g) Swiss cheese, shredded

Add olive oil to a large skillet and sauté mushrooms, onion, green bell pepper, zucchini, and tomato until soft, adding tomato last. Whisk together egg substitute, sour cream, and water until fluffy. Coat an omelet pan or skillet with nonstick vegetable spray and place over medium-high heat. Pour egg mixture into pan. Lift the edges as it cooks to allow uncooked egg to run underneath. When eggs are nearly set, cover half the eggs with the cheese and sautéed vegetables and fold the other half over. Continue cooking until eggs are completely set.

Yield: 2 servings

Per serving: 263 calories (46% from fat, 41% from protein, 13% from carbohydrate); 25 g protein; 13 g total fat; 3 g saturated fat; 6 g monounsaturated fat; 3 g polyunsaturated fat; 8 g carbohydrate; 2 g fiber; 4 g sugar; 386 mg phosphorus; 369 mg calcium; 3 mg iron; 309 mg sodium; 746 mg potassium; 962 IU vitamin A; 26 mg ATE vitamin E; 25 mg vitamin C; 17 mg cholesterol; 259 g water

Sausage Frittata

We like this for breakfast on those rare occasions when the entire family is around, but it also makes a good dinner with a salad and a slice of freshly baked bread.

1 cup (240 ml) egg substitute

¼ cup (60 ml) skim milk

8 ounces (225 g) Turkey Breakfast Sausage (see recipe page 64)

½ cup (75 g) green bell pepper, chopped

4 ounces (115 g) low fat cheddar cheese, shredded

Preheat broiler. Combine egg substitute and milk in medium bowl; whisk until well blended. Set aside. Place a 12-inch (30-cm) broiler-proof nonstick skillet over medium-high heat until hot. Add sausage; cook and stir for 4 minutes or until no longer pink, breaking up sausage with spoon. Drain sausage on paper towels; set aside. Add pepper to same skillet; cook and stir for 2 minutes, or until crisp-tender. Return sausage to skillet. Add egg mixture; stir until blended. Cover; cook over medium-low heat for 10 minutes, or until eggs are almost set. Sprinkle cheese over frittata. Broil for 2 minutes, or until cheese is melted and eggs are set. Cut into wedges.

Yield: 4 servings

Per serving: 245 calories (54% from fat, 40% from protein, 6% from carbohydrate); 24 g protein; 14 g total fat; 6 g saturated fat; 4 g monounsaturated fat; 3 g polyunsaturated fat; 4 g carbohydrate; 0 g fiber; 1 g sugar; 339 mg phosphorus; 193 mg calcium; 2 mg iron; 626 mg sodium; 398 mg potassium; 385 IU vitamin A; 26 mg ATE vitamin E; 32 mg vitamin C; 41 mg cholesterol; 137 g water

Vegetable Frittata

A frittata is an Italian-style omelet, with the filling mixed in with the eggs. It's cooked without turning and then the top set under the broiler. This version does not have any of the meat and potatoes that they often have, providing you with a filling weekend breakfast low in sodium, fat, and carbohydrates.

½ cup (75 g) red bell pepper, diced

½ cup (80 g) onion, chopped

1 cup (70 g) broccoli florets

8 ounces (225 g) mushrooms, sliced

1 cup (113 g) zucchini, sliced

1½ cups (355 ml) egg substitute

1 tablespoon (0.4 g) dried parsley

¼ teaspoon (0.5 g) black pepper

2 ounces (55 g) Swiss cheese, shredded

Spray a large oven-proof skillet with nonstick vegetable oil spray. Stir fry the red bell pepper, onions, and broccoli until crisp-tender. Add the mushrooms and zucchini and stir fry for 1 to 2 minutes more. Stir together the egg substitute, parsley, and pepper, and pour over vegetable mixture, spreading to cover. Cover and cook over medium heat for 10 to 12 minutes, or until eggs are nearly set. Sprinkle cheese over the top. Place under the broiler until eggs are set and cheese is melted.

Yield: 4 servings

Per serving: 140 calories (26% from fat, 51% from protein, 22% from carbohydrate); 18 g protein; 4 g total fat; 1 g saturated fat; 1 g monounsaturated fat; 2 g polyunsaturated fat; 8 g carbohydrate; 2 g fiber; 4 g sugar; 283 mg phosphorus; 209 mg calcium; 3 mg iron; 216 mg sodium; 721 mg potassium; 1618 IU vitamin A; 6 mg ATE vitamin E; 50 mg vitamin C; 6 mg cholesterol; 220 g water

Pasta Frittata

This makes a wonderful meatless meal. It's kind of like macaroni and cheese, only a little fancier.

2 tablespoons (30 ml) olive oil

1 cup (150 g) red bell pepper, diced

1 cup (160 g) onion, chopped

2 cups (100 g) cooked pasta

¼ cup (25 g) grated Parmesan

1 cup (235 ml) egg substitute

Heat a 10-inch (25-cm) nonstick skillet that is broiler safe. When the pan is hot, add the oil, then sauté red bell pepper and onion for 2 to 3 minutes, stirring frequently. Add the pasta to the pan, mixing well. When ingredients are thoroughly combined, press down on pasta with spatula to flatten it against the bottom of the pan. Let it cook a few minutes more. Whisk grated Parmesan into the egg substitute. Pour egg mixture over the top of the pasta, making sure the eggs spread evenly. Gently lift the edges of the pasta to let egg flow underneath and completely coat the pasta. Let the eggs cook for 6 to 9 minutes. Slide the pan into a preheated broiler and finish cooking.

Yield: 4 servings

Per serving: 360 calories (29% from fat, 20% from protein, 51% from carbohydrate); 18 g protein; 12 g total fat; 3 g saturated fat; 6 g monounsaturated fat; 2 g polyunsaturated fat; 46 g carbohydrate; 3 g fiber; 5 g sugar; 242 mg phosphorus; 125 mg calcium; 2 mg iron; 213 mg sodium; 469 mg potassium; 1421 IU vitamin A; 7 mg ATE vitamin E; 51 mg vitamin C; 6 mg cholesterol; 128 g water

Breakfast Potatoes

Sometimes called O'Brien potatoes, this is a traditional breakfast kind of dish, but it works just as well as a side dish at dinner.

4 potatoes

1 cup (160 g) onion, chopped

¼ cup (37 g) green bell peppers, chopped

1 tablespoon (14 g) unsalted margarine

½ teaspoon (1 g) freshly ground black pepper

Boil or microwave potatoes until almost cooked through. Drain. Coarsely chop potatoes and combine with onion and green bell pepper. Melt margarine in a heavy skillet. Add potato mixture. Sprinkle black pepper over the top. Fry until browned, turning frequently.

Yield: 6 servings

Per serving: 201 calories (10% from fat, 10% from protein, 81% from carbohydrate); 5 g protein; 2 g total fat; 1 g saturated fat; 1 g monounsaturated fat; 0 g polyunsaturated fat; 42 g carbohydrate; 5 g fiber; 4 g sugar; 161 mg phosphorus; 34 mg calcium; 2 mg iron; 37 mg sodium; 1174 mg potassium; 141 IU vitamin A; 23 mg ATE vitamin E; 28 mg vitamin C; 0 mg cholesterol; 229 g water

Banana Pancakes

While trying to use up some overripe bananas, I came up with this breakfast recipe.

1 cup (125 g) flour

1 tablespoon (13 g) sugar

1 tablespoon (14 g) baking powder

½ cup (120 ml) skim milk

¼ cup (60 ml) egg substitute

1 tablespoon (15 ml) canola oil

1 cup (225 g) banana, chopped

TIP *The griddle is hot enough when a drop of water sizzles and breaks up immediately.*

Stir together flour, sugar, and baking powder. Combine the milk, egg substitute, and oil. Stir in banana. Add milk mixture all at once to flour mixture. Stir until blended but still slightly lumpy. Pour about ¼ cup (60 ml) of batter onto a hot griddle sprayed with nonstick vegetable oil spray. Cook until browned on bottom (when bubbles form and then break on the top). Turn and cook on the other side until done. Repeat with remaining batter.

Yield: 4 servings

Per serving: 235 calories (17% from fat, 12% from protein, 71% from carbohydrate); 7 g protein; 5 g total fat; 1 g saturated fat; 2 g monounsaturated fat; 1 g polyunsaturated fat; 43 g carbohydrate; 2 g fiber; 10 g sugar; 175 mg phosphorus; 263 mg calcium; 2 mg iron; 413 mg sodium; 343 mg potassium; 155 IU vitamin A; 19 mg ATE vitamin E; 5 mg vitamin C; 1 mg cholesterol; 86 g water

French Toast

French toast is one of those breakfasts that we don't seem to have very often, but wonder why not every time we do.

½ cup (120 ml) egg substitute

¾ cup (180 ml) skim milk

2 teaspoons (10 ml) vanilla extract

½ teaspoon (1.2 g) cinnamon

8 slices day-old whole wheat bread

TIP

Top with confectioner's sugar and fresh fruit.

Combine egg substitute, milk, vanilla, and cinnamon in a wide bowl or dish. Dip bread in egg mixture, ensuring both sides are soaked. Coat a griddle or nonstick skillet with nonstick vegetable oil spray and place over medium-high heat. Place bread slices in skillet or griddle and cook for 3 minutes on each side, or until both sides of bread are golden brown.

Yield: 4 servings

Per serving: 185 calories (15% from fat, 25% from protein, 60% from carbohydrate); 11 g protein; 3 g total fat; 1 g saturated fat; 1 g monounsaturated fat; 1 g polyunsaturated fat; 27 g carbohydrate; 2 g fiber; 3 g sugar; 167 mg phosphorus; 157 mg calcium; 3 mg iron; 344 mg sodium; 284 mg potassium; 207 IU vitamin A; 28 mg ATE vitamin E; 1 mg vitamin C; 1 mg cholesterol; 86 g water

Breakfast Cookies

These are good for breakfast on the run. They are fairly soft, but they're portable and fat-free.

3 cups (675 g) mashed banana

⅓ cup (82 g) applesauce

2 cups (160 g) quick-cooking oats

¼ cup (60 ml) skim milk

½ cup (75 g) dried cranberries

1 teaspoon (5 ml) vanilla

1 teaspoon (2.3 g) cinnamon

1 tablespoon (13 g) sugar

½ cup (50 g) pecans, chopped

TIP *You can leave out the nuts if you prefer and substitute other dried fruit like raisins or dried apples for the cranberries.*

Preheat oven to 350°F (180°C, or gas mark 4). Mix all ingredients in a bowl until well combined. Let this mixture stand for at least 5 minutes. Heap the dough by teaspoonfuls onto a greased baking sheet. Bake for 15 to 20 minutes and let cool.

Yield: 20 servings

Per serving: 127 calories (22% from fat, 10% from protein, 68% from carbohydrate); 3 g protein; 3 g total fat; 0 g saturated fat; 1 g monounsaturated fat; 1 g polyunsaturated fat; 23 g carbohydrate; 3 g fiber; 8 g sugar; 101 mg phosphorus; 18 mg calcium; 1 mg iron; 3 mg sodium; 209 mg potassium; 30 IU vitamin A; 2 mg ATE vitamin E; 3 mg vitamin C; 0 mg cholesterol; 33 g water

Pumpkin Oatmeal

Oatmeal is one of the few foods that has been approved to claim it reduces cholesterol, so that makes it our friend. But it can get boring after a while. Adding pumpkin spices it up with a little fall flavor.

2 cups (160 g) quick-cooking oats

3 cups (710 ml) skim milk

½ cup (160 g) canned pumpkin

¼ teaspoon (0.5 g) pumpkin pie spice

⅛ teaspoon (0.3 g) cinnamon

¼ cup (40 g) raisins

Place oats in a microwave-safe bowl and stir in milk. Microwave on high for 2 to 3 minutes. Remove from microwave and stir in pumpkin, pumpkin pie spice, and cinnamon. Heat for 40 to 60 seconds, or until heated through. Stir in raisins.

Yield: 4 servings

Per serving: 273 calories (10% from fat, 21% from protein, 69% from carbohydrate); 14 g protein; 3 g total fat; 1 g saturated fat; 1 g monounsaturated fat; 1 g polyunsaturated fat; 48 g carbohydrate; 5 g fiber; 8 g sugar; 420 mg phosphorus; 300 mg calcium; 2 mg iron; 113 mg sodium; 619 mg potassium; 5141 IU vitamin A; 113 mg ATE vitamin E; 4 mg vitamin C; 4 mg cholesterol; 198 g water

Couscous Cereal with Fruit

I get bored with cereal sometimes. This is a little different take on hot breakfast cereal.

¾ cup (180 ml) water

½ cup (88 g) couscous

2 tablespoons (20 g) raisins

2 tablespoons (19 g) dried cranberries

1 tablespoon (15 ml) honey

½ teaspoon (1.2 g) cinnamon

(continued on page 76)

Bring water to a boil. Add the couscous and stir, then cover and remove from heat. Let stand for 5 minutes. Stir in the remaining ingredients.

Yield: 2 servings

Per serving: 250 calories (2% from fat, 9% from protein, 89% from carbohydrate); 6 g protein; 0 g total fat; 0 g saturated fat; 0 g monounsaturated fat; 0 g polyunsaturated fat; 57 g carbohydrate; 3 g fiber; 20 g sugar; 85 mg phosphorus; 27 mg calcium; 1 mg iron; 9 mg sodium; 161 mg potassium; 2 IU vitamin A; 0 mg ATE vitamin E; 0 mg vitamin C; 0 mg cholesterol; 97 g water

Cranberry Orange Smoothie

If you have a little cranberry sauce left (as I always seem to after the holidays), this is a tasty way to use it.

½ cup (135 g) cranberry sauce

½ cup (120 ml) orange juice

1 cup (230 g) plain nonfat yogurt

1 cup (225 g) banana, sliced

½ cup (120 ml) skim milk

Combine all ingredients in a blender and process until smooth.

Yield: 2 servings

Per serving: 326 calories (3% from fat, 13% from protein, 84% from carbohydrate); 11 g protein; 1 g total fat; 0 g saturated fat; 0 g monounsaturated fat; 0 g polyunsaturated fat; 72 g carbohydrate; 4 g fiber; 49 g sugar; 297 mg phosphorus; 346 mg calcium; 1 mg iron; 152 mg sodium; 963 mg potassium; 283 IU vitamin A; 40 mg ATE vitamin E; 33 mg vitamin C; 4 mg cholesterol; 341 g water

Banana Melon Smoothies

I like smoothies for a quick breakfast, but I find that I'm often hungry before noon. Adding some extra protein with the tofu seems to help fill me up longer.

6 ounces (170 g) soft tofu

1 banana

1 cup (155 g) cantaloupe

½ cup (120 ml) skim milk

½ cup (120 ml) apple juice

Place all ingredients in a blender and process until smooth.

Yield: 2 servings

Per serving: 230 calories (11% from fat, 14% from protein, 75% from carbohydrate); 9 g protein; 3 g total fat; 1 g saturated fat; 1 g monounsaturated fat; 1 g polyunsaturated fat; 46 g carbohydrate; 4 g fiber; 28 g sugar; 164 mg phosphorus; 131 mg calcium; 1 mg iron; 60 mg sodium; 979 mg potassium; 3190 IU vitamin A; 38 mg ATE vitamin E; 43 mg vitamin C; 1 mg cholesterol; 347 g water

Bananaberry Smoothies

I developed this as a way to store and use later those last couple of bananas that always seem to be near the end of their useful life just when you don't have a use for them. Peel bananas, cut in halves or thirds, and freeze in a resealable plastic bag to use them in smoothies later. Using frozen bananas also gives you a nice, thick smoothie that isn't diluted by ice.

½ cup (120 ml) orange juice

1½ cups (340 g) frozen bananas

½ cup (55 g) frozen strawberries

Pour juice into blender. Add frozen bananas and berries and blend until smooth.

Yield: 2 servings

Per serving: 190 calories (4% from fat, 5% from protein, 91% from carbohydrate); 3 g protein; 1 g total fat; 0 g saturated fat; 0 g monounsaturated fat; 0 g polyunsaturated fat; 48 g carbohydrate; 5 g fiber; 22 g sugar; 53 mg phosphorus; 21 mg calcium; 1 mg iron; 3 mg sodium; 781 mg potassium; 161 IU vitamin A; 0 mg ATE vitamin E; 58 mg vitamin C; 0 mg cholesterol; 216 g water

TIP *You can use apple juice or other fruit juice and any kind of fresh or frozen fruit.*

Peach Smoothies

The yogurt in this smoothie adds calcium, protein, and other nutrients, making it even more healthful than some of the fruit-only ones.

1 cup (235 ml) orange juice

1 cup (225 g) banana

1 cup (230 g) low fat vanilla yogurt

¾ cup (150 g) peaches, sliced and frozen

Place all ingredients in a blender and process until thick and smooth.

Yield: 1 serving

Per serving: 563 calories (7% from fat, 12% from protein, 81% from carbohydrate); 18 g protein; 5 g total fat; 2 g saturated fat; 1 g monounsaturated fat; 1 g polyunsaturated fat; 121 g carbohydrate; 8 g fiber; 71 g sugar; 431 mg phosphorus; 462 mg calcium; 1 mg iron; 166 mg sodium; 2034 mg potassium; 820 IU vitamin A; 29 mg ATE vitamin E; 111 mg vitamin C; 12 mg cholesterol; 685 g water

Strawberry Smoothie

1¼ cups (140 g) strawberries

1½ cups (355 ml) skim milk

1 tablespoon (13 g) sugar

1 teaspoon (5 ml) lemon juice

Put all ingredients in a blender and process until smooth.

Yield: 2 servings

Per serving: 131 calories (5% from fat, 24% from protein, 71% from carbohydrate); 8 g protein; 1 g total fat; 0 g saturated fat; 0 g monounsaturated fat; 0 g polyunsaturated fat; 24 g carbohydrate; 2 g fiber; 11 g sugar; 230 mg phosphorus; 279 mg calcium; 1 mg iron; 110 mg sodium; 484 mg potassium; 386 IU vitamin a; 113 mg ATE vitamin e; 59 mg vitamin c; 4 mg cholesterol; 254 g water

Yogurt Parfait

This makes a nice change of pace for breakfast. Even though the total fat may seem high, it's almost all from the walnuts, which provide a healthy fat.

1 cup (110 g) strawberries

2 tablespoons (26 g) sugar

8 ounces (225 g) plain fat-free yogurt

½ cup (50 g) granola

¼ cup (31 g) chopped walnuts

Chop the strawberries and toss with the sugar. Layer in parfait glasses in this order: fruit, yogurt, granola, and nuts. Repeat layers.

Yield: 2 servings

Per serving: 313 calories (29% from fat, 15% from protein, 55% from carbohydrate); 12 g protein; 11 g total fat; 1 g saturated fat; 3 g monounsaturated fat; 6 g polyunsaturated fat; 45 g carbohydrate; 4 g fiber; 32 g sugar; 333 mg phosphorus; 255 mg calcium; 1 mg iron; 166 mg sodium; 545 mg potassium; 23 IU vitamin A; 2 mg ATE vitamin E; 46 mg vitamin C; 2 mg cholesterol; 168 g water

5

Main Dishes:
Vegetarian

I have to admit that we never ate many vegetarian meals before my doctor warned me about my cholesterol. My wife sometimes claims to be a carnivore, and I have to admit to feeling that way myself sometimes. But as we learned to reduce the amount of saturated fats we were eating, we turned to vegetarian cooking more often. These recipes do contain cheese and other dairy products, so they wouldn't work without modification for vegan and other strict vegetarian diets. But for those of us looking for healthy alternatives to meat, they fill the bill.

Tomato and Basil Quiche

A great meatless quiche. If you want, you can put it in a crust, but we like it just as well without it.

1 tablespoon (15 ml) olive oil

1 cup (160 g) onion, sliced

2 cups (360 g) tomatoes, sliced

2 tablespoons (16 g) flour

2 teaspoons (1.4 g) dried basil

¾ cup (180 ml) egg substitute

½ cup (120 ml) skim milk

½ teaspoon (1 g) black pepper

1 cup (110 g) Swiss cheese, shredded

Preheat oven to 400°F (200°C, or gas mark 6). Heat olive oil in a large skillet over medium heat. Sauté onion until soft; remove from skillet. Sprinkle tomato slices with flour and basil, then sauté 1 minute on each side. In a small bowl, whisk together egg substitute and milk. Season with pepper. Spread half the cheese in the bottom of a pie pan sprayed with nonstick vegetable oil spray. Layer onions over the cheese and top with tomatoes. Pour the egg mixture over the vegetables. Sprinkle the remaining cheese over the top. Bake for 10 minutes. Reduce heat to 350°F (180°C, or gas mark 4), and bake for 15 to 20 minutes, or until filling is puffed and golden brown. Serve warm.

Yield: 4 servings

Per serving: 188 calories (33% from fat, 38% from protein, 29% from carbohydrate); 18 g protein; 7 g total fat; 2 g saturated fat; 3 g monounsaturated fat; 1 g polyunsaturated fat; 14 g carbohydrate; 2 g fiber; 2 g sugar; 327 mg phosphorus; 408 mg calcium; 2 mg iron; 196 mg sodium; 491 mg potassium; 781 IU vitamin A; 32 mg ATE vitamin E; 23 mg vitamin C; 13 mg cholesterol; 192 g water

Broccoli Wild Rice Casserole

This is another recipe that can be used as either a side dish or as a vegetarian main course.

1½ cups (240 g) wild rice

6 cups (420 g) broccoli

2 cups (484 g) reduced-sodium cream of mushroom soup

2 cups (225 g) low fat cheddar cheese, shredded

Preheat oven to 325°F (170°C, or gas mark 3). Prepare wild rice according to package directions. Layer rice in the bottom of a 9 × 9-inch (23 × 23-cm) casserole pan. Steam broccoli for 5 minutes and layer on top of rice. Mix soup and cheese together and spread on top of broccoli. Bake, uncovered, for 45 minutes.

Yield: 6 servings

Per serving: 293 calories (16% from fat, 27% from protein, 58% from carbohydrate); 20 g protein; 5 g total fat; 2 g saturated fat; 1 g monounsaturated fat; 1 g polyunsaturated fat; 44 g carbohydrate; 5 g fiber; 5 g sugar; 489 mg phosphorus; 245 mg calcium; 2 mg iron; 623 mg sodium; 800 mg potassium; 672 IU vitamin A; 28 mg ATE vitamin E; 81 mg vitamin C; 12 mg cholesterol; 185 g water

Potato and Winter Vegetable Casserole

A simple potato and vegetable casserole that's good for a winter's evening with rustic bread.

6 potatoes

2 tablespoons (30 ml) olive oil

1 cup (160 g) onion, sliced

2 cups (180 g) cabbage, chopped

2 cups (300 g) cauliflower, chopped

1 teaspoon (3 g) garlic, crushed

1 cup (230 g) plain fat-free yogurt

(continued on page 84)

2 cups (450 g) canned white kidney beans

¼ cup (16 g) fresh dill, chopped

½ teaspoon (1.3 g) paprika

Preheat oven to 325°F (170°C, or gas mark 3). Boil or microwave the potatoes until nearly done. When cool enough, peel if desired. Heat the olive oil in a large skillet over medium-high heat. Sauté the onions until soft. Add the cabbage, cauliflower, and garlic, and fry until the cabbage and cauliflower are just tender. Add the yogurt to the vegetable mixture. Drain and rinse the white beans and add to the vegetable mixture. Mix thoroughly and set aside. Slice the potatoes into rounds and put half the slices on the bottom of a 9 × 13-inch (23 × 33-cm) baking dish sprayed with nonstick vegetable oil spray. Spread the vegetable mixture over the potatoes. Cover with the remaining potatoes. Sprinkle with dill and paprika. Bake for 20 minutes.

Yield: 6 servings

Per serving: 462 calories (11% from fat, 15% from protein, 74% from carbohydrate); 17 g protein; 6 g total fat; 1 g saturated fat; 3 g monounsaturated fat; 1 g polyunsaturated fat; 88 g carbohydrate; 12 g fiber; 11 g sugar; 400 mg phosphorus; 235 mg calcium; 6 mg iron; 89 mg sodium; 2352 mg potassium; 289 IU vitamin A; 1 mg ATE vitamin E; 70 mg vitamin C; 1 mg cholesterol; 415 g water

Mexican Bean Bake

This makes a great Mexican-flavored vegetarian meal. We usually have it with a simple salad topped with guacamole.

2 cups (460 g) refried beans

4 cups (660 g) cooked rice

2 cups (450 g) canned black beans, drained

1 cup (225 g) salsa

1 cup (120 g) low fat cheddar cheese, shredded

Preheat oven to 375°F (190°C, or gas mark 5). In a 9 × 9-inch (23 × 23-cm) baking dish, spread out the refried beans. Layer cooked rice on top. Layer black beans on top of rice. Spread with salsa. Sprinkle with cheese. Bake for 15 to 20 minutes, or until heated through and cheese is melted.

Yield: 6 servings

Per serving: 334 calories (9% from fat, 22% from protein, 68% from carbohydrate); 19 g protein; 3 g total fat; 2 g saturated fat; 1 g monounsaturated fat; 0 g polyunsaturated fat; 57 g carbohydrate; 11 g fiber; 2 g sugar; 330 mg phosphorus; 168 mg calcium; 5 mg iron; 647 mg sodium; 630 mg potassium; 175 IU vitamin A; 13 mg ATE vitamin E; 6 mg vitamin C; 11 mg cholesterol; 228 g water

Eggplant and Fresh Mozzarella Bake

This again can be either a meal or a side dish with other Italian food. The fresh mozzarella adds a different flavor and has the benefit of being low in sodium.

6 ounces (170 g) fresh mozzarella

2 cups (470 ml) low sodium spaghetti sauce

1 eggplant, peeled and sliced

Preheat oven to 375°F (190°C, or gas mark 5). Slice mozzarella thinly and place on paper towels to soak up excess moisture. Cover the bottom of an 8 × 8-inch (20 × 20-cm) baking dish with spaghetti sauce, layer eggplant on top of sauce, then cheese on top of eggplant. Repeat layers, ending with a layer of sauce. Bake for 30 minutes or until bubbly and cheese is melted.

Yield: 6 servings

Per serving: 181 calories (41% from fat, 19% from protein, 39% from carbohydrate); 9 g protein; 9 g total fat; 3 g saturated fat; 4 g monounsaturated fat; 1 g polyunsaturated fat; 18 g carbohydrate; 5 g fiber; 12 g sugar; 180 mg phosphorus; 252 mg calcium; 1 mg iron; 202 mg sodium; 519 mg potassium; 669 IU vitamin A; 35 mg ATE vitamin E; 11 mg vitamin C; 18 mg cholesterol; 149 g water

Squash and Rice Bake

Another of those dishes that can be either a full meal or a side dish in a meal with meat.

½ cup (95 g) rice

2 tablespoons (30 ml) olive oil

¼ teaspoon (0.8 g) minced garlic

½ teaspoon (0.5 g) dried thyme

4 cups (450 g) yellow squash, sliced

2 ounces (55 g) low fat Swiss cheese, shredded

Preheat oven to 350°F (180°C, or gas mark 4). Cook rice according to package directions. Heat oil in a large skillet. Sauté garlic for a few minutes. Add thyme and squash. Sauté for a few minutes more. Stir the rice and cheese into the mixture. Turn into a 2-quart (1.9-L) baking dish that has been coated with nonstick vegetable oil spray. Bake for 25 minutes or until heated through.

Yield: 4 servings

Per serving: 128 calories (53% from fat, 18% from protein, 29% from carbohydrate); 6 g protein; 8 g total fat; 1 g saturated fat; 5 g monounsaturated fat; 1 g polyunsaturated fat; 10 g carbohydrate; 1 g fiber; 3 g sugar; 140 mg phosphorus; 160 mg calcium; 1 mg iron; 40 mg sodium; 325 mg potassium; 252 IU vitamin A; 6 mg ATE vitamin E; 19 mg vitamin C; 5 mg cholesterol; 129 g water

Zucchini Frittata

During the summer when the garden is producing I'm often looking for uses for zucchini, and this one was popular.

2 cups (250 g) shredded zucchini

2 tablespoons (30 ml) olive oil

½ cup (35 g) mushrooms, sliced

1 cup (235 ml) egg substitute

⅓ cup (37 g) Swiss cheese, shredded

Place the zucchini in a paper towel and squeeze out any excess moisture. Heat oil in a 10-inch (25-cm) skillet. Sauté the mushrooms briefly, then add the zucchini. Cook for 4 minutes, or until the squash is barely tender. Pour egg substitute over vegetables. Stir once quickly to coat vegetables. Cook over low heat until eggs begin to set. Sprinkle with the cheese. Place under the broiler until cheese browns. Let set for 2 to 3 minutes. Cut into wedges and serve.

Yield: 4 servings

Per serving: 144 calories (59% from fat, 32% from protein, 9% from carbohydrate); 12 g protein; 10 g total fat; 2 g saturated fat; 6 g monounsaturated fat; 2 g polyunsaturated fat; 3 g carbohydrate; 1 g fiber; 2 g sugar; 174 mg phosphorus; 149 mg calcium; 2 mg iron; 146 mg sodium; 410 mg potassium; 367 IU vitamin A; 4 mg ATE vitamin E; 11 mg vitamin C; 4 mg cholesterol; 125 g water

Lentils and Pasta

We usually eat this as a side dish, but it also could be the start of a complete meal, just by adding salad and bread.

1 cup (225 g) lentils

½ cup (50 g) celery, sliced

1½ cups (240 g) onion, coarsely chopped, divided

2 tablespoons (30 ml) olive oil

½ teaspoon (1.3 g) cumin

1 tablespoon (4 g) cilantro

6 ounces (170 g) fresh spinach

8 ounces (225 g) pasta (small shapes like orzo are best)

Cook lentils in 6 cups (1.4 L) water with celery and ½ cup (80 g) of the onion until soft, about 40 minutes. In a large skillet, heat the olive oil and sauté the remaining onions, cumin, and cilantro until onions are soft. Add spinach and sauté until wilted, another 4 to 5 minutes. Drain lentils and stir into onion-spinach mixture. Cook pasta according to package directions. Stir into mixture.

Yield: 6 servings

(continued on page 88)

Per serving: 245 calories (20% from fat, 15% from protein, 65% from carbohydrate); 10 g protein; 5 g total fat; 1 g saturated fat; 3 g monounsaturated fat; 1 g polyunsaturated fat; 40 g carbohydrate; 6 g fiber; 4 g sugar; 160 mg phosphorus; 72 mg calcium; 2 mg iron; 39 mg sodium; 378 mg potassium; 3492 IU vitamin A; 0 mg ATE vitamin E; 5 mg vitamin C; 0 mg cholesterol; 96 g water

Pasta with Garbanzos

Again this could be a main dish or a fantastic side dish. I often take leftovers of dishes like this for lunch, skipping the meat.

1 tablespoon (15 ml) olive oil

½ cup (80 g) onion, diced

⅛ teaspoon (0.2 g) red pepper flakes

½ teaspoon (1.5 g) minced garlic

1½ cups (360 g) garbanzo beans, cooked

8 ounces (225 g) pasta

¼ cup Parmesan, shredded

Heat oil in a large skillet over medium-high heat. Sauté onions, red pepper flakes, and garlic until onion is soft. Stir in cooked garbanzo beans. Cook pasta according to package directions and stir into mixture. Sprinkle with cheese.

Yield: 4 servings

Per serving: 383 calories (17% from fat, 15% from protein, 68% from carbohydrate); 15 g protein; 7 g total fat; 2 g saturated fat; 3 g monounsaturated fat; 1 g polyunsaturated fat; 65 g carbohydrate; 6 g fiber; 2 g sugar; 240 mg phosphorus; 115 mg calcium; 2 mg iron; 369 mg sodium; 321 mg potassium; 73 IU vitamin A; 7 mg ATE vitamin E; 5 mg vitamin C; 6 mg cholesterol; 88 g water

Cheese Pie

This is an ideal vegetarian main dish, needing only a salad to make it a complete meal.

4 ounces (115 g) feta cheese

16 ounces (455 g) low fat ricotta cheese

1 cup (235 ml) egg substitute

¼ cup (30 g) flour

¾ cup (180 ml) skim milk

¼ teaspoon (0.5 g) black pepper

Preheat oven to 375°F (190°C, or gas mark 5). Spray an ovenproof skillet or glass baking dish with nonstick vegetable oil spray. Mix the cheeses together, then stir in the egg substitute, flour, milk, and pepper. Pour the batter into the prepared pan. Bake for 40 minutes, or until golden and set. Cut into wedges.

Yield: 4 servings

Per serving: 332 calories (47% from fat, 33% from protein, 20% from carbohydrate); 27 g protein; 17 g total fat; 10 g saturated fat; 5 g monounsaturated fat; 2 g polyunsaturated fat; 16 g carbohydrate; 0 g fiber; 2 g sugar; 439 mg phosphorus; 549 mg calcium; 2 mg iron; 597 mg sodium; 460 mg potassium; 875 IU vitamin A; 183 mg ATE vitamin E; 1 mg vitamin C; 62 mg cholesterol; 194 g water

Spaghetti with Italian Vegetables

Fresh vegetables are all that's really needed to make a meal of spaghetti. This is a great summer dinner when the garden and farmer's market are overflowing.

12 ounces (340 g) spaghetti

2 tablespoons (30 ml) olive oil

1 cup (150 g) red bell pepper, cut in strips

1 cup (150 g) yellow bell pepper, cut in strips

1 cup (160 g) onion, thinly sliced

(continued on page 90)

½ teaspoon (1.5 g) minced garlic

1 teaspoon (0.7 g) Italian seasoning

½ cup (120 ml) dry white wine

30 cherry tomatoes, halved

¼ cup (20 g) Parmesan, shredded

Cook spaghetti according to package directions. Drain. Heat oil in large skillet or Dutch oven. Sauté peppers and onion until they begin to soften, then add the garlic, Italian seasoning, and wine and sauté a few minutes more, stirring to remove anything stuck to the pan. Add the tomatoes and sauté just until they begin to soften. Stir in the spaghetti. Top with cheese.

Yield: 4 servings

Per serving: 284 calories (32% from fat, 10% from protein, 58% from carbohydrate); 7 g protein; 10 g total fat; 2 g saturated fat; 6 g monounsaturated fat; 1 g polyunsaturated fat; 40 g carbohydrate; 7 g fiber; 4 g sugar; 149 mg phosphorus; 101 mg calcium; 1 mg iron; 101 mg sodium; 579 mg potassium; 2148 IU vitamin A; 7 mg ATE vitamin E; 160 mg vitamin C; 6 mg cholesterol; 198 g water

Vegetarian Lasagna

This recipe is the traditional way to assemble lasagna. It has no meat, but it still has lots of flavor. This is the kind of recipe that I like to tackle on the weekend when there's plenty of time, making a double batch and freezing the extra for a quick meal at some later date.

2 tablespoons (30 ml) olive oil

1 cup (160 g) onion, chopped

6 cups (1.4 L) low sodium spaghetti sauce

12 ounces (340 g) frozen spinach, thawed and drained

15 ounces (425 g) ricotta cheese

½ cup (40 g) Parmesan, shredded

4 ounces (115 g) part-skim mozzarella, shredded

2 tablespoons (0.8 g) dried parsley

½ cup (120 ml) egg substitute

12 ounces (340 g) lasagna noodles, cooked and drained

Preheat oven to 350°F (180°C, or gas mark 4). Heat olive oil in a large skillet over medium-high heat. Sauté onion until lightly browned. Stir in spaghetti sauce. In large bowl, mix the spinach, ricotta, Parmesan, mozzarella, parsley, and egg substitute. Spray a 9 × 13-inch (23 × 33-cm) baking pan with nonstick vegetable oil spray. Place a layer of tomato sauce in the bottom of the pan. Layer noodles, tomato sauce, and ricotta mixture in that order, making three layers of each. Add an additional layer of noodles and sauce on the top. Bake, covered with foil, for 60 to 75 minutes, or until bubbling and heated through. Remove the foil and bake 10 minutes longer.

Yield: 12 servings

Per serving: 376 calories (35% from fat, 17% from protein, 48% from carbohydrate); 16 g protein; 15 g total fat; 5 g saturated fat; 8 g monounsaturated fat; 1 g polyunsaturated fat; 46 g carbohydrate; 6 g fiber; 15 g sugar; 215 mg phosphorus; 309 mg calcium; 3 mg iron; 253 mg sodium; 726 mg potassium; 4477 IU vitamin A; 54 mg ATE vitamin E; 16 mg vitamin C; 21 mg cholesterol; 173 g water

Zucchini Lasagna

This simple vegetarian lasagna using no-boil noodles gets a flavor boost from zucchini.

2 pounds (900 g) zucchini

8 ounces (225 g) low fat ricotta cheese

8 ounces (225 g) part-skim mozzarella, shredded

½ cup (40 g) Parmesan, shredded

2½ cups (570 ml) low sodium spaghetti sauce

8 ounces (225 g) no-boil lasagna noodles

TIP *If you make multiple batches, this freezes well, so you can have it again without the same effort.*

Preheat oven to 350°F (180°C, or gas mark 4). Spray a 9 × 13-inch (23 × 33-cm) glass baking dish with nonstick vegetable oil spray. Slice zucchini lengthwise. Combine the ricotta, mozzarella, and Parmesan. Cover the bottom of the prepared dish with ½ cup (120 ml) of the spaghetti sauce. Cover with 3 noodles. Layer with one-third of the ricotta mixture, ½ cup (120 ml) sauce, and one-third of the zucchini. Repeat 3 times, ending with the remaining sauce. Bake for 40 minutes, or until bubbling and cheese is melted.

Yield: 6 servings

(continued on page 92)

Per serving: 451 calories (34% from fat, 21% from protein, 45% from carbohydrate); 24 g protein; 17 g total fat; 8 g saturated fat; 7 g monounsaturated fat; 1 g polyunsaturated fat; 51 g carbohydrate; 5 g fiber; 14 g sugar; 374 mg phosphorus; 539 mg calcium; 3 mg iron; 451 mg sodium; 767 mg potassium; 1169 IU vitamin A; 96 mg ATE vitamin E; 26 mg vitamin C; 43 mg cholesterol; 207 g water

Pizza Omelet

When you have a taste for pizza, but don't have the time or want to make the effort to make it yourself, try this instead. This is a dinner-sized omelet for two.

1 cup (235 ml) egg substitute

2 tablespoons (30 g) fat-free sour cream

2 tablespoons (30 ml) water

½ teaspoon (0.4 g) Italian seasoning

½ cup (35 g) mushrooms, sliced

¼ cup (40 g) onion, sliced

¼ cup (37 g) green bell pepper, coarsely chopped

¼ cup (60 ml) spaghetti sauce, heated

2 ounces (55 g) part-skim mozzarella, shredded

Whisk together egg substitute, sour cream, water, and Italian seasoning until fluffy. Sauté mushrooms, onion, and green bell pepper until onion begins to get soft. Pour egg mixture into a heated nonstick skillet or omelet pan sprayed with nonstick vegetable oil spray. Lift the edges as it cooks to allow uncooked egg to run underneath. When it is nearly set, cover half the omelet with the vegetables and fold the other half over the top. Remove to plate. Top with heated sauce and cheese.

Yield: 2 servings

Per serving: 232 calories (39% from fat, 45% from protein, 16% from carbohydrate); 24 g protein; 9 g total fat; 4 g saturated fat; 3 g monounsaturated fat; 2 g polyunsaturated fat; 9 g carbohydrate; 2 g fiber; 3 g sugar; 334 mg phosphorus; 323 mg calcium; 3 mg iron; 547 mg sodium; 699 mg potassium; 856 IU vitamin A; 51 mg ATE vitamin E; 20 mg vitamin C; 25 mg cholesterol; 224 g water

Ricotta Omelet

This makes a nice summer dinner, with a salad and bread. You could also add some vegetables if you like.

1 cup (235 ml) egg substitute

¼ teaspoon (0.8 g) garlic powder

¼ teaspoon (0.5 g) black pepper

½ cup (125 g) low fat ricotta cheese

2 tablespoons (30 ml) olive oil

Beat the egg substitute with the garlic powder, pepper, and ricotta. Heat the oil in a skillet or omelet pan. Add the egg mixture, and swirl to distribute evenly. Cook until nearly set, lifting edge to allow uncooked egg to run underneath. Fold over, cover, and cook until done.

Yield: 2 servings

Per serving: 311 calories (66% from fat, 29% from protein, 6% from carbohydrate); 22 g protein; 23 g total fat; 6 g saturated fat; 12 g monounsaturated fat; 4 g polyunsaturated fat; 4 g carbohydrate; 0 g fiber; 1 g sugar; 266 mg phosphorus; 235 mg calcium; 3 mg iron; 299 mg sodium; 498 mg potassium; 689 IU vitamin A; 65 mg ATE vitamin E; 0 mg vitamin C; 20 mg cholesterol; 150 g water

Spinach-Stuffed Tomatoes

This is another of those recipes that would also make a good side dish.

10 ounces (280 g) fresh spinach

4 tomatoes

1 cup (115 g) part-skim mozzarella, divided

¼ cup (40 g) onion, finely chopped

¼ cup (25 g) Parmesan, grated

⅛ teaspoon (0.3 g) pepper

2 tablespoons (8 g) fresh parsley, minced

(continued on page 94)

Preheat oven to 350°F (180°C, or gas mark 4). Steam spinach or microwave in a covered bowl until softened but still slightly crispy. Drain well and squeeze dry. Put in a large bowl. Slice and hollow out tomatoes, reserving the pulp. Discard seeds. Chop pulp finely and add to spinach. Add ½ cup (60 g) mozzarella cheese, onion, Parmesan, and pepper to spinach and blend well. Spoon into tomato shells. Sprinkle with remaining mozzarella and parsley. Arrange in an 8-inch (20 cm) round glass or ceramic baking dish and bake for 6 minutes, or until heated through.

Yield: 4 servings

Per serving: 158 calories (38% from fat, 32% from protein, 30% from carbohydrate); 14 g protein; 7 g total fat; 4 g saturated fat; 2 g monounsaturated fat; 1 g polyunsaturated fat; 13 g carbohydrate; 4 g fiber; 1 g sugar; 252 mg phosphorus; 412 mg calcium; 2 mg iron; 355 mg sodium; 602 mg potassium; 9802 IU vitamin A; 42 mg ATE vitamin E; 44 mg vitamin C; 24 mg cholesterol; 230 g water

Zucchini Patties

These taste like crab cakes but without the crab.

2½ cups (310 g) grated zucchini

¼ cup (60 ml) egg substitute

1 cup (115 g) bread crumbs

¼ cup (60 g) minced onion

1 teaspoon (2.4 g) Old Bay Seasoning

¼ cup (30 g) flour

2 tablespoons (30 ml) olive oil

In a large bowl, combine zucchini and egg substitute. Stir in bread crumbs, minced onion, and seasoning. Mix well. Shape mixture into patties. Dredge in flour. In a medium skillet, heat oil over medium-high heat until hot. Fry patties in oil until golden brown on both sides.

Yield: 6 servings

Per serving: 150 calories (36% from fat, 13% from protein, 51% from carbohydrate); 5 g protein; 6 g total fat; 1 g saturated fat; 4 g monounsaturated fat; 1 g polyunsaturated fat; 19 g carbohydrate; 2 g fiber; 2 g sugar; 70 mg phosphorus; 49 mg calcium; 2 mg iron; 156 mg sodium; 221 mg potassium; 141 IU vitamin A; 0 mg ATE vitamin E; 9 mg vitamin C; 0 mg cholesterol; 65 g water ·

Bean and Tomato Curry

This makes a good side dish with something like a grilled chicken breast or loin pork chop, but you can also use it for a vegetarian meal. In that case, serve over rice or with pita bread.

1 tablespoon (15 ml) canola oil

1 teaspoon (3.7 g) mustard seed

1 teaspoon (2.5 g) cumin seeds

1 cup (160 g) onion, chopped

1 tablespoon (6 g) fresh ginger, peeled and chopped

½ teaspoon (1.5 g) chopped garlic

4 cups (720 g) canned no-salt-added tomatoes

2 cups (450 g) kidney beans, drained and rinsed

1 teaspoon (2 g) curry powder

TIP *To lower the amount of sodium, use no-salt-added beans or cooked dried beans.*

Heat oil in large pot over medium heat and stir-fry the mustard and cumin seeds until they pop. Add onion, ginger, and garlic, and stir-fry until lightly colored. Add tomatoes with juice, beans, and curry powder. Simmer for about 20 minutes or until thick and saucy.

Yield: 6 servings

Per serving: 140 calories (19% from fat, 19% from protein, 62% from carbohydrate); 7 g protein; 3 g total fat; 0 g saturated fat; 2 g monounsaturated fat; 1 g polyunsaturated fat; 23 g carbohydrate; 6 g fiber; 5 g sugar; 131 mg phosphorus; 81 mg calcium; 4 mg iron; 163 mg sodium; 598 mg potassium; 196 IU vitamin A; 0 mg ATE vitamin E; 18 mg vitamin C; 0 mg cholesterol; 215 g water

Garbanzo Curry

Indian vegetarian slow cooker recipes like this curry will warm you up on a cold day. It's so easy, but it tastes as good as vegetarian Indian recipes you get at a restaurant.

2 tablespoons (30 ml) canola oil

1 cup (160 g) onion, diced

½ teaspoon (1.5 g) minced garlic

1 teaspoon (2.7 g) fresh ginger, peeled and grated

1 teaspoon (2.5 g) cumin

1 teaspoon (2 g) coriander

1 teaspoon (2.2 g) turmeric

2 cups (480 g) canned garbanzo beans,
   drained and rinsed

2 cups (360 g) canned no-salt-added tomatoes

½ teaspoon (1.2 g) garam masala

TIP *Garam masala is an Indian spice blend that you can find at larger grocery or specialty stores.*

Heat oil in a heavy skillet. Sauté onion, garlic, ginger, cumin, coriander, and turmeric until onion becomes soft. Place onion mixture and remaining ingredients in a slow cooker and cook on low for 8 to 10 hours or on high for 4 to 5 hours.

Yield: 4 servings

Per serving: 246 calories (31% from fat, 12% from protein, 57% from carbohydrate); 8 g protein; 9 g total fat; 1 g saturated fat; 5 g monounsaturated fat; 3 g polyunsaturated fat; 37 g carbohydrate; 7 g fiber; 5 g sugar; 148 mg phosphorus; 93 mg calcium; 4 mg iron; 377 mg sodium; 524 mg potassium; 185 IU vitamin A; 0 mg ATE vitamin E; 20 mg vitamin C; 0 mg cholesterol; 233 g water

Tofu Curry

This is one of the simplest vegetarian meals you'll find. Serve the curry over rice with whatever condiments you like.

3 tablespoons (45 ml) olive oil, divided

12 ounces (340 g) firm tofu, drained and cubed

1 cup (113 g) zucchini, sliced

1 cup (70 g) mushrooms, sliced

1 cup (235 ml) fat-free evaporated milk

2 teaspoons (4 g) curry powder

TIP *The possibilities for vegetable combinations are almost endless. Feel free to experiment.*

Heat 1 tablespoon (15 ml) oil in a large skillet or work. Fry tofu until the bottom gets golden, then carefully turn and fry the other sides. Remove to a plate. Heat remaining oil and stir-fry zucchini and mushrooms until crisp-tender. Add milk and curry powder and continue cooking until slightly thickened. Stir in tofu.

Yield: 4 servings

Per serving: 204 calories (55% from fat, 23% from protein, 22% from carbohydrate); 12 g protein; 13 g total fat; 2 g saturated fat; 8 g monounsaturated fat; 2 g polyunsaturated fat; 12 g carbohydrate; 1 g fiber; 9 g sugar; 232 mg phosphorus; 223 mg calcium; 2 mg iron; 109 mg sodium; 531 mg potassium; 325 IU vitamin A; 76 mg ATE vitamin E; 7 mg vitamin C; 3 mg cholesterol; 171 g water

Tofu and Broccoli Stir-Fry

This makes a quick and hearty meal with just rice as a base.

12 ounces (340 g) firm tofu

6 tablespoons (90 ml) Dick's Reduced-Sodium Soy Sauce (see recipe page 30)

2 tablespoons (30 ml) mirin wine

1 teaspoon (5 ml) sesame oil

¼ teaspoon (0.8 g) minced garlic

½ teaspoon (0.9 g) ground ginger

1 tablespoon (15 ml) olive oil

6 cups (420 g) broccoli florets

½ cup (35 g) mushrooms, sliced

Remove tofu from package and drain under a plate or other weight. Combine soy sauce, mirin, sesame oil, garlic, and ginger. Remove tofu from weight, cut into ¾-inch (2-cm) cubes, and place in soy sauce mixture. Heat olive oil in a wok or large skillet. Stir-fry broccoli and mushrooms until broccoli is crisp-tender. Remove from wok. Add tofu and cook until it begins to turn golden, then carefully turn and cook the other sides. Return vegetables to wok. Add remaining marinade. Cook and stir carefully until heated through.

Yield: 4 servings

Per serving: 155 calories (9% from fat, 5% from protein, 86% from carbohydrate); 9 g protein; 7 g total fat; 1 g saturated fat; 3 g monounsaturated fat; 5 g polyunsaturated fat; 156 g carbohydrate; 0 g fiber; 5 g sugar; 174 mg phosphorus; 92 mg calcium; 2 mg iron; 217 mg sodium; 606 mg potassium; 3204 IU vitamin A; 0 mg ATE vitamin E; 100 mg vitamin C; 0 mg cholesterol; 214 g water

Corn Chowder

This is great just the way it is, or you can add some cooked chicken or ground turkey if you like. We had it just like this with breadsticks and nothing else.

1 tablespoon (15 ml) olive oil

1 cup (160 g) onion, chopped

½ cup (50 g) celery, sliced

½ cup (65 g) carrot, sliced

2 tablespoons (16 g) flour

2 cups (475 ml) low sodium chicken broth

4 cups (945 ml) skim milk

2 potatoes, peeled and diced

3 cups (410 g) frozen corn, thawed

½ teaspoon (1 g) black pepper

Heat the oil in a large Dutch oven. Add the onion, celery, and carrots and cook over medium heat until just soft. Sprinkle on the flour and cook for 3 minutes, stirring frequently. Stir in the broth and milk. Add the potatoes and corn. Simmer for 25 minutes or until potatoes are tender. Sprinkle with pepper.

Yield: 6 servings

Per serving: 278 calories (12% from fat, 18% from protein, 70% from carbohydrate); 13 g protein; 4 g total fat; 1 g saturated fat; 2 g monounsaturated fat; 1 g polyunsaturated fat; 52 g carbohydrate; 5 g fiber; 6 g sugar; 346 mg phosphorus; 268 mg calcium; 2 mg iron; 148 mg sodium; 1148 mg potassium; 2176 IU vitamin A; 100 mg ATE vitamin E; 18 mg vitamin C; 3 mg cholesterol; 427 g water

Vegetarian Chili

This is a different kind of chili, but it's still very good. Garnish with fresh cilantro, crushed corn chips, shredded low fat cheese, or fat-free sour cream (or all of them!).

¼ cup (60 ml) dry sherry

1 tablespoon (15 ml) olive oil

2 cups (320 g) onion, chopped

½ cup (50 g) celery, chopped

½ cup (65 g) carrot, sliced

½ cup (75 g) red bell pepper, chopped

4 cups (900 g) cooked black beans

2 cups (475 ml) water

½ teaspoon (1.5 g) minced garlic

1 cup (180 g) plum tomato, chopped

2 teaspoons (5 g) ground cumin

4 teaspoons (10 g) chili powder

½ teaspoon (0.5 g) dried oregano

¼ cup (15 g) chopped fresh cilantro

2 tablespoons (30 ml) honey

2 tablespoons (30 ml) no-salt-added tomato paste

In a large, heavy pot over medium heat, combine sherry and oil and heat to simmering. Add onions and sauté 8 to 10 minutes. Add celery, carrots, and bell pepper and sauté 5 minutes more, stirring frequently. Add remaining ingredients and bring to a boil. Lower heat and simmer, covered, for 45 minutes to 1 hour. Mixture should be thick, with all water absorbed.

Yield: 8 servings

Per serving: 192 calories (12% from fat, 18% from protein, 69% from carbohydrate); 9 g protein; 3 g total fat; 0 g saturated fat; 1 g monounsaturated fat; 1 g polyunsaturated fat; 34 g carbohydrate; 10 g fiber; 9 g sugar; 155 mg phosphorus; 55 mg calcium; 3 mg iron; 35 mg sodium; 563 mg potassium; 2358 IU vitamin A; 0 mg ATE vitamin E; 20 mg vitamin C; 0 mg cholesterol; 201 g water

Grilled Veggie Subs

I particularly like these on focaccia bread, but they are also good on homemade rolls. You could add a slice of chicken or other leftover meat if you aren't into the all-veggie thing, but I don't see the need. Feel free to vary the vegetables as desired. I usually sprinkle a little homemade Italian dressing on them too.

4 slices red onion

½ cup (35 g) mushrooms, sliced

½ cup (56 g) zucchini, sliced

¾ cup (112 g) eggplant, sliced

1 cup (180 g) tomato, sliced

2 tablespoons (30 ml) olive oil

8 ounces (225 g) Swiss cheese, sliced

8 slices focaccia bread or 4 rolls

TIP

Be prepared with extra napkins—these are very juicy!

Preheat broiler. Brush onion, mushrooms, zucchini, eggplant, and tomato with oil. Grill or sauté until soft. Divide evenly between focaccia or rolls. Top each with a slice of Swiss cheese. Place under the broiler until cheese melts.

Yield: 4 servings

Per serving: 192 calories (46% from fat, 36% from protein, 18% from carbohydrate); 17 g protein; 10 g total fat; 3 g saturated fat; 6 g monounsaturated fat; 1 g polyunsaturated fat; 9 g carbohydrate; 2 g fiber; 4 g sugar; 381 mg phosphorus; 562 mg calcium; 0 mg iron; 153 mg sodium; 313 mg potassium; 432 IU vitamin A; 22 mg ATE vitamin E; 11 mg vitamin C; 20 mg cholesterol; 142 g water

Grilled Stuffed Portobellos

I discovered Portobello mushrooms not too long ago. We like them grilled on a bun, but these Mediterranean-flavored ones are better served with pasta or rice.

2/3 cup (120 g) plum tomato, chopped

2 ounces (55 g) part-skim mozzarella, shredded

1 teaspoon (5 ml) olive oil, divided

½ teaspoon (0.4 g) fresh rosemary

⅛ teaspoon (0.3 g) coarsely ground black pepper

¼ teaspoon (0.8 g) crushed garlic

4 Portobello mushroom caps, about 4 to 5 inches (10 to 12.5 cm) each

2 tablespoons (30 ml) lemon juice

2 teaspoons (2.6 g) fresh parsley

Prepare grill. Combine the tomato, cheese, ½ teaspoon (2.5 ml) oil, rosemary, pepper, and garlic in a small bowl. Remove brown gills from the undersides of mushroom caps using a spoon, and discard gills. Remove stems; discard. Combine remaining ½ teaspoon oil (2.5 ml) and lemon juice in a small bowl. Brush over both sides of mushroom caps. Place the mushroom caps, stem sides down, on grill rack sprayed with nonstick vegetable oil spray, and grill for 5 minutes on each side or until soft. Spoon one-quarter of the tomato mixture into each mushroom cap. Cover and grill 3 minutes or until cheese is melted. Sprinkle with parsley.

Yield: 4 servings

Per serving: 75 calories (40% from fat, 29% from protein, 32% from carbohydrate); 6 g protein; 4 g total fat; 2 g saturated fat; 1 g monounsaturated fat; 0 g polyunsaturated fat; 6 g carbohydrate; 2 g fiber; 3 g sugar; 181 mg phosphorus; 122 mg calcium; 1 mg iron; 95 mg sodium; 490 mg potassium; 331 IU vitamin A; 18 mg ATE vitamin E; 8 mg vitamin C; 9 mg cholesterol; 115 g water

Grilled Portobello Mushrooms

This is a fairly simple recipe for grilled Portobellos, but one that still provides a flavorful meat alternative.

4 portobello mushroom caps

¼ cup (60 ml) balsamic vinegar

1 tablespoon (15 ml) olive oil

1 teaspoon (0.7 g) dried basil

1 teaspoon (1 g) dried oregano

½ teaspoon (1.5 g) minced garlic

4 ounces (115 g) low fat provolone cheese, sliced

Place the mushroom caps smooth side up in a shallow dish. Mix together vinegar, oil, basil, oregano, and garlic. Pour over the mushrooms. Let stand at room temperature for 15 minutes, turning twice. Preheat grill to medium-high heat. Brush grate with oil. Place mushrooms on the grill, reserving marinade for basting. Grill for 5 to 8 minutes on each side, or until tender. Brush with marinade frequently. Top with cheese during the last 2 minutes of grilling.

Yield: 4 servings

Per serving: 156 calories (53% from fat, 30% from protein, 17% from carbohydrate); 9 g protein; 7 g total fat; 3 g saturated fat; 4 g monounsaturated fat; 1 g polyunsaturated fat; 5 g carbohydrate; 1 g fiber; 2 g sugar; 252 mg phosphorus; 230 mg calcium; 1 mg iron; 254 mg sodium; 466 mg potassium; 283 IU vitamin A; 65 mg ATE vitamin E; 0 mg vitamin C; 20 mg cholesterol; 102 g water

Hawaiian Portobello Burgers

We only recently started using Portobello mushrooms, but they have quickly become a popular addition to our diet. This recipe gives you a sandwich so flavorful you won't miss the meat.

2 Portobello mushrooms, cleaned and stems removed

2 tablespoons (30 ml) Dick's Reduced-Sodium Teriyaki Sauce (see recipe page 31)

2 slices pineapple

(continued on page 104)

2 slices low fat Monterey jack cheese

2 lettuce leaves

2 slices tomato

2 hamburger buns

1 tablespoon (14 g) low fat mayonnaise

Place mushrooms in a shallow dish. Spread teriyaki sauce over the mushrooms and marinate for 15 minutes. Grill the mushrooms and pineapple slices over low heat until tender. Add the cheese on top of the mushrooms and continue to grill briefly to melt cheese. Assemble burgers by placing 1 lettuce leaf and tomato slice on each bottom bun, then top with the mushrooms and pineapple. Spread each top bun with half of the mayonnaise.

Yield: 2 servings

Per serving: 248 calories (19% from fat, 25% from protein, 56% from carbohydrate); 17 g protein; 6 g total fat; 2 g saturated fat; 1 g monounsaturated fat; 1 g polyunsaturated fat; 39 g carbohydrate; 11 g fiber; 26 g sugar; 441 mg phosphorus; 276 mg calcium; 4 mg iron; 329 mg sodium; 1671 mg potassium; 4191 IU vitamin A; 17 mg ATE vitamin E; 29 mg vitamin C; 9 mg cholesterol; 909 g water

Roasted Vegetable Stuffed Pizza

My daughter found a picture of a recipe like this one in a bread book at Border's bookstore when she worked there part-time. We set out with what she remembered to try to recreate it. I have to say I liked it better than anything new we've had in quite a while. But then, I've always thought that pizza was the perfect food.

1 cup (235 ml) water

4 teaspoons (20 ml) olive oil

1½ cups (190 g) bread flour

1½ cups (190 g) whole wheat flour

1½ teaspoons (3.5 g) yeast

3 cups (210 g) mushrooms, quartered

2 cups (226 g) zucchini, sliced

1 cup (160 g) onion, sliced

1 cup (150 g) red bell pepper, sliced

1 cup (150 g) green bell pepper, sliced

1 tablespoon (15 ml) olive oil

1 cup (235 ml) low sodium spaghetti sauce

3 ounces (85 g) part-skim mozzarella, shredded

Preheat oven to 450°F (230°C, or gas mark 8). Place first 5 ingredients (through yeast) in a bread machine pan in the order specified by the manufacturer. Process on the dough cycle. Meanwhile, combine mushrooms, zucchini, onion, and red and green bell peppers and olive oil in a large baking pan. Bake vegetable mixture for 20 minutes, or until tender and browned on the edges. Stir in spaghetti sauce and set aside. Reduce oven heat to 350°F (180°C, or gas mark 4). Grease the bottom and sides of a 9-inch (23-cm) springform pan. When dough is done, remove from bread machine, punch down, and allow to rest 10 minutes. Separate into two balls, with about three-quarters of the dough in the largest one. Roll the large ball out to a 16-inch (40-cm) circle. Place in bottom and up the sides of the pan. Sprinkle half the cheese on the bottom. Place the vegetable mixture on top of the cheese, then sprinkle the remaining cheese over. Roll the smaller ball to a 9-inch (23-cm) circle. Place over the mixture. Fold the edges of the bottom crust over the top and seal. Bake for 30 to 40 minutes, or until golden brown. Cool in pan 20 minutes, then remove sides and cut into six wedges.

Yield: 6 servings

Per serving: 393 calories (24% from fat, 15% from protein, 61% from carbohydrate); 15 g protein; 11 g total fat; 3 g saturated fat; 6 g monounsaturated fat; 1 g polyunsaturated fat; 62 g carbohydrate; 8 g fiber; 9 g sugar; 296 mg phosphorus; 157 mg calcium; 4 mg iron; 113 mg sodium; 702 mg potassium; 1280 IU vitamin A; 18 mg ATE vitamin E; 66 mg vitamin C; 9 mg cholesterol; 228 g water

Zucchini Wraps

A nice change-of-pace zucchini dish, vegetarian and flavored with southwestern spices.

1 tablespoon (15 ml) olive oil

1 cup (160 g) onion, chopped

1 teaspoon (3 g) dry mustard

1 teaspoon (2.5 g) cumin

4 cups (500 g) zucchini, shredded

½ teaspoon (1.3 g) chili powder

¼ teaspoon (0.5 g) black pepper

4 tortillas

¼ cup (60 g) fat-free sour cream

In a medium wok or frying pan, heat the oil over medium-high heat. Add the onions, mustard, and cumin. Sauté until onions are soft. Add the shredded zucchini. Cook 5 to 10 minutes, stirring frequently, until the zucchini gets soft and tender. Stir in the chili powder and pepper. Warm the tortillas and place on a flat surface. Spread 1 tablespoon (15 g) of sour cream on each. Place one-quarter of the zucchini filling in the center of each tortilla. Roll up each tortilla.

Yield: 4 servings

Per serving: 131 calories (32% from fat, 12% from protein, 56% from carbohydrate); 4 g protein; 4 g total fat; 1 g saturated fat; 3 g monounsaturated fat; 1 g polyunsaturated fat; 17 g carbohydrate; 3 g fiber; 4 g sugar; 135 mg phosphorus; 66 mg calcium; mg iron; 33 mg sodium; 456 mg potassium; 406 IU vitamin A; 15 mg ATE vitamin E; 24 mg vitamin C; 6 mg cholesterol; 174 g water

Whole Wheat Apple Strata

This has become a traditional Christmas-morning breakfast. The original recipe called for ham, but no one seems to miss it. You could use any leftover bread, but I like honey wheat. If you can't find canned apples, you can use apple pie filling, although the result will be sweeter.

6 slices whole wheat bread, cubed

1 can (21-ounce, or 600 g) apples or apple pie filling

3 ounces (85 g) low fat cheddar cheese, shredded

1 cup (235 ml) egg substitute

¼ cup (60 ml) skim milk

Place bread in a 9-inch (23-cm) square pan coated with nonstick vegetable oil spray. Spoon apples over bread. Sprinkle with cheese. Combine egg substitute and milk and pour over bread mixture. Cover with plastic wrap and refrigerate overnight. Preheat oven to 350°F (180°C, or gas mark 4). Bake uncovered for 40 to 45 minutes, or until top is lightly browned and center is set.

Yield: 4 servings

Per serving: 232 calories (21% from fat, 31% from protein, 48% from carbohydrate); 18 g protein; 5 g total fat; 2 g saturated fat; 2 g monounsaturated fat; 2 g polyunsaturated fat; 28 g carbohydrate; 3 g fiber; 9 g sugar; 284 mg phosphorus; 189 mg calcium; 3 mg iron; 484 mg sodium; 376 mg potassium; 313 IU vitamin A; 22 mg ATE vitamin E; 2 mg vitamin C; 5 mg cholesterol; 125 g water

6

Main Dishes:
Fish

We already talked about fish in the Introduction and Chapter 1 and identified it as a major source of omega-3 fatty acids, which are helpful in reducing LDL cholesterol levels. That's the good news. The really good news is that fish comes in a variety of flavors, which makes it great as a stand-alone dish as well as being ideal for any number of recipes with herbs or sauces and in soups and stews. This chapter contains a wide range of recipes, so eating your two servings a week should not be a problem.

Baked Swordfish with Vegetables

This is a fairly simple recipe, with the flavor coming from the vegetables. It's good with pasta or plain brown rice.

4 ounces (115 g) mushrooms, sliced

1 cup (160 g) onion, sliced

2 tablespoons (19 g) green bell pepper, chopped

2 tablespoons (30 ml) lemon juice

¼ teaspoon (0.3 g) dried dill

1 pound (455 g) swordfish steaks

4 small bay leaves

2 tomatoes, sliced

Preheat oven to 400°F (200°C, or gas mark 6). In a bowl, combine mushrooms, onions, green bell pepper, lemon juice, and dill. Line a shallow baking pan with foil. Spread vegetable mixture in bottom then arrange swordfish steaks on top. Place a bay leaf on each swordfish steak. Place 2 tomato slices on each swordfish steak. Cover pan with foil and bake for 45 to 55 minutes or until fish flakes easily with a fork.

Yield: 4 servings

Per serving: 165 calories (26% from fat, 59% from protein, 15% from carbohydrate); 24 g protein; 5 g total fat; 1 g saturated fat; 2 g monounsaturated fat; 1 g polyunsaturated fat; 6 g carbohydrate; 1 g fiber; 3 g sugar; 339 mg phosphorus; 18 mg calcium; 1 mg iron; 126 mg sodium; 529 mg potassium; 168 IU vitamin A; 41 mg ATE vitamin E; 12 mg vitamin C; 44 mg cholesterol; 159 g water

Creole-Style Catfish

A simple, Creole-style recipe.

1 tablespoon (15 ml) olive oil

1 cup (160 g) onion, chopped

½ cup (50 g) celery, chopped

½ cup (75 g) green bell pepper, chopped

1 clove garlic, minced

2 cups (360 g) canned no-salt-added tomatoes

1 lemon, sliced

1 tablespoon (15 ml) Worcestershire sauce

1 tablespoon (7 g) paprika

1 bay leaf

¼ teaspoon (0.3 g) dried thyme

¼ teaspoon (1 ml) hot pepper sauce

2 pounds (905 g) catfish fillets

TIP *You can substitute any other white fish for the catfish.*

Heat the oil in a large skillet over medium heat. Add the onion, celery, green pepper, and garlic. Cook until soft. Add tomatoes and their liquid. Break the tomatoes with a spoon. Add lemon slices, Worcestershire sauce, paprika, bay leaf, thyme, and hot pepper sauce. Cook, stirring occasionally, for 15 minutes, or until the sauce is slightly thickened. Press fish pieces down into sauce and spoon some of the sauce over the top of the fish. Cover the pan and simmer gently for 10 minutes, or until the fish flakes easily with a fork. Serve over hot cooked rice.

Yield: 6 servings

Per serving: 260 calories (49% from fat, 38% from protein, 13% from carbohydrate); 25 g protein; 14 g total fat; 3 g saturated fat; 7 g monounsaturated fat; 3 g polyunsaturated fat; 9 g carbohydrate; 2 g fiber; 4 g sugar; 341 mg phosphorus; 55 mg calcium; 2 mg iron; 125 mg sodium; 746 mg potassium; 870 IU vitamin A; 23 mg ATE vitamin E; 31 mg vitamin C; 71 mg cholesterol; 242 g water

Herbed Fish

Simple baked fish made flavorful by a combination of herbs and spices.

2 pounds (905 g) perch, or other firm white fish

1 tablespoon (15 ml) olive oil

½ teaspoon (1.5 g) garlic powder

½ teaspoon (0.3 g) dried marjoram

½ teaspoon (0.5 g) dried thyme

⅛ teaspoon (0.3 g) white pepper

2 bay leaves

½ cup (80 g) onion, chopped

½ cup (120 ml) white wine

Preheat oven to 350°F (180°C, or gas mark 4). Wash fish, pat dry, and place in 9 × 13-inch (23 × 33-cm) dish. Combine oil with garlic powder, marjoram, thyme, and white pepper. Drizzle over fish. Top with bay leaves and onion. Pour wine over all. Bake, uncovered, for 20 to 30 minutes, or until fish flakes easily with a fork.

Yield: 4 servings

Per serving: 277 calories (26% from fat, 69% from protein, 5% from carbohydrate); 43 g protein; 7 g total fat; 1 g saturated fat; 4 g monounsaturated fat; 1 g polyunsaturated fat; 3 g carbohydrate; 0 g fiber; 1 g sugar; 503 mg phosphorus; 253 mg calcium; 2 mg iron; 173 mg sodium; 675 mg potassium; 100 IU vitamin A; 27 mg ATE vitamin E; 3 mg vitamin C; 95 mg cholesterol; 222 g water

Tuna Steaks

If you get them on sale, tuna steaks are a good bargain, as well as containing lots of omega-3 fatty acids. The key is not to overcook them and dry them out. It's fine for them to be medium or even medium-rare. Soaking in a simple marinade also helps to keep them moist and flavorful.

2 tablespoons (30 ml) olive oil

2 tablespoons (30 ml) lemon juice

6 ounces (170 g) tuna steaks

½ teaspoon (1 g) freshly ground black pepper

Combine the olive oil and lemon juice. Marinate the steaks in the mixture for at least 30 minutes, turning occasionally. Heat a skillet over high heat. Add the steaks and cook 2 minutes. Sprinkle with pepper, turn over, and cook 2 minutes longer.

Yield: 2 servings

Per serving: 247 calories (65% from fat, 32% from protein, 3% from carbohydrate); 20 g protein; 18 g total fat; 3 g saturated fat; 11 g monounsaturated fat; 3 g polyunsaturated fat; 2 g carbohydrate; 0 g fiber; 0 g sugar; 218 mg phosphorus; 10 mg calcium; 1 mg iron; 34 mg sodium; 240 mg potassium; 1861 IU vitamin A; 557 mg ATE vitamin E; 7 mg vitamin C; 32 mg cholesterol; 72 g water

Grilled Tuna Steaks

Tuna steaks tend to get tough if you cook them too long, so take them off the grill while they are still pink in the center to keep them juicy.

½ cup (120 ml) balsamic vinegar

2 tablespoons (26 g) sugar

1 tablespoon (2.1 g) Italian seasoning

½ teaspoon (1.5 g) garlic powder

1 tablespoon (15 ml) olive oil

1 pound (455 g) tuna steaks

1 tablespoon (15 ml) lemon juice

Combine all ingredients except tuna and lemon juice and pour in a 9 × 9-inch (23 × 23-cm) glass baking dish. Add tuna and marinate 15 minutes, turning frequently. Heat grill to high. Place fish on grill and grill until medium doneness, about 3 minutes per side. Place on serving plates and drizzle lemon juice over.

Yield: 4 servings

Per serving: 228 calories (37% from fat, 49% from protein, 14% from carbohydrate); 27 g protein; 9 g total fat; 2 g saturated fat; 4 g monounsaturated fat; 2 g polyunsaturated fat; 8 g carbohydrate; 0 g fiber; 7 g sugar; 294 mg phosphorus; 24 mg calcium; 2 mg iron; 46 mg sodium; 329 mg potassium; 2528 IU vitamin A; 743 mg ATE vitamin E; 2 mg vitamin C; 43 mg cholesterol; 109 g water

Grilled Tuna with Honey-Mustard Marinade

These tuna steaks can be grilled or broiled. If it's not good weather for outdoor grilling, they also work well on a contact grill like the George Foreman models.

⅓ cup (80 ml) red wine vinegar

1 tablespoon (15 g) spicy brown mustard

1 tablespoon (15 ml) honey

3 tablespoons (45 ml) extra-virgin olive oil

1 pound (455 g) tuna steaks

Combine the vinegar, mustard, honey, and olive oil in a jar or covered container; shake to mix well. Put tuna in a resealable plastic bag; add the mustard mixture. Seal the bag and let marinate for about 20 minutes. Heat the grill. Remove the tuna from the marinade and pour the marinade in a small saucepan. Bring marinade to a boil; remove from heat and set aside. Grill the tuna over high heat for about 2 minutes on each side, or to desired doneness. Drizzle with the hot marinade.

Yield: 4 servings

Per serving: 275 calories (53% from fat, 40% from protein, 7% from carbohydrate); 27 g protein; 16 g total fat; 3 g saturated fat; 9 g monounsaturated fat; 3 g polyunsaturated fat; 5 g carbohydrate; 0 g fiber; 4 g sugar; 294 mg phosphorus; 13 mg calcium; 1 mg iron; 89 mg sodium; 302 mg potassium; 2478 IU vitamin A; 743 mg ATE vitamin E; 0 mg vitamin C; 43 mg cholesterol; 100 g water

Asian Marinated Tuna Steaks

Marinating tuna steaks helps to keep them moist. Plus, it adds a nice extra bit of flavor. The other thing to remember to keep them juicy is to avoid cooking them too long.

1 tablespoon (15 ml) lemon juice

1 teaspoon (3 g) minced garlic

2 tablespoons (12 g) fresh ginger, peeled and minced

¼ cup (60 ml) Dick's Reduced-Sodium Teriyaki Sauce (see recipe page 31)

¼ cup (60 ml) olive oil

1 teaspoon (1.2 g) red pepper flakes

¼ teaspoon (0.5 g) black pepper

3 tablespoons (12 g) fresh cilantro, chopped

2 pounds (905 g) tuna steaks

Mix all ingredients except the tuna in a bowl or baking dish that is just big enough to hold the steaks in one layer. Add the steaks and turn them to coat. Marinate for 30 minutes. Grill or pan-fry the steaks, turning once, until medium to medium-rare, about 4 minutes per side.

Yield: 4 servings

Per serving: 392 calories (39% from fat, 56% from protein, 6% from carbohydrate); 53 g protein; 16 g total fat; 2 g saturated fat; 10 g monounsaturated fat; 2 g polyunsaturated fat; 5 g carbohydrate; 0 g fiber; 3 g sugar; 442 mg phosphorus; 42 mg calcium; 2 mg iron; 245 mg sodium; 1057 mg potassium; 453 IU vitamin A; 41 mg ATE vitamin E; 6 mg vitamin C; 102 mg cholesterol; 180 g water

Marinated Tuna Steaks

Marinated in a southwestern-flavored sauce, these tuna steaks go well with Spanish rice and corn.

2 tablespoons (30 ml) olive oil

2 teaspoons (5 g) cumin

2 tablespoons (30 ml) lime juice

2 teaspoons (2.6 g) cilantro

1 pound (455 g) tuna steaks

Combine first 4 ingredients in a shallow dish; add fish and turn to coat. Marinate for 20 minutes, turning occasionally. Heat the grill. Remove the tuna from the marinade and grill the tuna over high heat for 2 minutes on each side, or until desired doneness.

Yield: 4 servings

Per serving: 229 calories (50% from fat, 48% from protein, 2% from carb); 27 g protein; 13 g total fat; 2 g saturated fat; 7 g monounsaturated fat; 2 g polyunsaturated fat; 1 g carb; 0 g fiber; 0 g sugar; 294 mg phosphorus; 20 mg calcium; 2 mg iron; 46 mg sodium; 315 mg potassium; 2521 IU vitamin A; 743 mg ATE vitamin E; 3 mg vitamin C; 43 mg cholesterol; 85 g water

Poached Salmon

Poaching fish is a healthy way to cook it, as well as making sure it stays moist and adding a little extra flavor.

4 cups (946 ml) water

2 tablespoons (30 ml) lemon juice

¼ cup (30 g) carrot, thinly sliced

½ cup (80 g) onion, thinly sliced

1 bay leaf

1 tablespoon (4 g) fresh dill, chopped

½ pound (225 g) salmon fillets

Preheat oven to 350°F (180°C, or gas mark 4). Combine all ingredients except salmon in a saucepan and heat to boiling. Reduce heat and simmer 5 minutes. Place salmon in a glass baking dish large enough to hold salmon in a single layer; pour poaching liquid over. Cover and bake for 20 minutes, or until salmon flakes easily.

Yield: 2 servings

Per serving: 238 calories (47% from fat, 40% from protein, 13% from carbohydrate); 24 g protein; 12 g total fat; 3 g saturated fat; 4 g monounsaturated fat; 4 g polyunsaturated fat; 7 g carbohydrate; 1 g fiber; 3 g sugar; 291 mg phosphorus; 71 mg calcium; 1 mg iron; 97 mg sodium; 595 mg potassium; 2841 IU vitamin A; 17 mg ATE vitamin E; 16 mg vitamin C; 67 mg cholesterol; 614 g water

Maple Salmon

The sweetness of the maple syrup and the flavor of the balsamic vinegar really go well with salmon.

¼ cup (60 ml) balsamic vinegar

¼ cup (60 ml) water

2 tablespoons (30 ml) olive oil

2 tablespoons (30 ml) maple syrup

¼ teaspoon (0.8 g) garlic powder

½ pound (225 g) salmon fillets

Heat all ingredients except salmon in a large skillet, stirring to combine. Add salmon fillets. Cover and cook for 10 minutes, or until salmon is done, turning once.

Yield: 2 servings

Per serving: 387 calories (61% from fat, 24% from protein, 15% from carbohydrate); 23 g protein; 26 g total fat; 4 g saturated fat; 14 g monounsaturated fat; 6 g polyunsaturated fat; 14 g carbohydrate; 0 g fiber; 12 g sugar; 268 mg phosphorus; 31 mg calcium; 1 mg iron; 71 mg sodium; 478 mg potassium; 57 IU vitamin A; 17 mg ATE vitamin E; 4 mg vitamin C; 67 mg cholesterol; 142 g water

Grilled Salmon and Vegetables

On hot days, it's sometimes a good idea to not use the stove at all. This recipe gives you protein, vegetables, and starch in one easy grilled packet.

1 cup (195 g) instant rice, uncooked

1 cup (235 ml) low sodium chicken broth

½ cup (56 g) zucchini, sliced

½ cup (60 g) carrot, shredded

½ pound (225 g) salmon fillets

¼ teaspoon (0.5 g) black pepper

½ lemon, sliced

Heat grill to medium. Spray two large pieces of heavy-duty aluminum foil with nonstick vegetable oil spray. In a small bowl, mix together rice and broth. Let stand for 5 minutes, or until most of broth is absorbed. Stir in zucchini and carrots, and set aside. Place a salmon fillet in the center of each piece of foil. Sprinkle with pepper and place lemon slices on top. Place rice mixture around each fillet. Fold up foil and bring edges together. Fold over several times to seal. Fold in ends, allowing some room for the rice to expand during cooking. Place on the grill and cook for 10 to 15 minutes, or until salmon is done.

Yield: 2 servings

Per serving: 347 calories (35% from fat, 33% from protein, 32% from carbohydrate); 28 g protein; 14 g total fat; 3 g saturated fat; 5 g monounsaturated fat; 5 g polyunsaturated fat; 28 g carbohydrate; 2 g fiber; 3 g sugar; 369 mg phosphorus; 54 mg calcium; 2 mg iron; 130 mg sodium; 765 mg potassium; 5502 IU vitamin A; 17 mg ATE vitamin E; 19 mg vitamin C; 67 mg cholesterol; 320 g water

Grilled Salmon Fillets

You can use a whole salmon fillet for this recipe. It makes an impressive display, but it can be difficult to turn. I usually cut the fillet into serving-sized pieces, but then you need to be careful not to overcook them and dry them out. The sweetness of the sauce goes well with the salmon.

¼ cup (60 g) brown sugar

2 tablespoons (30 ml) cider vinegar

2 tablespoons (30 ml) honey

¼ teaspoon (1 ml) liquid smoke

¼ teaspoon (0.5 g) black pepper

¼ teaspoon (0.8 g) crushed garlic

2 pounds (905 g) salmon fillets

TIP *Be careful not to overcook the salmon; it will lose its juices and flavor if cooked too long.*

Preheat grill. In a small mixing bowl, combine the first 6 ingredients (through garlic). Mix well. Brush one side of the salmon with the basting sauce, then place the salmon (basted side down) on the grill. When the salmon is half finished cooking, baste the top portion of the salmon and flip the fillet so the fresh

(continued on page 118)

basting sauce is on the grill. When the fish is almost finished cooking, apply the basting sauce and flip the salmon again. Baste and flip the salmon once more and serve.

Yield: 6 Servings

Per serving: 110 g water ; 334 calories (45% from fat, 37% from protein, 18% from carbohydrate); 30 g protein; 16 g total fat; 3 g saturated fat; 6 g monounsaturated fat; 6 g polyunsaturated fat; 15 g carbohydrate; 0 g fiber; 15 g sugar; 355 mg phosphorus; 27 mg calcium; 1 mg iron; 93 mg sodium; 587 mg potassium; 76 IU vitamin a; 23 mg ATE vitamin e; 6 mg vitamin c; 89 mg cholesterol

Blackened Salmon

Salmon blackened the Cajun way. This is one of the spicier recipes in this book. You can reduce the amount of cayenne pepper to suit your taste buds.

2 tablespoons (14 g) paprika

1 tablespoon (5 g) cayenne pepper

1 tablespoon (9 g) onion powder

½ teaspoon (1 g) white pepper

½ teaspoon (1 g) black pepper

¼ teaspoon (0.3 g) dried thyme

¼ teaspoon (0.2 g) dried basil

¼ teaspoon (0.3 g) dried oregano

1 pound (455 g) salmon fillets

2 tablespoons (30 ml) olive oil

In a small bowl, mix paprika, cayenne pepper, onion powder, white pepper, black pepper, thyme, basil, and oregano. Brush salmon fillets on both sides with oil, and sprinkle evenly with the cayenne pepper mixture. Drizzle one side of each fillet with half the remaining oil. In a large, heavy skillet over high heat, cook salmon, oiled side down, for 2 to 5 minutes, or until blackened. Turn fillets, drizzle with remaining oil, and continue cooking until blackened and fish flakes easily with a fork.

Yield: 4 servings

Per serving: 289 calories (61% from fat, 32% from protein, 6% from carbohydrate); 23 g protein; 20 g total fat; 4 g saturated fat; 9 g monounsaturated fat; 6 g polyunsaturated fat; 5 g carbohydrate; 2 g fiber; 1 g sugar; 287 mg phosphorus; 33 mg calcium; 2 mg iron; 70 mg sodium; 541 mg potassium; 2439 IU vitamin A; 17 mg ATE vitamin E; 8 mg vitamin C; 67 mg cholesterol; 79 g water

Cedar-Planked Salmon

Grilling salmon on a cedar plank gives it a marvelous smoky flavor. You can grill it plain, but we like this honey-mustard sauce on it.

¼ cup (60 g) Dijon mustard

1 tablespoon (15 ml) honey

1 teaspoon (1 g) dried dill

1 pound (455 g) salmon fillets

TIP *You can find cedar planks at stores with grills and grilling equipment, such as Lowe's or The Home Depot.*

Mix mustard, honey, and dill. Pour over salmon in a glass baking dish and marinate while you prepare the grill. Preheat grill to medium and soak planks according to package directions. Place the plank on the heated grill and allow to preheat for 3 minutes. Turn the plank over and place salmon on plank. Close grill and cook for 12 minutes, or until fish flakes easily.

Yield: 4 servings

Per serving: 234 calories (50% from fat, 40% from protein, 9% from carbohydrate); 23 g protein; 13 g total fat; 3 g saturated fat; 5 g monounsaturated fat; 5 g polyunsaturated fat; 5 g carbohydrate; 1 g fiber; 4 g sugar; 282 mg phosphorus; 27 mg calcium; 1 mg iron; 238 mg sodium; 443 mg potassium; 82 IU vitamin A; 17 mg ATE vitamin E; 5 mg vitamin C; 67 mg cholesterol; 91 g water

Mediterranean Salmon

This complete meal makes a great presentation and tastes delicious.

1 pound (455 g) salmon fillets

1 cup (175 g) couscous

1 cup (113 g) zucchini, sliced

1 cup (160 g) red onion, peeled and sliced

4 ounces (115 g) mushrooms, sliced

½ cup (75 g) red bell pepper, cut in strips

2 tablespoons (30 ml) olive oil, divided

1 tablespoon (2.5 g) fresh basil

Prepare couscous according to package instructions. Meanwhile, preheat a skillet or griddle pan. Toss the zucchini, onion, mushrooms, and red bell pepper in 1 tablespoon (15 ml) oil. Sauté vegetables for 8 to 10 minutes, turning once. Remove from pan. Brush the salmon with the remaining 1 tablespoon (15 ml) oil and cook for 6 to 8 minutes, turning once. Add the vegetables and basil to the couscous and toss well. Serve the vegetable couscous topped with the salmon.

Yield: 4 servings

Per serving: 460 calories (39% from fat, 26% from protein, 35% from carbohydrate); 30 g protein; 20 g total fat; 4 g saturated fat; 9 g monounsaturated fat; 5 g polyunsaturated fat; 40 g carbohydrate; 4 g fiber; 3 g sugar; 392 mg phosphorus; 51 mg calcium; 2 mg iron; 78 mg sodium; 768 mg potassium; 752 IU vitamin A; 17 mg ATE vitamin E; 37 mg vitamin C; 67 mg cholesterol; 190 g water

Lemon-Baked Salmon

This method will give you a little more intense lemon flavor than most. You can use this same preparation for a number of kinds of fish.

1 lemon

1 pound (455 g) salmon fillets

¼ cup (60 ml) lemon juice

2 tablespoons (6 g) dill

2 teaspoons (10 ml) olive oil

Preheat oven to 350°F (180°C, or gas mark 4). Spray a 9 × 13-inch (23 × 33-cm) glass baking dish with nonstick vegetable oil spray. Slice lemon into ¼-inch (0.6-cm) slices and place in bottom of pan. Lay fillets over slices. Combine lemon juice, dill, and oil and pour over fillets. Bake for 12 to 15 minutes, or until fish flakes easily.

Yield: 4 servings

Per serving: 213 calories (55% from fat, 38% from protein, 7% from carbohydrate); 20 g protein; 13 g total fat; 2 g saturated fat; 5 g monounsaturated fat; 4 g polyunsaturated fat; 4 g carbohydrate; 1 g fiber; 1 g sugar; 242 mg phosphorus; 44 mg calcium; 1 mg iron; 62 mg sodium; 449 mg potassium; 146 IU vitamin A; 15 mg ATE vitamin E; 19 mg vitamin C; 58 mg cholesterol; 95 g water

Salmon with Dill

This is a simple stick-it-in-the-oven-and-wait type of dish. It goes well with boiled potatoes (you could make a little extra of the sauce to put on them).

2 tablespoons (30 ml) olive oil

1 teaspoon (1 g) dried dill

1 teaspoon (3 g) onion powder

½ teaspoon (1 g) black pepper

1 pound (455 g) salmon fillets

Preheat oven to 400°F (200°C, or gas mark 6). Mix together oil, dill, onion powder, and pepper. Place salmon in a 9 × 13-inch (23 × 33-cm) baking dish that has been coated with nonstick vegetable oil spray. Brush all of the olive oil mixture on the fish. Bake for 20 minutes, or until fish flakes easily.

Yield: 4 servings

Per serving: 271 calories (65% from fat, 34% from protein, 1% from carbohydrate); 23 g protein; 19 g total fat; 3 g saturated fat; 9 g monounsaturated fat; 5 g polyunsaturated fat; 1 g carbohydrate; 0 g fiber; 0 g sugar; 268 mg phosphorus; 22 mg calcium; 1 mg iron; 68 mg sodium; 428 mg potassium; 73 IU vitamin A; 17 mg ATE vitamin E; 5 mg vitamin C; 67 mg cholesterol; 78 g water

Teriyaki Fish

¼ cup (30 g) flour

⅛ teaspoon (0.3 g) black pepper

12 ounces (340 g) catfish fillets, cut in 1-inch (2.5-cm) cubes

2 tablespoons (30 ml) olive oil

¼ cup (60 ml) Dick's Reduced-Sodium Teriyaki Sauce (see recipe page 31)

¼ cup (50 g) sugar

½ teaspoon (2.5 ml) sesame oil

¼ cup (12 g) chives, chopped

Combine the flour and pepper in a resealable plastic bag. Add the fish and shake to coat. Heat the olive oil in a large skillet. Add the fish and cook until done. Remove from skillet. And the soy sauce and sugar to the pan. Cook and stir until the sugar is melted. Stir in the sesame oil. Add the fish and chives and stir to coat.

Yield: 4 servings

Per serving: 222 calories (21% from fat, 9% from protein, 70% from carbohydrate); 14 g protein; 14 g total fat; 3 g saturated fat; 8 g monounsaturated fat; 4 g polyunsaturated fat; 104 g carbohydrate; 0 g fiber; 2 g sugar; 194 mg phosphorus; 20 mg calcium; 1 mg iron; 149 mg sodium; 310 mg potassium; 179 IU vitamin A; 13 mg ATE vitamin E; 2 mg vitamin C; 40 mg cholesterol; 88 g water

Island Fish Grill

Jalapeños aren't really island fare, but their heat make this dish taste like the Caribbean.

2 tablespoons (30 ml) olive oil

1 teaspoon (3 g) minced garlic

1½ tablespoons (22 ml) lime juice

1 tablespoon (6 g) fresh ginger, peeled and minced

2 tablespoons (18 g) jalapeño peppers, seeded and sliced

1 pound (455 g) cod fillets

½ teaspoon (1 g) black pepper

Combine the olive oil with the garlic, lime juice, ginger, and jalapeño peppers in a mixing bowl. Add the fish fillets and turn to coat them well. Cover and refrigerate for 1 hour. Prepare grill. Remove the fillets from the marinade and scrape off most of the garlic and ginger pieces. Season the fish with black pepper and grill until done.

Yield: 4 servings

Per serving: 161 calories (43% from fat, 52% from protein, 5% from carbohydrate); 20 g protein; 8 g total fat; 1 g saturated fat; 5 g monounsaturated fat; 1 g polyunsaturated fat; 2 g carbohydrate; 0 g fiber; 0 g sugar; 235 mg phosphorus; 23 mg calcium; 1 mg iron; 62 mg sodium; 505 mg potassium; 73 IU vitamin A; 14 mg ATE vitamin E; 4 mg vitamin C; 49 mg cholesterol; 100 g water

Grilled Swordfish

We don't have swordfish all that often, but occasionally I'll find it on sale and buy some. It works well for this simple barbecue recipe because it's dense enough to hold together.

¼ cup (60 ml) barbecue sauce

1 tablespoon (15 ml) Worcestershire sauce

2 tablespoons (30 ml) fresh lime juice

2 tablespoons (20 g) chopped onion

½ teaspoon (1.5 g) minced garlic

2 swordfish steaks

Combine all ingredients except swordfish to make marinade. Marinate swordfish steaks for 6 hours or overnight, turning occasionally. When ready to grill, reserve marinade. Grill or cook as desired (do not overcook). Heat reserved marinade to boiling and pour over fish to serve.

Yield: 2 servings

Per serving: 242 calories (21% from fat, 47% from protein, 32% from carbohydrate); 28 g protein; 6 g total fat; 1 g saturated fat; 2 g monounsaturated fat; 1 g polyunsaturated fat; 19 g carbohydrate; 0 g fiber; 12 g sugar; 372 mg phosphorus; 11 mg calcium; 2 mg iron; 498 mg sodium; 487 mg potassium; 179 IU vitamin A; 49 mg ATE vitamin E; 20 mg vitamin C; 53 mg cholesterol; 147 g water

Brown Rice Tuna Bake

A variation on the traditional tuna casserole. Brown rice adds nutrients, and yogurt provides flavor and creaminess.

1¼ cups (238 g) uncooked brown rice

3 cups (710 ml) water

1 cup (100 g) chopped celery

½ cup (80 g) onion, finely diced

½ cup (115 g) plain fat-free yogurt

1 cup (235 ml) skim milk

¼ teaspoon (0.3 g) red pepper flakes

½ teaspoon (0.3 g) dried tarragon

14 ounces (395 g) water-packed canned tuna, drained

2 cups (280 g) frozen peas, thawed

¾ cup (90 g) low fat cheddar cheese, shredded

Preheat oven to 350°F (180°C, or gas mark 4). Combine rice and water in large saucepan. Bring to a boil. Reduce heat, cover, and cook for 35 minutes. Remove from heat. Add celery, onion, yogurt, and milk. Add red pepper flakes and tarragon; mix well. Flake the tuna with a fork and add it and thawed peas to the rice mixture; mix well. Pour into 2-quart (1.9-L) casserole dish. Bake for 30 minutes. Top with shredded cheese.

Yield: 6 servings

Per serving: 321 calories (9% from fat, 37% from protein, 54% from carbohydrate); 29 g protein; 3 g total fat; 1 g saturated fat; 1 g monounsaturated fat; 1 g polyunsaturated fat; 42 g carbohydrate; 4 g fiber; 5 g sugar; 445 mg phosphorus; 209 mg calcium; 3 mg iron; 537 mg sodium; 526 mg potassium; 1231 IU vitamin A; 47 mg ATE vitamin E; 7 mg vitamin C; 25 mg cholesterol; 302 g water

Spaghetti with Fish

My daughter made this after seeing a similar recipe on some cooking program on TV. It turned out really well and is just different enough from the way we typically serve pasta that we tend to go back to it when we want something a little different, especially since it fits my daughter's rule that if you don't know what to have, make something Italian.

8 ounces (225 g) spaghetti

1 pound (455 g) perch, or other white fish

2 tablespoons (30 ml) olive oil

½ teaspoon (1.5 g) minced garlic

2 tablespoons (30 ml) lemon juice

1 tablespoon (2.5 g) Italian seasoning

¼ teaspoon (0.5 g) black pepper

2 cups (360 g) canned no-salt-added tomatoes

¼ cup (60 ml) white wine

2 tablespoons (8 g) fresh parsley

Cook spaghetti according to package directions, drain and set aside. Cut fish into 1-inch (2.5-cm) cubes. In a large skillet heat olive oil. Add garlic, lemon juice, Italian seasoning, and pepper. Cook until garlic starts to brown. Add fish and cook until nearly done. Add tomatoes and reheat to boiling. Remove from heat. Stir in spaghetti and wine and toss to coat spaghetti with sauce. Sprinkle with parsley.

Yield: 4 servings

Per serving: 276 calories (31% from fat, 35% from protein, 34% from carbohydrate); 24 g protein; 9 g total fat; 1 g saturated fat; 6 g monounsaturated fat; 1 g polyunsaturated fat; 22 g carbohydrate; 4 g fiber; 3 g sugar; 317 mg phosphorus; 177 mg calcium; 3 mg iron; 103 mg sodium; 599 mg potassium; 430 IU vitamin A; 14 mg ATE vitamin E; 19 mg vitamin C; 48 mg cholesterol; 263 g water

Fish Sauce for Pasta

Even though this recipe may seem higher in fat than most of the others, it's the good kind of fat that comes from olive oil and fish. So enjoy it guilt-free.

¼ cup (60 ml) olive oil

12 ounces (340 g) salmon fillets, cubed

12 ounces (340 g) cod fillets, cubed

1 teaspoon (3 g) minced garlic

½ cup (120 ml) white wine

½ teaspoon (0.5 g) dried oregano

½ teaspoon (0.6 g) dried rosemary

1 teaspoon (0.1 g) dried parsley

1 tablespoon (10 g) onion, minced

Heat oil in a heavy skillet. Add salmon, cod, and garlic and sauté for a minute or two, until nearly cooked through. Add wine and remaining ingredients and continue cooking until sauce has been reduced to about half. Serve over pasta.

Yield: 6 servings

Per serving: 248 calories (61% from fat, 37% from protein, 2% from carbohydrate); 21 g protein; 16 g total fat; 3 g saturated fat; 9 g monounsaturated fat; 3 g polyunsaturated fat; 1 g carbohydrate; 0 g fiber; 0 g sugar; 252 mg phosphorus; 21 mg calcium; 1 mg iron; 66 mg sodium; 461 mg potassium; 76 IU vitamin A; 15 mg ATE vitamin E; 3 mg vitamin C; 58 mg cholesterol; 104 g water

Tuna Casserole

Ever have one of those nights where you can't think of a thing for dinner and end up pawing randomly through cookbooks looking for something that sounds good and that you have the ingredients for? This was the result. And it actually worked out well. The top layer is a quiche-like custard.

2 cups (330 g) cooked rice

1 cup (235 ml) egg substitute, divided

½ teaspoon (0.7 g) dried basil

1 tablespoon (10 g) onion, minced

7 ounces (200 g) water packed tuna

1 cup (235 ml) skim milk

4 ounces (115 g) Swiss cheese, shredded

Preheat oven to 350°F (180°C, or gas mark 4). Combine rice, ¼ cup (60 ml) egg substitute, basil, and onion. Press into the bottom of an 8 × 8-inch (20 × 20-cm) baking dish sprayed with nonstick vegetable oil spray. Spread tuna over the top. Combine remaining egg substitute, milk, and cheese and pour over the top. Bake for 40 to 45 minutes, or until a knife inserted near the center comes out clean.

Yield: 4 servings

Per serving: 285 calories (14% from fat, 48% from protein, 37% from carbohydrate); 33 g protein; 4 g total fat; 2 g saturated fat; 1 g monounsaturated fat; 1 g polyunsaturated fat; 26 g carbohydrate; 1 g fiber; 1 g sugar; 442 mg phosphorus; 417 mg calcium; 4 mg iron; 390 mg sodium; 519 mg potassium; 430 IU vitamin A; 57 mg ATE vitamin E; 1 mg vitamin C; 27 mg cholesterol; 219 g water

Tuna Noodle Casserole

This is traditional American comfort food.

1 tablespoon (15 ml) olive oil

2 tablespoons (16 g) flour

2 cups (470 ml) skim milk

¼ cup (30 g) low fat cheddar cheese, shredded

3 cups (450 g) cooked egg noodles

10-ounce (280 g) package frozen peas, thawed

7 ounces (200 g) water-packed tuna

4 ounces (115 g) mushrooms, sliced

¼ cup (37 g) chopped green bell pepper

⅛ teaspoon (0.3 g) black pepper

½ cup (60 g) bread crumbs

Preheat oven to 375°F (190°C, or gas mark 5). Heat oil in a large skillet over low heat; add flour, stirring until smooth. Cook 1 minute, stirring constantly. Gradually add milk; cook over medium heat, stirring constantly, until mixture is thickened and bubbly. Stir in cheese; cook over low heat, stirring constantly, until cheese melts. Remove from heat. Combine cheese sauce, noodles, and next 5 ingredients (through black pepper). Spoon mixture into a 2-quart (1.9-L) casserole dish coated with nonstick vegetable oil spray. Sprinkle evenly with bread crumbs. Bake for 35 minutes, or until the casserole is bubbly and the top is browned.

Yield: 6 servings

Per serving: 277 calories (14% from fat, 28% from protein, 58% from carbohydrate); 19 g protein; 4 g total fat; 1 g saturated fat; 2 g monounsaturated fat; 1 g polyunsaturated fat; 40 g carbohydrate; 7 g fiber; 3 g sugar; 303 mg phosphorus; 174 mg calcium; 2 mg iron; 414 mg sodium; 424 mg potassium; 1254 IU vitamin A; 59 mg ATE vitamin E; 11 mg vitamin C; 13 mg cholesterol; 211 g water

Swedish Salmon Stew

This recipe turned up one night during a fairly desperate search for something different to do with fish.

1½ pounds (680 g) potatoes, peeled and sliced

1½ pounds (680 g) salmon fillets

1 tablespoon (4 g) fresh dill, chopped

¼ cup (60 ml) olive oil, heated

½ cup (120 ml) white wine

¼ cup (60 ml) sherry

½ cup (115 g) fat-free sour cream

2 tablespoons (30 g) horseradish, grated

Preheat oven to 350°F (180°C, or gas mark 4). Boil potatoes for 10 to 15 minutes, or until almost done. Layer potato slices in a large ovenproof casserole. Place the salmon on top. Sprinkle with the dill and drizzle with the olive oil. Cover and bake for 25 minutes. Remove from the oven and pour the wine and sherry over. Continue to cook uncovered until salmon flakes easily with a fork. Stir together sour cream and horseradish and pour over the top.

Yield: 6 servings

Per serving: 372 calories (50% from fat, 24% from protein, 26% from carbohydrate); 19 g protein; 18 g total fat; 3 g saturated fat; 6 g monounsaturated fat; 8 g polyunsaturated fat; 22 g carbohydrate; 2 g fiber; 3 g sugar; 288 mg phosphorus; 57 mg calcium; 1 mg iron; 82 mg sodium; 891 mg potassium; 154 IU vitamin A; 32 mg ATE vitamin E; 15 mg vitamin C; 56 mg cholesterol; 193 g water

Greek Fish Stew

This is a soup to warm you on a cold night. A slice of bread is all that's needed to make it a meal.

4 ounces (115 g) orzo, or other small pasta

½ cup (80 g) onion, chopped

½ teaspoon (1.5 g) minced garlic

1 teaspoon (2 g) fennel seed

2 cups (360 g) canned no-salt-added tomatoes

2 cups (470 g) low sodium chicken broth

1 tablespoon (0.4 g) dried parsley

½ teaspoon (1 g) black pepper

¼ teaspoon (0.6 g) turmeric

12 ounces (340 g) cod fillets, cut in 1-inch (2.5-cm) cubes

Cook pasta according to package directions. Drain and set aside. In a large nonstick saucepan coated with nonstick vegetable oil spray, cook onions, garlic, and fennel seed until onion is tender. Add tomatoes, broth, parsley, pepper, and turmeric. Reduce heat and simmer for 10 minutes. Add fish and simmer for 5 minutes, or until fish is cooked through. Divide pasta among four bowls. Ladle soup over pasta.

Yield: 4 servings

Per serving: 226 calories (8% from fat, 40% from protein, 53% from carbohydrate); 23 g protein; 2 g total fat; 0 g saturated fat; 1 g monounsaturated fat; 1 g polyunsaturated fat; 30 g carbohydrate; 3 g fiber; 5 g sugar; 295 mg phosphorus; 75 mg calcium; 3 mg iron; 101 mg sodium; 794 mg potassium; 255 IU vitamin A; 10 mg ATE vitamin E; 15 mg vitamin C; 37 mg cholesterol; 319 g water

Fish Wine Chowder

My daughter fixed this one rainy cold night. Since she isn't a fish lover, I figured it must be the amount of wine in it that appealed to her. It turns out to be a liberal modification of a recipe in a *Better Homes and Gardens* soup cookbook. It turned out quite well, and even she had to admit that fish isn't bad this way. You could use whatever fish you have on hand or that you prefer; the salmon and perch just happened to be what was in our freezer.

1 pound (455 g) salmon

1 pound (455 g) perch

4 slices low sodium bacon

½ cup (80 g) onion, chopped

½ cup (50 g) celery, chopped

¼ teaspoon (0.8 g) minced garlic

1½ cups (355 ml) white wine

1½ cups (355 ml) water

2 potatoes, cubed

¼ teaspoon (0.3 g) thyme

1 teaspoon (0.1 g) parsley

3 tablespoons (24 g) flour

3 tablespoons (45 ml) water

½ cup (60 ml) skim milk

Cut fish into cubes; set aside. Cook bacon in a Dutch oven; crumble and set aside. Drain grease from pan. Sauté onion, celery, and garlic until tender. Add wine, water, potatoes, thyme, and parsley. Simmer for 20 minutes, or until potatoes are almost done. Add fish, cover and simmer 10 minutes more. Mix together flour and water to form a paste. Stir into soup and simmer until thickened. Stir in milk and reserved bacon.

Yield: 8 servings

Per serving: 306 calories (30% from fat, 39% from protein, 31% from carbohydrate); 26 g protein; 9 g total fat; 2 g saturated fat; 3 g monounsaturated fat; 3 g polyunsaturated fat; 21 g carbohydrate; 2 g fiber; 2 g sugar; 368 mg phosphorus; 113 mg calcium; 2 mg iron; 142 mg sodium; 913 mg potassium; 133 IU vitamin A; 25 mg ATE vitamin E; 13 mg vitamin C; 62 mg cholesterol; 285 g water

Tuna Chowder

We like this for dinner with some freshly baked bread. It makes a nice warm meal on a cool evening, and it's the kind of thing you can throw together quickly when you haven't planned something for dinner.

2 cups (470 ml) water

2 cups (470 ml) low sodium chicken broth

6 potatoes, diced

14 ounces (400 g) water-packed tuna

½ cup (65 g) carrots, sliced

½ cup (50 g) celery, sliced

½ cup (80 g) onion, diced

½ cup (82 g) frozen corn, thawed

½ teaspoon (0.3 g) dried basil

½ teaspoon (0.5 g) dried dill

1 tablespoon (0.4 g) dried parsley

½ cup (120 ml) skim milk

In a large saucepan, mix water with broth. Add potatoes and simmer for 10 to 15 minutes, or until tender. Remove cooked potatoes from broth, reserving liquid. Purée cooked potatoes with ¼ cup (60 ml) reserved broth. Add tuna, carrots, celery, onion, corn, basil, dill, parsley, and puréed potatoes to remaining broth in saucepan. Simmer for 8 to 10 minutes, or until vegetables are tender. Stir in milk and heat to serving temperature, but do not boil.

Yield: 6 servings

Per serving: 379 calories (4% from fat, 28% from protein, 68% from carbohydrate); 27 g protein; 2 g total fat; 0 g saturated fat; 0 g monounsaturated fat; 1 g polyunsaturated fat; 66 g carbohydrate; 7 g fiber; 5 g sugar; 398 mg phosphorus; 93 mg calcium; 4 mg iron; 300 mg sodium; 2047 mg potassium; 2000 IU vitamin A; 24 mg ATE vitamin E; 35 mg vitamin C; 20 mg cholesterol; 562 g water

Oven-Fried Fish

This nice crunchy coating is low in fat and sodium, and it goes really well with oven-fried potatoes.

¼ cup (60 ml) egg substitute

2 tablespoons (30 ml) skim milk

½ cup (30 g) dried mashed potato flakes

¼ teaspoon (0.5 g) black pepper

1 pound (455 g) catfish fillets

Preheat oven to 325°F (170°C, or gas mark 3). Mix egg substitute and milk together. Stir together potatoes and pepper. Dip fish in egg mixture, then potato flakes. Dip fish again in egg and then potato flakes. Place on baking sheet. Coat fish with nonstick vegetable oil spray. Bake for 15 minutes, or until fish flakes easily.

Yield: 4 servings

Per serving: 196 calories (43% from fat, 43% from protein, 14% from carbohydrate); 20 g protein; 9 g total fat; 2 g saturated fat; 4 g monounsaturated fat; 2 g polyunsaturated fat; 7 g carbohydrate; 1 g fiber; 0 g sugar; 269 mg phosphorus; 32 mg calcium; 1 mg iron; 100 mg sodium; 489 mg potassium; 130 IU vitamin A; 22 mg ATE vitamin E; 7 mg vitamin C; 54 mg cholesterol; 106 g water

Salmon Patties

When I was growing up, canned salmon was cheaper than tuna. We had salmon patties fairly often because they were a quick and tasty meal. Salmon is no longer quite the bargain, but the patties still taste just as good.

14-ounce (400-g) can salmon, drained and flaked

½ cup (120 ml) egg substitute

¾ cup (90 g) bread crumbs

½ cup (80 g) onion, chopped

Salt and pepper to taste

1 tablespoon (15 ml) olive oil

(continued on page 134)

In a large bowl, combine salmon, egg substitute, bread crumbs, onion, salt, and pepper; shape into six equal-sized patties. Heat oil in a large frying pan over medium heat. Add salmon patties and brown on both sides.

Yield: 6 servings

Per serving: 217 calories (46% from fat, 33% from protein, 21% from carbohydrate); 18 g protein; 11 g total fat; 2 g saturated fat; 5 g monounsaturated fat; 3 g polyunsaturated fat; 11 g carbohydrate; 1 g fiber; 2 g sugar; 206 mg phosphorus; 47 mg calcium; 1 mg iron; 175 mg sodium; 354 mg potassium; 109 IU vitamin A; 10 mg ATE vitamin E; 4 mg vitamin C; 39 mg cholesterol; 76 g water

Thai-Style Fish

A complex blend of flavors, this Asian fish stew will become a favorite.

2 pounds (905 g) catfish fillets, cut in 2-inch (5-cm) pieces

¼ cup (60 ml) lime juice

¼ teaspoon (0.3 g) red pepper flakes

1 tablespoon (15 ml) sesame oil

1 cup (160 g) onion, thinly sliced

1 cup (100 g) celery, sliced

1 cup (70 g) bok choy, shredded

1 teaspoon (1.8 g) ground ginger

1 teaspoon (3 g) minced garlic

1 tablespoon (6.3 g) curry powder

8 cups (1.9 L) low sodium chicken broth

2 cups (330 g) cooked rice

Mix catfish, lime juice, and red pepper flakes; set aside. Heat sesame oil in a large saucepan or Dutch oven. Sauté onion, celery, bok choy, ginger, and garlic for 1 minute. Sprinkle with curry powder. Reduce heat and sauté until onion is soft. Add chicken broth and bring to a boil. Stir in catfish mixture and simmer for 3 minutes, or until catfish is done. To serve, place rice in the center of soup bowls and ladle soup over.

Yield: 8 servings

Per serving: 275 calories (39% from fat, 35% from protein, 26% from carbohydrate); 24 g protein; 12 g total fat; 3 g saturated fat; 5 g monounsaturated fat; 3 g polyunsaturated fat; 18 g carbohydrate; 1 g fiber; 2 g sugar; 339 mg phosphorus; 47 mg calcium; 2 mg iron; 177 mg sodium; 668 mg potassium; 155 IU vitamin A; 17 mg ATE vitamin E; 6 mg vitamin C; 53 mg cholesterol; 393 g water

Pecan-Crusted Catfish

A delightful southern treat. Serve with rice pilaf.

6 tablespoons (90 g) Dijon mustard

¼ cup (60 ml) skim milk

1 cup (100 g) pecans, ground

1 pound (455 g) catfish fillets

Preheat oven to 450°F (230°C, or gas mark 8). Coat a baking sheet with nonstick vegetable oil spray. Mix mustard and milk in a shallow dish. Spread pecans in another dish. Dip fillets in mustard mixture, then roll in pecans to coat. Place on prepared pan. Bake 10 to 12 minutes, or until fish flakes easily.

Yield: 4 servings

Per serving: 364 calories (70% from fat, 23% from protein, 6% from carbohydrate); 22 g protein; 29 g total fat; 4 g saturated fat; 16 g monounsaturated fat; 8 g polyunsaturated fat; 6 g carbohydrate; 3 g fiber; 1 g sugar; 346 mg phosphorus; 64 mg calcium; 2 mg iron; 325 mg sodium; 510 mg potassium; 119 IU vitamin A; 26 mg ATE vitamin E; 1 mg vitamin C; 54 mg cholesterol; 119 g water

Sesame Fish

Sesame seeds add crunch as well as flavor to this Asian baked fish dish.

1 pound (455 g) halibut fillets

½ cup (120 ml) Dick's Reduced-Sodium Teriyaki Sauce (see recipe page 31)

2 tablespoons (16 g) sesame seeds

1 tablespoon (8 g) flour

½ teaspoon (1 g) white pepper

Place fillets in a shallow baking dish. Pour teriyaki sauce over fish. Cover and refrigerate 30 minutes or overnight. Preheat oven to 450°F (230°C, or gas mark 8). Combine sesame seeds with flour and pepper. Dip each fillet in the flour mixture. Coat a nonstick baking pan with nonstick vegetable oil spray and place fillets on the pan in a single layer. Lightly spray the top of each fillet with nonstick vegetable oil spray. Bake for 10 to 15 minutes, or until golden brown and fish flakes easily when pricked with a fork.

Yield: 4 servings

Per serving: 163 calories (15% from fat, 66% from protein, 19% from carbohydrate); 26 g protein; 3 g total fat; 0 g saturated fat; 1 g monounsaturated fat; 1 g polyunsaturated fat; 7 g carbohydrate; 0 g fiber; 5 g sugar; 310 mg phosphorus; 63 mg calcium; 2 mg iron; 86 mg sodium; 594 mg potassium; 178 IU vitamin A; 53 mg ATE vitamin E; 0 mg vitamin C; 36 mg cholesterol; 113 g water

Oven-Steamed Salmon and Vegetables

I've also cooked this on a gas grill.

8 ounces (225 g) salmon fillets

2 medium potatoes, diced

½ cup (56 g) yellow squash, thinly sliced

½ cup (65 g) carrot, thinly sliced

¼ cup (25 g) scallions, thinly sliced

½ cup (35 g) mushrooms, sliced

2 teaspoons (10 ml) white wine

½ teaspoon (0.5 g) dried dill

½ teaspoon (1.5 g) minced garlic

¼ teaspoon (0.5 g) black pepper, fresh ground

Preheat oven to 425°F (220°C, or gas mark 7). Place a baking sheet in the oven to preheat as well. Meanwhile, spray the center of two 12-inch (30-cm) squares of aluminum foil with nonstick vegetable oil spray. Combine salmon, potatoes, squash, carrots, scallions, and mushrooms and divide evenly among the prepared foil sheets. Sprinkle with wine, dill, garlic, and pepper; fold diagonally to form a triangle; tightly seal edges. Place foil package on preheated baking sheet, then return to oven and bake 10 to 15 minutes, or until salmon is opaque and vegetables are tender.

Yield: 2 servings

Per serving: 498 calories (23% from fat, 25% from protein, 52% from carbohydrate); 31 g protein; 13 g total fat; 3 g saturated fat; 4 g monounsaturated fat; 5 g polyunsaturated fat; 65 g carbohydrate; 8 g fiber; 6 g sugar; 535 mg phosphorus; 82 mg calcium; 4 mg iron; 116 mg sodium; 2374 mg potassium; 5659 IU vitamin A; 17 mg ATE vitamin E; 46 mg vitamin C; 67 mg cholesterol; 464 g water

7

Main Dishes:
Chicken and Turkey

Chicken and turkey are great choices for a low cholesterol diet. You can hardly find any other meat with lower saturated fat than chicken or turkey breast. And the rest of the birds are healthy too, as long as you avoid eating the skin. There are a lot of chicken breast recipes here because they are a staple of a low fat diet. The only potential problem with chicken breasts is they can be dry and tough if you aren't careful cooking them. Many of these recipes contain sauces and marinades that help to keep them moist and give them extra flavor. There also are healthy recipes here for whole birds and ground turkey, so you don't need to worry about variety. I've even included some recipes that give you the taste of fried chicken, while still holding the line on fat.

Baked Italian Chicken Breasts

This is really "oven-fried" chicken. Using boneless breasts cuts way back on the saturated fat. And the sun-dried tomatoes and Italian seasoning give it a different flavor. We had this recently with roasted vegetables that we also sprinkled with Italian seasoning.

2 boneless chicken breasts

½ cup (60 g) bread crumbs

¼ cup (28 g) oil-packed sun-dried tomatoes

¼ teaspoon (0.8 g) garlic powder

1 teaspoon (0.7 g) Italian seasoning

¼ cup (60 ml) egg substitute

Preheat oven to 400°F (200°C, or gas mark 6). Split each chicken breast in half to make two thin cutlets. Combine bread crumbs, tomatoes, garlic powder, and Italian seasoning in a food processor. Process until well blended. Dip chicken in egg substitute and then in crumb mixture to coat thoroughly. Place in an ovenproof casserole dish. Bake for 20 minutes, or until chicken is cooked through.

Yield: 2 servings

Per serving: 243 calories (20% from fat, 41% from protein, 39% from carbohydrate); 25 g protein; 5 g total fat; 1 g saturated fat; 2 g monounsaturated fat; 2 g polyunsaturated fat; 23 g carbohydrate; 2 g fiber; 2 g sugar; 243 mg phosphorus; 88 mg calcium; 3 mg iron; 336 mg sodium; 565 mg potassium; 339 IU vitamin A; 4 mg ATE vitamin E; 15 mg vitamin C; 41 mg cholesterol; 88 g water

Chicken with Red Pepper Sauce

This was a recipe that sat in my "I need to try that" file for a while. It had a great flavor, but wasn't overly hot.

For Chicken:

¼ cup (30 g) flour

½ teaspoon (1.3 g) paprika

¼ teaspoon (0.5 g) black pepper

2 pounds (905 g) boneless chicken breasts

For Sauce:

1 tablespoon (15 ml) canola oil

¾ cup (113 g) red bell pepper, cut in 1-inch (2.5-cm) cubes

¼ cup (25 g) scallions, sliced

2 tablespoons (16 g) flour

1 cup (235 ml) low sodium chicken broth

2 tablespoons (26 g) sugar

½ tablespoon (2.5 g) cayenne pepper

⅓ cup (80 ml) cider vinegar

TIP *If you want something a little spicier, just increase the amount of cayenne pepper.*

Preheat oven to 375°F (190°C, or gas mark 5).

To make the chicken: In a plastic bag, combine flour, paprika, and pepper. Add chicken, a few pieces at a time, to the bag, shaking to coat well. Arrange chicken in a shallow baking pan. Coat with nonstick vegetable oil spray to moisten the flour. Bake for 20 minutes.

To make the sauce: Heat the oil in a medium saucepan; cook red bell pepper and scallions until tender. Stir in flour. Add chicken broth, sugar, and cayenne pepper. Cook and stir until thickened and bubbly. Cook and stir for 1 minute more. Remove from heat, stir in vinegar, and cool slightly. Spoon sauce over chicken. Bake for 20 minutes more, or until done, basting with the sauce 2 or 3 times during baking.

Yield: 6 servings

Per serving: 249 calories (18% from fat, 61% from protein, 21% from carbohydrate); 37 g protein; 5 g total fat; 1 g saturated fat; 2 g monounsaturated fat; 1 g polyunsaturated fat; 13 g carbohydrate; 1 g fiber; 5 g sugar; 326 mg phosphorus; 26 mg calcium; 2 mg iron; 113 mg sodium; 503 mg potassium; 942 IU vitamin A; 9 mg ATE vitamin E; 27 mg vitamin C; 88 mg cholesterol; 186 g water

Chili Chicken Breasts

These make a good meal with some Spanish-style rice.

2 tablespoons (30 ml) olive oil

⅓ cup (80 ml) lime juice

2 tablespoons (6 ml) chopped green chilis

¼ teaspoon (0.8 g) garlic powder

4 boneless chicken breasts

4 ounces (115 g) low fat Swiss cheese

Salsa, for serving

In a 9-inch (23-cm) square baking pan stir together the olive oil, lime juice, chilis, and garlic powder. Add chicken breasts; marinate in the refrigerator for at least 45 minutes, turning once. Remove chicken from marinade; drain. Grill or sauté chicken for 7 minutes; turn over and continue cooking for 6 to 8 minutes, or until done. Top each chicken breast with a slice of cheese. Continue cooking until cheese begins to melt. Serve with salsa.

Yield: 4 servings

Per serving: 195 calories (43% from fat, 51% from protein, 6% from carbohydrate); 25 g protein; 9 g total fat; 2 g saturated fat; 6 g monounsaturated fat; 1 g polyunsaturated fat; 3 g carbohydrate; 0 g fiber; 1 g sugar; 315 mg phosphorus; 285 mg calcium; 1 mg iron; 138 mg sodium; 243 mg potassium; 74 IU vitamin A; 15 mg ATE vitamin E; 8 mg vitamin C; 51 mg cholesterol; 92 g water

Grilled Marinated Chicken Breasts

These thin grilled chicken breasts make great sandwiches. They are also good sliced on top of a salad or stirred into a pasta salad.

¼ cup (60 ml) olive oil

¼ cup (60 ml) red wine vinegar

¼ teaspoon (0.8 g) minced garlic

1 teaspoon (3 g) onion powder

(continued on page 142)

1½ teaspoons (1 g) Italian seasoning

½ teaspoon (0.5 g) dried thyme

2 boneless chicken breasts

Combine all ingredients except chicken in a resealable plastic bag and mix well. Slice breasts in half crosswise, making two thin fillets from each. Add the chicken to the bag, seal, and marinate for at least 2 hours, turning occasionally. Remove chicken from marinade and grill over medium heat until done, turning once.

Yield: 4 servings

Per serving: 165 calories (77% from fat, 20% from protein, 2% from carbohydrate); 8 g protein; 14 g total fat; 2 g saturated fat; 10 g monounsaturated fat; 2 g polyunsaturated fat; 1 g carbohydrate; 0 g fiber; 0 g sugar; 74 mg phosphorus; 16 mg calcium; 1 mg iron; 25 mg sodium; 110 mg potassium; 38 IU vitamin A; 2 mg ATE vitamin E; 1 mg vitamin C; 21 mg cholesterol; 41 g water

Honey-Mustard Fruit-Sauced Chicken

I was looking for something a little different, and this just came to me. It is a true original.

6 boneless chicken breasts

1 cup (240 g) fruit cocktail, in juice

2 tablespoons (30 ml) red wine vinegar

2 tablespoons (30 ml) honey

2 tablespoons (30 ml) honey mustard

Preheat oven to 350°F (180°C, or gas mark 4). Place chicken breasts in a roasting pan. Purée fruit cocktail, vinegar, honey, and mustard in a blender. Pour over chicken. Bake for 50 to 60 minutes, or until done.

Yield: 6 servings

Per serving: 122 calories (8% from fat, 56% from protein, 36% from carbohydrate); 17 g protein; 1 g total fat; 0 g saturated fat; 0 g monounsaturated fat; 0 g polyunsaturated fat; 11 g carbohydrate; 1 g fiber; 10 g sugar; 151 mg phosphorus; 15 mg calcium; 1 mg iron; 105 mg sodium; 231 mg potassium; 139 IU vitamin A; 4 mg ATE vitamin E; 2 mg vitamin C; 41 mg cholesterol; 98 g water

Indian Chicken

A slightly tangy, not overly hot chicken flavored like the classic Tandoori chicken. If you like hotter food, you can add more cayenne pepper.

1 cup (230 g) plain fat-free yogurt

½ teaspoon (0.9 g) cardamom

½ teaspoon (1.3 g) ground cumin

½ teaspoon (1.1 g) turmeric

⅛ teaspoon (0.3 g) cayenne pepper

1 teaspoon (0.6 g) bay leaf, crushed

½ teaspoon (1.5 g) garlic powder

¾ teaspoon (1.4 g) ground ginger

¼ cup (40 g) onion, minced

¼ cup (60 ml) lime juice

¼ teaspoon (0.5 g) black pepper

1 teaspoon (2.3 g) cinnamon

1 teaspoon (2 g) ground coriander

8 boneless chicken breasts

Combine yogurt and remaining ingredients except chicken, mixing well. Prick chicken with a fork. In a resealable plastic bag or glass pan large enough to hold chicken, cover chicken with yogurt marinade, making sure all surfaces of chicken are coated. Cover and refrigerate at least 3 hours, or overnight. Turn at least once while marinating. Grill over medium heat until done or preheat oven to 375°F (190°C, or gas mark 5) and place chicken in a greased roasting pan with marinade and cook for 45 minutes to 1 hour, or until chicken is tender.

Yield: 8 servings

Per serving: 103 calories (9% from fat, 73% from protein, 17% from carbohydrate); 18 g protein; 1 g total fat; 0 g saturated fat; 0 g monounsaturated fat; 0 g polyunsaturated fat; 4 g carbohydrate; 0 g fiber; 3 g sugar; 193 mg phosphorus; 79 mg calcium; 1 mg iron; 71 mg sodium; 293 mg potassium; 44 IU vitamin A; 5 mg ATE vitamin E; 4 mg vitamin C; 42 mg cholesterol; 91 g water

Lemon Rosemary Chicken

This technique has become my new favorite way of grilling chicken. It allows it to cook relatively quickly, stay juicy, and not get too blackened. Plus, you usually have some left over for sandwiches or salads the next day. Whole chickens can be very low in saturated fat as long as you don't eat the skin.

1 whole chicken, 3 to 4 pounds (1.4 to 1.8 kg)

½ cup (120 ml) lemon juice

1 teaspoon (1.2 g) dried rosemary

Split chicken in half, cutting along backbone and breast bone. Place in resealable plastic bag with lemon juice and rosemary. Marinate at least two hours, turning frequently. Preheat grill, making one side hot and the other low heat. Cook over the low side with grill covered, turning several times, for about 1 hour or until done. Discard the skin.

Yield: 8 servings

Per serving: 33 calories (20% from fat, 64% from protein, 16% from carbohydrate); 5 g protein; 1 g total fat; 0 g saturated fat; 0 g monounsaturated fat; 0 g polyunsaturated fat; 1 g carbohydrate; 0 g fiber; 0 g sugar; 44 mg phosphorus; 4 mg calcium; 0 mg iron; 19 mg sodium; 76 mg potassium; 18 IU vitamin A; 4 mg ATE vitamin E; 8 mg vitamin C; 17 mg cholesterol; 32 g water

Rotisserie-Flavored Chicken Breasts

This recipe gives you a flavor reminiscent of carryout rotisserie chicken, but with lower-fat chicken breasts as the basis.

¼ cup (60 ml) honey

1 teaspoon (2.5 g) paprika

1 teaspoon (3 g) onion powder

½ teaspoon (1 g) black pepper

½ teaspoon (0.5 g) dried thyme

¼ teaspoon (0.8 g) garlic powder

4 boneless chicken breasts

Preheat oven to 325°F (170°C, or gas mark 3). Mix honey, paprika, onion powder, black pepper, thyme, and garlic powder. Rub onto chicken. Roast for 45 minutes, or until done, basting occasionally with pan juices.

Yield: 4 servings

Per serving: 148 calories (6% from fat, 44% from protein, 50% from carbohydrate); 17 g protein; 1 g total fat; 0 g saturated fat; 0 g monounsaturated fat; 0 g polyunsaturated fat; 19 g carbohydrate; 0 g fiber; 18 g sugar; 145 mg phosphorus; 16 mg calcium; 1 mg iron; 48 mg sodium; 217 mg potassium; 324 IU vitamin A; 4 mg ATE vitamin E; 2 mg vitamin C; 41 mg cholesterol; 57 g water

Chicken with Asparagus

My wife came home with some asparagus recently, and this recipe came up while searching our recipe file. It had been a long time since we made it, but it turned out very well. It's definitely something we will keep in mind for the future.

4 boneless chicken breasts

1 tablespoon (4 g) cilantro, chopped

2 tablespoons (30 ml) olive oil

½ pound (225 g) asparagus, cut in 3-inch (7.5-cm) lengths

1½ cups (355 ml) low sodium chicken broth

1 tablespoon (8 g) cornstarch

1 tablespoon (15 ml) lemon juice

½ teaspoon (1 g) black pepper

Slice the chicken breasts into strips about ¼-inch (62-mm) thick. Sprinkle with cilantro and toss to coat. Heat the oil in a large frying pan and fry the chicken quickly in small batches, 1 to 2 minutes per side. Remove from pan when no longer pink. Add asparagus and chicken broth to pan and bring to a boil. Cook for 4 to 5 minutes, or until asparagus is tender. Mix the cornstarch with a little water and stir into the broth. Cook until thickened. Add the chicken. Stir in the lemon juice and pepper. Cook until chicken is heated through.

Yield: 4 servings

(continued on page 146)

Per serving: 170 calories (49% from fat, 43% from protein, 8% from carbohydrate); 18 g protein; 9 g total fat; 2 g saturated fat; 6 g monounsaturated fat; 1 g polyunsaturated fat; 3 g carbohydrate; 0 g fiber; 0 g sugar; 148 mg phosphorus; 14 mg calcium; 1 mg iron; 66 mg sodium; 225 mg potassium; 67 IU vitamin A; 3 mg ATE vitamin E; 2 mg vitamin C; 44 mg cholesterol; 126 g water

Chicken Pot Pie

This makes a large amount and is good for a family meal or leftovers for lunch.

2 pounds (905 g) boneless chicken breasts

2 cups (470 ml) low sodium chicken broth

1 cup (160 g) onion, coarsely chopped

1 cup (130 g) carrot, sliced

1⅓ cups (170 g) frozen peas, thawed

⅔ cup (84 g) flour

1 cup (235 g) water

1 tablespoon (0.4 g) dried parsley

1 teaspoon (1 g) dried thyme

6 potatoes, peeled and diced

1 cup (235 ml) skim milk

Preheat broiler. Place chicken and broth in a slow cooker or Dutch oven and cook until chicken is done. Remove chicken from broth, chop coarsely. Strain any fat from broth and add enough water to make 5 cups (1.2 L). Return broth to Dutch oven. Add onions, carrots, and peas and cook for 15 minutes, or until carrots are tender. Add flour to water in a jar with a tight-fitting lid. Shake until dissolved. Add to broth and cook until thickened. Stir in chicken, parsley, and thyme. While chicken mixture is cooking boil potatoes until done. Mash with milk. Drop mashed potatoes by spoonful onto top of chicken mixture. Broil until potatoes start to brown.

Yield: 8 servings

Per serving: 411 calories (5% from fat, 35% from protein, 59% from carbohydrate); 36 g protein; 2 g total fat; 1 g saturated fat; 1 g monounsaturated fat; 1 g polyunsaturated fat; 61 g carbohydrate; 7 g fiber; 5 g sugar; 486 mg phosphorus; 109 mg calcium; 4 mg iron; 209 mg sodium; 1791 mg potassium; 3265 IU vitamin A; 26 mg ATE vitamin E; 30 mg vitamin C; 66 mg cholesterol; 474 g water

Reduced-Fat Chicken and Dumplings

This is classic comfort food any time of year, but especially as the weather gets colder. You can also make the dumplings using 2 cups (250 g) of Reduced-Fat Biscuit Mix (see recipe page 437) rather than the flour, baking powder, and margarine called for here.

For Chicken:

1½ cups (165 g) chicken breast, cooked and cubed

3 cups (710 ml) low sodium chicken broth

3 cups (710 ml) water

1½ cups (195 g) carrot, sliced

6 potatoes, peeled and cubed

1 cup (160 g) onion, chopped

For Dumplings:

2 cups (250 g) flour

1 tablespoon (14 g) baking powder

2 tablespoons (28 g) margarine

²/₃ cup (160 g) skim milk

To make the chicken: Place chicken, broth, water, carrots, potatoes, and onion in a large pan. Bring to a boil.

To make the dumplings: Stir together the flour and baking powder. Cut in margarine until mixture resembles coarse crumbs. Stir in milk until dough holds together in a ball. Drop dumplings on top of boiling chicken mixture by spoonfuls. Reduce heat and simmer uncovered for 10 minutes. Cover and simmer 10 minutes more.

Yield: 6 servings

Per serving: 556 calories (11% from fat, 19% from protein, 71% from carbohydrate); 26 g protein; 7 g total fat; 2 g saturated fat; 3 g monounsaturated fat; 1 g polyunsaturated fat; 100 g carbohydrate; 9 g fiber; 7 g sugar; 488 mg phosphorus; 251 mg calcium; 6 mg iron; 413 mg sodium; 2113 mg potassium; 5668 IU vitamin A; 65 mg ATE vitamin E; 36 mg vitamin C; 30 mg cholesterol; 637 g water

Chicken Zucchini Pie

An easy and tasty one-dish meal based on the concept of the Bisquick impossible pies, which make their own crust.

1 cup (110 g) cooked chicken breast, cubed

1 cup (113 g) zucchini, cubed

1 cup (180 g) tomatoes, chopped

1 cup (160 g) onion, chopped

¼ cup (20 g) Parmesan cheese, shredded

1 cup (235 ml) skim milk

½ cup (60 g) Reduced-Fat Biscuit Mix (see recipe page 437)

½ cup (120 ml) egg substitute

¼ teaspoon (0.5 g) black pepper

Preheat oven to 400°F (200°C, or gas mark 6) and coat a 9-inch (23-cm) pie plate with nonstick vegetable oil spray. Mix chicken, zucchini, tomatoes, onion, and cheese and spoon evenly into prepared pie plate. Beat remaining ingredients in a blender or with a wire whisk until smooth. Pour evenly over chicken mixture. Bake for 35 minutes, or until a knife inserted in center comes out clean. Let stand 5 minutes before cutting.

Yield: 6 servings

Per serving: 156 calories (23% from fat, 38% from protein, 39% from carbohydrate); 15 g protein; 4 g total fat; 1 g saturated fat; 1 g monounsaturated fat; 1 g polyunsaturated fat; 15 g carbohydrate; 1 g fiber; 2 g sugar; 231 mg phosphorus; 160 mg calcium; 2 mg iron; 157 mg sodium; 433 mg potassium; 423 IU vitamin a; 41 mg ATE vitamin e; 12 mg vitamin c; 25 mg cholesterol; 138 g water

Chicken and Spaghetti Bake

This comes more or less directly from my daughter's theory of cooking, namely, if you can't think of anything else for dinner, make something Italian. Works for me!

8 ounces (225 g) spaghetti

½ cup (120 ml) egg substitute

1 cup (225 g) fat-free cottage cheese

1 pound (455 g) boneless chicken breast, sliced

½ cup (80 g) onion, chopped

½ cup (75 g) green bell pepper, chopped

2 cups (360 g) canned no-salt-added tomatoes

6 ounces (170 g) no-salt-added tomato paste

1 teaspoon (4 g) sugar

1 teaspoon (1 g) dried oregano

½ teaspoon (1.5 g) garlic powder

½ cup (60 g) mozzarella, shredded

Preheat oven to 350°F (180°C, or gas mark 4). Cook spaghetti according to package directions. Drain. Mix in egg substitute. Form into a "crust" in a greased 10-inch (25-cm) pie pan. Top with cottage cheese. In a large skillet cook chicken, onion, and green bell pepper until meat is done and vegetables are tender. Add remaining ingredients except mozzarella and heat through. Spread over spaghetti and cottage cheese. Bake for 20 minutes. Sprinkle with mozzarella about 5 minutes before the end of baking.

Yield: 6 servings

Per serving: 218 calories (9% from fat, 50% from protein, 41% from carbohydrate); 27 g protein; 2 g total fat; 1 g saturated fat; 1 g monounsaturated fat; 1 g polyunsaturated fat; 22 g carbohydrate; 4 g fiber; 8 g sugar; 274 mg phosphorus; 70 mg calcium; 3 mg iron; 128 mg sodium; 766 mg potassium; 704 IU vitamin A; 7 mg ATE vitamin E; 26 mg vitamin C; 46 mg cholesterol; 239 g water

Pasta with Chicken and Vegetables

This is a good way to use up a few fresh vegetables. These were what we had available, but you can vary them to match what you have. It makes a simple one-dish meal that's perfect for a warm evening with just a little homemade bread.

8 ounces (225 g) linguine or spaghetti

2 tablespoons (30 ml) olive oil

1 cup (113 g) zucchini, cut in strips

½ cup (35 g) mushrooms, sliced

½ teaspoon (0.3 g) dried basil

½ teaspoon (1.5 g) minced garlic

1 cup (235 ml) skim milk

2 cups (220 g) chicken breast, cooked and cubed

1 cup (180 g) roma tomatoes, sliced

2 tablespoons (10 g) Parmesan cheese, grated

⅛ teaspoon (0.3 g) black pepper

Cook linguini or spaghetti according to package directions. Meanwhile, heat the oil in a skillet. Add zucchini, mushrooms, basil, and garlic. Cook and stir for 2 to 3 minutes, or until zucchini is crisp-tender. Drain pasta and return to saucepan. Stir in milk, chicken, and zucchini mixture and heat through. Add tomatoes, cheese, and pepper. Toss and serve.

Yield: 6 servings

Per serving: 297 calories (26% from fat, 31% from protein, 42% from carbohydrate); 23 g protein; 9 g total fat; 2 g saturated fat; 5 g monounsaturated fat; 1 g polyunsaturated fat; 31 g carbohydrate; 2 g fiber; 2 g sugar; 278 mg phosphorus; 110 mg calcium; 1 mg iron; 102 mg sodium; 424 mg potassium; 379 IU vitamin A; 37 mg ATE vitamin E; 7 mg vitamin C; 74 mg cholesterol; 119 g water

Turkey and Zucchini Meatloaf

The glaze gives this a nice sweet-tart taste. The turkey keeps it low in fat. The zucchini keeps it moist. What more could you ask?

1¼ pounds (570 g) ground turkey

1 cup (125 g) zucchini, grated

½ cup (60 g) low sodium bread crumbs

¼ cup (60 ml) egg substitute

1 tablespoon (0.4 g) dried parsley

½ teaspoon (1 g) black pepper

½ teaspoon (1.5 g) garlic powder

1 teaspoon (3 g) onion powder

¼ cup (80 g) peach preserves

2 teaspoons (10 g) Dijon mustard

Preheat oven to 350°F (180°C, or gas mark 4). Combine first 8 ingredients (through onion powder) in a large bowl and mix well. Shape mixture into a loaf on a baking sheet. Bake for 45 minutes. Stir preserves and mustard together. Spread on top of loaf. Return to the oven and bake for 20 minutes, or until the internal temperature is 165°F (74°C).

Yield: 8 servings

Per serving: 144 calories (12% from fat, 51% from protein, 37% from carbohydrate); 18 g protein; 2 g total fat; 1 g saturated fat; 0 g monounsaturated fat; 1 g polyunsaturated fat; 13 g carbohydrate; 1 g fiber; 6 g sugar; 162 mg phosphorus; 32 mg calcium; 2 mg iron; 126 mg sodium; 282 mg potassium; 100 IU vitamin A; 0 mg ATE vitamin E; 4 mg vitamin C; 52 mg cholesterol; 80 g water

Chicken Curry

I'm fond of curries. They make a particularly nice slow-cooker meal because they fill the house with such a great aroma for you to come home to. This one calls for a number of spices that are typical of curry powder. If you have a favorite curry powder on the shelf, you could substitute a couple of tablespoons of that for the other spices.

5 medium potatoes, diced

¾ cup (112 g) green bell peppers, coarsely chopped

¾ cup (120 g) onion, coarsely chopped

1 pound (455 g) boneless chicken breasts, cubed

2 cups (360 g) canned no-salt-added tomatoes

1 tablespoon (6 g) ground coriander

1½ tablespoons (10.5 g) paprika

1 tablespoon (5.5 g) ground ginger

¼ teaspoon (0.5 g) cayenne pepper

½ teaspoon (1.1 g) turmeric

¼ teaspoon (0.6 g) cinnamon

⅛ teaspoon (0.3 g) ground cloves

1 cup (235 ml) low sodium chicken broth

2 tablespoons (60 ml) cold water

¼ cup (32 g) cornstarch

Place potatoes, green bell peppers, and onion in slow cooker. Place chicken on top. Mix together tomatoes and the next 8 ingredients (through chicken broth). Pour over chicken. Cook on low 8 to 10 hours or on high 5 to 6 hours. Remove chicken and vegetables. Turn heat to high. Stir cornstarch into water. Add to cooker. Cook for 15 to 20 minutes, or until sauce is slightly thickened.

Yield: 5 servings

Per serving: 438 calories (5% from fat, 28% from protein, 67% from carbohydrate); 30 g protein; 2 g total fat; 1 g saturated fat; 0 g monounsaturated fat; 1 g polyunsaturated fat; 74 g carbohydrate; 8 g fiber; 8 g sugar; 448 mg phosphorus; 87 mg calcium; 5 mg iron; 126 mg sodium; 2235 mg potassium; 1394 IU vitamin A; 5 mg ATE vitamin E; 71 mg vitamin C; 53 mg cholesterol; 484 g water

Turkey Cutlets Scaloppini

I don't usually pay the price they want for turkey cutlets, but I do occasionally buy a turkey breast and slice it into "cutlets," freezing most for later use and making soup of the carcass once most of the meat has been removed.

1¼ pounds (570 g) turkey cutlets

1½ teaspoons (3 g) lemon pepper

1 tablespoon (7 g) paprika

3 tablespoons (45 ml) lemon juice

3/8 cups (90 ml) water

1 tablespoon (15 ml) olive oil

Coat a skillet with nonstick vegetable oil spray. Flatten cutlets to about ¼-inch (0.6 cm) thickness. Place in skillet. Sprinkle with lemon pepper and paprika. Cook 3 to 4 minutes, turn over, and cook 4 to 5 minutes more or until done. Remove turkey from skillet. Add lemon juice, water, and oil. Heat until hot, stirring up any browned bits stuck on the bottom of the skillet. Serve sauce over cutlets.

Yield: 4 servings

Per serving: 257 calories (29% from fat, 67% from protein, 4% from carbohydrate); 42 g protein; 8 g total fat; 2 g saturated fat; 4 g monounsaturated fat; 2 g polyunsaturated fat; 2 g carbohydrate; 1 g fiber; 0 g sugar; 314 mg phosphorus; 29 mg calcium; 3 mg iron; 77 mg sodium; 460 mg potassium; 914 IU vitamin A; 0 mg ATE vitamin E; 7 mg vitamin C; 128 mg cholesterol; 129 g water

Turkey and Zucchini Moussaka

A variation of the typical Greek dish using ground turkey and zucchini, rather than the more common lamb and eggplant.

6 cups (675 g) zucchini, sliced lengthwise

½ pound (225 g) ground turkey

1 cup (160 g) onion, chopped

2 teaspoons (6 g) garlic, minced

½ teaspoon (1.2 g) cinnamon

½ teaspoon (0.5 g) dried oregano

1 cup (235 ml) low sodium chicken broth

⅔ cup (130 g) rice

8 ounces (235 ml) no-salt-added tomato sauce

2 tablespoons (30 ml) olive oil

¼ cup (30 g) flour

1½ cups (355 ml) skim milk

½ cup (120 ml) egg substitute

¼ teaspoon (0.6 g) nutmeg

Preheat oven to 350°F (180°C, or gas mark 4). Lightly grease a shallow 2-quart (1.9-L) baking dish. Bring 3 cups (705 ml) water to boil in a large nonstick skillet. Add zucchini, cover, reduce heat, and simmer 10 minutes or until crisp-tender. Remove to paper towels to drain. Wipe out skillet. Add turkey, onion, and garlic. Cook until turkey is no longer pink. Stir in cinnamon and oregano, then broth and rice. Cover and simmer 10 minutes, stirring two or three times. Stir in tomato sauce. Remove from heat. Heat oil in a 2-quart (1.9-L) saucepan. Whisk in flour and cook, stirring 1 to 2 minutes without letting mixture brown. Gradually whisk in milk. Cook, whisking constantly, 4 to 5 minutes until thickened and smooth. Whisk one-third of the hot mixture into the egg substitute, then whisk egg mixture into remaining sauce. Remove from heat; stir in nutmeg.

To assemble: Cover the bottom of prepared baking dish with half the zucchini slices. Spoon the turkey mixture over the slices, then cover with remaining zucchini. Pour the milk mixture over everything. Bake for 20 to 25 minutes, or until hot and bubbly and top is lightly golden.

Yield: 4 servings

Per serving: 327 calories (27% from fat, 32% from protein, 41% from carbohydrate); 26 g protein; 10 g total fat; 2 g saturated fat; 6 g monounsaturated fat; 2 g polyunsaturated fat; 34 g carbohydrate; 4 g fiber; 8 g sugar; 390 mg phosphorus; 217 mg calcium; 4 mg iron; 190 mg sodium; 1259 mg potassium; 879 IU vitamin A; 56 mg ATE vitamin E; 44 mg vitamin C; 44 mg cholesterol; 491 g water

Turkey Skillet Pie

This is a great dish to make with leftover holiday turkey and stuffing.

1 tablespoon (15 ml) olive oil

⅓ cup (35 g) celery, chopped

2 tablespoons (20 g) onion, finely chopped

⅔ cup (160 ml) fat-free evaporated milk

2 cups (400 g) prepared stuffing

3 cups (525 g) cooked turkey, chopped

1 cup (110 g) low fat Swiss cheese, shredded

Heat olive oil in a small skillet; cook celery and onion until soft. In a large bowl, combine milk, stuffing, and onion mixture. Stir in turkey. Pour into a large skillet and sprinkle with cheese. Cook until heated through, about 10 minutes.

Yield: 6 servings

Per serving: 305 calories (33% from fat, 42% from protein, 25% from carbohydrate); 31 g protein; 11 g total fat; 3 g saturated fat; 5 g monounsaturated fat; 3 g polyunsaturated fat; 19 g carbohydrate; 2 g fiber; 5 g sugar; 359 mg phosphorus; 325 mg calcium; 2 mg iron; 501 mg sodium; 364 mg potassium; 370 IU vitamin A; 113 mg ATE vitamin E; 1 mg vitamin C; 77 mg cholesterol; 133 g water

Turkey-Stuffed Zucchini

This is perfect for those times when you don't get back to check the garden as often as you should and find a couple of zucchini that would make great softball bats. Discard the seeds and any center part of the squash that has gotten hard or stringy, and put the rest of what you scoop out into the filling.

3 large zucchini

1¼ pounds (570 g) ground turkey

1 cup (160 g) onion, chopped

2 cloves garlic, crushed

2 cups (360 g) canned no-salt-added tomatoes

1½ cups (250 g) cooked rice, or small pasta

1 teaspoon (0.7 g) dried basil

12 ounces (340 g) Swiss cheese, sliced

Preheat broiler. Cut the zucchini in half lengthwise. Scrape out the center, leaving a thickness of about ½ inch (1.2 cm). Discard the seeds and chop the remainder of the flesh; set aside. In a large skillet, cook the turkey, onion, and garlic until turkey is done. Stir in tomatoes, rice, basil, and chopped zucchini flesh. Cook the zucchini halves in boiling water until it begins to soften. Drain and place in baking pan. Divide the filling between the zucchini halves. Place a slice of cheese on top of each. Place under broiler until cheese is melted and bubbly.

Yield: 6 servings

Per serving: 309 calories (15% from fat, 54% from protein, 32% from carbohydrate); 42 g protein; 5 g total fat; 2 g saturated fat; 1 g monounsaturated fat; 1 g polyunsaturated fat; 24 g carbohydrate; 4 g fiber; 7 g sugar; 633 mg phosphorus; 625 mg calcium; 4 mg iron; 236 mg sodium; 1012 mg potassium; 563 IU vitamin A; 22 mg ATE vitamin E; 41 mg vitamin C; 89 mg cholesterol; 408 g water

Baked Chicken Nuggets

You can greatly reduce the amount of fat in chicken nuggets by baking them instead of frying them. The flavor is just as good, and they are a lot better for you.

½ cup (14 g) crushed corn flakes

2 tablespoons (15 g) nonfat dry milk

1 tablespoon (0.4 g) dried parsley

1 tablespoon (7 g) paprika

1 teaspoon (3 g) onion powder

¼ teaspoon (0.8 g) garlic powder

½ teaspoon (0.4 g) poultry seasoning

1 pound (455 g) boneless chicken breasts, cut in strips

¼ cup (60 ml) egg substitute

Preheat oven to 350°F (180°C, or gas mark 4). Mix together crushed corn flakes and next 6 ingredients (through poultry seasoning) in a resealable plastic bag. Dip chicken pieces in egg substitute, then place in bag. Shake to coat evenly. Place on baking sheet coated with nonstick vegetable oil spray. Bake for 20 minutes, or until chicken is done and coating is crispy.

Yield: 4 servings

Per serving: 167 calories (12% from fat, 73% from protein, 14% from carbohydrate); 29 g protein; 2 g total fat; 1 g saturated fat; 1 g monounsaturated fat; 1 g polyunsaturated fat; 6 g carbohydrate; 1 g fiber; 2 g sugar; 274 mg phosphorus; 61 mg calcium; 2 mg iron; 116 mg sodium; 442 mg potassium; 1088 IU vitamin A; 22 mg ATE vitamin E; 3 mg vitamin C; 66 mg cholesterol; 98 g water

Grilled Southwestern Chicken Breasts

The cilantro and lime give these chicken breasts a nice southwestern flavor.

4 boneless chicken breasts

¼ cup (60 ml) olive oil

2 tablespoons (30 g) Dijon mustard

1 tablespoon (15 ml) rice wine vinegar

1 teaspoon (2 g) black pepper

dash hot pepper sauce

¼ cup (60 ml) lime juice

2 tablespoons (8 g) cilantro

TIP

Serve with rice and grilled corn.

Pound the chicken breasts to ½-inch (1.3-cm) thickness and place all ingredients in a 1-gallon (3.8-L) resealable plastic bag or a bowl and cover. Marinate in the refrigerator for at least 30 minutes. Grill over medium heat for 20 minutes, or until done.

Yield: 4 servings

Per serving: 209 calories (64% from fat, 32% from protein, 4% from carbohydrate); 17 g protein; 15 g total fat; 2 g saturated fat; 10 g monounsaturated fat; 2 g polyunsaturated fat; 2 g carbohydrate; 0 g fiber; 0 g sugar; 151 mg phosphorus; 18 mg calcium; 1 mg iron; 133 mg sodium; 226 mg potassium; 117 IU vitamin A; 4 mg ATE vitamin E; 6 mg vitamin C; 41 mg cholesterol; 78 g water

Grilled Roaster

If you cook a large chicken on the weekend, you can have a great meal and lots of leftovers to use during the week. This one has a smoky flavor, but not so much as to overpower other ingredients.

1 large roasting chicken, 5 to 6 pounds (2.3 to 2.7 kg)

2 tablespoons (30 ml) olive oil

1 teaspoon (2.5 g) paprika

1 teaspoon (3 g) onion powder

½ teaspoon (1 g) black pepper

½ teaspoon (0.5 g) dried thyme

¼ teaspoon (0.8 g) garlic powder

1 teaspoon (5 ml) liquid smoke

Split chicken in half along the backbone and breastbone. Mix together remaining ingredients and rub into both sides of chicken halves. Grill over indirect heat, turning occasionally, for 1½ to 2 hours, or until done. Place over low heat the last 15 minutes to brown skin.

Yield: 12 servings

Per serving: 289 calories (69% from fat, 30% from protein, 1% from carbohydrate); 22 g protein; 22 g total fat; 6 g saturated fat; 9 g monounsaturated fat; 4 g polyunsaturated fat; 1 g carbohydrate; 0 g fiber; 0 g sugar; 2 mg phosphorus; 15 mg calcium; 2 mg iron; 0 mg sodium; 255 mg potassium; 209 IU vitamin A; 0 mg ATE vitamin E; 3 mg vitamin C; 113 mg cholesterol; 0 g water

Cajun Grilled Chicken

Nice Cajun flavor off the grill. Serve with rice and a steamed vegetable.

4 boneless chicken breasts

5 teaspoons (10 g) Cajun blackening spice mix

Cut slashes into the chicken ½-inch (1.3-cm) deep to allow spices to penetrate the meat. Rub the spices into the chicken. Cook on a medium grill for about 25 minutes, or until done.

Yield: 4 servings

Per serving: 78 calories (11% from fat, 89% from protein, 0% from carbohydrate); 16 g protein; 1 g total fat; 0 g saturated fat; 0 g monounsaturated fat; 0 g polyunsaturated fat; 0 g carbohydrate; 0 g fiber; 0 g sugar; 139 mg phosphorus; 8 mg calcium; 1 mg iron; 46 mg sodium; 181 mg potassium; 15 IU vitamin A; 4 mg ATE vitamin E; 1 mg vitamin C; 41 mg cholesterol; 53 g water

Jerk Chicken Breasts

A simple recipe for jerk-flavored chicken. You could also cook this on the grill or a rotisserie.

½ cup (80 g) onion, finely chopped

6 boneless chicken breasts

1 teaspoon (2.5 g) paprika

2 teaspoons (6 g) garlic powder

3 tablespoons (19 g) jerk seasoning

Preheat oven to 350°F (180°C, or gas mark 4). Rub the onion into the chicken, inside and out. Combine the paprika, garlic powder, and jerk seasoning. Rub all over the chicken and allow the chicken to marinate for at least 2 hours. Roast in oven for 45 minutes to an hour, or until done.

Yield: 6 servings

Per serving: 88 calories (10% from fat, 80% from protein, 10% from carbohydrate); 17 g protein; 1 g total fat; 0 g saturated fat; 0 g monounsaturated fat; 0 g polyunsaturated fat; 2 g carbohydrate; 0 g fiber; 1 g sugar; 148 mg phosphorus; 12 mg calcium; 1 mg iron; 47 mg sodium; 220 mg potassium; 217 IU vitamin A; 4 mg ATE vitamin E; 2 mg vitamin C; 41 mg cholesterol; 65 g water

Smoked Turkey

If you have a smoker, this makes a sweet and juicy meal for a crowd, with a slightly southwestern flavor. Remember to discard the skin. It has most of the saturated fat, and it tends to get rubbery in the smoker anyway, so you're less tempted to cheat.

10-pound (4.5 kg) turkey

1 apple, quartered

1 onion, quartered

1 cup (100 g) celery, sliced

¼ cup (60 ml) honey

¼ cup (60 ml) lime juice

½ teaspoon (1.3 g) paprika

1 tablespoon (7 g) cumin

½ teaspoon (0.9 g) cayenne pepper

½ teaspoon (1.5 g) garlic powder

Place apple, onion, and celery inside turkey cavity. Combine remaining ingredients. Loosen the skin of the breast, legs, and thighs. Rub the honey spice mixture under the skin, spreading it as far as possible. Smoke for 8 to 10 hours, or until done.

Yield: 20 servings

Per serving: 271 calories (13% from fat, 79% from protein, 9% from carbohydrate); 51 g protein; 4 g total fat; 1 g saturated fat; 1 g monounsaturated fat; 1 g polyunsaturated fat; 6 g carbohydrate; 0 g fiber; 5 g sugar; 424 mg phosphorus; 35 mg calcium; 4 mg iron; 144 mg sodium; 634 mg potassium; 79 IU vitamin A; 0 mg ATE vitamin E; 2 mg vitamin C; 166 mg cholesterol; 191 g water

Reduced-Fat Chicken Salad

This makes great sandwiches, and the food processor makes it easy. A few seconds will give you perfectly ground and mixed salad. I often cook a whole chicken in the slow cooker and then use the meat for this and other recipes.

1 cup (110 g) chicken, cooked

¼ cup (25 g) celery, chopped

2 tablespoons (28 g) low fat mayonnaise

2 tablespoons (30 g) fat-free sour cream

½ teaspoon (1.5 g) onion powder

Place chicken and celery in food processor and process until finely ground. Add remaining ingredients and process until well mixed.

Yield: 4 servings

Per serving: 104 calories (49% from fat, 45% from protein, 6% from carbohydrate); 10 g protein; 5 g total fat; 1 g saturated fat; 1 g monounsaturated fat; 1 g polyunsaturated fat; 1 g carbohydrate; 0 g fiber; 1 g sugar; 82 mg phosphorus; 17 mg calcium; 0 mg iron; 98 mg sodium; 118 mg potassium; 89 IU vitamin A; 13 mg ATE vitamin E; 0 mg vitamin C; 37 mg cholesterol; 39 g water

Pulled Chicken

Here's a good use for leftover smoked or grilled chicken. Try it with the onion rolls and a scoop of coleslaw on it and you won't even miss the expensive sandwiches at your favorite barbecue restaurant.

8 ounces (225 g) no-salt-added tomato sauce

¼ cup (60 ml) vinegar

¼ cup (60 ml) molasses

½ teaspoon (1.5 g) onion powder

½ teaspoon (1.3 g) chili powder

½ teaspoon (1.5 g) dry mustard

¼ teaspoon (0.5 g) cayenne pepper

¼ teaspoon (0.8 g) garlic powder

2 cups (220 g) smoked chicken, shredded

6 onion rolls

Mix the first 8 ingredients (through garlic powder). Add chicken and stir to combine or place chicken on rolls and spoon sauce over chicken.

Yield: 6 servings

Per serving: 146 calories (23% from fat, 39% from protein, 38% from carbohydrate); 14 g protein; 4 g total fat; 1 g saturated fat; 1 g monounsaturated fat; 1 g polyunsaturated fat; 14 g carbohydrate; 1 g fiber; 8 g sugar; 116 mg phosphorus; 45 mg calcium; 3 mg iron; 227 mg sodium; 475 mg potassium; 490 IU vitamin A; 7 mg ATE vitamin E; 3 mg vitamin C; 42 mg cholesterol; 76 g water

Oven-Fried Chicken

Fried chicken doesn't have to be as unhealthy as it usually is. Get rid of the skin and "fry" the chicken in the oven, and it's a perfectly acceptable food. Not to mention that it tastes good.

¼ cup (55 g) unsalted margarine, melted

¼ teaspoon (0.5 g) black pepper

3 pounds (1.4 kg) chicken, cut into pieces, skin removed

1 cup (56 g) corn flake crumbs

Preheat oven to 350°F (180°C, or gas mark 4). Combine margarine and pepper. Roll chicken in margarine mixture , then corn flake crumbs. Place in an ungreased baking pan and bake about 1 hour, or until done.

Yield: 8 servings

Per serving: 267 calories (38% from fat, 57% from protein, 5% from carbohydrate); 37 g protein; 11 g total fat; 2 g saturated fat; 4 g monounsaturated fat; 3 g polyunsaturated fat; 3 g carbohydrate; 0 g fiber; 0 g sugar; 297 mg phosphorus; 22 mg calcium; 3 mg iron; 159 mg sodium; 395 mg potassium; 423 IU vitamin A; 104 mg ATE vitamin E; 6 mg vitamin C; 119 mg cholesterol; 130 g water

Potato-Coated Oven-Fried Chicken

This is my favorite recipe for oven-fried chicken.

¼ cup (60 ml) egg substitute

2 tablespoons (30 ml) water

¼ cup (25 g) Parmesan cheese, grated

3 pounds (1.4 kg) chicken, cut into pieces, skin removed

1 cup (60 g) instant mashed potato flakes

Preheat oven to 375°F (190°C, or gas mark 5). Combine egg, water, and cheese. Dip chicken in egg mixture, then roll in potato flakes. Place in ungreased baking pan. Bake for 1 hour, or until done.

Yield: 8 servings

Per serving: 249 calories (24% from fat, 65% from protein, 10% from carbohydrate); 39 g protein; 6 g total fat; 2 g saturated fat; 2 g monounsaturated fat; 1 g polyunsaturated fat; 6 g carbohydrate; 0 g fiber; 0 g sugar; 338 mg phosphorus; 61 mg calcium; 2 mg iron; 201 mg sodium; 502 mg potassium; 131 IU vitamin A; 31 mg ATE vitamin E; 10 mg vitamin C; 122 mg cholesterol; 140 g water

8

Main Dishes:
Beef

Beef producers tell us that "it's what's for dinner," and I have to admit that in our household this was often true. We had beef three or four times a week. However, current dietary guidelines often recommend limiting yourself to no more than one or two meals a week of red meat. But that doesn't mean we need to give up the taste we love completely. The key is being selective about the cuts of beef that you buy. An ounce of chuck or prime rib contains over 6 grams of fat, but the same amount of round steak only has about 1 gram. Ground beef comes in a range of 5% fat to 20% fat, which is marked right on the package. The ground beef I buy, and what is specified in the following recipes, in 93% lean. You will need to be more careful how you cook your lean beef to get maximum flavor and tenderness out of it. The recipes in this chapter will show you how you can enjoy beef and still keep to your cholesterol-healthy diet.

Big Juicy Burgers

Extra lean ground beef doesn't have to be dry. If you prefer your burger medium or medium rare, you can have great grilled burgers that are still juicy without the fat content. If you prefer a more well done burger, you might try this recipe, where low fat beef broth provides the extra moistness.

1 cup (235 ml) low sodium beef broth

2 slices white bread, torn into pieces

1½ pounds (680 g) extra-lean ground beef (93% lean)

2 tablespoons (30 ml) egg substitute

½ teaspoon (1 g) black pepper

Microwave broth in a glass bowl for 30 seconds. Add bread pieces and combine with your hands. Combine broth mixture and remaining ingredients. Shape into 5 patties. Grill patties over medium-high heat 6 to 8 minutes on each side or to desired doneness.

Yield: 5 servings

Per serving: 328 calories (43% from fat, 56% from protein, 0% from carbohydrate); 27 g protein; 9 g total fat; 4 g saturated fat; 4 g monounsaturated fat; 0 g polyunsaturated fat; 0 g carbohydrate; 0 g fiber; 0 g sugar; 206 mg phosphorus; 17 mg calcium; 3 mg iron; 129 mg sodium; 436 mg potassium; 23 IU vitamin A; 0 mg ATE vitamin E; 0 mg vitamin C; 94 mg cholesterol; 138 g water

Italian Burgers

A little added flavor for the meat accompaniment to your pasta. The sun-dried tomatoes add moistness as well as flavor.

1 pound (455 g) extra-lean ground beef (93% lean)

½ cup (55 g) oil-packed sun-dried tomatoes, chopped

¼ teaspoon (0.8 g) garlic powder

½ teaspoon (0.7 g) dried basil

½ teaspoon (0.5 g) dried oregano

Mix all ingredients together. Form into patties and grill or fry to desired doneness.

Yield: 4 servings

Per serving: 296 calories (45% from fat, 47% from protein, 7% from carbohydrate); 22 g protein; 9 g total fat; 3 g saturated fat; 4 g monounsaturated fat; 1 g polyunsaturated fat; 3 g carbohydrate; 1 g fiber; 0 g sugar; 180 mg phosphorus; 18 mg calcium; 3 mg iron; 112 mg sodium; 544 mg potassium; 194 IU vitamin A; 0 mg ATE vitamin E; 14 mg vitamin C; 78 mg cholesterol; 79 g water

Asian Grilled Burgers

There used to be a packaged mix for these, as well as a number of other Asian dishes, but they seem to have faded from the scene before I had a chance to banish them because of the sodium content. The oriental vegetable mix I use contains bean sprouts, mushrooms, water chestnuts, bamboo shoots, and red peppers, but you can use whatever vegetable mix you like.

1½ pounds (680 g) extra-lean ground beef (93% lean)

1 can (15 ounces, or 420 g) oriental vegetable mix

½ teaspoon (1 g) oriental seasoning

¼ teaspoon (0.5 g) ground ginger

¼ cup (60 ml) Dick's Reduced-Sodium Soy Sauce (see recipe page 30)

Combine all ingredients. Shape into 6 patties. Grill or fry to desired doneness.

Yield: 6 servings

Per serving: 274 calories (16% from fat, 21% from protein, 63% from carbohydrate); 21 g protein; 7 g total fat; 3 g saturated fat; 3 g monounsaturated fat; 2 g polyunsaturated fat; 65 g carbohydrate; 0 g fiber; 1 g sugar; 168 mg phosphorus; 13 mg calcium; 2 mg iron; 144 mg sodium; 349 mg potassium; 4 IU vitamin A; 0 mg ATE vitamin E; 0 mg vitamin C; 78 mg cholesterol; 85 g water

Barbecued Beef

This is a quick sandwich meal that will cook while you are out. Small children and teenagers seem to like this too, so it's great for a party or family get-together.

1½ pounds (680 g) extra-lean ground beef (93% lean)

1 onion, chopped

1 cup (240 g) low sodium ketchup

1 green bell pepper, chopped

2 tablespoons (30 g) brown sugar

½ teaspoon (1.5 g) garlic powder

2 tablespoons (30 g) prepared mustard

3 tablespoons (45 ml) vinegar

1 tablespoon (15 ml) Worcestershire sauce

1 teaspoon (2.6 g) chili powder

In a skillet, brown beef and onion. Drain. Stir together remaining ingredients in slow cooker. Stir in meat and onion mixture. Cook on low for 6 to 8 hours or on high for 3 to 4 hours.

Yield: 8 servings

Per serving: 249 calories (32% from fat, 40% from protein, 28% from carbohydrate); 17 g protein; 6 g total fat; 2 g saturated fat; 2 g monounsaturated fat; 0 g polyunsaturated fat; 12 g carbohydrate; 0 g fiber; 10 g sugar; 135 mg phosphorus; 18 mg calcium; 2 mg iron; 85 mg sodium; 402 mg potassium; 377 IU vitamin A; 0 mg ATE vitamin E; 8 mg vitamin C; 59 mg cholesterol; 80 g water

Meatloaf

This meatloaf, with variations as our diet has changed, has been a family favorite for years. It's a simple loaf with only a few ingredients, which my kids seemed to appreciate. The sauce is the real star here, a sweet and sour barbecue-y marvel that is worlds away from plain tomato sauce or, heaven forbid, tomato soup. It gives the whole house a wonderful aroma while it cooks. I always make at least a double recipe. It makes great sandwiches. You can also use ground turkey and make a lower-fat version.

1½ pounds (680 g) extra-lean ground beef (93% lean)

1 cup (115 g) bread crumbs

1 onion, finely chopped

¼ cup (60 ml) egg substitute

¼ teaspoon (0.5 g) black pepper

8 ounces (225 g) no-salt-added tomato sauce, divided

½ cup (120 ml) water

2 teaspoons (10 ml) Worcestershire sauce

3 tablespoons (45 ml) vinegar

2 tablespoons (30 g) mustard

3 tablespoons (45 g) brown sugar

Preheat oven to 350°F (180°C, or gas mark 4). Mix together beef, bread crumbs, onion, egg substitute, pepper, and half the tomato sauce. Form into one large loaf or two small ones; mix remaining tomato sauce and remaining ingredients together; pour over loaves. Bake for 1 to 1½ hours.

Yield: 6 servings

Per serving: 393 calories (29% from fat, 37% from protein, 33% from carbohydrate); 26 g protein; 9 g total fat; 3 g saturated fat; 3 g monounsaturated fat; 1 g polyunsaturated fat; 23 g carbohydrate; 1 g fiber; 9 g sugar; 218 mg phosphorus; 62 mg calcium; 4 mg iron; 249 mg sodium; 585 mg potassium; 175 IU vitamin A; 0 mg ATE vitamin E; 8 mg vitamin C; 78 mg cholesterol; 142 g water

Reduced-Fat Meatballs

This meatball recipe has been in the family for years, long before we were concerned with heart-healthy cooking. It's been modified a number of times as our diets changed, first to reduce the sodium, and later to make it lower in fat. The meatballs are good by themselves, but they're better if allowed to simmer in the sauce in a slow cooker for a few hours.

1½ pounds (680 g) extra-lean ground beef (93% lean)

¾ cup (180 ml) egg substitute

½ cup Parmesan cheese, shredded

½ teaspoon (1.5 g) garlic powder

1 tablespoon (0.4 g) dried parsley

½ tablespoon (1.5 g) dried oregano

4 slices bread, crumbled

2 cups (320 g) onion, chopped

6 ounces (170 g) no-salt-added tomato paste

1½ cups (355 ml) water

½ cup (120 ml) red wine vinegar

3 tablespoons (45 g) brown sugar

Preheat oven to 375°F (190°C, or gas mark 5). Combine beef, egg substitute, cheese, garlic powder, parsley, oregano, and bread. Form into 1-inch (2.5 cm) balls. Bake for 30 to 40 minutes, turning once. Pour a few tablespoons (45 ml) of meat drippings into a skillet; sauté onion. Combine onions, tomato paste, water, vinegar, and brown sugar and place in slow cooker. Add meatballs. Stir to mix and cook on low for several hours.

Yield: 6 servings

Per serving: 457 calories (31% from fat, 37% from protein, 32% from carbohydrate); 32 g protein; 12 g total fat; 5 g saturated fat; 4 g monounsaturated fat; 1 g polyunsaturated fat; 28 g carbohydrate; 4 g fiber; 15 g sugar; 340 mg phosphorus; 173 mg calcium; 5 mg iron; 398 mg sodium; 887 mg potassium; 653 IU vitamin A; 10 mg ATE vitamin E; 11 mg vitamin C; 86 mg cholesterol; 254 g water

German Meatballs

These German-flavored meatballs would traditionally be served over spaetzle, but they are also good with noodles, rice, or mashed potatoes.

¼ cup (60 ml) egg substitute

¼ cup (60 ml) skim milk

¼ cup (29 g) bread crumbs

¼ teaspoon (0.2 g) poultry seasoning

1 pound (455 g) extra-lean ground beef (93% lean)

2 cups (470 ml) low sodium beef broth

½ cup (35 g) mushrooms, sliced

½ cup (80 g) onion, chopped

1 cup (230 g) fat-free sour cream

1 tablespoon (8 g) flour

1 teaspoon (2.1 g) caraway seed

Combine egg substitute and milk. Stir in bread crumbs and poultry seasoning. Add beef and mix well. Form into 24 meatballs, each about 1½ inches (3.8 cm). Brown meatballs in skillet. Drain. Add broth, mushrooms, and onion to the skillet. Cover and simmer for 30 minutes. Stir together sour cream, flour, and caraway seed. Add to skillet. Cook and stir until thickened.

Yield: 6 servings

Per serving: 281 calories (32% from fat, 47% from protein, 21% from carbohydrate); 19 g protein; 6 g total fat; 2 g saturated fat; 2 g monounsaturated fat; 1 g polyunsaturated fat; 8 g carbohydrate; 1 g fiber; 1 g sugar; 199 mg phosphorus; 87 mg calcium; 2 mg iron; 172 mg sodium; 417 mg potassium; 212 IU vitamin A; 47 mg ATE vitamin E; 2 mg vitamin C; 68 mg cholesterol; 194 g water

Stuffed Banana Peppers

Another recipe that uses some excess peppers. The original recipe I used to develop this one called for frying, but I decided to make them in the oven instead to reduce the amount of fat, since the meat and cheese already have a significant amount.

12 banana peppers, hot or sweet

1 pound (455 g) extra-lean ground beef (93% lean)

½ cup (80 g) onion, finely chopped

½ cup (55 g) Swiss cheese, shredded

¼ cup (60 ml) egg substitute

¼ teaspoon (0.5 g) black pepper

¼ cup (30 g) flour

Preheat oven to 350°F (180°C, or gas mark 4). Wash and clean peppers, then cut off the top and a small part of the bottom of peppers. In a large skillet, sauté ground beef and onions until meat is browned. Stir in cheese. Stuff mixture into peppers. Whisk egg substitute and black pepper in a bowl. Dip peppers in egg mixture. Roll in flour, dip in egg again, and roll in flour again. Place in 9 x 13-inch (23 x 33-cm) baking dish and coat surface with nonstick vegetable oil spray until flour is moistened. Bake for 20 minutes, or until cheese is melted and coating begins to brown.

Yield: 4 servings

Per serving: 372 calories (32% from fat, 47% from protein, 21% from carbohydrate); 30 g protein; 9 g total fat; 4 g saturated fat; 4 g monounsaturated fat; 1 g polyunsaturated fat; 14 g carbohydrate; 4 g fiber; 3 g sugar; 325 mg phosphorus; 195 mg calcium; 3 mg iron; 159 mg sodium; 685 mg potassium; 419 IU vitamin A; 7 mg ATE vitamin E; 83 mg vitamin C; 84 mg cholesterol; 204 g water

Chili Casserole

A Mexican meal in one pan. This is a fairly mild version, but you could increase the chili powder or add a chopped jalapeño to either the chili or the cornbread if you wanted to make it spicier.

1 pound (455 g) extra-lean ground beef (93% lean)

½ cup (80 g) onion, chopped

½ cup (75 g) red bell pepper, chopped

2 cups (450 g) no-salt-added kidney beans

2 cups (360 g) tomatoes, chopped and drained

1 cup (164 g) frozen corn

1 tablespoon (7.5 g) chili powder

1 teaspoon (2.5 g) cumin

½ teaspoon (1.5 g) garlic powder

½ cup (60 g) flour

½ cup (70 g) yellow cornmeal

2 tablespoons (26 g) sugar

1½ teaspoons (7 g) baking powder

1 cup (235 ml) skim milk

¼ cup (60 ml) egg substitute, or 1 egg

1 tablespoon (15 ml) olive oil

Preheat oven to 425°F (220°C, or gas mark 7). Brown beef with onions and red bell pepper until beef is no longer pink. Add beans, tomatoes, corn, chili powder, cumin, and garlic powder and simmer for 5 minutes. In a large bowl, stir together flour, cornmeal, sugar, and baking powder. In a medium bowl, combine milk, egg, and oil and pour into flour mixture, stirring until just moistened. Spread beef mixture in a greased 8 x 8-inch (20 x 20-cm) baking dish. Spread cornmeal mixture over top. Bake for 10 to 12 minutes, or until cornbread is done.

Yield: 4 servings

Per serving: 669 calories (20% from fat, 28% from protein, 52% from carbohydrate); 39 g protein; 13 g total fat; 4 g saturated fat; 6 g monounsaturated fat; 2 g polyunsaturated fat; 74 g carbohydrate; 13 g fiber; 10 g sugar; 506 mg phosphorus; 288 mg calcium; 8 mg iron; 357 mg sodium; 1247 mg potassium; 1838 IU vitamin A; 38 mg ATE vitamin E; 49 mg vitamin C; 80 mg cholesterol; 340 g water

Mexican Skillet Meal

This is one of those one-pan meals that you used to buy in a box. I have to say I think the flavor of this one is better than anything Hamburger Helper ever did.

1 pound (455 g) extra-lean ground beef (93% lean)

½ cup (80 g) onion, chopped

¼ cup (37 g) green bell peppers, chopped

¼ cup (37 g) red bell pepper, chopped

½ teaspoon (1.5 g) minced garlic

1½ cups (290 g) rice

3 cups (710 ml) water

2 teaspoons (4 g) low sodium beef bouillon

2 cups (360 g) canned no-salt-added tomatoes

1 tablespoon (7.5 g) chili powder

½ teaspoon (1.3 g) cumin

¼ teaspoon (0.3 g) dried oregano

12 ounces (340 g) frozen corn, thawed

Sauté beef, onion, green and red bell peppers, and garlic in a large skillet until beef is browned and vegetables are tender. Add rice and sauté 2 minutes longer. Stir in remaining ingredients. Bring to boil. Reduce heat, cover, and simmer for 20 minutes, or until rice is tender and liquid is absorbed.

Yield: 5 servings

Per serving: 357 calories (22% from fat, 31% from protein, 47% from carbohydrate); 22 g protein; 7 g total fat; 2 g saturated fat; 3 g monounsaturated fat; 1 g polyunsaturated fat; 33 g carbohydrate; 4 g fiber; 6 g sugar; 225 mg phosphorus; 64 mg calcium; 4 mg iron; 98 mg sodium; 653 mg potassium; 826 IU vitamin A; 0 mg ATE vitamin E; 29 mg vitamin C; 63 mg cholesterol; 404 g water

Enchilada Bake

An easy casserole dish with the taste of enchiladas.

1 pound (455 g) extra-lean ground beef (93% lean)

¼ cup (40 g) onion, chopped

1 cup (235 ml) egg substitute

8 ounces (225 g) no-salt-added tomato sauce

⅔ cup (160 ml) fat-free evaporated milk

2 tablespoons (5 g) taco seasoning

¼ cup (34 g) ripe olives, sliced

1 cup (28 g) corn chips

¾ cup (90 g) low fat cheddar cheese, shredded

Preheat oven to 350°F (180°C, or gas mark 4). In a skillet, cook beef and onion until meat is brown and onion is soft. Drain. Spread in the bottom of a 9-inch (23-cm) square baking dish that has been coated with nonstick vegetable oil spray. Beat together egg substitute, tomato sauce, milk, and taco seasoning. Pour over meat. Sprinkle with olives. Top with corn chips. Bake for 25 minutes, or until set in the center. Sprinkle cheese on top and return to oven just until cheese melts, about 3 minutes.

Yield: 6 servings

Per serving: 339 calories (38% from fat, 41% from protein, 22% from carbohydrate); 27 g protein; 11 g total fat; 3 g saturated fat; 4 g monounsaturated fat; 2 g polyunsaturated fat; 14 g carbohydrate; 1 g fiber; 6 g sugar; 322 mg phosphorus; 206 mg calcium; 3 mg iron; 455 mg sodium; 621 mg potassium; 586 IU vitamin A; 44 mg ATE vitamin E; 6 mg vitamin C; 57 mg cholesterol; 160 g water

Beef Stroganoff

Serve this creamy beef dish over noodles. Lima beans always seem to go well as an accompaniment to me.

1 pound (455 g) beef round steak

2 tablespoons (30 ml) olive oil

1½ cups (105 g) mushrooms, sliced

½ cup (120 ml) dry sherry

¼ cup (60 ml) low sodium beef broth

1 cup (230 g) fat-free sour cream

Cut beef into ¼-inch (63-mm) strips. Heat oil in skillet. Cook beef quickly, 2 to 4 minutes. Remove beef from skillet. Add mushrooms to skillet and cook for 2 to 3 minutes. Remove mushrooms. Add sherry and broth to skillet and cook until liquid is reduced to about ⅓ cup (80 ml). Stir in sour cream. Stir in beef and mushrooms. Heat through, but do not boil.

Yield: 4 servings

Per serving: 419 calories (36% from fat, 55% from protein, 9% from carbohydrate); 44 g protein; 13 g total fat; 3 g saturated fat; 7 g monounsaturated fat; 1 g polyunsaturated fat; 7 g carbohydrate; 0 g fiber; 1 g sugar; 341 mg phosphorus; 72 mg calcium; 4 mg iron; 89 mg sodium; 576 mg potassium; 225 IU vitamin A; 61 mg ATE vitamin E; 1 mg vitamin C; 126 mg cholesterol; 175 g water

Steak Cacciatore

Serve this over pasta or just stir some pre-cooked pasta in along with the zucchini.

2 pounds (905 g) beef round steak

¼ teaspoon (0.5 g) black pepper

½ cup (80 g) onion, sliced

½ cup (75 g) green bell pepper, cut in strips

1 jar (28 ounces, 795 g) low sodium spaghetti sauce

1 cup (113 g) zucchini, sliced

Cut beef into serving-sized pieces. Sprinkle with pepper. Layer beef, onion, and green pepper in slow cooker. Pour spaghetti sauce over. Cover and cook on low for 8 to 10 hours. Stir in zucchini, cover, turn heat to high and cook 15 to 20 minutes more, or until zucchini is tender.

Yield: 6 servings

Per serving: 456 calories (28% from fat, 51% from protein, 21% from carbohydrate); 58 g protein; 14 g total fat; 3 g saturated fat; 7 g monounsaturated fat; 1 g polyunsaturated fat; 24 g carbohydrate; 5 g fiber; 17 g sugar; 404 mg phosphorus; 51 mg calcium; 6 mg iron; 111 mg sodium; 1110 mg potassium; 900 IU vitamin A; 0 mg ATE vitamin E; 29 mg vitamin C; 136 mg cholesterol; 232 g water

London Broil

London broil is traditionally made with flank steak. But now you'll find top round steak labeled as London broil. That is what we'll use here. Cooking under the broiler to medium-rare and slicing thin against the grain give you a tender piece of meat from a lean cut.

¼ cup (60 ml) olive oil

1 teaspoon (5 ml) cider vinegar

¼ teaspoon (0.8 g) minced garlic

¼ teaspoon (0.5 g) freshly ground black pepper

1½ pounds (680 g) beef round steak

TIP *We often grill this recipe, rather than broiling.*

Score steak on both sides. Combine oil, vinegar, garlic and pepper in a resealable plastic bag. Add steak and marinate for several hours, turning occasionally. Preheat broiler. Remove steak from marinade and broil 3 inches (7.5 cm) from heat for 4 to 5 minutes. Turn and broil 4 to 5 minutes longer, or until medium-rare. Carve in thin slices against the grain.

Yield: 5 servings

Per serving: 367 calories (45% from fat, 55% from protein, 0% from carbohydrate); 49 g protein; 18 g total fat; 4 g saturated fat; 11 g monounsaturated fat; 1 g polyunsaturated fat; 0 g carbohydrate; 0 g fiber; 0 g sugar; 308 mg phosphorus; 6 mg calcium; 5 mg iron; 62 mg sodium; 457 mg potassium; 0 IU vitamin A; 0 mg ATE vitamin E; 0 mg vitamin C; 122 mg cholesterol; 81 g water

Oven Swiss Steak

This is an easy recipe for Swiss steak. It's good served with noodles or rice to soak up the sauce.

1½ pounds (690 g) beef round steak

¼ cup (30 g) flour

2 tablespoons (30 ml) olive oil

2 cups (360 g) canned no-salt-added tomatoes

½ cup (50 g) celery, finely chopped

½ cup (65 g) carrot, finely chopped

1 tablespoon (15 ml) Worcestershire sauce

Preheat oven to 350°F (180°C, or gas mark 4). Cut meat into serving-sized pieces. Dredge in flour. Heat oil in a heavy skillet. Brown meat on both sides in oil. Transfer meat to a glass baking dish. Blend any remaining flour into pan drippings. Stir in remaining ingredients. Cook and stir until thickened and bubbly. Pour over meat. Bake, covered, for 1½ hours, or until tender.

Yield: 6 servings

Per serving: 306 calories (31% from fat, 57% from protein, 12% from carbohydrate); 42 g protein; 10 g total fat; 3 g saturated fat; 6 g monounsaturated fat; 1 g polyunsaturated fat; 9 g carbohydrate; 1 g fiber; 3 g sugar; 286 mg phosphorus; 37 mg calcium; 5 mg iron; 100 mg sodium; 611 mg potassium; 1927 IU vitamin A; 0 mg ATE vitamin E; 13 mg vitamin C; 102 mg cholesterol; 161 g water

Italian Beef Roast

Not only does this make a great meal with spaghetti or other pasta, but when it's cold it's also easy to cut into thin slices that make wonderful sandwiches.

½ cup (120 ml) dry red wine

2 tablespoons (4.2 g) Italian seasoning

4 pounds (1.8 kg) beef round tip roast

1 cup (235 ml) low sodium spaghetti sauce

1 cup (160 g) onion, sliced

1 cup (100 g) celery, sliced

1 cup (70 g) mushrooms, sliced

½ cup (115 g) fat-free sour cream

¼ cup (60 ml) water

¼ cup (30 g) flour

Combine wine and Italian seasoning. Marinate roast in mixture overnight. In a Dutch oven, combine marinade and spaghetti sauce. Add roast. Cover and simmer for 1½ hours. Add onion, celery, and mushrooms, cover, and simmer for 1 hour, or until meat is tender. Remove roast and vegetables. Skim fat off pan juices and return 2 cups (470 ml) liquid to pan. Combine sour cream and water. Stir in flour. Stir sour cream mixture into the pan juices and simmer until thickened. Serve sauce with meat.

Yield: 10 servings

Per serving: 298 calories (25% from fat, 61% from protein, 14% from carbohydrate); 40 g protein; 7 g total fat; 2 g saturated fat; 3 g monounsaturated fat; 0 g polyunsaturated fat; 10 g carbohydrate; 2 g fiber; 4 g sugar; 409 mg phosphorus; 75 mg calcium; 4 mg iron; 128 mg sodium; 823 mg potassium; 286 IU vitamin A; 12 mg ATE vitamin E; 5 mg vitamin C; 101 mg cholesterol; 212 g water

Sauerbraten

Round roasts are not the tenderest cut of beef. But marinating followed by slow, moist cooking makes this one a treat to eat and gives it great flavor. Serve with egg noodles.

For Marinade:

2½ cups (590 ml) water

1½ cups (355 ml) red wine vinegar

1 tablespoon (13 g) sugar

¼ teaspoon (0.5 g) ground ginger

12 whole cloves

6 bay leaves

2 cups (320 g) onion, sliced

(continued on page 180)

For Meat

4 pounds (1.8 kg) beef round roast

2 tablespoons (30 ml) olive oil

½ cup (65 g) carrot, finely chopped

½ cup (50 g) celery, finely chopped

½ cup (80 g) onion, finely chopped

1 cup (100 g) gingersnaps, crushed

⅔ cup (160 ml) water

To make the marinade: In a large bowl combine the marinade ingredients. Add roast. Cover and refrigerate for 1½ to 2 days, turning occasionally. Remove meat and wipe dry. Strain and reserve marinade liquid.

To make the meat: In a Dutch oven, brown meat in oil on all sides. Add reserved marinade, carrots, celery, and chopped onion. Cover and simmer until meat is tender, 2 to 2½ hours. Remove meat to platter and slice thinly. Reserve 2 cups of cooking liquid in pot. Add gingersnaps and water. Cook and stir until thickened. Serve sauce with meat.

Yield: 10 servings

Per serving: 323 calories (30% from fat, 54% from protein, 16% from carbohydrate); 41 g protein; 10 g total fat; 3 g saturated fat; 5 g monounsaturated fat; 1 g polyunsaturated fat; 12 g carbohydrate; 1 g fiber; 5 g sugar; 419 mg phosphorus; 62 mg calcium; 4 mg iron; 183 mg sodium; 792 mg potassium; 1100 IU vitamin A; 0 mg ATE vitamin E; 4 mg vitamin C; 91 mg cholesterol; 288 g water

Beef Kabobs

The marinade helps to give these kabobs a nice flavor as well as making the leaner cut of meat more tender. You could also cook these in the oven if you don't want to grill them.

¼ cup (60 ml) olive oil

⅓ cup (80 ml) Dick's Reduced-Sodium Soy Sauce (see recipe page 30)

¼ cup (60 ml) lemon juice

2 tablespoons (30 ml) Worcestershire sauce

½ teaspoon (1.5 g) minced garlic

1 teaspoon (2 g) coarsely ground black pepper

1 pound (455 g) beef round steak, cut in 1-inch (2.5-cm) cubes

2 cups (140 g) mushrooms

Mix together all ingredients except beef and mushrooms. Add beef cubes. Cover and refrigerate overnight, turning meat occasionally. Thread meat and mushrooms on skewers. Grill over hot fire to desired doneness, turning often.

Yield: 4 servings

Per serving: 380 calories (20% from fat, 19% from protein, 61% from carbohydrate); 42 g protein; 19 g total fat; 4 g saturated fat; 12 g monounsaturated fat; 4 g polyunsaturated fat; 135 g carbohydrate; 1 g fiber; 4 g sugar; 313 mg phosphorus; 20 mg calcium; 5 mg iron; 266 mg sodium; 628 mg potassium; 21 IU vitamin A; 0 mg ATE vitamin E; 21 mg vitamin C; 102 mg cholesterol; 142 g water

Peasant Soup

A quick soup using leftover roast beef. A round roast, trimmed of fat, is a good choice. This is a warming meal on a cold evening, needing just bread to make it complete.

1 pound (455 g) leftover roast beef, chopped

2 cups (470 ml) low sodium beef broth

1 cup (180 g) canned no-salt-added tomatoes

1 pound (455 g) frozen mixed vegetables, thawed

1 cup (70 g) cabbage, shredded

½ cup (75 g) turnips, cubed

Combine all ingredients in a large Dutch oven. Simmer until vegetables are tender.

Yield: 6 servings

Per serving: 198 calories (24% from fat, 50% from protein, 26% from carbohydrate); 25 g protein; 5 g total fat; 2 g saturated fat; 2 g monounsaturated fat; 0 g polyunsaturated fat; 13 g carbohydrate; 4 g fiber; 4 g sugar; 197 mg phosphorus; 51 mg calcium; 3 mg iron; 503 mg sodium; 467 mg potassium; 3295 IU vitamin A; 0 mg ATE vitamin E; 13 mg vitamin C; 67 mg cholesterol; 254 g water

Beef and Mushroom Stew

This is a simple and hearty slow-cooker stew, but one with a lot of flavor. It goes well with just a simple multigrain bread to make a complete meal.

1½ pounds (680 g) beef round steak, cut into ½-inch (1.3-cm) cubes

1 can (14 ounces, or 395 g) low sodium beef broth

½ cup (120 ml) red wine

¼ teaspoon (0.5 g) freshly ground black pepper

5 medium potatoes, cubed

1⅓ cups (195 g) carrot, sliced

1 cup (70 g) mushrooms, sliced

1 bay leaf

¼ teaspoon (0.3 g) dried rosemary

2 cups (360 g) canned no-salt-added tomatoes

3 tablespoons (24 g) flour

¼ cup (60 ml) water

Combine first 9 ingredients (through rosemary) and place in slow cooker. Cover and cook on low for 8 to 10 hours. About 45 minutes to 1 hour before done, turn heat to high. Add tomatoes. Stir flour and water together to make a paste and stir into stew. Cook until slightly thickened.

Yield: 6 servings

Per serving: 507 calories (12% from fat, 40% from protein, 48% from carbohydrate); 50 g protein; 7 g total fat; 2 g saturated fat; 2 g monounsaturated fat; 1 g polyunsaturated fat; 59 g carbohydrate; 7 g fiber; 7 g sugar; 501 mg phosphorus; 79 mg calcium; 7 mg iron; 158 mg sodium; 2140 mg potassium; 4898 IU vitamin A; 0 mg ATE vitamin E; 36 mg vitamin C; 102 mg cholesterol; 549 g water

Fall Stew

Apple cider gives this stew its unique flavor.

3 tablespoons (24 g) flour

¼ teaspoon (0.5 g) black pepper

¼ teaspoon (0.3 g) dried thyme

2 pounds (905 g) beef round steak, cut in 1-inch (2.5-cm) cubes

3 tablespoons (45 ml) olive oil

2 cups (470 ml) apple cider

2 tablespoons (30 ml) cider vinegar

3 medium potatoes, peeled and quartered

1½ cups (195 g) carrot, sliced

1 cup (160 g) onion, quartered

½ cup (50 g) celery, sliced

Combine flour, pepper, and thyme. Dredge meat in flour mixture. Heat oil in Dutch oven. Brown half the meat at a time in the oil. Return all meat to the pan. Stir in cider and vinegar. Cook and stir until mixture boils. Reduce heat, cover and simmer 1¼ hours, or until the meat is tender. Stir in potatoes, carrot, onion, and celery. Cover and cook until vegetables are done, about 30 minutes more.

Yield: 8 servings

Per serving: 430 calories (24% from fat, 42% from protein, 34% from carbohydrate); 44 g protein; 11 g total fat; 3 g saturated fat; 6 g monounsaturated fat; 1 g polyunsaturated fat; 36 g carbohydrate; 3 g fiber; 10 g sugar; 361 mg phosphorus; 36 mg calcium; 5 mg iron; 89 mg sodium; 1193 mg potassium; 4077 IU vitamin A; 0 mg ATE vitamin E; 18 mg vitamin C; 102 mg cholesterol; 256 g water

Cabbage Beef Soup

This is one of those throw-together meals that turned out to be a keeper. It's quick and easy and has a lot of flavor.

½ pound (225 g) extra-lean ground beef (93% lean)

½ cup (80 g) onion, chopped

1 cup (70 g) cabbage, shredded

1 cup (180 g) canned no-salt-added tomatoes

2 cups (450 g) Mexican beans

1 cup (235 ml) water

TIP *For variety, replace the cabbage with packaged coleslaw or broccoli slaw mix.*

Brown beef and onion in a large saucepan. Drain. Add cabbage and continue cooking until cabbage is soft, about 5 minutes. Add tomatoes, beans, and water. Bring to a boil and simmer 10 minutes to blend the flavors.

Yield: 5 servings

Per serving: 213 calories (16% from fat, 37% from protein, 47% from carbohydrate); 16 g protein; 3 g total fat; 1 g saturated fat; 1 g monounsaturated fat; 0 g polyunsaturated fat; 20 g carbohydrate; 8 g fiber; 2 g sugar; 179 mg phosphorus; 77 mg calcium; 4 mg iron; 44 mg sodium; 570 mg potassium; 76 IU vitamin A; 0 mg ATE vitamin E; 13 mg vitamin C; 31 mg cholesterol; 199 g water

Beef and Black Bean Stew

Not quite a chili, but with a definite southwestern flavor, this one is always a big hit at our house.

2 pounds (905 g) extra-lean ground beef (93% lean)

½ teaspoon (1.5 g) minced garlic

1 cup (160 g) onion, chopped

2 cups (360 g) canned no-salt-added tomatoes

1 cup (225 g) salsa

1 teaspoon (2.5 g) ground cumin

½ teaspoon (1 g) freshly ground black pepper

1 cup (170 g) frozen corn, thawed

2 cups (450 g) black beans, drained and rinsed

1 tablespoon (4 g) chopped fresh cilantro

TIP *To make a meal, top with grated cheese, guacamole, or sour cream, and serve with tortilla chips or cornbread.*

In a large skillet, brown ground beef with garlic and onion. Drain and transfer to a slow cooker. Add tomatoes, salsa, cumin, pepper, corn, and black beans. Cook on low 6 to 8 hours or on high for 3 to 4 hours. Add cilantro during the last hour of cooking.

Yield: 8 servings

Per serving: 369 calories (28% from fat, 41% from protein, 32% from carbohydrate); 27 g protein; 8 g total fat; 3 g saturated fat; 3 g monounsaturated fat; 1 g polyunsaturated fat; 21 g carbohydrate; 6 g fiber; 4 g sugar; 268 mg phosphorus; 55 mg calcium; 4 mg iron; 282 mg sodium; 779 mg potassium; 238 IU vitamin A; 0 mg ATE vitamin E; 9 mg vitamin C; 78 mg cholesterol; 220 g water

Scottish Oxtail Soup

Oxtails may be difficult to find, although you might get some from an old-fashioned butcher or meat market. Here, in the metropolitan Washington, DC, area, I can occasionally get oxtails from the meat department at some of the big supermarkets.

1 bay leaf

2 tablespoons (4.8 g) fresh thyme

¼ cup (15 g) fresh parsley

½ cup (50 g) celery, chopped, plus one 4-inch (10-cm) piece celery stalk

2 scallions

4 cups (946 ml) low sodium beef broth

1 pound (455 g) oxtail, cut into pieces, fat removed

½ cup (80 g) onion, chopped

½ cup (65 g) carrot, chopped

4 ounces (115 g) no-salt-added tomato sauce

1 tablespoon (8 g) flour

3 tablespoons (45 ml) port wine

Make a spice bag by placing bay leaf, thyme, parsley (including stalks), one 4-inch (10-cm) piece celery stalk with leaves, and scallions in the center of a square of double thickness cheesecloth. Fold up the sides of the cheesecloth and tie off the top very tightly. Pour the beef broth into a saucepan and add the oxtail and onion, carrot, tomato sauce, and remaining celery, as well as the spice bag. Bring to a boil, and then transfer to a slow cooker and cook on high for 1½-2 hours (or longer if necessary) until the meat is tender. Strain the stock, cut all the meat from the bones and then return the stock and meat to the saucepan. Bring to a boil. Mix the flour and port together and add to the soup. Simmer for 5 minutes before serving.

Yield: 6 servings

Per serving: 148 calories (23% from fat, 56% from protein, 21% from carbohydrate); 19 g protein; 3 g total fat; 1 g saturated fat; 2 g monounsaturated fat; 0 g polyunsaturated fat; 7 g carbohydrate; 2 g fiber; 3 g sugar; 198 mg phosphorus; 63 mg calcium; 4 mg iron; 161 mg sodium; 566 mg potassium; 2187 IU vitamin A; 0 mg ATE vitamin E; 9 mg vitamin C; 29 mg cholesterol; 269 g water

9

Main Dishes:
Pork

Like beef, pork used to be a staple of our diet. Growing up in a home with German heritage, pork was on our menu often, and that carried over to my adult life. And like beef, pork can contain a lot of saturated fat if you aren't careful about the cut. However, also like beef, there is good news out there. For the past few years, I've been able to find whole pork loins at stores like BJ's or Sam's Club for around USD $2.00 a pound. These can easily be cut into great tasting, lean chops, as well as into any size roast you want. And most of your favorite pork recipes can be adapted to use a cut from the loin instead of the fattier cuts you may have been used to. In this chapter, you'll find recipes not just for chops and roasts, but for everything from soups and stir-fries to your favorite barbecue recipes.

Italian Breaded Pork Chops

You can easily vary the flavor of these chops by changing the seasonings. I was looking for an Italian flavor, but you could just as easily make them southern, Mexican or barbecue.

4 pork loin chops

½ cup (60 g) bread crumbs

1 tablespoon (0.4 g) dried parsley

1 tablespoon (2.1 g) Italian seasoning

1 teaspoon (2 g) black pepper

1 teaspoon (3 g) onion powder

Preheat oven to 350°F (180°C, or gas mark 4). Moisten chops with water. Combine bread crumbs and remaining ingredients in a plastic bag. Add chops and shake until evenly covered. Coat a baking sheet with nonstick vegetable oil spray. Place the chops on the sheet and spray the tops with more of the vegetable oil spray. Bake for 20 to 30 minutes depending on thickness of chops, or until done.

Yield: 4 servings

Per serving: 189 calories (25% from fat, 51% from protein, 24% from carbohydrate); 23 g protein; 5 g total fat; 2 g saturated fat; 2 g monounsaturated fat; 1 g polyunsaturated fat; 11 g carbohydrate; 1 g fiber; 1 g sugar; 247 mg phosphorus; 55 mg calcium; 2 mg iron; 152 mg sodium; 430 mg potassium; 139 IU vitamin A; 2 mg ATE vitamin E; 3 mg vitamin C; 64 mg cholesterol; 76 g water

Apple and Pork Chop Skillet

A newsletter subscriber originally sent in this recipe. It's just spicy enough to satisfy even those people who aren't on a diet.

1 tablespoon (15 ml) olive oil

½ cup (80 g) onion, chopped

3 pork loin chops

2 tablespoons (13 g) fresh ginger, peeled and thinly sliced

1 apple, peeled and thinly sliced

½ cup (120 ml) water

Heat oil in a nonstick skillet over medium heat. Sauté the chopped onion for 2 to 4 minutes, or until lightly browned. Push the onion pieces to one side of the skillet and place the chops in the center of the skillet. Brown the chops on each side. Spoon the onion pieces on top of each chop, dividing evenly. Layer each chop with sliced ginger and apple. Add the water to the skillet and cover tightly. Cook over low heat for 30 to 40 minutes depending on the thickness of the pork chops.

Yield: 3 servings

Per serving: 213 calories (39% from fat, 42% from protein, 20% from carbohydrate); 22 g protein; 9 g total fat; 2 g saturated fat; 5 g monounsaturated fat; 1 g polyunsaturated fat; 10 g carbohydrate; 1 g fiber; 6 g sugar; 238 mg phosphorus; 27 mg calcium; 1 mg iron; 55 mg sodium; 500 mg potassium; 29 IU vitamin A; 2 mg ATE vitamin E; 5 mg vitamin C; 64 mg cholesterol; 175 g water

Asian Pork Chops

These are good either as an Asian-style meal with stir-fried vegetables and rice or in a more American setting with pasta or potatoes.

1 tablespoon (15 ml) vegetable oil

4 pork loin chops

¼ teaspoon (0.5 g) black pepper

1 teaspoon (1.8 g) ground ginger

¼ cup (60 ml) orange juice

Heat oil in a large skillet over medium heat. Brown chops on both sides. Sprinkle with pepper and ginger and pour orange juice over. Cover and cook for 10 to 15 minutes, or until done.

Yield: 4 servings

Per serving: 168 calories (43% from fat, 53% from protein, 5% from carbohydrate); 21 g protein; 8 g total fat; 2 g saturated fat; 3 g monounsaturated fat; 2 g polyunsaturated fat; 2 g carbohydrate; 0 g fiber; 0 g sugar; 223 mg phosphorus; 16 mg calcium; 1 mg iron; 52 mg sodium; 411 mg potassium; 20 IU vitamin A; 2 mg ATE vitamin E; 6 mg vitamin C; 64 mg cholesterol; 88 g water

Grilled Pork Chops

A quick and easy grill recipe for a summer evening. You could make a little extra of the marinade and put it on zucchini slices to grill as a side dish.

2 tablespoons (30 ml) honey

¼ cup (60 ml) Worcestershire sauce

¼ teaspoon (0.5 g) black pepper

¼ teaspoon (0.8 g) garlic powder

4 boneless pork loin chops

In a shallow glass dish or bowl, mix together honey, Worcestershire sauce, pepper, and garlic powder. Add pork chops and toss to coat. Cover and refrigerate for no more than 4 hours. Lightly oil grill and preheat to medium. Remove pork chops from marinade. Grill 20 to 30 minutes, or until cooked through, turning often.

Yield: 4 servings

Per serving: 174 calories (22% from fat, 50% from protein, 27% from carbohydrate); 22 g protein; 4 g total fat; 1 g saturated fat; 2 g monounsaturated fat; 0 g polyunsaturated fat; 12 g carbohydrate; 0 g fiber; 9 g sugar; 238 mg phosphorus; 14 mg calcium; 2 mg iron; 199 mg sodium; 503 mg potassium; 24 IU vitamin A; 2 mg ATE vitamin E; 28 mg vitamin C; 64 mg cholesterol; 80 g water

Stuffed Pork Chops

These make an elegant meal. If possible, get the meat cutter at the store to cut the slit in the chops. The idea is to open it up inside, but not cut the whole way around the chop, so it's easier to close back up.

6 pork loin chops, cut 1½ inches (3.8 cm) thick

1 tablespoon (15 ml) olive oil

¼ cup (37 g) green bell peppers, chopped

¼ cup (40 g) onion, chopped

TIP *If you have some stale raisin bread on hand, this recipe is a great way to use it.*

¼ cup (60 ml) egg substitute

1½ cups (120 g) bread cubes

¼ teaspoon (0.6 g) cumin

Make a slit in each chop to allow for stuffing. Heat oil in a small skillet over medium heat. Cook green bell pepper and onion until soft. Combine egg substitute, bread, and cumin in a bowl. Pour pepper and onion mixture over bread mixture and toss to combine. Spoon an equal amount of the stuffing into the pocket of each chop. Secure with a wooden toothpick or skewer. Grill over medium heat about 20 minutes. Turn and grill 15 minutes more, or until done.

Yield: 6 servings

Per serving: 193 calories (36% from fat, 50% from protein, 14% from carbohydrate); 24 g protein; 7 g total fat; 2 g saturated fat; 4 g monounsaturated fat; 1 g polyunsaturated fat; 7 g carbohydrate; 1 g fiber; 1 g sugar; 245 mg phosphorus; 27 mg calcium; 2 mg iron; 123 mg sodium; 440 mg potassium; 69 IU vitamin A; 2 mg ATE vitamin E; 6 mg vitamin C; 64 mg cholesterol; 95 g water

Pineapple-Stuffed Pork Chops

Feel like you need a trip to the islands? Let these pineapple-stuffed chops ferry you away.

4 pork loin chops, 1 inch (2.5-cm) thick

8 ounces (225 g) pineapple slices canned in juice, undrained

¼ cup (60 g) low sodium ketchup

1 tablespoon (6 g) scallions, chopped

½ teaspoon (1.5 g) dry mustard

Cut a pocket in each chop to make room for pineapple. Drain pineapple, reserving liquid. Cut two pineapple slices in half; cut up remaining pineapple and set aside. Place a half pineapple slice in the pocket of each chop. Heat grill to medium and grill about 20 minutes, turning once. Meanwhile, in a small saucepan combine ketchup, scallions, mustard and the reserved pineapple juice and pieces. Heat to boiling, reduce heat and simmer 10 minutes. Grill chops 5 minutes more, brushing with sauce and turning several times.

Yield: 4 servings

(continued on page 192)

Per serving: 189 calories (21% from fat, 46% from protein, 33% from carbohydrate); 22 g protein; 4 g total fat; 1 g saturated fat; 2 g monounsaturated fat; 0 g polyunsaturated fat; 15 g carbohydrate; 1 g fiber; 13 g sugar; 230 mg phosphorus; 25 mg calcium; 1 mg iron; 55 mg sodium; 495 mg potassium; 171 IU vitamin A; 2 mg ATE vitamin E; 8 mg vitamin C; 64 mg cholesterol; 131 g water

Skillet Pork Chops

This is a great skillet meal. Not exactly typical Hamburger Helper fare, but the kind of thing that you would want to serve on the patio after a summer day of working in the yard.

6 pork loin chops

1 tablespoon (15 ml) olive oil

1 cup (160 g) onion, chopped

½ teaspoon (1.5 g) minced garlic

½ cup (120 ml) low sodium chicken broth

½ cup (120 ml) barbecue sauce

4 cups (900 g) no-salt-added canned pinto beans, drained

2 jalapeño peppers, chopped

In a large skillet, sear pork chops in oil for 5 minutes, or until brown. Remove pork chops and place on a plate. Add onion and garlic to skillet; cook 10 minutes. Stir in broth, barbecue sauce, beans, and jalapeños. Heat mixture to a boil. Return pork to skillet. Reduce heat; cover and simmer 50 to 60 minutes, stirring sauce and turning chops occasionally until meat is fork-tender.

Yield: 6 servings

Per serving: 370 calories (18% from fat, 35% from protein, 47% from carbohydrate); 33 g protein; 7 g total fat; 2 g saturated fat; 4 g monounsaturated fat; 1 g polyunsaturated fat; 43 g carbohydrate; 11 g fiber; 9 g sugar; 403 mg phosphorus; 73 mg calcium; 3 mg iron; 261 mg sodium; 938 mg potassium; 45 IU vitamin A; 2 mg ATE vitamin E; 6 mg vitamin C; 64 mg cholesterol; 206 g water

Barbecue Pork Chops

A nice sweet-and-sour sort of barbecue sauce gives these chops great flavor.

4 pork loin chops, 1 inch (2.5 cm) thick

1 cup (160 g) onion, finely chopped

2 tablespoons (30 ml) vinegar

1 tablespoon (15 ml) canola oil

½ teaspoon (1.5 g) dry mustard

1 tablespoon (15 ml) Worcestershire sauce

1 teaspoon (2 g) black pepper

1 tablespoon (13 g) sugar

½ teaspoon (1.3 g) paprika

Score the edges of the chops to prevent curling. Place into a large baking pan; set aside. Combine remaining ingredients and mix well. Pour over the chops to coat well. Cover and chill for 2 to 4 hours. Grill chops to desired doneness, basting often.

Yield: 4 servings

Per serving: 196 calories (37% from fat, 46% from protein, 17% from carbohydrate); 22 g protein; 8 g total fat; 2 g saturated fat; 4 g monounsaturated fat; 2 g polyunsaturated fat; 8 g carbohydrate; 1 g fiber; 5 g sugar; 238 mg phosphorus; 26 mg calcium; 1 mg iron; 91 mg sodium; 482 mg potassium; 166 IU vitamin A; 2 mg ATE vitamin E; 11 mg vitamin C; 64 mg cholesterol; 118 g water

Southern Pork Chops

Slow-cooked stuffed pork chops. Great with greens and cornbread.

4 pork loin chops, 1 inch (2.5 cm) thick

2 cups (215 g) cornbread stuffing mix

2 tablespoons (30 ml) low sodium chicken broth

⅓ cup (80 ml) orange juice

(continued on page 194)

1 tablespoon (8 g) pecans, finely chopped

¼ cup (60 ml) light corn syrup

½ teaspoon (0.9 g) grated orange peel

With a sharp knife, cut a horizontal slit in side of each chop forming a pocket for stuffing. Combine stuffing with remaining ingredients. Fill pockets with stuffing mixture. Place chops on a metal rack in a slow cooker. Cover and cook on low for 6 to 8 hours. Uncover; turn to high and brush with sauce. Cook on high for 15 to 20 minutes.

Yield: 4 servings

Per serving: 322 calories (19% from fat, 31% from protein, 50% from carbohydrate); 25 g protein; 7 g total fat; 2 g saturated fat; 3 g monounsaturated fat; 1 g polyunsaturated fat; 41 g carbohydrate; 4 g fiber; 7 g sugar; 262 mg phosphorus; 42 mg calcium; 2 mg iron; 431 mg sodium; 485 mg potassium; 70 IU vitamin A; 2 mg ATE vitamin E; 9 mg vitamin C; 64 mg cholesterol; 106 g water

Oriental Grilled Pork Chops

Using loin chops reduces the amount of fat in this Asian-flavored dish. Good with steamed mixed vegetables and rice.

¼ cup (60 ml) sweet and sour sauce

2 tablespoons (30 ml) Dick's Reduced-Sodium Soy Sauce (see recipe page 30)

4 pork loin chops

Combine sauces and brush on chops. Grill over medium heat for 15 minutes, or until done, turning once.

Yield: 4 servings

Per serving: 170 calories (11% from fat, 24% from protein, 64% from carbohydrate); 21 g protein; 4 g total fat; 2 g saturated fat; 2 g monounsaturated fat; 2 g polyunsaturated fat; 57 g carbohydrate; 0 g fiber; 1 g sugar; 230 mg phosphorus; 19 mg calcium; 1 mg iron; 206 mg sodium; 442 mg potassium; 18 IU vitamin A; 2 mg ATE vitamin E; 1 mg vitamin C; 64 mg cholesterol; 95 g water

Italian Pork Skillet

There's plenty enough sauce here to serve over rice or pasta to make a complete meal.

2 tablespoons (30 ml) olive oil

4 pork loin chops

1 cup (160 g) onion, chopped

½ cup (75 g) green bell pepper, chopped

½ teaspoon (1.5 g) minced garlic

2 cups (360 g) canned no-salt-added tomatoes

1 teaspoon (0.7 g) Italian seasoning

¼ teaspoon (0.5 g) black pepper

In a large skillet, heat the oil and brown the pork chops for 2 to 3 minutes per side. Remove the chops from the skillet and cover to keep warm. Add the onion, green bell pepper, and garlic to the skillet and sauté for 3 to 5 minutes, until tender and lightly browned. Stir in the tomatoes, Italian seasoning, and black pepper. Return the pork chops to the skillet; reduce the heat to low, cover, and simmer for 30 minutes, or until the chops are cooked through.

Yield: 4 servings

Per serving: 227 calories (44% from fat, 40% from protein, 16% from carbohydrate); 23 g protein; 11 g total fat; 2 g saturated fat; 7 g monounsaturated fat; 1 g polyunsaturated fat; 9 g carbohydrate; 2 g fiber; 5 g sugar; 256 mg phosphorus; 65 mg calcium; 2 mg iron; 69 mg sodium; 665 mg potassium; 166 IU vitamin A; 2 mg ATE vitamin E; 15 mg vitamin C; 64 mg cholesterol; 223 g water

Hawaiian Kabobs

Serve these with rice for an island treat.

½ cup (120 ml) Dick's Reduced-Sodium Soy Sauce (see recipe page 30)

2 tablespoons (30 ml) olive oil

1 tablespoon (15 g) brown sugar

½ teaspoon (1.5 g) minced garlic

1 teaspoon (3 g) dry mustard

1 teaspoon (1.8 g) ground ginger

2 pounds (905 g) pork tenderloin, cut in 1-inch (2.5-cm) cubes

2 cups (300 g) green bell peppers, cut in 1-inch (2.5-cm) pieces

20 cherry tomatoes

6 ounces (170 g) pineapple chunks

In a large bowl combine soy sauce, oil, brown sugar, garlic, mustard, and ginger. Add pork cubes; cover and refrigerate overnight. Drain meat, reserving marinade. Thread meat, green bell pepper, tomatoes, and pineapple on skewers. Grill over medium-hot fire for 15 minutes, or until pork is done. Baste with marinade with cooking.

Yield: 6 servings

Per serving: 279 calories (11% from fat, 17% from protein, 72% from carbohydrate); 33 g protein; 10 g total fat; 2 g saturated fat; 6 g monounsaturated fat; 4 g polyunsaturated fat; 140 g carbohydrate; 2 g fiber; 8 g sugar; 370 mg phosphorus; 34 mg calcium; 2 mg iron; 217 mg sodium; 867 mg potassium; 566 IU vitamin A; 3 mg ATE vitamin E; 54 mg vitamin C; 98 mg cholesterol; 213 g water

Stir-Fried Pork and Cabbage

Not a traditional Asian stir-fry, but it still as an interesting flavor combination and is good served over rice.

1 pound (455 g) pork loin chops, sliced thinly

1 tablespoon (15 ml) olive oil

1 cup (150 g) apple, sliced thinly

3 tablespoons (45 ml) honey

4 cups (280 g) cabbage, shredded

Slice pork. Heat oil in wok or skillet, add pork and stir-fry until no longer pink, about 5 minutes. Add apples and honey, stir-fry 1 minute. Add cabbage and stir-fry for 30 to 45 seconds, or until heated through, but still crispy.

Yield: 4 servings

Per serving: 259 calories (28% from fat, 38% from protein, 33% from carbohydrate); 25 g protein; 8 g total fat; 2 g saturated fat; 5 g monounsaturated fat; 1 g polyunsaturated fat; 22 g carbohydrate; 3 g fiber; 19 g sugar; 274 mg phosphorus; 53 mg calcium; 2 mg iron; 75 mg sodium; 604 mg potassium; 106 IU vitamin A; 2 mg ATE vitamin E; 35 mg vitamin C; 71 mg cholesterol; 192 g water

Apple Cranberry Stuffed Pork Roast

When I said I was going to make this, my wife wondered about going to the trouble of butterflying the roast, but the results were worth what turned out to be not a lot of effort. This is the kind of meal you could serve to anyone without worrying that it seems like a special "diet" food.

2/3 cup (160 ml) apple cider

1/4 cup (60 ml) cider vinegar

1/2 cup (115 g) light brown sugar, packed

1 tablespoon (0.9 g) dried shallots

(continued on page 198)

1 cup (86 g) dried apples

½ cup (75 g) dried cranberries

1 teaspoon (1.8 g) ground ginger

½ teaspoon (1.9 g) mustard seed

½ teaspoon (0.8 g) ground allspice

⅛ teaspoon (0.3 g) cayenne pepper

2 pounds (905 g) boneless pork loin roast

Combine all ingredients except pork in medium saucepan and bring to a simmer over medium-high heat. Cover; reduce heat to low, and cook until apples are very soft, about 20 minutes. Strain through a fine-mesh sieve, using a rubber spatula to press against the apple mixture in the sieve to extract as much liquid as possible; reserve the liquid. Return liquid to saucepan and simmer over medium-high heat until reduced to ½ cup (120 ml), about 5 minutes. Remove from heat, set aside, and reserve for use as a glaze.

Preheat oven to 350°F (180°C, or gas mark 4) or prepare your grill for indirect heat. Lay the roast down, fat side up. Insert a knife into the roast ½ inch (1.3 cm) horizontally from the bottom of the roast, along the long side of the roast. Make a long cut along the bottom of the roast, stopping ½ inch (1.3 cm) before the edge of the roast. You might find it easier to handle by starting at a corner of the roast. Open up the roast and continue to cut through the thicker half of the roast, again keeping ½ inch (1.3 cm) from the bottom. Repeat until the roast is an even ½-inch (1.3-cm) thickness all over when laid out. Spread out the filling on the roast, leaving a ½-inch (1.3-cm) border from the edges. Starting with the short side of the roast, roll it up very tightly. Secure with kitchen twine at 1-inch (2.5-cm) intervals. If baking, place the roast on a rack in a roasting pan and cook on the middle rack of the oven. If you are grilling using indirect heat, preheat the grill and wipe the grates with olive oil. Place roast, fat side up, on the side of the grill that has no coals underneath. Cover the grill with the lid. Cook for 45 to 60 minutes (if you are grilling, turn roast halfway through the cooking). Brush the roast with half of the glaze and cook for 5 minutes longer. Remove the roast from the oven or grill. Place it on a cutting board. Cover with foil to rest and keep warm for 15 minutes before slicing. Slice into ½-inch (1.3-cm) pieces, removing the cooking twine as you cut the roast. Serve with remaining glaze.

Yield: 8 servings

Per serving: 269 calories (26% from fat, 38% from protein, 37% from carbohydrate); 25 g protein; 8 g total fat; 3 g saturated fat; 3 g monounsaturated fat; 1 g polyunsaturated fat; 24 g carbohydrate; 1 g fiber; 22 g sugar; 245 mg phosphorus; 24 mg calcium; 1 mg iron; 58 mg sodium; 581 mg potassium; 41 IU vitamin A; 2 mg ATE vitamin E; 1 mg vitamin C; 62 mg cholesterol; 121 g water

Glazed Pork Roast

You can also grill this using indirect heat. Place a pan of water under the roast and mound the charcoal around it. Close the grill. This makes excellent sandwiches, too.

¼ cup (60 ml) honey

1 tablespoon (9 g) dry mustard

¼ cup (60 ml) white wine vinegar

1 teaspoon (2.6 g) chili powder

2 pounds (905 g) pork tenderloin

Preheat oven to 350°F (180°C, or gas mark 4). Mix together the first 4 ingredients. Trim excess fat from pork roast. Brush with honey glaze. Roast for 1 to 1½ hours, or until done, brushing with additional glaze occasionally.

Yield: 8 servings

Per serving: 173 calories (22% from fat, 57% from protein, 21% from carbohydrate); 24 g protein; 4 g total fat; 1 g saturated fat; 2 g monounsaturated fat; 0 g polyunsaturated fat; 9 g carbohydrate; 0 g fiber; 9 g sugar; 258 mg phosphorus; 9 mg calcium; 2 mg iron; 61 mg sodium; 436 mg potassium; 101 IU vitamin A; 2 mg ATE vitamin E; 1 mg vitamin C; 74 mg cholesterol; 94 g water

Stuffed Pork Roast

This pork loin is filled with a traditional cornbread stuffing. If you put a drip pan under the roast during the indirect cooking phase and add some water to it, you will end up with the makings of a delicious gravy. Remember not to let the drip pan dry out.

2 tablespoons (30 ml) olive oil

½ cup (160 g) onion, chopped

1 teaspoon (3 g) minced garlic

1 tablespoon (2 g) dried sage, chopped

4 cups (600 g) Lower-Fat Cornbread, cubed (see recipe page 439)

(continued on page 200)

¼ cup (60 ml) egg substitute

1 cup (235 ml) low sodium chicken broth

2 pounds (905 g) pork loin roast

In a skillet, heat oil over medium-high heat. Add onions and garlic and cook until tender. Add sage and cook for about 30 seconds. Remove from heat and add cornbread, onion mixture, and egg substitute. Stir, adding the chicken broth slowly until it becomes spreadable (it should look like stuffing). Butterfly the pork loin. Spread stuffing over the pork loin and roll up. Secure with kitchen twine at 1-inch (2.5-cm) intervals. Preheat grill and prepare for indirect grilling. Place pork loin on grill over direct heat. Turn every two minutes until the surface of the pork loin is seared. Move to indirect portion of grill and continue cooking for about 30 minutes or until the meat reaches an internal temperature of 155°F (68°C). Remove from grill and let rest for 5 minutes. Slice and serve.

Yield: 8 servings

Per serving: 371 calories (31% from fat, 38% from protein, 31% from carbohydrate); 28 g protein; 10 g total fat; 3 g saturated fat; 6 g monounsaturated fat; 2 g polyunsaturated fat; 24 g carbohydrate; 3 g fiber; 4 g sugar; 303 mg phosphorus; 53 mg calcium; 2 mg iron; 222 mg sodium; 552 mg potassium; 391 IU vitamin A; 75 mg ATE vitamin E; 3 mg vitamin C; 72 mg cholesterol; 193 g water

Pork Loin Roast

This pork roast has a Latin flavor. The sauce is good over rice or noodles.

3 pounds (1.4 kg) pork loin roast

1 tablespoon (7.5 g) chili powder

½ cup (120 ml) lime juice

1 teaspoon (2.5 g) cumin

1 teaspoon (1 g) dried oregano

½ teaspoon (1 g) black pepper

½ teaspoon (1.5 g) minced garlic

6 ounces (170 g) orange juice concentrate, thawed, divided

¼ cup (60 ml) dry white wine

½ cup (115 g) fat-free sour cream

Place pork roast in a shallow glass dish. Mix chili powder, lime juice, cumin, oregano, pepper, garlic, and ¼ cup (60 ml) of orange juice concentrate and brush mixture onto the pork roast. Cover and refrigerate at least 8 hours. Preheat oven to 325°F (170°C, or gas mark 3). Place pork on a rack in a shallow roasting pan. Roast uncovered for 1½ to 2 hours, or until thermometer registers 170°F (77°C). Remove pork and rack from the pan. Strain the drippings from the pan and set aside. Add enough water to remaining orange juice concentrate to measure ¾ cup (180 ml); stir juice and wine into the drippings, then stir in the sour cream. Serve with the pork roast.

Yield: 9 servings

Per serving: 255 calories (26% from fat, 57% from protein, 17% from carbohydrate); 33 g protein; 7 g total fat; 2 g saturated fat; 3 g monounsaturated fat; 1 g polyunsaturated fat; 10 g carbohydrate; 1 g fiber; 7 g sugar; 361 mg phosphorus; 49 mg calcium; 2 mg iron; 93 mg sodium; 748 mg potassium; 397 IU vitamin A; 16 mg ATE vitamin E; 32 mg vitamin C; 100 mg cholesterol; 151 g water

Pork Loin Roast with Asian Vegetables

Serve this Asian-style pork roast with rice for a complete meal.

1 teaspoon (1.8 g) ground ginger

2 tablespoons (30 ml) olive oil

2 pounds (905 g) pork loin roast

1¼ cups (295 ml) water, divided

1 cup (160 g) onion, coarsely chopped

¼ cup (60 ml) Dick's Reduced-Sodium Soy Sauce (see recipe page 30)

¼ cup (60 ml) red wine vinegar

2 tablespoons (30 g) brown sugar

½ teaspoon (1.5 g) garlic powder

¼ teaspoon (0.5 g) black pepper

4 cups (250 g) snow pea pods

(continued on page 202)

2 cups (360 g) canned no-salt-added tomatoes, undrained

8 ounces (225 g) water chestnuts

1 cup mushrooms (70 g), sliced

2 tablespoons (16 g) cornstarch

In a large Dutch oven, sauté ginger in oil for 30 seconds. Add pork roast and brown meat on all sides. Add 1 cup (235 ml) water, onion, soy sauce, vinegar, brown sugar, garlic powder, and pepper. Cover and simmer for 1½ hours, or until tender. Add pea pods, tomatoes and liquid, water chestnuts, and mushrooms. Cover and simmer for 3 to 5 minutes, or until crisp-tender. Remove vegetables and meat. Skim any fat from pan juices. Blend the remaining ¼ cup (60 ml) water with the cornstarch and stir into the pot. Cook and stir until bubbly. Serve sauce with vegetables and meat.

Yield: 8 servings

Per serving: 273 calories (16% from fat, 23% from protein, 60% from carbohydrate); 27 g protein; 8 g total fat; 2 g saturated fat; 5 g monounsaturated fat; 2 g polyunsaturated fat; 70 g carbohydrate; 3 g fiber; 10 g sugar; 325 mg phosphorus; 72 mg calcium; 3 mg iron; 128 mg sodium; 893 mg potassium; 615 IU vitamin A; 2 mg ATE vitamin E; 39 mg vitamin C; 71 mg cholesterol; 285 g water

Italian Pork Roast

This can be part of a great Italian meal, but it also makes the best Italian pork sub sandwiches that you will ever have.

½ teaspoon (1 g) ground allspice

1 teaspoon (2 g) fennel seed, crushed

1 teaspoon (1.2 g) dried rosemary

1 teaspoon (2 g) black pepper

2½ pound (1.1 kg) pork loin roast

Preheat oven to 325°F (170°C, or gas mark 3). Combine allspice, fennel, rosemary, and pepper and mix well. Rub this mixture thoroughly into all sides of the roast. Marinate in the refrigerator overnight. Bake for 30 to 40 minutes per pound, until internal temperature is 170°F (77°C).

Yield: 8 servings

Per serving: 42 calories (31% from fat, 66% from protein, 4% from carbohydrate); 7 g protein; 1 g total fat; 0 g saturated fat; 1 g monounsaturated fat; 0 g polyunsaturated fat; 0 g carbohydrate; 0 g fiber; 0 g sugar; 71 mg phosphorus; 9 mg calcium; 0 mg iron; 17 mg sodium; 126 mg potassium; 6 IU vitamin A; 1 mg ATE vitamin E; 0 mg vitamin C; 20 mg cholesterol; 23 g water

Winter Pork Stew

One of those meals that just takes too long to fix when you get home from work, transformed into an easy slow-cooker creation.

4 sweet potatoes, peeled and sliced

2 pounds (905 g) pork loin roast

½ cup (115 g) brown sugar

¼ teaspoon (0.5 g) cayenne pepper

¼ teaspoon (0.5 g) black pepper

¼ teaspoon (0.8 g) garlic powder

½ teaspoon (1.5 g) onion powder

Place sweet potatoes in the bottom of a slow cooker. Place pork on top. Combine remaining ingredients and sprinkle over pork and potatoes. Cover and cook on low 8 to 10 hours. Remove pork and slice. Serve juices over pork and potatoes.

Yield: 8 servings

Per serving: 256 calories (18% from fat, 40% from protein, 43% from carbohydrate); 25 g protein; 5 g total fat; 2 g saturated fat; 2 g monounsaturated fat; 1 g polyunsaturated fat; 27 g carbohydrate; 2 g fiber; 18 g sugar; 276 mg phosphorus; 48 mg calcium; 2 mg iron; 84 mg sodium; 645 mg potassium; 11915 IU vitamin A; 2 mg ATE vitamin E; 11 mg vitamin C; 71 mg cholesterol; 144 g water

Pork Chops with Red Cabbage

Make your own sweet-and-sour red cabbage while cooking flavorful pork chops.

4 cups (280 g) red cabbage, shredded

½ cup (80 g) onion, chopped

1 apple, peeled and chopped

½ cup (115 g) brown sugar

½ cup (120 ml) cider vinegar

4 pork loin chops

Place cabbage, onion, and apple in a slow cooker. Combine sugar and vinegar, pour over vegetables and stir to mix. Place pork chops on top of mixture. Cook on low for 7 to 8 hours.

Yield: 4 servings

Per serving: 290 calories (14% from fat, 32% from protein, 55% from carbohydrate); 23 g protein; 4 g total fat; 2 g saturated fat; 2 g monounsaturated fat; 1 g polyunsaturated fat; 40 g carbohydrate; 3 g fiber; 34 g sugar; 265 mg phosphorus; 85 mg calcium; 2 mg iron; 89 mg sodium; 765 mg potassium; 1013 IU vitamin A; 2 mg ATE vitamin E; 54 mg vitamin C; 64 mg cholesterol; 229 g water

Barbecued Pork

This recipe for pulled pork is made in the oven, but it could also be cooked in a smoker or using indirect heat on a grill.

3 pounds (1.4 kg) pork loin roast

1 teaspoon (1.2 g) red pepper flakes

1 teaspoon (2 g) black pepper

1 cup (235 ml) apple cider

1 cup (235 ml) apple cider vinegar

1 cup (160 g) onion, sliced

½ teaspoon (1.5 g) minced garlic

Preheat oven to 300°F (160°C, or gas mark 2). Coat a large baking pan with nonstick vegetable oil spray. Rub the pork with the red pepper flakes and pepper and place in the prepared baking pan. Pour the cider and vinegar over and around the pork. Scatter the onions and garlic over and around the pork. Cover with aluminum foil. Roast for 3 hours. Uncover and continue to roast for 1 hour, or until an instant-read thermometer inserted into the thickest part of the pork registers 180°F (82°C). Remove the pork from the oven and transfer to a plate. Let stand for 1 hour. Using two forks, shred the pork by steadying the meat with one fork and pulling it away with the other, discarding any fat.

Yield: 12 servings

Per serving: 165 calories (28% from fat, 62% from protein, 10% from carbohydrate); 24 g protein; 5 g total fat; 2 g saturated fat; 2 g monounsaturated fat; 1 g polyunsaturated fat; 4 g carbohydrate; 0 g fiber; 3 g sugar; 255 mg phosphorus; 22 mg calcium; 1 mg iron; 60 mg sodium; 484 mg potassium; 70 IU vitamin A; 2 mg ATE vitamin E; 2 mg vitamin C; 71 mg cholesterol; 132 g water

Pork Chops with Scalloped Potatoes

Real comfort food—pork chops and potatoes baked together in a flavorful sauce.

3 tablespoons (45 ml) canola oil, divided

3 tablespoons (24 g) flour

¼ teaspoon (0.5 g) black pepper

2 cups (470 ml) low sodium chicken broth

6 pork loin chops, ¾-inch (1.9-cm) thick

6 medium potatoes, thinly sliced

1 cup (160 g) onion, sliced

Preheat oven to 350°F (180°C, or gas mark 4). In a saucepan, heat 2 tablespoons (30 ml) oil, stir in flour and pepper. Add chicken broth; cook and stir constantly until mixture boils. Cook for 1 minute; remove from heat and set aside. In a skillet, brown pork chops in remaining 1 tablespoon (15 ml) oil. In a greased 9 x 13-inch (23 x 33-cm) baking dish, layer potatoes and onion. Pour the broth mixture over. Place pork chops on top. Cover and bake for 1 hour; uncover and bake 30 minutes longer, or until potatoes are tender.

Yield: 6 servings

(continued on page 206)

Per serving: 624 calories (24% from fat, 34% from protein, 42% from carbohydrate); 52 g protein; 17 g total fat; 4 g saturated fat; 8 g monounsaturated fat; 3 g polyunsaturated fat; 65 g carbohydrate; 6 g fiber; 6 g sugar; 692 mg phosphorus; 63 mg calcium; 4 mg iron; 164 mg sodium; 2489 mg potassium; 49 IU vitamin A; 4 mg ATE vitamin E; 42 mg vitamin C; 127 mg cholesterol; 479 g water

Pork and Apple Curry

Curry flavor creates a new kind of pork dish.

2 tablespoons (30 ml) olive oil

4 pork loin chops

½ cup (80 g) onion, thinly sliced

¼ teaspoon (0.8 g) minced garlic

1 apple, peeled and sliced

½ cup (75 g) red bell pepper, cut in strips

½ cup (120 ml) low sodium chicken broth

1 teaspoon (2 g) cornstarch

1 teaspoon (2 g) curry powder

½ teaspoon (1.3 g) ground cumin

½ teaspoon (1.2 g) cinnamon

¼ teaspoon (0.5 g) freshly ground black pepper

TIP *Serve with quick-cooking couscous flavored with chopped scallions and raisins.*

In a heavy frying pan, heat oil over medium-high heat. Cook pork chops until browned on both sides and almost cooked through; remove from pan and set aside. Over medium heat, cook the onion, garlic, apple, and red bell pepper strips for 2 minutes or until softened. Blend chicken broth with cornstarch; add to pan along with curry powder, cumin, and cinnamon; cook for 1 or 2 minutes, or until slightly reduced and thickened. Return pork chops to frying pan. Cook for 1 or 2 minutes or until heated through. Serve pork chops with sauce and sprinkle with pepper.

Yield: 4 servings

Per serving: 228 calories (45% from fat, 39% from protein, 15% from carbohydrate); 23 g protein; 11 g total fat; 3 g saturated fat; 7 g monounsaturated fat; 1 g polyunsaturated fat; 9 g carbohydrate; 2 g fiber; 5 g sugar; 247 mg phosphorus; 31 mg calcium; 2 mg iron; 63 mg sodium; 513 mg potassium; 612 IU vitamin A; 2 mg ATE vitamin E; 28 mg vitamin C; 64 mg cholesterol; 166 g water

Caribbean Grilled Pork

Grilled pork, seasoned with a spicy sauce. The pork tenderloin is low in fat, but still very tender. Be careful not to overcook.

2 pounds (905 g) pork tenderloin
½ cup (120 ml) bottled jerk sauce

Make shallow cuts in the roast and rub in the sauce. Marinate overnight. Grill at lowest possible setting for 15 to 20 minutes, or until done. Adding apple or other aromatic wood to the fire will add to the flavor.

Yield: 4 servings

Per serving: 307 calories (24% from fat, 65% from protein, 11% from carbohydrate); 48 g protein; 8 g total fat; 3 g saturated fat; 4 g monounsaturated fat; 1 g polyunsaturated fat; 8 g carbohydrate; 0 g fiber; 6 g sugar; 516 mg phosphorus; 14 mg calcium; 3 mg iron; 144 mg sodium; 878 mg potassium; 68 IU vitamin A; 5 mg ATE vitamin E; 2 mg vitamin C; 147 mg cholesterol; 184 g water

10

Soups, Stews, and Chilis

I love soups and stews, especially during cooler weather. And the moist, slow cooking in a Dutch oven or slow cooker can turn even the leanest cuts of meat into tender morsels. They tend to make very healthy meals, low in fat, full of other good nutrition, and often needing only a slice of bread to make a complete meal. In this chapter, you'll find all the traditional favorite soups, as well as a selection of recipes with flavors from around the globe and a few that probably have never been seen anywhere else.

Amish Chicken Soup

When I was growing up along the Maryland/Pennsylvania border, Amish chicken corn soup was always one of the highlights at volunteer fire company carnivals and suppers. This soup has a similar flavor.

4 cups (946 ml) low sodium chicken broth

2 cups (220 g) chicken, cooked and chopped

½ cup (50 g) celery, chopped

½ cup (65 g) carrot, sliced

½ cup (80 g) onion, chopped

1 tablespoon (0.4 g) dried parsley

¼ teaspoon (0.8 g) garlic powder

2 cups (470 ml) water

12 ounces (340 g) egg noodles

Place all ingredients in a large kettle and simmer until noodles are tender (see package directions for approximate time).

Yield: 8 servings

Per serving: 148 calories (22% from fat, 37% from protein, 41% from carbohydrate); 14 g protein; 4 g total fat; 1 g saturated fat; 1 g monounsaturated fat; 1 g polyunsaturated fat; 15 g carbohydrate; 3 g fiber; 1 g sugar; 144 mg phosphorus; 20 mg calcium; 1 mg iron; 49 mg sodium; 262 mg potassium; 1456 IU vitamin A; 6 mg ATE vitamin E; 2 mg vitamin C; 31 mg cholesterol; 248 g water

Ham and Bean Soup

Bean soup is one of those classic comfort foods. Add a big slice of dark bread and everything is right with your world.

1 pound (455 g) dried navy beans

8 cups (1.9 L) water

½ pound (225 g) ham, cubed

2 medium potatoes, peeled and cubed

½ cup (50 g) celery, sliced

½ cup (65 g) carrots, sliced

½ cup (80 g) onion, chopped

¼ teaspoon (0.5 g) black pepper

Soak beans in water overnight. Do not drain. Bring beans to a boil in the soaking liquid. Add ham, reduce heat, cover, and simmer for 1 hour or until beans are nearly done. Add remaining ingredients, cover, and simmer for 30 minutes more, or until vegetables are done.

Yield: 10 servings

Per serving: 148 calories (13% from fat, 26% from protein, 61% from carbohydrate); 10 g protein; 2 g total fat; 1 g saturated fat; 1 g monounsaturated fat; 0 g polyunsaturated fat; 23 g carbohydrate; 4 g fiber; 2 g sugar; 162 mg phosphorus; 42 mg calcium; 2 mg iron; 464 mg sodium; 594 mg potassium; 1104 IU vitamin A; 0 mg ATE vitamin E; 8 mg vitamin C; 9 mg cholesterol; 313 g water

Caribbean Turkey Soup

This makes a flavorful soup that is also a good way to use up leftover holiday turkey.

1½ pounds (680 g) turkey breast, cut into bite-sized pieces

1 teaspoon (2.5 g) paprika

1 cup (160 g) onion, coarsely chopped

½ cup (75 g) green bell pepper, coarsely chopped

½ teaspoon (1.5 g) finely chopped garlic

1 cup (100 g) celery, coarsely chopped

½ cup (35 g) mushrooms, sliced

2 cups (360 g) canned no-salt-added tomatoes

1 cup (235 ml) low sodium chicken broth

1 cup (134 g) frozen peas, thawed

¼ teaspoon (0.5 g) black pepper

¼ teaspoon (0.3 g) dried thyme

2 medium potatoes, peeled and chopped

1 tablespoon (0.4 g) dried parsley

¼ teaspoon (0.3 g) dried oregano

In a large skillet or saucepan, combine turkey and paprika. Cook over medium heat, about 5 minutes. Remove turkey and set aside. Place onions, green bell pepper, garlic, celery, and mushrooms in skillet. Cook, stirring, about 4 minutes. Add remaining ingredients; mix well. Add turkey; cook, covered, over low heat about 40 minutes.

Yield: 6 servings

Per serving: 277 calories (8% from fat, 47% from protein, 45% from carbohydrate); 33 g protein; 3 g total fat; 1 g saturated fat; 0 g monounsaturated fat; 1 g polyunsaturated fat; 31 g carbohydrate; 6 g fiber; 6 g sugar; 379 mg phosphorus; 77 mg calcium; 4 mg iron; 203 mg sodium; 1274 mg potassium; 1044 IU vitamin A; 0 mg ATE vitamin E; 34 mg vitamin C; 68 mg cholesterol; 376 g water

Chicken Barley Soup

This soup is full of both flavor and nutrition, low in fat, and high in fiber.

4 cups (946 ml) low sodium chicken broth

4 cups (720 g) canned no-salt-added tomatoes

3 cups (710 ml) water

3 cups (480 g) onions, chopped

¾ cup (98 g) carrot, chopped

1²/₃ cups (280 g) frozen corn, thawed

1 cup (150 g) red bell pepper, chopped

1 cup (165 g) frozen lima beans, thawed

½ cup (50 g) celery, chopped

¼ cup (56 g) lentils

¼ cup (50 g) pearl barley

¼ cup (50 g) split peas

1½ tablespoons (3 g) dried sage

2 cups (220 g) cooked chicken breast, diced

Combine all ingredients except chicken in large, heavy pot or Dutch oven. Bring to boil over medium-high heat. Reduce heat to medium. Simmer for 45 minutes, or until all vegetables and legumes are tender and soup is thick, stirring occasionally. Stir in chicken and heat through.

Yield: 8 servings

Per serving: 222 calories (11% from fat, 33% from protein, 55% from carbohydrate); 20 g protein; 3 g total fat; 1 g saturated fat; 1 g monounsaturated fat; 1 g polyunsaturated fat; 32 g carbohydrate; 7 g fiber; 9 g sugar; 256 mg phosphorus; 89 mg calcium; 3 mg iron; 109 mg sodium; 864 mg potassium; 2913 IU vitamin A; 2 mg ATE vitamin E; 44 mg vitamin C; 30 mg cholesterol; 479 g water

Potato Leek Chowder

Warm and filling, this is the kind of soup you want to sip in front of the fire on a cold night.

1 cup leeks, sliced

1 cup (130 g) carrot, sliced

1 medium potato, cubed

1 cup (235 ml) low sodium chicken broth

2 cups (470 ml) fat-free evaporated milk

1 cup (170 g) frozen corn, thawed

2 tablespoons (8 g) fresh parsley, chopped

In medium saucepan, combine leeks, carrot, potato, and chicken broth. Cover and simmer 10 minutes or until vegetables are tender. Purée. Add milk and corn. Heat, without boiling, to serving temperature. Serve sprinkled with parsley.

Yield: 4 servings

Per serving: 240 calories (5% from fat, 24% from protein, 71% from carbohydrate); 15 g protein; 1 g total fat; 0 g saturated fat; 0 g monounsaturated fat; 0 g polyunsaturated fat; 44 g carbohydrate; 4 g fiber; 19 g sugar; 379 mg phosphorus; 407 mg calcium; 2 mg iron; 208 mg sodium; 1151 mg potassium; 6509 IU vitamin A; 151 mg ATE vitamin E; 21 mg vitamin C; 5 mg cholesterol; 297 g water

Vegetable Soup

A good cold-weather meal that makes use of the best late fall and winter vegetables. Feel free to vary the vegetables to meet availability and individual likes.

1½ pounds (680 g) beef round steak

6 cups (1.4 L) water

½ cup (80 g) onion, chopped

1 teaspoon (2 g) black pepper

1 teaspoon (0.7 g) dried basil

(continued on page 214)

2 cups (360 g) canned no-salt-added tomatoes

3 medium potatoes, peeled and diced

2 medium turnips, peeled and diced

½ cup (65 g) carrot, peeled and sliced

½ cup (50 g) celery, sliced

12 ounces (340 g) frozen mixed vegetables, thawed

2 cups (140 g) cabbage, shredded

Trim fat from beef and cut into ½-inch (1.3-cm) cubes. Place beef, water, onion, pepper, and basil in a large pot. Simmer until beef is tender. Add remaining ingredients and continue cooking until vegetables are done.

Yield: 8 servings

Per serving: 334 calories (13% from fat, 43% from protein, 44% from carbohydrate); 36 g protein; 5 g total fat; 2 g saturated fat; 2 g monounsaturated fat; 0 g polyunsaturated fat; 36 g carbohydrate; 6 g fiber; 8 g sugar; 332 mg phosphorus; 81 mg calcium; 5 mg iron; 126 mg sodium; 1270 mg potassium; 3305 IU vitamin A; 0 mg ATE vitamin E; 40 mg vitamin C; 77 mg cholesterol; 490 g water

Indian Vegetable Soup

A great vegetarian meal. The amount of ginger gives it a sneaky sort of spiciness. I prefer mild curry powder, but if you want something even hotter you could use hot curry powder.

1 eggplant, peeled and cubed

1 pound (455 g) potatoes, cubed

2 cups (360 g) canned no-salt-added tomatoes

1½ cups (360 g) cooked garbanzo beans

1 cup (160 g) onion, coarsely chopped

1½ teaspoons (3 g) curry powder

1½ teaspoons (2.7 g) ground ginger

1 teaspoon (2 g) ground coriander

¼ teaspoon (0.5 g) black pepper

4 cups (946 ml) low sodium vegetable broth

In a slow cooker combine the eggplant, potatoes, tomatoes, garbanzo beans, and onion. Sprinkle curry powder, ginger, coriander, and pepper over top. Pour the broth over all. Cover and cook on low for 8 to 10 hours or on high for 4 to 5 hours.

Yield: 6 servings

Per serving: 196 calories (9% from fat, 18% from protein, 73% from carbohydrate); 9 g protein; 2 g total fat; 0 g saturated fat; 1 g monounsaturated fat; 1 g polyunsaturated fat; 38 g carbohydrate; 8 g fiber; 6 g sugar; 193 mg phosphorus; 76 mg calcium; 3 mg iron; 246 mg sodium; 969 mg potassium; 146 IU vitamin A; 0 mg ATE vitamin E; 21 mg vitamin C; 0 mg cholesterol; 426 g water

African Peanut Stew

A spicy vegetarian stew with sweet potatoes and other vegetables, flavored with peanut butter.

2 sweet potatoes, cubed

2 tablespoons (30 ml) canola oil

½ teaspoon (1.5 g) minced garlic

3 tablespoons fresh ginger, minced

2 tablespoons (12 g) ground coriander

½ teaspoon (0.9 g) cayenne pepper

4 cups (640 g) onion, chopped

1 cup (180 g) tomatoes, chopped

1 eggplant, cubed

½ cup (120 ml) water

1 cup (113 g) zucchini, chopped

1 cup (150 g) green bell pepper, chopped

2 cups (470 ml) low sodium tomato juice

½ cup (130 g) reduced-fat peanut butter

Steam or boil sweet potato cubes until tender. Heat oil in a large skilled over medium-high heat. Sauté garlic, ginger, coriander, and cayenne pepper for 1 minute. Add onions and cook until soft. Add tomatoes, eggplant, and water; simmer 10 minutes. Add zucchini and bell pepper; continue

(continued on page 216)

to simmer for 20 minutes, or until all vegetables are tender. Add sweet potatoes to stew along with tomato juice and peanut butter. Stir well and simmer on very low heat.

Yield: 6 servings

Per serving: 173 calories (25% from fat, 9% from protein, 66% from carbohydrate); 4 g protein; 5 g total fat; 0 g saturated fat; 3 g monounsaturated fat; 2 g polyunsaturated fat; 31 g carbohydrate; 7 g fiber; 13 g sugar; 104 mg phosphorus; 69 mg calcium; 2 mg iron; 35 mg sodium; 829 mg potassium; 8694 IU vitamin A; 0 mg ATE vitamin E; 65 mg vitamin C; 0 mg cholesterol; 370 g water

Chicken Minestrone

A richly flavored version of minestrone, with cubed chicken breast adding to the mix.

½ cup (80 g) onion, chopped

½ cup (65 g) carrot, diced

1 cup (113 g) zucchini, sliced

2 cloves garlic, crushed

3 boneless chicken breasts, cubed

2 cups (470 ml) low sodium chicken broth

2 cups (500 g) dried great northern beans

1 teaspoon (0.7 g) dried basil

1 teaspoon (1 g) dried oregano

2 cups (360 g) canned no-salt-added tomatoes

Parmesan cheese (optional)

Sauté onions, carrot, zucchini, and garlic until tender. Add to soup pot with remaining ingredients and simmer 1 to 1½ hours. Add additional water if needed. Garnish with Parmesan cheese, if desired.

Yield: 6 servings

Per serving: 147 calories (6% from fat, 41% from protein, 53% from carbohydrate); 16 g protein; 1 g total fat; 0 g saturated fat; 0 g monounsaturated fat; 0 g polyunsaturated fat; 20 g carbohydrate; 5 g fiber; 4 g sugar; 197 mg phosphorus; 71 mg calcium; 3 mg iron; 229 mg sodium; 663 mg potassium; 1958 IU vitamin A; 2 mg ATE vitamin E; 14 mg vitamin C; 21 mg cholesterol; 260 g water

Winter Vegetable Soup

A good meal for a winter's evening. With no potatoes or pasta, it's also low in carbohydrates for an entire meal. Using a lean cut of meat like round steak also makes it low in fat.

1 pound (455 g) beef round steak

2 cups (470 ml) low sodium beef broth

2 cups (360 g) canned no-salt-added tomatoes

1 cup (150 g) turnips, diced

6 ounces (170 g) frozen green beans, thawed

6 ounces (170 g) frozen broccoli, thawed

6 ounces (170 g) frozen cauliflower, thawed

½ cup (65 g) carrot, sliced

½ cup (80 g) onion, diced

½ cup (50 g) celery, diced

Combine all ingredients in a slow cooker and cook on low for 8 to 10 hours or high 4 to 5 hours. Remove meat and cut into bite-sized pieces or shred. Return to slow cooker and stir until warmed through.

Yield: 4 servings

Per serving: 317 calories (19% from fat, 59% from protein, 23% from carbohydrate); 47 g protein; 7 g total fat; 2 g saturated fat; 2 g monounsaturated fat; 1 g polyunsaturated fat; 18 g carbohydrate; 7 g fiber; 8 g sugar; 377 mg phosphorus; 119 mg calcium; 6 mg iron; 188 mg sodium; 1135 mg potassium; 3451 IU vitamin A; 0 mg ATE vitamin E; 82 mg vitamin C; 102 mg cholesterol; 493 g water

Beef Vegetable Soup

This is a pretty classic beef vegetable soup, the kind that country mothers have been making for years (except they probably didn't use the slow cooker).

1½ pounds (680 g) round steak, cut in ½-inch (1.3-cm) pieces

1 cup (160 g) onion, coarsely chopped

½ cup (50 g) celery, sliced

4 potatoes, cubed

4 cups (946 ml) reduced-sodium beef broth

1 cup (70 g) cabbage, coarsely chopped

4 cups (750 g) frozen mixed vegetables, thawed

2 cups (360 g) canned no-salt-added tomatoes

Brown meat in a skillet and transfer to slow cooker. Add onion, celery, and potatoes. Pour broth over. Cook on low for 8 to 10 hours. Add cabbage, mixed vegetables, and tomatoes. Turn to high and cook for 30 minutes to 1 hour, or until vegetables are done.

Yield: 8 servings

Per serving: 373 calories (10% from fat, 39% from protein, 51% from carbohydrate); 37 g protein; 4 g total fat; 1 g saturated fat; 2 g monounsaturated fat; 0 g polyunsaturated fat; 48 g carbohydrate; 8 g fiber; 8 g sugar; 367 mg phosphorus; 85 mg calcium; 5 mg iron; 446 mg sodium; 1525 mg potassium; 4015 IU vitamin A; 0 mg ATE vitamin E; 31 mg vitamin C; 49 mg cholesterol; 486 g water

Beef Goulash

This is the kind of stew that has been popular in the United States since colonial days. And with good reason—you couldn't ask for a better cold-weather meal.

5 tablespoons (40 g) flour, divided

¼ teaspoon (0.5 g) black pepper

2 pounds (905 g) beef round steak, cut in 1-inch (2.5-cm) cubes

2 tablespoons (30 ml) olive oil

1½ cups (240 g) onion, sliced

1 cup (235 ml) apple juice

1⅓ cups (320 ml) water, divided

4 cups (560 g) rutabagas, cut in 1-inch (2.5-cm) cubes

3 cups (390 g) carrot, sliced

½ teaspoon (0.1 g) dried parsley

½ teaspoon (0.3 g) dried marjoram

½ teaspoon (0.5 g) dried thyme

6 potatoes, peeled, cooked, and mashed

Combine 2 tablespoons (16 g) of the flour with the pepper in a resealable plastic bag. Add meat a little at a time and shake to coat. Brown the meat in the oil in a Dutch oven, half at a time. Return all meat to Dutch oven, add onions, juice, and 1 cup (235 ml) of the water. Cover and simmer about 1¼ hours, or until meat is tender. Add rutabagas, carrot, parsley, marjoram, and thyme. Cover and simmer about 30 minutes more, until vegetables are done. Blend the remaining ⅓ cup (80 ml) water and the remaining 3 tablespoons (24 g) of the flour and stir into stew. Cook and stir until thickened and bubbly. Spoon mashed potatoes around the edge of the stew to serve.

Yield: 8 servings

Per serving: 538 calories (16% from fat, 36% from protein, 48% from carbohydrate); 48 g protein; 10 g total fat; 3 g saturated fat; 5 g monounsaturated fat; 1 g polyunsaturated fat; 64 g carbohydrate; 9 g fiber; 14 g sugar; 499 mg phosphorus; 94 mg calcium; 7 mg iron; 120 mg sodium; 2117 mg potassium; 8103 IU vitamin A; 0 mg ATE vitamin E; 47 mg vitamin C; 102 mg cholesterol; 489 g water

Italian Kitchen Sink Soup

Okay, so the name's kind of strange. But it sure seems like it has everything in it. In truth, it's a heartier version of the Italian Wedding Soup that's become popular in recent years. This one is truly a meal in a bowl. And it's low in fat and sodium, but high in fiber and vitamins.

4 cups (946 ml) water

2 cups (320 g) onion, chopped

2 red potatoes, diced

1 cup (250 g) dried great northern beans

½ cup (65 g) carrot, sliced

½ cup (35 g) mushrooms, sliced

½ cup (100 g) uncooked pearl barley

½ pound (225 g) round steak, cubed

2 cups (360 g) canned no-salt-added tomatoes

2 cups (470 ml) low sodium beef broth

1 tablespoon (2.1 g) Italian seasoning

½ teaspoon (1.5 g) minced garlic

1 cup (113 g) zucchini, sliced

1 cup (20 g) fresh spinach, torn into bite-sized pieces

½ cup (75 g) small pasta

1 tablespoon (3.3 g) dried rosemary

½ teaspoon (1 g) black pepper

Combine first 12 ingredients (through garlic) in a large electric slow cooker. Cover with lid, and cook on high for 6 hours or low for 10 to 12 hours. Add remaining ingredients, cover and cook on high-heat setting for an additional 30 minutes, or until beans are tender.

Yield: 8 servings

Per serving: 209 calories (9% from fat, 30% from protein, 61% from carbohydrate); 16 g protein; 2 g total fat; 1 g saturated fat; 1 g monounsaturated fat; 0 g polyunsaturated fat; 33 g carbohydrate; 8 g fiber; 4 g sugar; 203 mg phosphorus; 112 mg calcium; 4 mg iron; 256 mg sodium; 689 mg potassium; 4349 IU vitamin A; 0 mg ATE vitamin E; 15 mg vitamin C; 18 mg cholesterol; 366 g water

Savory Beef Stew

Here is the kind of meal you need as the weather starts to turn cooler (seems like I say that about a lot of recipes!). It has a wonderful aroma and flavor, thanks to a couple of unusual ingredients. And it can cook while you're away, so it's ready when you arrive home.

2 tablespoons (16 g) flour

1 pound (455 g) beef round steak, cubed

2 tablespoons (30 ml) olive oil

4 medium potatoes, cubed

1 cup (130 g) carrot, sliced

½ cup (80 g) onion, coarsely chopped

1 cup (235 ml) low sodium beef broth

2 cups (360 g) canned no-salt-added tomatoes

½ cup (120 ml) water

2 tablespoons (30 g) brown sugar

1 tablespoon (15 ml) Worcestershire sauce

1 tablespoon (15 ml) vinegar

1½ teaspoons (1.5 g) instant coffee

1 teaspoon (2.5 g) cumin

½ teaspoon (0.9 g) ground ginger

¼ teaspoon (0.5 g) ground allspice

Place flour in a plastic bag. Add beef and shake to coat. Heat oil in a large skillet over medium heat. Brown beef on all sides. Place potatoes, carrots, and onion in a slow cooker. Top with beef. Combine remaining ingredients and pour over meat and vegetables. Cover and cook on low for 8 to 10 hours or on high 4 to 5 hours.

Yield: 6 servings

Per serving: 424 calories (19% from fat, 32% from protein, 49% from carbohydrate); 34 g protein; 9 g total fat; 2 g saturated fat; 5 g monounsaturated fat; 1 g polyunsaturated fat; 53 g carbohydrate; 6 g fiber; 10 g sugar; 361 mg phosphorus; 74 mg calcium; 6 mg iron; 126 mg sodium; 1682 mg potassium; 3705 IU vitamin A; 0 mg ATE vitamin E; 35 mg vitamin C; 68 mg cholesterol; 413 g water

Pork Stew

It's nice to have dinner finished when you get home once in a while. You can serve this over rice or noodles or just have it with a big slice of freshly baked bread (the delay bake option on the bread machine works *so* well with the slow cooker).

1 pound (455 g) pork loin

¾ cup (120 g) onion, sliced

2 cups (360 g) canned no-salt-added tomatoes

½ cup (75 g) green bell pepper, coarsely chopped

2 cups (470 ml) low sodium chicken broth

1 cup (70 g) mushrooms, quartered

1 tablespoon (0.4 g) dried parsley

1 teaspoon (1 g) dried thyme

¼ cup (15 g) fresh cilantro, chopped

¼ cup (30 g) flour

Cube pork. Layer all ingredients except the flour in a slow cooker, reserving half the chicken broth. Cook on low for 6 to 8 hours. Stir the flour into the remaining chicken broth. Add to slow cooker. Turn to high and cook an additional 30 minutes, or until slightly thickened.

Yield: 4 servings

Per serving: 242 calories (35% from fat, 35% from protein, 30% from carbohydrate); 22 g protein; 10 g total fat; 4 g saturated fat; 4 g monounsaturated fat; 1 g polyunsaturated fat; 18 g carbohydrate; 3 g fiber; 70 mg calcium; 3 mg iron; 91 mg sodium; 801 mg potassium; 1073 IU vitamin A; 54 mg vitamin C; 52 mg cholesterol

Mock Crab Soup

This soup is typical of Maryland crab soup in flavor. The only big difference is the lack of crab meat, which is high in both sodium and cholesterol. In its place we have fish. I happened to have some flounder fillets available, but any white fish would do. This is also one of our spicier recipes. You can reduce the amount of pepper if you prefer a milder version.

1 pound (455 g) flounder

2 cups (470 ml) low sodium chicken broth

2 cups (360 g) canned no-salt-added tomatoes, diced

½ cup (82 g) frozen corn, thawed

½ cup (67 g) frozen peas, thawed

1½ teaspoons (3 g) seafood seasoning

½ teaspoon (1 g) black pepper

½ teaspoon (0.9 g) cayenne pepper

Shred the fish (processing in a food processor with a little of the broth does this easily). Place all ingredients in a large saucepan and simmer for 10 minutes, or until fish and vegetables are cooked.

Yield: 4 servings

Per serving: 178 calories (12% from fat, 58% from protein, 30% from carbohydrate); 26 g protein; 2 g total fat; 1 g saturated fat; 1 g monounsaturated fat; 1 g polyunsaturated fat; 14 g carbohydrate; 3 g fiber; 5 g sugar; 298 mg phosphorus; 70 mg calcium; 2 mg iron; 242 mg sodium; 810 mg potassium; 742 IU vitamin A; 11 mg ATE vitamin E; 16 mg vitamin C; 54 mg cholesterol; 350 g water

Fish Stew

An Italian- or Mediterranean-flavored fish stew, great for a cold evening.

2 tablespoons (30 ml) olive oil

1 cup (160 g) onions, thinly sliced

1 teaspoon (3 g) minced garlic

¼ cup (60 ml) dry sherry

1½ cups (270 g) tomatoes, chopped

3 potatoes, cubed

2 whole cloves

2 bay leaves

1 tablespoon (4 g) fresh parsley, minced

½ teaspoon dried tarragon

½ teaspoon (0.7 g) fresh marjoram

¼ teaspoon (0.5 g) pepper

2 quarts (1.9 L) water

2 pounds (905 g) cod, halibut, or pollock fillets

½ cup (40 g) Parmesan cheese, shredded

Fresh parsley, for garnish

Heat oil in a large Dutch oven and sauté onion and garlic. Add sherry and next 9 ingredients (through water). Cover and simmer for 1 hour. Uncover and reduce liquid for two hours on a low simmer. Cut fish into large chunks. Add to stew and simmer for 10 minutes. Serve stew in soup bowls and top each with one tablespoon (5 g) Parmesan cheese. Garnish with parsley.

Yield: 8 servings

Per serving: 276 calories (21% from fat, 39% from protein, 40% from carbohydrate); 26 g protein; 6 g total fat; 2 g saturated fat; 3 g monounsaturated fat; 1 g polyunsaturated fat; 27 g carbohydrate; 3 g fiber; 3 g sugar; 371 mg phosphorus; 114 mg calcium; 2 mg iron; 182 mg sodium; 1196 mg potassium; 345 IU vitamin A; 21 mg ATE vitamin E; 26 mg vitamin C; 54 mg cholesterol; 466 g water

Italian Fish Stew

A fish stew in the tradition of southern Italy.

2 tablespoons (30 ml) olive oil

1 cup (160 g) red onion, chopped

½ teaspoon (1.5 g) chopped garlic

1 cup (60 g) fresh parsley, chopped

2 teaspoons (1.4 g) dried basil

1½ cups (270 g) tomatoes, peeled, seeded, and finely chopped

1 cup (235 ml) water

½ cup (120 ml) dry white wine

1 pound (455 g) cod fillets

¼ cup (25 g) Parmesan cheese, grated

Heat the olive oil in a wide, heavy pot over medium heat. Add the onions and garlic and cook, stirring occasionally, for 5 minutes, or until onions are translucent. Add the parsley, basil, and tomatoes. Raise the heat and bring to a simmer. Add water and wine. Cook, partially covered, for 10 minutes. Add the fish, cover, and simmer for 12 to 15 minutes. Ladle into bowls and top with grated cheese.

Yield: 4 servings

Per serving: 239 calories (40% from fat, 44% from protein, 16% from carbohydrate); 24 g protein; 10 g total fat; 2 g saturated fat; 6 g monounsaturated fat; 1 g polyunsaturated fat; 9 g carbohydrate; 2 g fiber; 2 g sugar; 317 mg phosphorus; 133 mg calcium; 2 mg iron; 175 mg sodium; 777 mg potassium; 1718 IU vitamin A; 21 mg ATE vitamin E; 39 mg vitamin C; 54 mg cholesterol; 279 g water

Fish Chowder

This makes a great chowder, thick and rich. You can substitute other fish, or a combination of different types of fish, for the cod.

2 tablespoons (30 ml) olive oil

2 cups (320 g) chopped onion

½ cup (35 g) mushrooms, sliced

½ cup (50 g) celery, chopped

5 cups (1.2 L) low sodium chicken broth, divided

4 medium potatoes, diced

2 pounds (905 g) cod, diced into ½-inch (1.3-cm) cubes

⅛ teaspoon (0.3 g) seafood seasoning

¼ teaspoon (0.5 g) black pepper

½ cup (60 g) flour

3 cups (710 ml) fat-free evaporated milk

In a large stockpot, heat oil over medium heat. Sauté onions, mushrooms, and celery until tender. Add 4 cups (946 ml) chicken broth and potatoes; simmer for 10 minutes. Add fish, and simmer another 10 minutes. Season to taste with seafood seasoning and pepper. Mix together remaining broth and flour until smooth; stir into soup. Cook until slightly thickened. Remove from heat and stir in evaporated milk.

Yield: 8 servings

Per serving: 397 calories (13% from fat, 35% from protein, 52% from carbohydrate); 35 g protein; 6 g total fat; 1 g saturated fat; 3 g monounsaturated fat; 1 g polyunsaturated fat; 52 g carbohydrate; 4 g fiber; 15 g sugar; 600 mg phosphorus; 334 mg calcium; 3 mg iron; 236 mg sodium; 1854 mg potassium; 468 IU vitamin A; 127 mg ATE vitamin E; 21 mg vitamin C; 53 mg cholesterol; 508 g water

Caribbean Fish Stew

This is a fairly spicy stew if you use the habanero pepper. I use a jalapeño instead, which still gives you some heat, but in moderation.

½ cup (65 g) carrot, sliced

1 cup (160 g) onion, sliced

2 tablespoons (28 g) grated fresh ginger

½ teaspoon (1.5 g) minced garlic

½ teaspoon (1 g) ground cloves

½ teaspoon (1 g) ground allspice

½ teaspoon (1 g) cardamom

½ teaspoon (1.1 g) turmeric

2 teaspoons (4 g) ground coriander

4 cups (360 g) canned no-salt-added tomatoes

12 ounces (355 ml) beer

1 habanero or jalapeño pepper

2 medium potatoes, diced

1 pound tilapia (455 g) fillets, cut into 2-inch (5-cm) pieces

1 tablespoon (4 g) cilantro, chopped

½ cup (120 ml) lime juice

In a Dutch oven, sauté the carrot and onion until slightly soft, then add the ginger and garlic. When the vegetables are soft, add the cloves, allspice, cardamom, turmeric, and coriander and sauté about 1 minute longer. Add the tomatoes and beer and bring to a boil. Add the habanero pepper. Reduce the heat and let simmer for 20 minutes, then add the potatoes. When the potatoes are tender, add the fish. Cook another 5 minutes. Then add the cilantro and lime juice. Stir and serve.

Yield: 4 servings

Per serving: 395 calories (9% from fat, 32% from protein, 59% from carbohydrate); 31 g protein; 4 g total fat; 1 g saturated fat; 1 g monounsaturated fat; 1 g polyunsaturated fat; 56 g carbohydrate; 8 g fiber; 11 g sugar; 454 mg phosphorus; 181 mg calcium; 6 mg iron; 131 mg sodium; 2078 mg potassium; 3282 IU vitamin A; 53 mg ATE vitamin E; 59 mg vitamin C; 36 mg cholesterol; 589 g water

Basic Chili

I never seem to make chili the same way twice, so I keep coming up with new recipes. One thing that's become fairly constant, though, is sautéing the spices, which seems to give it a deeper flavor.

1 pound (455 g) dried kidney beans

2 pounds (905 g) beef round steak

1 tablespoon (15 ml) olive oil

½ cup (80 g) onion, coarsely chopped

½ teaspoon (1.5 g) minced garlic

½ cup (75 g) green bell pepper, coarsely chopped

4 ounces (115 g) canned jalapeño peppers

2 tablespoons (15 g) chili powder

1 tablespoon (7 g) cumin

1 teaspoon (1 g) dried oregano

1 tablespoon (4 g) cilantro

2 cups (360 g) canned no-salt-added tomatoes

2 cups (360 g) canned no-salt-added crushed tomatoes

Soak kidney beans overnight. Drain and add fresh water. Simmer for 1½ hours, or until almost tender. Coarsely grind beef or chop into small cubes no bigger than ½ inch (1.3 cm). Heat oil in a skillet and sauté beef, onion, garlic, green bell pepper, and jalapeños until beef is browned on all sides. Add chili powder, cumin, oregano, and cilantro and sauté an additional 5 minutes. Transfer to slow cooker. Stir in tomatoes. Drain beans and add to slow cooker. Stir to mix, cover, and cook on low 4 to 5 hours.

Yield: 8 servings

Per serving: 353 calories (22% from fat, 54% from protein, 24% from carbohydrate); 48 g protein; 8 g total fat; 2 g saturated fat; 4 g monounsaturated fat; 1 g polyunsaturated fat; 21 g carbohydrate; 6 g fiber; 4 g sugar; 379 mg phosphorus; 77 mg calcium; 8 mg iron; 223 mg sodium; 948 mg potassium; 884 IU vitamin A; 0 mg ATE vitamin E; 28 mg vitamin C; 102 mg cholesterol; 249 g water

Cincinnati-Style Chili

Cincinnati, Ohio, claims to be where chili was created. Cincinnati-style chili is quite different from the more familiar Tex-Mex variety. The chili is thinner and contains an unusual blend of spices that includes cinnamon, chocolate or cocoa, allspice, and Worcestershire sauce. It's usually served over spaghetti, although it's good in a bowl by itself or as a hot dog topping.

1 cup (160 g) onion, chopped

1 pound (455 g) extra-lean ground beef (93% lean)

¼ teaspoon (0.8 g) minced garlic

1 tablespoon (7.5 g) chili powder

1 teaspoon (1.9 g) ground allspice

1 teaspoon (2.3 g) cinnamon

1 teaspoon (2.5 g) cumin

½ teaspoon (0.9 g) cayenne pepper

1½ tablespoons (8 g) unsweetened cocoa powder

16 ounces (455 g) no-salt-added tomato sauce

1 tablespoon (15 ml) Worcestershire sauce

1 tablespoon (15 ml) cider vinegar

½ cup (120 ml) water

In a large frying pan over medium-high heat, sauté onion, ground beef, garlic, and chili powder until ground beef is slightly cooked. Add remaining ingredients. Reduce heat to low and simmer, uncovered, 1½ hours.

To serve the traditional Cincinnati way, ladle chili over cooked spaghetti and serve with toppings of your choice. Oyster crackers are served on the side. Cincinnati chili is ordered by number:

- Two-Way Chili: Chili served on spaghetti
- Three-Way Chili: Additionally topped with shredded cheddar cheese
- Four-Way Chili: Additionally topped with chopped onions
- Five-Way Chili: Additionally topped with kidney beans

Yield: 6 servings

(continued on page 230)

Per serving: 227 calories (32% from fat, 41% from protein, 27% from carbohydrate); 16 g protein; 6 g total fat; 2 g saturated fat; 2 g monounsaturated fat; 0 g polyunsaturated fat; 10 g carbohydrate; 3 g fiber; 4 g sugar; 156 mg phosphorus; 38 mg calcium; 3 mg iron; 98 mg sodium; 598 mg potassium; 688 IU vitamin A; 0 mg ATE vitamin E; 17 mg vitamin C; 52 mg cholesterol; 158 g water

Black Bean Chili

This could be the perfect chili. Not only does it taste great, but it's good for you, high in fiber, and low in fat. And it cooks in only 20 minutes. Plus, it's a great way to use up leftover turkey.

1 cup (250 g) dried black beans

1 tablespoon (15 ml) canola oil

1 cup (160 g) onion, chopped

½ cup (75 g) red bell pepper, cubed

1 teaspoon (3 g) minced garlic

2 jalapeño peppers, seeded and chopped

2 cups (360 g) canned no-salt-added tomatoes

2 tablespoons (15 g) chili powder

1 teaspoon (2.5 g) cumin

1 teaspoon (2 g) coriander

1 teaspoon (0.6 g) dried marjoram

¼ teaspoon (0.3 g) red pepper flakes

¼ teaspoon (0.6 g) cinnamon

2 cups (225 g) cooked turkey breast, cubed

⅓ cup fresh (20 g) cilantro, coarsely chopped

4 teaspoons (8 g) low fat cheddar cheese, shredded

Soak and cook black beans according to package directions. Heat oil in a 3-quart (2.8-L) saucepan and sauté onion, bell pepper, garlic, and jalapeño peppers until crisp-tender. Add all other ingredients except turkey, cilantro, and cheese. Bring to a boil, then simmer for 10 to 15 minutes. Stir in turkey and cilantro and cook until heated throughout. To serve, ladle into bowls and top with cheese.

Yield: 4 servings

Per serving: 153 calories (27% from fat, 17% from protein, 56% from carbohydrate); 7 g protein; 5 g total fat; 1 g saturated fat; 2 g monounsaturated fat; 2 g polyunsaturated fat; 23 g carbohydrate; 8 g fiber; 6 g sugar; 133 mg phosphorus; 97 mg calcium; 3 mg iron; 77 mg sodium; 608 mg potassium; 2208 IU vitamin A; 2 mg ATE vitamin E; 46 mg vitamin C; 1 mg cholesterol; 207 g water

Steak Chili

This is a guy's kind of chili—spicy and full of just meat, with none of those beans for fillers.

2 tablespoons (30 ml) canola oil

3 pounds (1.4 kg) beef round steak

2 cups (470 ml) low sodium beef broth

8 ounces (225 g) no-salt-added tomato sauce

2 cups (360 g) canned no-salt-added tomatoes

4 ounces (115 g) canned chili peppers

¾ cup (175 ml) beer

2 tablespoons (15 g) chili powder

1 teaspoon (3 g) garlic powder

1 tablespoon (9 g) onion powder

1 teaspoon (5 ml) hot pepper sauce

1 tablespoon (7 g) cumin

Heat oil in a skillet and sauté beef until done; drain well. Put beef and broth in a large pot and bring to a slow simmer. Add remaining ingredients and simmer slowly for about 1½ hours, or until meat is tender.

Yield: 10 servings

Per serving: 370 calories (27% from fat, 58% from protein, 15% from carbohydrate); 52 g protein; 11 g total fat; 3 g saturated fat; 5 g monounsaturated fat; 2 g polyunsaturated fat; 14 g carbohydrate; 5 g fiber; 7 g sugar; 362 mg phosphorus; 45 mg calcium; 7 mg iron; 129 mg sodium; 921 mg potassium; 3599 IU vitamin A; 0 mg ATE vitamin E; 12 mg vitamin C; 122 mg cholesterol; 209 g water

Black Bean and Squash Chili

Winter squash adds color and a seasonal twist to this vegetarian chili.

1 medium butternut squash

1 tablespoon (15 ml) olive oil

1 cup (160 g) onion, chopped

½ teaspoon (1.5 g) minced garlic

¾ cup (112 g) green bell pepper, chopped

4 cups (900 g) canned black beans, drained and rinsed

4 cups (720 g) canned no-salt-added tomatoes

4 ounces (115 g) canned chili peppers

1 teaspoon (2.5 g) ground cumin

½ teaspoon (0.5 g) dried oregano

Cut squash in half and scoop out and discard seeds. Place squash in a microwave-safe container with ¼-inch (63 mm) of water. Cover and microwave until tender, allowing 2 to 3 minutes per squash half. Remove squash and let cool, then peel and cut into chunks. In a large pot, heat oil over medium heat. Add onion and cook, stirring often, for 5 minutes or until soft. Add remaining ingredients except squash and mix well. Bring to a boil. Reduce heat and simmer gently for 15 minutes. Stir in squash and heat through.

Yield: 10 servings

Per serving: 199 calories (11% from fat, 17% from protein, 72% from carbohydrate); 9 g protein; 3 g total fat; 0 g saturated fat; 1 g monounsaturated fat; 1 g polyunsaturated fat; 39 g carbohydrate; 12 g fiber; 10 g sugar; 167 mg phosphorus; 92 mg calcium; 4 mg iron; 28 mg sodium; 951 mg potassium; 9267 IU vitamin A; 0 mg ATE vitamin E; 66 mg vitamin C; 0 mg cholesterol; 247 g water

11

Salads and Salad Dressings

Salads can be one of those good-news, bad-news kind of things when you are watching your diet. The salad itself is often very healthy, but the dressing may not be. You'll need to be careful about what kind of fat is in that bottle you pick up off the grocer's shelf. Many contain 2 to 3 grams of saturated fat and as much as 15 grams of total fat per serving. I've provided some tasty alternatives here with less than half that. There also are recipes for some meal-sized salads, side salads that aren't just the same old thing, and reduced-fat versions of favorites like potato salad.

Lower-Fat Peppercorn Dressing

This is my favorite dressing recipe. It's similar to a ranch dressing, but with a little extra pop from the peppercorns.

1 cup (225 g) low fat mayonnaise

1 cup (235 ml) low fat buttermilk

2 teaspoons (0.2 g) dried parsley

1 teaspoon (3 g) onion powder

¼ teaspoon (0.8 g) garlic powder

¼ teaspoon (0.3 g) dried dill

1 teaspoon (1.7 g) black peppercorns, coarsely cracked

TIP *You can crack the peppercorns by putting them in a plastic bag and beating on them with a mallet or rolling pin.*

Mix all ingredients together well. Refrigerate overnight before using.

Yield: 16 servings

Per serving: 51 calories (87% from fat, 1% from protein, 12% from carbohydrate); 0 g protein; 5 g total fat; 1 g saturated fat; 0 g monounsaturated fat; 0 g polyunsaturated fat; 2 g carbohydrate; 0 g fiber; 1 g sugar; 10 mg phosphorus; 3 mg calcium; 0 mg iron; 120 mg sodium; 13 mg potassium; 42 IU vitamin A; 0 mg ATE vitamin E; 0 mg vitamin C; 5 mg cholesterol; 8 g water

Onion Ranch Dressing

This dressing is better if you make it ahead of time and let it sit at least overnight so the herbs soften and the flavor develops.

½ cup (120 ml) buttermilk

1 cup (225 g) low fat mayonnaise

1 teaspoon (3 g) onion powder

1 teaspoon (0.1 g) dried parsley

1½ teaspoons (6 g) sugar

½ teaspoon (1.5 g) garlic powder

½ teaspoon (1.5 g) dry mustard

¼ teaspoon (0.2 g) dried thyme

¼ teaspoon (0.2 g) dried basil

¼ teaspoon (0.3 g) dried oregano

¼ teaspoon (0.3 g) dried rosemary

¼ teaspoon (0.2 g) dried sage

¼ teaspoon (0.5 g) freshly ground black pepper

Mix all the ingredients together. Store in the refrigerator in a tightly covered jar.

Yield: 12 servings

Per serving: 75 calories (81% from fat, 3% from protein, 16% from carbohydrate); 1 g protein; 7 g total fat; 1 g saturated fat; 0 g monounsaturated fat; 0 g polyunsaturated fat; 3 g carbohydrate; 0 g fiber; 2 g sugar; 22 mg phosphorus; 16 mg calcium; 0 mg iron; 170 mg sodium; 32 mg potassium; 53 IU vitamin A; 1 mg ATE vitamin E; 0 mg vitamin C; 7 mg cholesterol; 20 g water

Reduced-Fat Buttermilk Dressing

I've had a difficult time finding low fat buttermilk around here, but when I can, this is one of the things I make. You can also make this with nonfat buttermilk powder. You can vary the herbs depending on what you like.

¼ cup (56 g) low fat mayonnaise

½ cup (120 ml) low fat buttermilk

1 tablespoon (10 g) onion, minced

2 teaspoons (2 g) dried dill

1 teaspoon (0.7 g) dried basil

1 tablespoon (0.4 g) dried parsley

¼ teaspoon (0.8 g) garlic powder

⅛ teaspoon (0.3 g) cayenne pepper

(continued on page 236)

Combine ingredients in a blender or food processor and process until smooth. Refrigerate several hours before serving to allow flavor to develop.

Yield: 6 servings

Per serving: 44 calories (71% from fat, 8% from protein, 21% from carbohydrate); 1 g protein; 4 g total fat; 1 g saturated fat; 0 g monounsaturated fat; 0 g polyunsaturated fat; 2 g carbohydrate; 0 g fiber; 2 g sugar; 28 mg phosphorus; 34 mg calcium; 0 mg iron; 102 mg sodium; 59 mg potassium; 123 IU vitamin A; 1 mg ATE vitamin E; 1 mg vitamin C; 4 mg cholesterol; 26 g water

Reduced-Fat Blue Cheese Dressing

I tried a number of recipes for blue cheese dressing when I first started low sodium cooking. The ones that were really low in sodium weren't all that tasty. The key seems to be the use of "real" blue cheese for flavor. Moving from there to a reduced-fat version was easier, by simply using low fat and fat-free products wherever available. This version has 5 total grams of fat per serving, compared to 11 grams in my original recipe.

2 ounces (55 g) blue cheese
1 cup (225 g) low fat mayonnaise
½ cup (115 g) fat-free sour cream
½ cup (120 ml) low fat buttermilk

Combine ingredients and chill overnight.

Yield: 20 servings

Per serving: 61 calories (80% from fat, 8% from protein, 12% from carbohydrate); 1 g protein; 5 g total fat; 1 g saturated fat; 0 g monounsaturated fat; 0 g polyunsaturated fat; 2 g carbohydrate; 0 g fiber; 1 g sugar; 29 mg phosphorus; 29 mg calcium; 0 mg iron; 144 mg sodium; 31 mg potassium; 68 IU vitamin A; 12 mg ATE vitamin E; 0 mg vitamin C; 9 mg cholesterol; 18 g water

Sun-Dried Tomato Vinaigrette

Nice flavor with a little more fat than most recipes here. But it's the good kind from olive oil, so I left it that way.

3 tablespoons (45 ml) white wine vinegar

¼ cup (28 g) oil-packed sun-dried tomatoes, chopped

1 teaspoon (5 ml) Worcestershire sauce

1 clove garlic, minced

½ teaspoon (2 g) sugar

½ teaspoon (1 g) white pepper

¼ cup (60 ml) olive oil

Shake ingredients together in a jar with a tight-fitting lid.

Yield: 8 servings

Per serving: 70 calories (91% from fat, 1% from protein, 8% from carbohydrate); 0 g protein; 7 g total fat; 1 g saturated fat; 5 g monounsaturated fat; 1 g polyunsaturated fat; 1 g carbohydrate; 0 g fiber; 0 g sugar; 6 mg phosphorus; 3 mg calcium; 0 mg iron; 16 mg sodium; 63 mg potassium; 45 IU vitamin A; 0 mg ATE vitamin E; 5 mg vitamin C; 0 mg cholesterol; 7 g water

Reduced-Fat Italian Dressing

This makes an Italian dressing that is every bit as good as the commercial ones, with less fat and fewer calories. It also has a lot less sodium for those who are watching their intake.

2 tablespoons (30 ml) olive oil

½ cup (120 ml) cider vinegar

2 tablespoons (30 g) Dijon mustard

½ teaspoon (1.5 g) garlic powder

½ teaspoon (1 g) black pepper

½ teaspoon (2 g) sugar

(continued on page 238)

1 teaspoon (0.7 g) dried basil

1 teaspoon (1 g) dried oregano

½ teaspoon (0.6 g) dried rosemary

Combine all ingredients in a jar with a tight-fitting lid. Shake well.

Yield: 6 servings

Per serving: 51 calories (87% from fat, 3% from protein, 10% from carbohydrate); 0 g protein; 5 g total fat; 1 g saturated fat; 3 g monounsaturated fat; 1 g polyunsaturated fat; 1 g carbohydrate; 0 g fiber; 1 g sugar; 9 mg phosphorus; 11 mg calcium; 0 mg iron; 58 mg sodium; 33 mg potassium; 28 IU vitamin A; 0 mg ATE vitamin E; 0 mg vitamin C; 0 mg cholesterol; 23 g water

Creamy Raspberry Vinaigrette

A fresh and fruity creamy salad dressing that is excellent on fruit salads.

1 cup (230 g) plain fat-free yogurt

½ cup (55 g) raspberries

1 tablespoon (15 ml) red wine vinegar

2 tablespoons (26 g) sugar

In a blender, combine the yogurt, raspberries, vinegar, and sugar. Blend until smooth and refrigerate until chilled.

Yield: 6 servings

Per serving: 45 calories (3% from fat, 22% from protein, 76% from carbohydrate); 2 g protein; 0 g total fat; 0 g saturated fat; 0 g monounsaturated fat; 0 g polyunsaturated fat; 9 g carbohydrate; 1 g fiber; 8 g sugar; 67 mg phosphorus; 84 mg calcium; 0 mg iron; 32 mg sodium; 121 mg potassium; 6 IU vitamin A; 1 mg ATE vitamin E; 3 mg vitamin C; 1 mg cholesterol; 46 g water

Honey-Mustard Cranberry Dressing

Here's a use for the leftover cranberry sauce that always seems to be the last thing left from Thanksgiving. You can use either the jellied or whole berry sauce.

1½ tablespoons (22 g) honey mustard

⅔ cup (185 g) cranberry sauce

¼ cup (60 ml) rice wine vinegar

¼ cup (60 ml) olive oil

In a food processor mix together the mustard, cranberry sauce, and the rice wine vinegar. With the machine running, slowly pour in the oil until the dressing is thickened. Store, covered, in the refrigerator.

Yield: 12 Servings

Per serving: 65 calories (62% from fat, 1% from protein, 37% from carbohydrate); 0 g protein; 5 g total fat; 1 g saturated fat; 3 g monounsaturated fat; 1 g polyunsaturated fat; 6 g carbohydrate; 0 g fiber; 6 g sugar; 3 mg phosphorus; 2 mg calcium; 0 mg iron; 26 mg sodium; 10 mg potassium; 8 IU vitamin A; 0 mg ATE vitamin E; 0 mg vitamin C; 0 mg cholesterol; 16 g water

Pepper Steak Salad

Although this doesn't actually contain any soy sauce, the flavor is definitely Asian.

For Marinade/Dressing:

¼ cup (60 ml) balsamic vinegar

2 tablespoons (30 ml) sesame oil

½ teaspoon (0.9 g) ground ginger

1 tablespoon (13 g) sugar

¼ teaspoon (0.8 g) minced garlic

1 ounce (28 g) sesame seeds

4 ounces (115 g) leftover roast beef

(continued on page 240)

For Salad:

½ pound (225 g) lettuce, shredded

4 ounces (115 g) snow peas

½ cup (65 g) carrots, sliced

1 cup (70 g) cabbage, shredded

4 ounces (115 g) mushrooms, sliced

½ cup (75 g) red bell pepper, sliced

4 ounces (115 g) mung bean sprouts

To make the marinade/dressing: Combine vinegar, sesame oil, ginger, sugar, garlic, and sesame seeds. Pour into a resealable plastic bag. Slice beef and add to marinade in bag for 1 to 2 hours. Drain, reserving liquid.

To make the salad: Toss salad ingredients, top with beef slices. Spoon remaining dressing over.

Yield: 4 servings

Per serving: 216 calories (51% from fat, 23% from protein, 26% from carbohydrate); 13 g protein; 13 g total fat; 2 g saturated fat; 5 g monounsaturated fat; 5 g polyunsaturated fat; 15 g carbohydrate; 5 g fiber; 8 g sugar; 184 mg phosphorus; 121 mg calcium; 3 mg iron; 38 mg sodium; 491 mg potassium; 3932 IU vitamin A; 0 mg ATE vitamin E; 54 mg vitamin C; 25 mg cholesterol; 217 g water

Asian Pork Salad

Another main dish salad for those hot days. This one uses fresh Asian-style vegetables and marinated pork chops to give you a taste of Asia in a cool meal.

For Marinade

4 boneless pork loin chops

¼ cup (60 ml) Dick's Reduced-Sodium Soy Sauce (see recipe page 30)

1 tablespoon (15 ml) sesame oil

1 tablespoon (15 ml) rice vinegar

1 tablespoon (13 g) sugar

For Salad:

½ pound (225 g) lettuce, shredded

4 ounces (115 g) snow peas

½ cup (65 g) carrot, sliced

1 cup (70 g) cabbage, shredded

4 ounces (115 g) mushrooms, sliced

½ cup (75 g) red bell pepper, sliced

4 ounces (115 g) mung bean sprouts

For Dressing:

¼ cup (60 ml) Dick's Reduced-Sodium Soy Sauce (see recipe page 30)

2 tablespoons (30 ml) rice vinegar

2 tablespoons (30 ml) mirin wine

½ teaspoon (0.9 g) ground ginger

1 tablespoon (8 g) sesame seeds

Thinly slice chops. Combine soy sauce, sesame oil, vinegar, and sugar. Place pork and marinade in a resealable plastic bag and marinate for 1 to 2 hours. Drain and stir-fry until cooked through. Toss salad ingredients, top with pork slices. Combine all dressing ingredients and spoon dressing over salad to serve.

Yield: 6 servings

Per serving: 173 calories (7% from fat, 10% from protein, 83% from carbohydrate); 17 g protein; 5 g total fat; 1 g saturated fat; 2 g monounsaturated fat; 4 g polyunsaturated fat; 140 g carbohydrate; 2 g fiber; 9 g sugar; 222 mg phosphorus; 52 mg calcium; 2 mg iron; 191 mg sodium; 564 mg potassium; 2634 IU vitamin A; 1 mg ATE vitamin E; 37 mg vitamin C; 42 mg cholesterol; 209 g water

Mexican Bean Salad

A simple and tasty South-of-the-border bean salad. Cook dry beans according to package directions or drain canned beans.

2 cups (450 g) cooked kidney beans

2 cups (450 g) cooked garbanzo beans

1 cup (180 g) tomatoes, chopped

¾ cup (105 g) cucumber, peeled and chopped

2 tablespoons (20 g) onion, diced

½ cup (115 g) avocado, mashed

½ cup (115 g) plain fat-free yogurt

¼ teaspoon (0.8 g) minced garlic

½ teaspoon (1.3 g) cumin

4 cups (80 g) lettuce, shredded

In a large bowl, toss together the kidney beans, garbanzo beans, tomatoes, cucumber, and onion. In a small bowl, mix the avocado, yogurt, garlic, and cumin. Stir the avocado mixture into the bean mixture and chill. Serve on top of shredded lettuce.

Yield: 8 servings

Per serving: 172 calories (17% from fat, 19% from protein, 64% from carbohydrate); 9 g protein; 3 g total fat; 0 g saturated fat; 2 g monounsaturated fat; 1 g polyunsaturated fat; 29 g carbohydrate; 7 g fiber; 2 g sugar; 164 mg phosphorus; 75 mg calcium; 3 mg iron; 303 mg sodium; 506 mg potassium; 346 IU vitamin A; 0 mg ATE vitamin E; 11 mg vitamin C; 0 mg cholesterol; 159 g water

Chicken Main-Dish Salad

A meal-on-a-plate. This makes a good hot weather dinner when you don't really feel like doing much cooking

For Dressing:

6 tablespoons (90 ml) olive oil

¼ teaspoon (0.8 g) minced garlic

1 tablespoon (15 ml) lemon juice

2 tablespoons (30 ml) red wine vinegar

½ teaspoon (2.5 ml) Worcestershire sauce

For Salad:

1 pound (455 g) boneless chicken breasts

12 ounces (340 g) romaine lettuce

1 cup (30 g) croutons

¼ cup (25 g) Parmesan cheese, grated

¼ teaspoon (0.5 g) freshly ground black pepper

Combine dressing ingredients in a jar with a tight-fitting lid and shake well. Place half of dressing in a resealable plastic bag with chicken breasts and marinate several hours. Remove chicken and discard dressing. Grill chicken until done and slice into strips. Place lettuce on plates and top with chicken. Add croutons, sprinkle with cheese and pepper. Serve with remaining dressing.

Yield: 4 servings

Per serving: 290 calories (44% from fat, 43% from protein, 13% from carbohydrate); 31 g protein; 14 g total fat; 3 g saturated fat; 8 g monounsaturated fat; 2 g polyunsaturated fat; 9 g carbohydrate; 2 g fiber; 1 g sugar; 304 mg phosphorus; 117 mg calcium; 2 mg iron; 235 mg sodium; 531 mg potassium; 4992 IU vitamin A; 14 mg ATE vitamin E; 25 mg vitamin C; 71 mg cholesterol; 178 g water

Asian-Flavored Chicken Salad

A great use for leftover chicken, whether roasted, grilled, or smoked.

6 cups (120 g) iceberg lettuce, torn into bite-sized pieces

¼ cup (25 g) scallions, sliced

½ cup (30 g) cilantro, chopped

½ cup (30 g) fresh parsley, chopped

½ cup (50 g) celery, sliced

¼ cup (60 ml) rice vinegar

1 tablespoon (15 ml) sesame oil

¼ cup (60 ml) Dick's Reduced-Sodium Soy Sauce (see recipe page 30)

1 tablespoon (8 g) sesame seeds

2 cups (220 g) cooked chicken breast, chopped

½ cup (100 g) mandarin oranges

¼ cup (31 g) slivered almonds

Chop lettuce, scallions, cilantro, parsley, and celery and toss together. For dressing, combine vinegar, sesame oil, soy sauce, and sesame seeds. Marinate the chopped chicken in the dressing for a few hours or overnight. Just before serving, add oranges, almonds, and chicken with dressing to salad. Toss well.

Yield: 4 servings

Per serving: 247 calories (15% from fat, 16% from protein, 68% from carbohydrate); 25 g protein; 11 g total fat; 2 g saturated fat; 5 g monounsaturated fat; 5 g polyunsaturated fat; 108 g carbohydrate; 3 g fiber; 8 g sugar; 253 mg phosphorus; 89 mg calcium; 2 mg iron; 188 mg sodium; 608 mg potassium; 1935 IU vitamin A; 4 mg ATE vitamin E; 27 mg vitamin C; 60 mg cholesterol; 241 g water

Curried Broccoli and Tomato Salad

A nice change of pace, with the broccoli and curry flavors adding an unusual twist.

½ pound (225 g) broccoli florets

1 cup (230 g) fat-free sour cream

¼ cup (60 ml) skim milk

½ teaspoon (1 g) curry powder

¼ teaspoon (0.8 g) dry mustard

2½ cups (50 g) lettuce

3 cups (540 g) tomatoes, cut in wedges

Steam broccoli for 5 minutes, or until crisp-tender. Drain and cool. Combine sour cream, milk, curry powder, and mustard. Pour over broccoli and refrigerate for 2 to 3 hours. To serve, divide lettuce between plates and arrange tomatoes and broccoli on top.

Yield: 5 servings

Per serving: 108 calories (8% from fat, 27% from protein, 65% from carbohydrate); 4 g protein; 1 g total fat; 0 g saturated fat; 0 g monounsaturated fat; 0 g polyunsaturated fat; 10 g carbohydrate; 1 g fiber; 1 g sugar; 119 mg phosphorus; 102 mg calcium; 1 mg iron; 51 mg sodium; 486 mg potassium; 2307 IU vitamin A; 56 mg ATE vitamin E; 67 mg vitamin C; 19 mg cholesterol; 209 g water

Black Bean Salad

This is a main-dish salad, with black beans and smoked turkey. If you don't have any smoked turkey, regular leftover turkey breast will do just as well. This salad has a lot of flavor, and the curry powder adds color. I use a fat-free vinaigrette dressing and don't miss the oil at all.

¾ cup (188 g) dried black beans

¾ cup (188 g) dried black-eyed peas

1 cup (160 g) onion, chopped

2 cups (225 g) smoked turkey breast

1 cup (235 ml) low fat Italian salad dressing

(continued on page 246)

1 cup (100 g) scallions, chopped

1⅓ cups (200 g) red bell pepper, chopped

1¼ cups (205 g) frozen corn, thawed

¼ cup (15 g) cilantro, chopped

2 teaspoons (4 g) curry powder

½ teaspoon (0.6 g) red pepper flakes

Place beans and peas in separate saucepans. Cover with water. Add half of onion to each. Bring to a boil and boil for 1 minute. Remove from heat, cover, and let stand for 1 hour. Add additional water to saucepans if needed. Divide turkey between pans. Simmer one hour or until beans are tender. Drain. Combine beans, black-eyed peas, and turkey in a large bowl. Pour Italian dressing over while hot. Add scallions, red bell pepper, corn, cilantro, curry powder, and red pepper flakes. Toss to mix. Cover and refrigerate overnight or serve warm.

Yield: 8 servings

Per serving: 161 calories (19% from fat, 36% from protein, 45% from carbohydrate); 15 g protein; 4 g total fat; 1 g saturated fat; 1 g monounsaturated fat; 1 g polyunsaturated fat; 19 g carbohydrate; 4 g fiber; 5 g sugar; 156 mg phosphorus; 37 mg calcium; 2 mg iron; 439 mg sodium; 421 mg potassium; 1059 IU vitamin A; 0 mg ATE vitamin E; 37 mg vitamin C; 26 mg cholesterol; 143 g water

Grilled Vegetable Orzo Salad

We made this to have with a grilled chicken breast, thinking we might as well put the rest of the grill to use while it was on. The leftovers provided lunch for several days.

1 cup (124 g) zucchini, cut into 1-inch (2.5-cm) cubes

½ cup (75 g) red bell pepper, cut into 1-inch (2.5-cm) cubes

½ cup (75 g) yellow bell pepper, cut into 1-inch (2.5-cm) cubes

1 cup (160 g) red onion, cut into 1-inch (2.5-cm) cubes

½ teaspoon (1.5 g) minced garlic

3 tablespoons (45 ml) olive oil, divided

1 teaspoon (2 g) freshly ground black pepper, divided

8 ounces (225 g) orzo

⅓ cup (80 ml) lemon juice

¼ cup (35 g) pine nuts, toasted

Prepare the grill. Toss zucchini, bell peppers, onion, and garlic with 1 tablespoon (15 ml) olive oil and ½ teaspoon (1 g) pepper in a large bowl. Transfer to a grill basket. Grill for 15 to 20 minutes, or until browned, stirring occasionally. Meanwhile, cook the orzo according to package directions. Drain and transfer to a large serving bowl. Add the roasted vegetables to the pasta. Combine the lemon juice and remaining olive oil and pepper and pour on the pasta and vegetables. Let cool to room temperature. Stir in the pine nuts.

Yield: 8 servings

Per serving: 201 calories (37% from fat, 10% from protein, 53% from carbohydrate); 5 g protein; 9 g total fat; 1 g saturated fat; 5 g monounsaturated fat; 2 g polyunsaturated fat; 27 g carbohydrate; 2 g fiber; 3 g sugar; 99 mg phosphorus; 19 mg calcium; 2 mg iron; 5 mg sodium; 244 mg potassium; 373 IU vitamin A; 0 mg ATE vitamin E; 63 mg vitamin C; 0 mg cholesterol; 75 g water

Roasted Corn Salad

I know this one sounds a little strange, but it turned out really well. It has a sort of Mexican flavor.

4 ears corn

¼ cup (38 g) red bell pepper, chopped

¼ cup (40 g) onion, chopped

2 tablespoons (30 ml) honey

¼ cup (60 ml) lime juice

1 tablespoon (4 g) fresh coriander

¼ teaspoon (0.6 g) cumin

Husk and clean corn. Wrap in aluminum foil. Grill over medium heat until tender, turning often. Cut corn from cobs. Stir in pepper and onion. Mix together remaining ingredients. Pour over vegetables. Stir to mix. Refrigerate at least 2 hours or overnight before serving.

Yield: 4 servings

(continued on page 248)

Per serving: 101 calories (3% from fat, 8% from protein, 89% from carbohydrate); 2 g protein; 0 g total fat; 0 g saturated fat; 0 g monounsaturated fat; 0 g polyunsaturated fat; 26 g carbohydrate; 2 g fiber; 12 g sugar; 51 mg phosphorus; 15 mg calcium; 1 mg iron; 6 mg sodium; 184 mg potassium; 329 IU vitamin A; 0 mg ATE vitamin E; 22 mg vitamin C; 0 mg cholesterol; 88 g water

Spinach Salad

This different kind of salad recipe comes from one of my wife's co-workers. It is a request for every luncheon and get-together they have, and it's easy to understand why. We made a main dish out of it by topping it with some grilled boneless chicken breast that had been marinating in extra dressing.

For Salad:
½ pound (225 g) spinach

½ pound (225 g) strawberries, hulled and halved

¼ cup (40 g) red onion, sliced

½ cup (50 g) cucumber, sliced

⅓ cup (30 g) almonds, sliced

For Dressing:
1 lemon

2 tablespoons (30 ml) white wine vinegar

1 tablespoon (15 ml) olive oil

⅓ cup (68 g) sugar

Combine salad ingredients. Zest the lemon and squeeze juice into a small bowl. Mix juice with other dressing ingredients. Toss salad and dressing just before serving.

Yield: 6 servings

Per serving: 142 calories (39% from fat, 10% from protein, 51% from carbohydrate); 4 g protein; 7 g total fat; 1 g saturated fat; 4 g monounsaturated fat; 1 g polyunsaturated fat; 20 g carbohydrate; 3 g fiber; 14 g sugar; 73 mg phosphorus; 87 mg calcium; 1 mg iron; 40 mg sodium; 267 mg potassium; 4576 IU vitamin A; 0 mg ATE vitamin E; 29 mg vitamin C; 0 mg cholesterol; 96 g water

Tofu Salad

Fresh Asian-style vegetables and tofu along with an Asian dressing give this main-dish salad a different kind of flavor.

For Salad:

½ pound (225 g) lettuce, shredded

4 ounces (115 g) snow peas

½ cup (65 g) carrot, shredded

1 cup (70 g) cabbage, shredded

½ cup (35 g) mushrooms, sliced

½ cup (75 g) red bell pepper, sliced

4 ounces (115 g) mung bean sprouts

½ cup (90 g) tomato, sliced

12 ounces (340 g) tofu, drained and cubed

For Dressing:

1 tablespoon (15 ml) rice vinegar

2 tablespoons (30 ml) sesame oil

3 tablespoons (45 ml) Dick's Reduced-Sodium Soy Sauce (see recipe page 30)

2 cloves garlic, crushed

1 tablespoon (8 g) sesame seeds

½ teaspoon (0.9 g) ground ginger

To make the salad: Toss salad ingredients.

To make the dressing: Combine dressing ingredients and spoon dressing over salad.

Yield: 6 servings

Per serving: 111 calories (19% from fat, 7% from protein, 75% from carbohydrate); 5 g protein; 6 g total fat; 1 g saturated fat; 2 g monounsaturated fat; 4 g polyunsaturated fat; 57 g carbohydrate; 3 g fiber; 5 g sugar; 92 mg phosphorus; 55 mg calcium; 1 mg iron; 72 mg sodium; 365 mg potassium; 2728 IU vitamin A; 0 mg ATE vitamin E; 38 mg vitamin C; 0 mg cholesterol; 185 g water

Coleslaw

This makes a fairly sour slaw, which is just fine with me, especially if you are planning to put it on barbecue sandwiches. You could add more sugar or a little honey if you like it sweeter.

2 cups (140 g) cabbage, shredded

⅓ cup (40 g) carrot, shredded

¼ cup (56 g) low fat mayonnaise

¼ cup (60 g) fat-free sour cream

2 tablespoons (30 ml) vinegar

2 tablespoons (26 g) sugar

¼ teaspoon (0.5 g) celery seed

¼ teaspoon (0.8 g) onion powder

Stir dressing ingredients together. Pour over cabbage and stir to mix.

Yield: 6 servings

Per serving: 75 calories (46% from fat, 5% from protein, 49% from carbohydrate); 1 g protein; 3 g total fat; 1 g saturated fat; 0 g monounsaturated fat; 0 g polyunsaturated fat; 8 g carbohydrate; 1 g fiber; 6 g sugar; 27 mg phosphorus; 28 mg calcium; 0 mg iron; 95 mg sodium; 97 mg potassium; 1281 IU vitamin A; 10 mg ATE vitamin E; 11 mg vitamin C; 7 mg cholesterol; 52 g water

Reduced-Fat Potato Salad

Time for a little picnic stuff. Feel free to vary the vegetables to whatever suits you best.

6 medium potatoes

½ cup (115 g) low fat mayonnaise

¼ cup (60 g) fat-free sour cream

2 teaspoons (6 g) dry mustard

1 teaspoon (3 g) onion powder

2 tablespoons (30 ml) honey

½ teaspoon (1 g) black pepper

1 tablespoon (0.4 g) dried parsley

½ teaspoon (1 g) celery seed

¼ teaspoon (0.3 g) dried dill

¼ cup (37 g) green bell pepper, chopped

¼ cup (25 g) celery, sliced

½ cup (65 g) carrot, sliced

TIP *Unless you have very small potatoes to boil whole, cut them into smaller pieces before cooking.*

Boil potatoes until done. Rinse in cold water and allow to cool. Mix together mayonnaise, sour cream, mustard, onion powder, honey, black pepper, parsley, celery seed, and dill. Pour over potatoes and stir to coat. Fold in green bell pepper, celery, and carrot.

Yield: 6 servings

Per serving: 371 calories (18% from fat, 8% from protein, 74% from carbohydrate); 8 g protein; 7 g total fat; 1 g saturated fat; 0 g monounsaturated fat; 0 g polyunsaturated fat; 69 g carbohydrate; 7 g fiber; 11 g sugar; 256 mg phosphorus; 63 mg calcium; 3 mg iron; 198 mg sodium; 1778 mg potassium; 1993 IU vitamin A; 10 mg ATE vitamin E; 39 mg vitamin C; 11 mg cholesterol; 339 g water

Tomato Pasta Salad

A cool and pleasing side dish with a simple dressing.

2 cups (300 g) dried pasta

1 cup (230 g) fat-free sour cream

¼ cup (60 ml) skim milk

1 tablespoon (4 g) fresh dill

1 tablespoon (15 ml) vinegar

½ teaspoon (1 g) black pepper

2 cups (270 g) cucumber, chopped

2 cups (360 g) tomatoes, chopped

Cook pasta in boiling salted water until al dente. Drain and rinse in cold water. Transfer cooked pasta to a large serving bowl. In a separate bowl, mix together sour cream, milk, dill, vinegar, and pepper. Set dressing aside. Mix cucumbers and tomatoes into the pasta. Pour dressing over pasta mixture and toss thoroughly to combine. Cover, and refrigerate at least 1 hour and preferably overnight. Stir just before serving.

Yield: 8 servings

Per serving: 91 calories (9% from fat, 19% from protein, 72% from carbohydrate); 3 g protein; 1 g total fat; 0 g saturated fat; 0 g monounsaturated fat; 0 g polyunsaturated fat; 11 g carbohydrate; 1 g fiber; 1 g sugar; 76 mg phosphorus; 57 mg calcium; 1 mg iron; 23 mg sodium; 211 mg potassium; 409 IU vitamin A; 35 mg ATE vitamin E; 11 mg vitamin C; 19 mg cholesterol; 92 g water

Garbanzo and Pasta Salad

Garbanzo beans can be purchased dried or canned. If using dried beans, cook according to package directions. For canned beans, be sure to drain and rinse them before using.

4 ounces (115 g) pasta

2 cups (480 g) cooked garbanzo beans

½ cup (75 g) red bell pepper, chopped

⅓ cup (33 g) celery, sliced

⅓ cup (43 g) carrot, sliced

¼ cup (25 g) scallions, chopped

3 tablespoons (45 ml) balsamic vinegar

2 tablespoons (28 g) low fat mayonnaise

2 teaspoons (10 g) mustard

½ teaspoon (1 g) black pepper

¼ teaspoon (0.2 g) dried Italian seasoning

4 cups (80 g) leaf lettuce, torn into bite-sized pieces

TIP *This recipe can also be used as a vegetarian main dish, yielding 4 servings.*

Cook pasta according to directions, omitting salt. Drain and rinse well under cold water until pasta is cool; drain well. Combine pasta, garbanzo beans, red bell pepper, celery, carrot, and scallions in medium bowl. Whisk together vinegar, mayonnaise, mustard, black pepper, and Italian seasoning in small bowl until blended. Pour over salad; toss to coat evenly. Cover and refrigerate up to 8 hours. Arrange lettuce on individual plates. Spoon salad over lettuce.

Yield: 8 servings

Per serving: 150 calories (16% from fat, 15% from protein, 69% from carbohydrate); 6 g protein; 3 g total fat; 0 g saturated fat; 0 g monounsaturated fat; 1 g polyunsaturated fat; 26 g carbohydrate; 4 g fiber; 1 g sugar; 103 mg phosphorus; 39 mg calcium; 1 mg iron; 226 mg sodium; 239 mg potassium; 2589 IU vitamin A; 2 mg ATE vitamin E; 18 mg vitamin C; 13 mg cholesterol; 87 g water

12

Potatoes, Pasta, and Rice

Starches like potatoes, pasta, and rice are not, by themselves, bad for you. However, the way they are prepared can affect how healthy they are. This chapter has a selection of recipes that will give you variety in your meals and still be heart-healthy. Just as a note here, I have converted almost totally to using whole-grain pasta and brown rice. This not only provides an extra whole-grain nutrition and fiber boost, but I've discovered that I actually prefer the taste.

Grilled Potatoes

This makes a very tasty variation on baked potatoes when you grill a steak or chops. It can also be cooked in the oven those days when you aren't firing up the grill.

4 potatoes

1 onion, sliced

Scrub potatoes and make 2 or 3 crosswise slices almost through. Place an onion slice in each cut. Wrap potatoes in heavy-duty foil and grill for 30 to 45 minutes, or until done.

Yield: 4 servings

Per serving: 274 calories (2% from fat, 10% from protein, 88% from carbohydrate); 7 g protein; 1 g total fat; 0 g saturated fat; 0 g monounsaturated fat; 0 g polyunsaturated fat; 62 g carbohydrate; 7 g fiber; 5 g sugar; 237 mg phosphorus; 46 mg calcium; 3 mg iron; 24 mg sodium; 1737 mg potassium; 27 IU vitamin A; 0 mg ATE vitamin E; 35 mg vitamin C; 0 mg cholesterol; 334 g water

Baked Fried Potatoes

Instead of French fries, make these baked fries. The texture and taste is similar to the frozen steak fries in the supermarket.

4 large potatoes

1 tablespoon (15 ml) olive oil

Preheat oven to 400°F (200°C, or gas mark 6). Scrub potatoes. Cut each in half lengthwise. Cut each half into 4 spears. Place potatoes in a large pot of boiling water, bring water back to a boil, and boil for 3 minutes. Drain in a colander. Coat a cooking sheet with nonstick vegetable oil spray. Mix the olive oil and potatoes in bowl and toss to coat. Bake for 15 minutes, or until tender. Drain on paper towels.

Yield: 4 servings

TIP *You can vary these with any combination of herbs and spices that appeal to you. Just toss them with the potatoes after coating them in the oil.*

Per serving: 288 calories (12% from fat, 9% from protein, 79% from carbohydrate); 7 g protein; 4 g total fat; 1 g saturated fat; 2 g monounsaturated fat; 1 g polyunsaturated fat; 59 g carbohydrate; 6 g fiber; 4 g sugar; 225 mg phosphorus; 37 mg calcium; 3 mg iron; 22 mg sodium; 1679 mg potassium; 26 IU vitamin A; 0 mg ATE vitamin E; 32 mg vitamin C; 0 mg cholesterol; 299 g water

Potato Pie

This is a great side dish—sort of a cross between scalloped potatoes and macaroni and cheese.

2 large potatoes, peeled and shredded

6 ounces (170 g) shredded low fat cheddar cheese, divided

½ cup (120 ml) skim milk

½ cup (80 g) onion, chopped

½ teaspoon (1 g) black pepper

1 cup (235 ml) egg substitute

Preheat oven to 350°F (180°C, or gas mark 4). Spray a 9-inch (23-cm) pie plate with nonstick vegetable oil spray. Mix potatoes and ½ cup (58 g) cheese. Press into bottom and up sides of prepared pie plate. Stir onion, pepper, remaining cheese, and egg substitute together. Pour into crust. Bake for 45 to 50 minutes, or until a knife inserted near the center comes out clean. Let stand 5 minutes before serving.

Yield: 6 servings

Per serving: 184 calories (18% from fat, 33% from protein, 49% from carbohydrate); 15 g protein; 4 g total fat; 2 g saturated fat; 1 g monounsaturated fat; 1 g polyunsaturated fat; 23 g carbohydrate; 2 g fiber; 2 g sugar; 290 mg phosphorus; 185 mg calcium; 2 mg iron; 268 mg sodium; 775 mg potassium; 260 IU vitamin A; 30 mg ATE vitamin E; 12 mg vitamin C; 7 mg cholesterol; 182 g water

Italian Potato Bake

Although we don't usually think of potatoes as Italian food, this potato casserole will change your mind. It's a great side dish with just a piece of grilled meat.

6 large potatoes

2 tablespoons (30 ml) canola oil

½ cup (80 g) chopped onions

½ teaspoon (0.4 g) dried basil

¼ teaspoon (0.5 g) black pepper

1 tablespoon (2.1 g) Italian seasoning

8 ounces (225 g) part-skim mozzarella, shredded

2 cups (470 ml) egg substitute

Preheat oven to 400°F (200°C, or gas mark 6). Peel potatoes and dice into large pieces. Boil potatoes until almost done. Heat oil in a frying pan over medium-high heat. Add potatoes, onion, basil, pepper, and Italian seasoning. Sauté and stir until potatoes are tender and lightly browned, like hash browns. Spray a casserole dish with nonstick vegetable oil spray. Layer potatoes in the bottom of the dish. Sprinkle mozzarella over the top. Pour egg substitute into casserole dish to cover the potatoes. Bake for approximately 40 minutes, or until eggs are done in the middle. Remove from oven and serve hot.

Yield: 8 servings

Per serving: 355 calories (26% from fat, 22% from protein, 52% from carbohydrate); 20 g protein; 11 g total fat; 4 g saturated fat; 4 g monounsaturated fat; 2 g polyunsaturated fat; 46 g carbohydrate; 5 g fiber; 4 g sugar; 380 mg phosphorus; 292 mg calcium; 4 mg iron; 304 mg sodium; 1513 mg potassium; 415 IU vitamin A; 35 mg ATE vitamin E; 25 mg vitamin C; 19 mg cholesterol; 300 g water

Baked Potato Casserole

This is a casserole version of hot-topped potatoes. It makes a nice presentation and allows everyone to take exactly how much they want.

6 large potatoes

6 slices low sodium bacon, cooked, drained, and crumbled

1 cup (115 g) low fat cheddar cheese, shredded

2 cups (300 g) frozen broccoli, thawed

¼ cup (25 g) scallions, sliced

Preheat oven to 350°F (180°C, or gas mark 4). Boil, bake, or microwave the potatoes until tender. Cut potatoes in half, leaving the skins on, and arrange in a large casserole dish. Press down with a fork. Spread bacon bits over potatoes. Boil or steam broccoli, chop, and add to top of casserole. Spread grated cheese over top. Bake for 20 to 25 minutes or until hot and cheese is melted. Garnish with scallions.

Yield: 6 servings

Per serving: 351 calories (14% from fat, 18% from protein, 68% from carbohydrate); 16 g protein; 6 g total fat; 2 g saturated fat; 2 g monounsaturated fat; 1 g polyunsaturated fat; 62 g carbohydrate; 7 g fiber; 4 g sugar; 396 mg phosphorus; 146 mg calcium; 3 mg iron; 250 mg sodium; 1846 mg potassium; 305 IU vitamin A; 14 mg ATE vitamin E; 60 mg vitamin C; 13 mg cholesterol; 344 g water

Fat-Free Mashed Potatoes

These make a flavorful addition to any meal, spicing up a piece of plain grilled meat.

4 medium red potatoes

½ teaspoon (1.5 g) roasted garlic

2 tablespoons (30 g) fat-free cream cheese

¼ cup (60 ml) skim milk

1 teaspoon (1 g) chives

1 tablespoon (4 g) fresh parsley, chopped.

TIP *If you don't want to roast your own garlic, you can find jars of it in the fresh vegetable sections of many large grocery stores.*

Cube the potatoes (you may peel them or leave unpeeled). Place in a saucepan of water, bring to a boil, and simmer until potatoes are soft, but not mushy. Drain very well. Place potatoes in a large mixing bowl; add garlic, cream cheese, and milk. Beat mixture until it reaches desired consistency, adding more milk if needed, then add the chives and parsley and mix well.

Yield: 4 servings

Per serving: 139 calories (2% from fat, 12% from protein, 86% from carbohydrate); 4 g protein; 0 g total fat; 0 g saturated fat; 0 g monounsaturated fat; 0 g polyunsaturated fat; 28 g carbohydrate; 5 g fiber; 1 g sugar; 88 mg phosphorus; 52 mg calcium; 4 mg iron; 44 mg sodium; 380 mg potassium; 178 IU vitamin A; 23 mg ATE vitamin E; 10 mg vitamin C; 5 mg cholesterol; 47 g water

Slow-Cooker Scalloped Potatoes

Another one of those classic comfort foods. In this version, I simplify the preparation by using the slow cooker to create tender, creamy potatoes.

2 cups (470 ml) water

1 teaspoon (3 g) cream of tartar

5 medium potatoes, thinly sliced

¼ cup (30 g) all-purpose flour

⅛ teaspoon (0.3 g) freshly ground black pepper

1½ cups (355 ml) skim milk

1 cup (115 g) low fat cheddar cheese, shredded

Combine water and cream of tartar in large bowl. Stir. Add potatoes and stir well. This will help keep potatoes from darkening. Drain. Pour potatoes into a slow cooker. Stir flour and pepper together in a saucepan. Whisk in milk gradually until no lumps remain. Heat and stir until boiling and thickened. Stir in cheese to melt. Pour over potatoes in cooker. Cover. Cook on low for 6 to 8 hours.

Yield: 6 servings

Per serving: 305 calories (6% from fat, 19% from protein, 75% from carbohydrate); 14 g protein; 2 g total fat; 1 g saturated fat; 1 g monounsaturated fat; 0 g polyunsaturated fat; 57 g carbohydrate; 5 g fiber; 4 g sugar; 360 mg phosphorus; 205 mg calcium; 2 mg iron; 204 mg sodium; 1573 mg potassium; 195 IU vitamin A; 51 mg ATE vitamin E; 32 mg vitamin C; 6 mg cholesterol; 339 g water

German Potato Bake

The flavor of German potato salad in casserole. Great with pork or chicken.

6 slices low sodium bacon

2 tablespoons (16 g) flour

¼ cup (60 ml) cider vinegar

2 cups (470 ml) low sodium chicken broth

2 tablespoons (30 g) brown sugar

¼ cup (25 g) scallions, sliced diagonally

¼ teaspoon (0.5 g) celery seed

6 medium potatoes, cooked and sliced

Preheat oven to 400°F (200°C, or gas mark 6). In a skillet, cook bacon until crisp; remove to a paper towel-lined plate to drain. Wipe out skillet. Shake flour and vinegar together in a jar with a tight-fitting lid until dissolved. Pour into skillet and add remaining ingredients except potatoes. Cook, stirring until thickened. In 1½-quart (1.4-L) shallow baking dish arrange potatoes; pour broth mixture over the top. Bake for 30 minutes. Garnish with bacon.

Yield: 6 servings

Per serving: 345 calories (11% from fat, 13% from protein, 75% from carbohydrate); 12 g protein; 4 g total fat; 1 g saturated fat; 2 g monounsaturated fat; 1 g polyunsaturated fat; 67 g carbohydrate; 6 g fiber; 8 g sugar; 298 mg phosphorus; 51 mg calcium; 3 mg iron; 132 mg sodium; 1832 mg potassium; 70 IU vitamin A; 1 mg ATE vitamin E; 33 mg vitamin C; 9 mg cholesterol; 390 g water

Spicy Baked French Fries

Southwestern flavors blend with spicy mustard for a zippy alternative to deep-fried fries. Feel free to increase the cayenne, red pepper, and chili powder if you like them spicier.

2 tablespoons (30 ml) olive oil

2 tablespoons (30 ml) lime juice

½ teaspoon (1.5 g) minced garlic

½ teaspoon (0.6 g) red pepper flakes

¼ teaspoon (0.5 g) cayenne pepper

1 teaspoon (2.6 g) chili powder

2 tablespoons (30 g) mustard

½ teaspoon (1 g) black pepper

4 medium potatoes, peeled and cut into ¼ inch (63 mm)–thick fries

Preheat oven to 400°F (200°C, or gas mark 6). In a large bowl, stir together the olive oil, lime juice, garlic, red pepper flakes, cayenne pepper, chili powder, mustard, and pepper. Add the potato slices, and stir until evenly coated. Arrange fries in a single layer on a large baking sheet. Bake for 20 minutes. Turn the fries over and continue to bake for 10 to 15 more minutes, or until crispy and browned.

Yield: 6 servings

Per serving: 221 calories (21% from fat, 9% from protein, 70% from carbohydrate); 5 g protein; 5 g total fat; 1 g saturated fat; 3 g monounsaturated fat; 1 g polyunsaturated fat; 40 g carbohydrate; 4 g fiber; 3 g sugar; 153 mg phosphorus; 31 mg calcium; 2 mg iron; 19 mg sodium; 1150 mg potassium; 239 IU vitamin A; 0 mg ATE vitamin E; 23 mg vitamin C; 0 mg cholesterol; 204 g water

Sweet Potato Fries

Try these instead of regular French fries. Sweet potatoes are lower in carbohydrates and are particularly rich in vitamin A. The egg coating that makes them nice and crisp can be used for regular potatoes too.

3 sweet potatoes

2 tablespoons (30 ml) egg substitute

¼ teaspoon (0.6 g) cinnamon

Preheat oven to 450°F (230°C, or gas mark 8). Cut potatoes into strips. In a bowl, beat together the egg substitute and cinnamon until frothy. Stir in potatoes and toss to coat well. Spread in a single layer on a baking sheet coated with nonstick vegetable oil spray. Bake for 20 to 25 minutes, or until crispy on the outside and soft inside.

Yield: 6 servings

Per serving: 62 calories (4% from fat, 11% from protein, 85% from carbohydrate); 2 g protein; 0 g total fat; 0 g saturated fat; 0 g monounsaturated fat; 0 g polyunsaturated fat; 13 g carbohydrate; 2 g fiber; 4 g sugar; 31 mg phosphorus; 24 mg calcium; 1 mg iron; 30 mg sodium; 191 mg potassium; 11903 IU vitamin A; 0 mg ATE vitamin E; 10 mg vitamin C; 0 mg cholesterol; 65 g water

Brown Rice Pilaf

When I make something like this, it makes me wonder why I don't cook brown rice more often. It has such a nice flavor and crunchy texture. And it's so simple.

2 cups (470 ml) low sodium chicken broth

½ cup (120 ml) water

1 cup (190 g) brown rice

2 tablespoons (20 g) minced onion

⅛ teaspoon (0.4 g) garlic powder

Place broth and water in a saucepan. Bring to boil. Add rice, onion, and garlic powder. Reduce heat, cover, and simmer for 45 minutes or until rice is done.

Yield: 4 servings

Per serving: 199 calories (9% from fat, 13% from protein, 78% from carbohydrate); 6 g protein; 2 g total fat; 0 g saturated fat; 1 g monounsaturated fat; 1 g polyunsaturated fat; 39 g carbohydrate; 2 g fiber; 1 g sugar; 198 mg phosphorus; 23 mg calcium; 1 mg iron; 41 mg sodium; 248 mg potassium; 1 IU vitamin A; 0 mg ATE vitamin E; 2 mg vitamin C; 0 mg cholesterol; 150 g water

Herbed Brown Rice

Flavored with dill and thyme, this is great with fish.

2 tablespoons (30 ml) olive oil

1 cup (160 g) onion, chopped

½ teaspoon (1.5 g) chopped garlic

1 cup (190 g) brown rice

2½ cups (590 ml) water

2 teaspoons (2 g) dried dill

½ teaspoon (0.7 g) thyme

½ teaspoon (1 g) black pepper

In a medium pot, heat the oil. Add onions, garlic, and rice, and sauté for 5 minutes, stirring frequently. Add the water, dill, thyme, and pepper. Stir until well combined. Bring to a boil, then reduce heat and simmer, covered, for 40 minutes, or until the water is absorbed. After 30 minutes, check to see if there is a lot of water left in the pot; if so, remove the cover for the remainder of the cooking time. Let the cooked rice stand in the pot, covered, for 15 minutes.

Yield: 4 servings

Per serving: 250 calories (29% from fat, 7% from protein, 64% from carbohydrate); 4 g protein; 8 g total fat; 1 g saturated fat; 5 g monounsaturated fat; 1 g polyunsaturated fat; 40 g carbohydrate; 2 g fiber; 2 g sugar; 170 mg phosphorus; 38 mg calcium; 1 mg iron; 11 mg sodium; 186 mg potassium; 37 IU vitamin A; 0 mg ATE vitamin E; 3 mg vitamin C; 0 mg cholesterol; 188 g water

Brown Rice with Spinach

Baked brown rice and spinach, with just enough cheese to add a little extra flavor.

1 cup (190 g) brown rice

1 pound (455 g) fresh spinach

1 tablespoon (15 ml) olive oil

¾ cup (120 g) onion, minced

¼ teaspoon (0.8 g) minced garlic

1 teaspoon (1 g) dried thyme, chopped

¼ cup (15 g) minced fresh parsley

¼ cup (30 g) low fat provolone cheese, shredded

¾ cup (180 ml) egg substitute

Preheat oven to 350°F (180°C, or gas mark 4). Cook rice according to package directions until tender but still undercooked (about 30 minutes). Drain, rinse with cold water, drain again, and set aside. Wash spinach and remove stems. In a large skillet, cook the spinach in the water that clings to the leaves until the spinach is wilted. Remove from skillet, cool, and chop coarsely. In the same skillet, heat the oil and sauté the onion until softened. Add the garlic and thyme. Combine the rice, spinach, onion mixture, parsley, provolone, and egg substitute. Coat a 1½-quart (1.4 L) baking dish with nonstick vegetable oil spray and add the spinach mixture. Cover with foil and bake for 25 minutes. Remove foil and cook for 5 minutes more.

Yield: 4 servings

Per serving: 320 calories (23% from fat, 21% from protein, 57% from carbohydrate); 16 g protein; 8 g total fat; 2 g saturated fat; 4 g monounsaturated fat; 2 g polyunsaturated fat; 45 g carbohydrate; 7 g fiber; 3 g sugar; 320 mg phosphorus; 289 mg calcium; 5 mg iron; 272 mg sodium; 680 mg potassium; 14245 IU vitamin A; 19 mg ATE vitamin E; 10 mg vitamin C; 6 mg cholesterol; 178 g water

Wild Rice and Fruit Pilaf

This sounds like a holiday sort of recipe, but it would be good any time of year.

2 cups (470 ml) low sodium chicken broth

1 cup (160 g) uncooked wild rice, rinsed

1 tablespoon (15 ml) olive oil

1 cup (160 g) onion, sliced in thin wedges

2 teaspoons (10 g) brown sugar, firmly packed

¼ cup (38 g) golden raisins

¼ cup (38 g) dried cranberries

¼ cup (60 ml) orange juice

1 teaspoon (1.7 g) orange peel

¼ teaspoon (0.5 g) white pepper

Combine chicken broth and wild rice in a medium saucepan; bring to a boil. Reduce heat, cover, and simmer for 40 minutes, or until rice is almost tender. Heat the oil in a small saucepan and sauté onion and brown sugar. Cook for 10 minutes, stirring occasionally, until onion is tender and lightly browned. Add cooked onions, raisins, cranberries, orange juice, orange peel, and pepper to rice mixture. Cover and simmer for 10 minutes, or until rice is tender.

Yield: 6 servings

Per serving: 186 calories (15% from fat, 13% from protein, 73% from carbohydrate); 6 g protein; 3 g total fat; 1 g saturated fat; 2 g monounsaturated fat; 1 g polyunsaturated fat; 36 g carbohydrate; 3 g fiber; 11 g sugar; 157 mg phosphorus; 22 mg calcium; 1 mg iron; 29 mg sodium; 301 mg potassium; 15 IU vitamin A; 0 mg ATE vitamin E; 6 mg vitamin C; 0 mg cholesterol; 114 g water

Vegetable Paella

This would be a good dish to try for those people who think they don't like vegetarian cooking. It has plenty of flavor and substance to satisfy.

2 tablespoons (30 ml) olive oil

1¼ cups (240 g) brown rice

1 cup (160 g) onion, sliced

2 cloves garlic, crushed

⅛ teaspoon (0.1 g) saffron

3 cups (710 ml) water

1 teaspoon (1.7 g) lemon peel

¼ teaspoon (0.5 g) freshly ground black pepper

2 cups (240 g) leeks, cut in 1-inch (2.5-cm) pieces

¼ cup (34 g) frozen peas, thawed

¼ cup (25 g) black olives

TIP *To add even more flavor and protein, sprinkle with nuts.*

Heat the oil in a large, deep pan. Add the brown rice and onion slices and stir until the rice is coated and begins to turn opaque. Add the garlic, saffron, water, lemon peel, and pepper. Mix well, then bring to a boil. Mix again to distribute the saffron. Arrange the leeks, peas, and olives on top of the rice. Bring to a boil. Cover and simmer for 45 minutes. Serve straight from the pan.

Yield: 4 servings

Per serving: 335 calories (25% from fat, 7% from protein, 67% from carbohydrate); 6 g protein; 10 g total fat; 1 g saturated fat; 6 g monounsaturated fat; 1 g polyunsaturated fat; 57 g carbohydrate; 4 g fiber; 4 g sugar; 230 mg phosphorus; 66 mg calcium; 2 mg iron; 126 mg sodium; 291 mg potassium; 987 IU vitamin A; 0 mg ATE vitamin E; 10 mg vitamin C; 0 mg cholesterol; 271 g water

Risotto with Sun-Dried Tomatoes

Every once in a while, when I'm looking for something different, I decide that risotto is worth the effort. We had this one with fish topped with a sun-dried tomato mixture. In order to get the real Italian-type risotto, you need to buy short-grained rice like Arborio.

4 cups (946 ml) low sodium chicken broth

2 tablespoons (30 ml) olive oil

½ cup (80 g) onion, chopped

½ cup (75 g) yellow bell peppers, chopped

1½ cups (300 g) Arborio rice

½ cup (120 ml) white wine

¼ cup (28 g) oil-packed sun-dried tomatoes, drained

Heat the broth in a large saucepan to almost boiling; reduce heat and keep hot. Sauté the onion and pepper in the olive oil in a large skillet or Dutch oven until softened. Add the rice and sauté until translucent, but not brown. Add the wine and simmer until liquid is almost completely absorbed. Add 1 cup (235 ml) of the broth and simmer until liquid is almost completely absorbed, stirring occasionally. Continue adding broth 1 cup (235 ml) at a time, stirring frequently and allowing it to cook until liquid is absorbed after each addition. After all broth is added, stir until rice is tender, about 20 minutes total cooking time. Stir in sun-dried tomatoes and simmer until heated through.

Yield: 4 servings

Per serving: 224 calories (40% from fat, 14% from protein, 46% from carbohydrate); 7 g protein; 9 g total fat; 2 g saturated fat; 6 g monounsaturated fat; 1 g polyunsaturated fat; 24 g carbohydrate; 1 g fiber; 2 g sugar; 131 mg phosphorus; 34 mg calcium; 2 mg iron; 94 mg sodium; 447 mg potassium; 135 IU vitamin A; 0 mg ATE vitamin E; 51 mg vitamin C; 0 mg cholesterol; 341 g water

Reduced-Fat Macaroni and Cheese

This isn't exactly the same as the boxes of macaroni and cheese. On the other hand, this recipe contains only 3 grams of saturated fat and has the nutritional advantage of having real cheese.

12 ounces (340 g) elbow macaroni

½ cup (120 ml) skim milk

1 cup (250 g) low fat ricotta cheese

¼ cup (40 g) onion, diced

¼ teaspoon (0.5 g) black pepper

1 cup (115 g) shredded low fat cheddar cheese, divided

Preheat oven to 350°F (180°C, or gas mark 4). Cook macaroni according to package directions, omitting salt. Drain. In a food processor or blender combine milk, ricotta cheese, onion, and pepper. Process until smooth. Pour into a bowl and add macaroni and ¼ cup (30 g) cheddar cheese. Mix well. Spray a 1-quart (946 ml) baking dish with nonstick vegetable oil spray. Pour in macaroni mixture and top with remaining cheese. Cover and bake for 30 minutes. Uncover and bake an additional 10 minutes.

Yield: 6 servings

Per serving: 316 calories (16% from fat, 24% from protein, 60% from carbohydrate); 18 g protein; 6 g total fat; 3 g saturated fat; 2 g monounsaturated fat; 0 g polyunsaturated fat; 47 g carbohydrate; 2 g fiber; 2 g sugar; 314 mg phosphorus; 246 mg calcium; 2 mg iron; 202 mg sodium; 240 mg potassium; 245 IU vitamin A; 69 mg ATE vitamin E; 1 mg vitamin C; 18 mg cholesterol; 74 g water

Couscous with Peppers and Onions

For anyone not familiar with couscous, it's a very small Middle Eastern pasta. It can be used as a base for curries, tomato sauces, or any number of other things, or by itself as a side dish. This variation adds a few vegetables for flavor and color.

1 tablespoon (15 ml) olive oil

¼ cup (40 g) onion, finely chopped

¼ cup (38 g) red bell pepper, finely chopped

¼ cup (25 g) celery, finely chopped

1½ cups (355 ml) low sodium chicken broth

1 cup (175 g) dry couscous

Heat oil in a skillet and sauté onion, red bell pepper, and celery until tender. In a large saucepan, bring broth to a boil. Stir in couscous and sautéed vegetables. Cover and let stand 5 minutes. Fluff with a fork before serving.

Yield: 4 servings

Per serving: 214 calories (18% from fat, 14% from protein, 68% from carbohydrate); 8 g protein; 4 g total fat; 1 g saturated fat; 3 g monounsaturated fat; 1 g polyunsaturated fat; 36 g carbohydrate; 3 g fiber; 1 g sugar; 107 mg phosphorus; 20 mg calcium; 1 mg iron; 37 mg sodium; 200 mg potassium; 320 IU vitamin A; 0 mg ATE vitamin E; 13 mg vitamin C; 0 mg cholesterol; 114 g water

Italian Orzo

This is kind of the quick-and-easy alternative to risotto. Made with rice-shaped orzo pasta, it has the same creaminess as risotto but doesn't require a half hour of stirring.

1 tablespoon (15 ml) olive oil

8 ounces (225 g) orzo

1¼ cups (300 ml) low sodium chicken broth

1¼ cups (300 ml) water

¼ cup (20 g) Parmesan cheese, shredded

1 teaspoon (0.7 g) dried basil

¼ teaspoon (0.5 g) black pepper

¼ cup (35 g) pine nuts, toasted

Heat oil in a saucepan over medium heat. Add orzo and cook for 3 minutes, stirring constantly. Stir in broth and water; bring to a boil. Reduce heat and simmer for 15 minutes, or until liquid is absorbed and orzo is done. Remove from heat; stir in Parmesan, basil, and pepper. Sprinkle with pine nuts. Serve immediately.

Yield: 6 servings

Per serving: 224 calories (32% from fat, 15% from protein, 53% from carbohydrate); 8 g protein; 8 g total fat; 2 g saturated fat; 3 g monounsaturated fat; 2 g polyunsaturated fat; 30 g carbohydrate; 1 g fiber; 1 g sugar; 150 mg phosphorus; 61 mg calcium; 2 mg iron; 83 mg sodium; 172 mg potassium; 31 IU vitamin A; 5 mg ATE vitamin E; 0 mg vitamin C; 4 mg cholesterol; 102 g water

Asian Noodles

A great Asian side dish.

8 ounces (225 g) angel hair pasta

1 tablespoon (15 ml) olive oil

½ tablespoon (8 ml) sesame oil

2 cups (140 g) cabbage, shredded

½ cup (50 g) scallions, sliced

¼ cup (60 ml) Dick's Reduced-Sodium Soy Sauce
   (see recipe page 30)

1 cup (104 g) bean sprouts, drained

TIP
You can add meat to the dish to make a complete meal.

Cook pasta according to package directions. Drain. Heat olive oil and sesame oil in a skillet. Sauté cabbage and scallions for 5 minutes. Add pasta, soy sauce, and bean sprouts and heat through.

Yield: 4 servings

Per serving: 147 calories (9% from fat, 2% from protein, 89% from carbohydrate); 3 g protein; 6 g total fat; 1 g saturated fat; 3 g monounsaturated fat; 3 g polyunsaturated fat; 118 g carbohydrate; 4 g fiber; 4 g sugar; 81 mg phosphorus; 40 mg calcium; 1 mg iron; 158 mg sodium; 174 mg potassium; 209 IU vitamin A; 0 mg ATE vitamin E; 19 mg vitamin C; 0 mg cholesterol; 141 g water

13

Side Dishes

I don't know about you, but I tend to get bored where food is concerned. Sure, you could eat plain vegetables all the time, and they would be great from a nutritional standpoint, but I like something different every once in a while. If you're like me, this chapter is for you. These recipes are just as good for you, but they aren't *ordinary*. As a bonus, if you are looking to include more meatless meals in your diet, there are several choices here that could easily be the main dish of a very satisfying meal.

Mexican Zucchini Oven Fries

These make a great alternative to French fries with a burger or other grilled meat.

2 medium zucchini

1 tablespoon (3 g) dried oregano

1 tablespoon (7 g) cumin

Preheat oven to 500°F (250°C, or gas mark 10). Cut zucchini in ¼ × 3-inch (0.6 × 7.5-cm) sticks, like French fries. Arrange zucchini on a nonstick baking sheet. Spray zucchini with nonstick vegetable oil spray. Combine oregano and cumin and sprinkle over the zucchini fries. Bake for 15 to 18 minutes. Serve hot with low sodium taco sauce or salsa for dipping.

Yield: 4 servings

Per serving: 18 calories (21% from fat, 20% from protein, 59% from carbohydrate); 1 g protein; 1 g total fat; 0 g saturated fat; 0 g monounsaturated fat; 0 g polyunsaturated fat; 3 g carbohydrate; 1 g fiber; 1 g sugar; 33 mg phosphorus; 35 mg calcium; 2 mg iron; 9 mg sodium; 202 mg potassium; 195 IU vitamin A; 0 mg ATE vitamin E; 11 mg vitamin C; 0 mg cholesterol; 59 g water

Roasted Vegetables

This is the perfect side dish with an Italian meat like the chicken breasts in Chapter 14.

2 tablespoons (30 ml) olive oil

½ teaspoon (1.5 g) minced garlic

½ teaspoon (0.4 g) dried basil

½ teaspoon (0.5 g) dried oregano

½ cup (80 g) onion, sliced into wedges

½ cup (75 g) green bell pepper, cut in 1-inch (2.5-cm) pieces

¼ cup (45 g) plum tomato halves

½ cup (56 g) zucchini, cut in 1-inch (2.5-cm) slices

½ cup (35 g) mushrooms, cut in half

Preheat oven to 400°F (200°C, or gas mark 6). Combine oil, garlic, basil, and oregano in a resealable plastic bag. Add onion, green bell pepper, tomatoes, zucchini, and mushrooms and shake to coat evenly. Coat a 9 × 13-inch (23 × 33-cm) roasting pan with nonstick vegetable oil spray. Place the vegetables in a single layer in the pan. Roast for 20 minutes, or until crisp.

Yield: 4 servings

Per serving: 79 calories (75% from fat, 5% from protein, 20% from carbohydrate); 1 g protein; 7 g total fat; 1 g saturated fat; 5 g monounsaturated fat; 1 g polyunsaturated fat; 4 g carbohydrate; 1 g fiber; 2 g sugar; 26 mg phosphorus; 15 mg calcium; 0 mg iron; 4 mg sodium; 159 mg potassium; 195 IU vitamin A; 0 mg ATE vitamin E; 21 mg vitamin C; 0 mg cholesterol; 67 g water

Green Beans and Tomatoes

A different twist on green beans. Good with grilled meat.

½ pound (225 g) green beans

1 tablespoon (15 ml) olive oil

¼ cup (38 g) red bell pepper, chopped

¼ cup (40 g) onion, chopped

1 cup (180 g) tomatoes, chopped

½ teaspoon (0.4 g) dried basil

½ teaspoon (0.6 g) dried rosemary

Cook green beans in boiling water until tender. Drain and set aside. In a skillet, heat oil and sauté red bell pepper and onion until soft. Add tomatoes, basil, and rosemary. Stir in green beans and heat through.

Yield: 4 servings

Per serving: 62 calories (48% from fat, 9% from protein, 43% from carbohydrate); 2 g protein; 4 g total fat; 1 g saturated fat; 2 g monounsaturated fat; 0 g polyunsaturated fat; 7 g carbohydrate; 3 g fiber; 2 g sugar; 36 mg phosphorus; 28 mg calcium; 1 mg iron; 8 mg sodium; 239 mg potassium; 925 IU vitamin A; 0 mg ATE vitamin E; 32 mg vitamin C; 0 mg cholesterol; 104 g water

Bean Salad

This makes a fairly traditional three-bean salad. You can use either low sodium canned kidney beans or cook dried beans ahead of time.

½ cup (120 ml) cider vinegar

¼ cup (50 g) sugar

¼ cup (60 ml) oil

¼ teaspoon (0.8 g) garlic powder

¼ teaspoon (0.5 g) black pepper

12 ounces (340 g) frozen green beans, thawed

12 ounces (340 g) frozen yellow (wax) beans, thawed

1 cup (225 g) cooked kidney beans

¼ cup (40 g) onion, diced

¼ cup (37 g) green bell peppers, diced

TIP *This will keep in the refrigerator for up to a week, but it probably won't last that long.*

Combine vinegar, sugar, oil, garlic powder, and black pepper in a saucepan. Heat until sugar melts. In a skillet, cook green, yellow, and kidney beans with onions and peppers until just tender. Combine vinegar mixture and vegetables and stir to mix. Refrigerate overnight.

Yield: 6 servings

Per serving: 194 calories (42% from fat, 9% from protein, 49% from carbohydrate); 5 g protein; 9 g total fat; 1 g saturated fat; 3 g monounsaturated fat; 5 g polyunsaturated fat; 24 g carbohydrate; 6 g fiber; 10 g sugar; 90 mg phosphorus; 54 mg calcium; 2 mg iron; 79 mg sodium; 394 mg potassium; 476 IU vitamin A; 0 mg ATE vitamin E; 24 mg vitamin C; 0 mg cholesterol; 153 g water

Vegetable-Stuffed Peppers

This dish could become a main dish with the addition of some ground turkey or cheese for protein. As it is, it makes a nice-looking, as well as tasty, side dish. The vegetable mixture, basically succotash in a pepper, can also be served alone.

2 green bell peppers

1 tablespoon (15 ml) olive oil

¼ cup (40 g) onion, chopped

6 ounces (170 g) frozen corn, thawed

2 cups (360 g) canned no-salt-added tomatoes, drained

6 ounces (170 g) frozen lima beans, thawed

¼ teaspoon (0.8 g) garlic powder

½ teaspoon (0.4 g) dried basil

½ cup (60 g) bread crumbs

Preheat oven to 350°F (180°C, or gas mark 4). Cut the green bell peppers in half lengthwise. Remove the tops and discard the seeds. Heat enough water in a saucepan to cover the peppers and boil for 3 to 5 minutes, or until just beginning to get soft. Drain. In a large skillet, heat olive oil and cook onion until soft, but not brown. Stir in corn, tomatoes, lima beans, garlic powder, and basil. Mix well. Place peppers in an 8 × 8-inch (20 × 20-cm) baking dish. Fill with vegetable mixture. Sprinkle bread crumbs on top. Bake for 20 minutes.

Yield: 4 servings

Per serving: 202 calories (20% from fat, 14% from protein, 66% from carbohydrate); 8 g protein; 5 g total fat; 1 g saturated fat; 3 g monounsaturated fat; 1 g polyunsaturated fat; 36 g carbohydrate; 7 g fiber; 8 g sugar; 136 mg phosphorus; 87 mg calcium; 3 mg iron; 132 mg sodium; 639 mg potassium; 497 IU vitamin A; 0 mg ATE vitamin E; 76 mg vitamin C; 0 mg cholesterol; 256 g water

Vegetable Bake

We were getting a little tired of the same old plain vegetables, so I threw together something a little different to have with roast beef.

12 ounces (340 g) frozen winter vegetable mix

6 ounces (170 g) brussels sprouts

1 cup (235 ml) skim milk

½ cup (115 g) fat-free sour cream

2 tablespoons (16 g) cornstarch

4 ounces (115 g) water chestnuts

2 ounces (55 g) low fat cheddar cheese, shredded

Preheat oven to 350°F (180°C, or gas mark 4). Cook winter vegetable mix and brussels sprouts according to package directions. Mix milk, sour cream, and cornstarch until blended. Cook and stir until bubbly and thickened. Stir in vegetables and water chestnuts. Sprinkle with cheese. Place in 9 × 13-inch (23 × 33-cm) baking dish and bake for 10 minutes, or until cheese is melted.

Yield: 6 servings

Per serving: 120 calories (9% from fat, 29% from protein, 62% from carbohydrate); 7 g protein; 1 g total fat; 1 g saturated fat; 0 g monounsaturated fat; 0 g polyunsaturated fat; 16 g carbohydrate; 4 g fiber; 2 g sugar; 158 mg phosphorus; 141 mg calcium; 1 mg iron; 113 mg sodium; 312 mg potassium; 2778 IU vitamin A; 51 mg ATE vitamin E; 23 mg vitamin C; 11 mg cholesterol; 131 g water

Zucchini Cakes

These are a light, flavorful way to use up some of that extra zucchini when the garden is really producing.

4 cups (500 g) zucchini, grated

½ cup (120 ml) egg substitute

¼ teaspoon (0.8 g) minced garlic

1 tablespoon (0.4 g) dried parsley

1 tablespoon (5 g) lemon zest

1 cup (115 g) bread crumbs

¼ cup (60 ml) olive oil

Stir together zucchini, egg substitute, garlic, parsley, lemon zest, and bread crumbs. Divide into 6 balls. Heat half of the oil in a large skillet. Shape 3 balls into patties about ½-inch (1.3-cm) thick. Fry until the bottom is golden, then turn and fry the other side. Repeat with remaining balls and oil.

Yield: 6 servings

Per serving: 182 calories (52% from fat, 13% from protein, 35% from carbohydrate); 6 g protein; 11 g total fat; 2 g saturated fat; 7 g monounsaturated fat; 2 g polyunsaturated fat; 16 g carbohydrate; 2 g fiber; 3 g sugar; 87 mg phosphorus; 59 mg calcium; 2mg iron; 178 mg sodium; 327 mg potassium; 294 IU vitamin A; 0 mg ATE vitamin E; 16 mg vitamin C; 0 mg cholesterol; 98 g water

Zucchini Squares

Another quiche-like recipe, featuring shredded zucchini.

2 tablespoons (30 ml) olive oil

1 cup (160 g) onion, chopped

1 teaspoon (3 g) minced garlic

¼ cup (15 g) fresh parsley, minced

½ cup (35 g) mushrooms, sliced

6 cups (745 g) zucchini, shredded

1½ cups (355 ml) egg substitute

½ cup (60 g) low fat sharp cheddar cheese, grated

1 cup (100 g) Parmesan cheese, grated

1 teaspoon (0.6 g) dried marjoram

½ cup (60 g) bread crumbs, toasted

Preheat oven to 350°F (180°C, or gas mark 4). Heat oil in a large skillet and sauté onion, garlic, parsley, and mushrooms. Add zucchini and sauté until barely softened. Mix egg substitute, cheeses, and marjoram. Add zucchini mixture to mixing bowl. Mix well and pour into a 9 × 13-inch (23 × 33-cm) glass baking dish that has been coated with nonstick vegetable oil spray. Sprinkle with bread crumbs. Bake for 30 to 40 minutes, or until a knife inserted near the center comes out clean. Allow to cool and cut into 2-inch (5-cm) squares to serve.

Yield: 35 servings

Per serving: 43 calories (45% from fat, 31% from protein, 23% from carbohydrate); 3 g protein; 2 g total fat; 1 g saturated fat; 1 g monounsaturated fat; 0 g polyunsaturated fat; 3 g carbohydrate; 0 g fiber; 1 g sugar; 56 mg phosphorus; 53 mg calcium; 0 mg iron; 88 mg sodium; 112 mg potassium; 135 IU vitamin A; 4 mg ATE vitamin E; 5 mg vitamin C; 3 mg cholesterol; 36 g water

Corn and Zucchini Bake

Something a little different in a vegetable side dish, with corn and zucchini contributing to a cheese-flavored custard.

3 cups (340 g) zucchini, sliced

1 tablespoon (15 ml) olive oil

¼ cup (40 g) onion, chopped

10 ounces (280 g) frozen corn, thawed

1 cup (110 g) low fat Swiss cheese, shredded

½ cup (120 ml) egg substitute

¼ cup (30 g) bread crumbs

2 tablespoons (13 g) Parmesan cheese, grated

Preheat oven to 350°F (180°C, or gas mark 4). Cook zucchini in boiling water until soft. Drain and mash with fork. Heat oil in a small skillet and sauté onion until soft. Combine zucchini, onion, corn, Swiss cheese, and egg substitute. Pour into a 1-quart (946 ml) casserole dish coated with nonstick vegetable oil spray. Combine bread crumbs and Parmesan, sprinkle over top. Place casserole dish on a baking sheet and bake, uncovered, for 40 minutes, or until a knife inserted near the center comes out clean.

Yield: 6 servings

Per serving: 154 calories (29% from fat, 31% from protein, 40% from carbohydrate); 12 g protein; 5 g total fat; 2 g saturated fat; 2 g monounsaturated fat; 1 g polyunsaturated fat; 16 g carbohydrate; 2 g fiber; 4 g sugar; 233 mg phosphorus; 267 mg calcium; 1 mg iron; 168 mg sodium; 347 mg potassium; 243 IU vitamin A; 11 mg ATE vitamin E; 12 mg vitamin C; 10 mg cholesterol; 132 g water

Cheesy Squash Bake

This is a great way to use extra yellow squash from the garden. It makes a good summer meal with just a simple piece of grilled chicken.

6 cups (680 g) yellow squash, sliced

1 cup (230 g) fat-free sour cream

½ cup (120 ml) egg substitute

2 tablespoons (16 g) flour

1 cup (115 g) low fat cheddar cheese, shredded

⅓ cup (38 g) bread crumbs

Preheat oven to 350°F (180°C, or gas mark 4). Slice squash and cook in boiling water until tender. Combine sour cream, egg substitute, and flour. In a 9 × 13-inch (23 × 33-cm) baking dish coated with nonstick vegetable oil spray, layer half the squash, half the egg mixture, and half the cheese. Repeat layers. Sprinkle bread crumbs on top. Bake for 20 to 25 minutes, or until set.

Yield: 8 servings

Per serving: 121 calories (21% from fat, 38% from protein, 41% from carbohydrate); 9 g protein; 2 g total fat; 1 g saturated fat; 1 g monounsaturated fat; 0 g polyunsaturated fat; 9 g carbohydrate; 1 g fiber; 2 g sugar; 169 mg phosphorus; 129 mg calcium; 1 mg iron; 176 mg sodium; 335 mg potassium; 373 IU vitamin A; 40 mg ATE vitamin E; 15 mg vitamin C; 15 mg cholesterol; 128 g water

Scalloped Zucchini

We sometimes make a meal of this by adding 1 pound (455 g) of browned ground turkey.

4 cups (500 g) zucchini, chopped

½ cup (80 g) onion, chopped

2 tablespoons (30 ml) olive oil

½ cup (50 g) Parmesan cheese, grated

½ cup (50 g) cracker crumbs

½ cup (120 ml) egg substitute

Preheat oven to 350°F (180°C, or gas mark 4). Cook zucchini in boiling water until nearly done. Drain, reserving ½ cup (120 ml) of liquid, and chop coarsely. Heat oil in a skillet and cook onion until soft. Stir all ingredients together and pour into a 1½-quart (1.4-L) baking dish coated with nonstick vegetable oil spray. Bake for 40 minutes, or until set.

Yield: 8 servings

Per serving: 111 calories (49% from fat, 21% from protein, 29% from carbohydrate); 6 g protein; 6 g total fat; 2 g saturated fat; 3 g monounsaturated fat; 1 g polyunsaturated fat; 8 g carbohydrate; 1 g fiber; 2 g sugar; 102 mg phosphorus; 102 mg calcium; 1 mg iron; 179 mg sodium; 250 mg potassium; 208 IU vitamin A; 7 mg ATE vitamin E; 11 mg vitamin C; 6 mg cholesterol; 82 g water

Cheese-Sauced Cauliflower

The sight of a whole head of cauliflower is an impressive display for what is usually considered a lowly vegetable.

1 medium head of cauliflower

2 tablespoons (16 g) flour

⅛ teaspoon (0.3 g) white pepper

2 tablespoons (30 ml) olive oil

1 cup (235 ml) skim milk

¾ cup (90 g) low fat cheddar cheese, shredded

1 teaspoon (5 g) mustard

Bring 1 cup (235 ml) of water to boil in a saucepan large enough to hold the cauliflower head. Add the cauliflower to the pan, cover, and cook for 20 minutes, or until tender. Transfer to a serving plate. Blend flour and pepper into oil in a saucepan. Stir in milk. Cook and stir until thickened. Stir in cheese and mustard, and heat until cheese melts. Pour over cauliflower.

Yield: 6 servings

Per serving: 124 calories (44% from fat, 25% from protein, 30% from carbohydrate); 8 g protein; 6 g total fat; 1 g saturated fat; 4 g monounsaturated fat; 1 g polyunsaturated fat; 10 g carbohydrate; 3 g fiber; 3 g sugar; 168 mg phosphorus; 148 mg calcium; 1 mg iron; 144 mg sodium; 266 mg potassium; 133 IU vitamin A; 35 mg ATE vitamin E; 55 mg vitamin C; 4 mg cholesterol; 163 g water

Broccoli Casserole

A delightful way to make broccoli something a little different.

6 cups (420 g) broccoli florets

10 ounces (280 g) low sodium cream of mushroom soup

¼ cup (60 g) low fat mayonnaise

¼ cup (30 g) low fat cheddar cheese

1 tablespoon (15 ml) lemon juice

⅓ cup (33 g) cracker crumbs

Preheat oven to 350°F (180°C, or gas mark 4). Cook broccoli in boiling water for 10 to 15 minutes, or until soft. Pour into a 1½-quart (1.4-L) casserole dish coated with nonstick vegetable oil spray. Combine remaining ingredients except cracker crumbs. Pour over broccoli. Top with crumbs. Bake, uncovered, for 35 minutes.

Yield: 6 servings

Per serving: 112 calories (39% from fat, 17% from protein, 45% from carbohydrate); 5 g protein; 5 g total fat; 1 g saturated fat; 0 g monounsaturated fat; 1 g polyunsaturated fat; 13 g carbohydrate; 1 g fiber; 2 g sugar; 113 mg phosphorus; 75 mg calcium; 1 mg iron; 203 mg sodium; 431 mg potassium; 2164 IU vitamin A; 4 mg ATE vitamin E; 67 mg vitamin C; 6 mg cholesterol; 117 g water

Mock Spaghetti

This makes a nice meat-free meal with just a salad for accompaniment. I've found that microwaving a spaghetti squash seems to work out better than baking it. It stays soft and juicy and takes less than half the time.

1 medium spaghetti squash

2 cups (360 g) canned no-salt-added diced tomatoes

2 cups (140 g) mushrooms, sliced

½ cup (65 g) carrot, grated

½ cup (75 g) green bell pepper, chopped

½ cup (67 g) frozen peas, thawed

1 tablespoon (2.1 g) Italian seasoning

½ tablespoon (5 g) garlic powder

¼ cup (60 ml) red wine

4 ounces (115 g) part-skim mozzarella, shredded

Pierce squash to center in several places. Microwave on high for 20 minutes, turning several times during cooking if microwave does not have a turntable. Slice in half lengthwise. When cool enough to handle, remove seeds and shred squash into strands with a fork. Place tomatoes, mushrooms, carrot, green bell pepper, peas, Italian seasoning, garlic powder, and red wine in a heavy saucepan and bring to a boil. Reduce heat, cover, and simmer for 15 to 20 minutes, or until vegetables are tender and sauce is thickened. Serve sauce over squash. Sprinkle with cheese.

Yield: 4 servings

Per serving: 171 calories (30% from fat, 25% from protein, 45% from carbohydrate); 11 g protein; 6 g total fat; 3 g saturated fat; 1 g monounsaturated fat; 1 g polyunsaturated fat; 19 g carbohydrate; 3 g fiber; 3 g sugar; 228 mg phosphorus; 275 mg calcium; 2 mg iron; 278 mg sodium; 570 mg potassium; 3881 IU vitamin A; 35 mg ATE vitamin E; 41 mg vitamin C; 18 mg cholesterol; 270 g water

Creamed Spinach

Creamed spinach is one of those dishes that kids tend to hate. Then they grow up and realize how good it really is.

3 tablespoons (24 g) flour

2 cups (470 ml) skim milk

½ cup (40 g) Parmesan cheese, shredded

1 tablespoon (15 ml) olive oil

½ cup (80 g) onion, finely chopped

½ teaspoon (1.5 g) minced garlic

12 ounces (340 g) frozen chopped spinach, thawed and squeezed dry

Shake flour and milk together in a jar with a tight-fitting lid until flour is dissolved. Pour into a saucepan, cook over medium heat and stir until thickened. Add Parmesan and stir until melted. In another pot, heat the oil and sauté the onion and garlic; add spinach. Cook for 10 minutes, or until spinach is hot and onion is translucent. Add sauce and mix thoroughly.

Yield: 4 servings

Per serving: 191 calories (35% from fat, 28% from protein, 37% from carbohydrate); 14 g protein; 8 g total fat; 3 g saturated fat; 4 g monounsaturated fat; 1 g polyunsaturated fat; 18 g carbohydrate; 4 g fiber; 1 g sugar; 284 mg phosphorus; 451 mg calcium; 2 mg iron; 347 mg sodium; 533 mg potassium; 10563 IU vitamin A; 90 mg ATE vitamin E; 5 mg vitamin C; 13 mg cholesterol; 207 g water

Greens

A traditional, long-cooked southern vegetable—none of this crisp-tender stuff for these people.

2 pounds (905 g) collard greens or kale

3 slices low sodium bacon

¼ cup (40 g) onion, chopped

½ teaspoon (1.5 g) black pepper

1 tablespoon (13 g) sugar

Rinse greens thoroughly. Cut off stems and chop coarsely. Brown bacon in the bottom of a stew pot or Dutch oven. Remove. Place greens, onion, pepper, and sugar in the pot. Add enough water to cover. Cover and cook for 45 minutes to 1 hour, or until tender. Drain. Crumble bacon over.

Yield: 6 servings

Per serving: 78 calories (24% from fat, 24% from protein, 52% from carbohydrate); 5 g protein; 2 g total fat; 1 g saturated fat; 1 g monounsaturated fat; 0 g polyunsaturated fat; 11 g carbohydrate; 6 g fiber; 3 g sugar; 39 mg phosphorus; 222 mg calcium; 0 mg iron; 72 mg sodium; 290 mg potassium; 10084 IU vitamin A; 0 mg ATE vitamin E; 54 mg vitamin C; 4 mg cholesterol; 143 g water

Southern-Style Greens

This makes a perfect accompaniment to grilled or smoked pork. The spices and honey make it more special than just boiled greens.

2 pounds (905 g) kale or collard greens

½ cup (80 g) onion, chopped

½ cup (75 g) red bell pepper, chopped

½ cup (75 g) green bell pepper, chopped

½ cup (120 ml) cider vinegar

1 tablespoon (15 ml) honey

½ teaspoon (1.5 g) garlic powder

½ teaspoon (1.5 g) freshly ground black pepper

1 teaspoon (5 ml) hot pepper sauce

Combine all ingredients in a large pot with 4 cups (946 ml) water. Bring to a boil, cover, reduce heat, and simmer for 1½ hours.

Yield: 6 servings

Per serving: 103 calories (9% from fat, 19% from protein, 72% from carbohydrate); 5 g protein; 1 g total fat; 0 g saturated fat; 0 g monounsaturated fat; 1 g polyunsaturated fat; 21 g carbohydrate; 4 g fiber; 4 g sugar; 97 mg phosphorus; 212 mg calcium; 3 mg iron; 73 mg sodium; 765 mg potassium; 23697 IU vitamin A; 0 mg ATE vitamin E; 208 mg vitamin C; 0 mg cholesterol; 183 g water

Scalloped Tomatoes

My mother used to make scalloped tomatoes, but for some reason we never did. We recently rediscovered them, and they are now a regular treat on our table.

2 tablespoons (30 ml) olive oil

½ cup (80 g) onion, chopped

2 slices bread, coarsely crumbled

3 cups (540 g) tomatoes, sliced

Preheat oven to 350°F (180°C, or gas mark 4). Heat oil in a skillet and cook onion until softened. Add bread crumbs and stir to coat. Layer half the tomatoes in a 1-quart (946-ml) casserole dish. Top with half the crumb mixture. Repeat layers. Bake for 30 minutes.

Yield: 6 servings

Per serving: 88 calories (50% from fat, 8% from protein, 42% from carbohydrate); 2 g protein; 5 g total fat; 1 g saturated fat; 3 g monounsaturated fat; 1 g polyunsaturated fat; 10 g carbohydrate; 2 g fiber; 2 g sugar; 41 mg phosphorus; 17 mg calcium; 1 mg iron; 59 mg sodium; 207 mg potassium; 464 IU vitamin A; 0 mg ATE vitamin E; 20 mg vitamin C; 0 mg cholesterol; 86 g water

Amish-Style Red Cabbage

Sweet and sour red cabbage recipe from Amish country, where sweets and sours are a part of life.

¼ cup (60 g) brown sugar, packed

¼ cup (60 ml) cider vinegar

½ teaspoon (1 g) caraway seed

⅛ teaspoon (0.2 g) red pepper flakes

¼ cup (60 ml) water

4 cups (280 g) red cabbage, shredded

2 cups (300 g) apple, cubed

Combine first 5 ingredients (through water) in a saucepan and heat until sugar is dissolved. Stir in cabbage and apples. Cook about 15 minutes for crisp cabbage or longer for softer cabbage.

Yield: 5 servings

Per serving: 88 calories (2% from fat, 5% from protein, 93% from carbohydrate); 1 g protein; 0 g total fat; 0 g saturated fat; 0 g monounsaturated fat; 0 g polyunsaturated fat; 22 g carbohydrate; 2 g fiber; 18 g sugar; 31 mg phosphorus; 46 mg calcium; 1 mg iron; 25 mg sodium; 263 mg potassium; 815 IU vitamin A; 0 mg ATE vitamin E; 42 mg vitamin C; 0 mg cholesterol; 126 g water

Japanese Salad

A great side dish with a plain piece of meat marinated in a little more of the dressing.

For Salad:

½ pound (225 g) lettuce, shredded

4 ounces (115 g) snow peas

½ cup (65 g) carrot, sliced

1 cup (70 g) cabbage, shredded

4 ounces (115 g) mushrooms, sliced

½ cup (75 g) red bell pepper, sliced

4 ounces (115 g) mung bean sprouts

For Dressing:

¼ cup (60 ml) Dick's Reduced-Sodium Soy Sauce (see recipe page 30)

2 tablespoons (30 ml) rice vinegar

2 tablespoons (30 ml) mirin wine

½ teaspoon (0.9 g) ground ginger

1 tablespoon (8 g) sesame seeds

To make the salad: Toss all salad ingredients.

To make the dressing: Mix all dressing ingredients until well combined. Spoon dressing over salad.

Yield: 6 servings

Per serving: 50 calories (1% from fat, 3% from protein, 95% from carbohydrate); 3 g protein; 0 g total fat; 0 g saturated fat; 0 g monounsaturated fat; 2 g polyunsaturated fat; 72 g carbohydrate; 2 g fiber; 5 g sugar; 67 mg phosphorus; 38 mg calcium; 1 mg iron; 87 mg sodium; 287 mg potassium; 2625 IU vitamin A; 0 mg ATE vitamin E; 36 mg vitamin C; 0 mg cholesterol; 144 g water

Corn Relish

This makes a nice addition to salads as well as being useful just as a relish. It will keep for at least a week in the refrigerator.

10 ounces (280 g) frozen corn

½ cup (100 g) sugar

1 tablespoon (8 g) cornstarch

½ cup (120 ml) cider vinegar

⅓ cup (80 ml) water

2 tablespoons (15 g) celery, finely chopped

2 tablespoons (19 g) green bell pepper, finely chopped

2 tablespoons (20 g) onion, finely chopped

2 tablespoons (24 g) pimentos, chopped

1 teaspoon (2.2 g) turmeric

½ teaspoon (1.5 g) dry mustard

Cook corn according to package directions; set aside. In saucepan combine sugar and cornstarch. Stir in vinegar and water. Add corn and remaining ingredients. Cook and stir until thickened and bubbly. Cover and refrigerate.

Yield: 8 servings

Per serving: 90 calories (5% from fat, 6% from protein, 90% from carbohydrate); 1 g protein; 1 g total fat; 0 g saturated fat; 0 g monounsaturated fat; 0 g polyunsaturated fat; 21 g carbohydrate; 1 g fiber; 14 g sugar; 36 mg phosphorus; 5 mg calcium; 0 mg iron; 8 mg sodium; 132 mg potassium; 170 IU vitamin A; 0 mg ATE vitamin E; 7 mg vitamin C; 0 mg cholesterol; 60 g water

Butternut Squash Bake

¾ cup (94 g) flour

¾ cup (170 g) brown sugar

2 teaspoons (4.6 g) cinnamon

1 teaspoon (1.9 g) ground allspice

¼ cup (55 g) unsalted margarine

1 butternut squash

1 cup (235 ml) maple syrup

½ cup (50 g) pecans, chopped

Preheat oven to 350°F (180°C, or gas mark 4). In a bowl, combine flour, sugar, cinnamon, and allspice. Cut in margarine until crumbly. Peel squash and cut into ½-inch (1.3-cm) thick slices, removing seeds. Place half of squash in a greased 8 × 8-inch (20 × 20-cm) baking dish. Sprinkle with half of the flour mixture. Repeat layers. Drizzle with maple syrup. Sprinkle pecans on top. Cover with foil. Bake for 1 hour. Remove foil. Bake for 10 minutes more.

Yield: 10 servings

Per serving: 285 calories (26% from fat, 3% from protein, 71% from carbohydrate); 2 g protein; 9 g total fat; 2 g saturated fat; 5 g monounsaturated fat; 2 g polyunsaturated fat; 53 g carbohydrate; 2 g fiber; 37 g sugar; 51 mg phosphorus; 78 mg calcium; 2 mg iron; 61 mg sodium; 362 mg potassium; 6198 IU vitamin A; 55 mg ATE vitamin E; 12 mg vitamin C; 0 mg cholesterol; 61 g water

Sweet Potatoes, Squash, and Apples

This makes a great side dish with pork.

2 cups (266 g) sweet potatoes, cut in 1-inch (2.5-cm) cubes

2 cups (280 g) butternut squash, cut in 1-inch (2.5-cm) cubes

1 cup (150 g) apple, peeled and sliced

¼ cup (60 ml) apple juice concentrate

½ teaspoon (1.2 g) cinnamon

Cook sweet potatoes and squash in water until almost soft. Drain, return to pan. Add apple and juice concentrate. Cook until apple is tender. Sprinkle with cinnamon.

Yield: 6 servings

Per serving: 113 calories (2% from fat, 7% from protein, 91% from carbohydrate); 2 g protein; 0 g total fat; 0 g saturated fat; 0 g monounsaturated fat; 0 g polyunsaturated fat; 27 g carbohydrate; 4 g fiber; 9 g sugar; 53 mg phosphorus; 55 mg calcium; 1 mg iron; 31 mg sodium; 433 mg potassium; 22177 IU vitamin A; 0 mg ATE vitamin E;25 mg vitamin C; 0 mg cholesterol; 144 g water

Spicy Sweet Potatoes

A slightly spicy, different way to serve sweet potatoes.

2 sweet potatoes, peeled and cubed

1 teaspoon (5 ml) canola oil

¼ cup (38 g) red bell pepper, chopped

¼ cup (40 g) onion, chopped

¼ cup (60 g) brown sugar

¼ cup (60 ml) orange juice

2 teaspoons (10 ml) lime juice

1½ teaspoons (3 g) jerk seasoning

Cook sweet potatoes in boiling water until just tender. Drain well. Heat oil in large skillet. Add sweet potatoes, red bell peppers, and onions to pan and mix well. Cook until vegetables caramelize. Combine brown sugar, orange and lime juices, and jerk seasoning in a small bowl. Add juice mixture to pan with vegetables and cook over medium heat to reduce liquid until syrupy.

Yield: 4 servings

Per serving: 133 calories (9% from fat, 4% from protein, 87% from carbohydrate); 1 g protein; 1 g total fat; 0 g saturated fat; 1 g monounsaturated fat; 0 g polyunsaturated fat; 30 g carbohydrate; 2 g fiber; 18 g sugar; 35 mg phosphorus; 37 mg calcium; 1 mg iron; 27 mg sodium; 288 mg potassium; 12189 IU vitamin A; 0 mg ATE vitamin E; 28 mg vitamin C; 0 mg cholesterol; 94 g water

14

Italian

There are several problems with most Italian meals from a cholesterol standpoint. One is the amount of cheese in many recipes. Whole milk cheeses contain a lot of saturated fat, which is one of the things we are most trying to avoid. As a start, I've included a number of good Italian recipes that don't contain any cheese at all. When you are shopping for cheese for the recipes that need it, look for the lowest fat varieties available. All stores should have low fat ricotta and part-skim mozzarella. If you look carefully, you may even be able to find fat-free varieties. By the time you get it into the recipe with all the other herbs and flavors, you won't be able to tell the difference. The other issue with many Italian recipes is the meat. We've already talked about using the leanest ground beef you can find. There also are some options where sausage comes in. I've included a recipe for making your own low fat Italian sausage from ground turkey. If you have a grinder, you can also make low fat pork sausage by grinding up some well-trimmed pork loin.

Chicken and Sun-Dried Tomato Pasta

Easy and delicious pasta with chicken. Serve with crusty bread and salad for a quick dinner.

12 ounces (340 g) bow-tie, fusilli or other shape pasta

½ teaspoon (2.5 ml) olive oil

½ teaspoon (1.5 g) minced garlic

2 boneless chicken breasts, cut into bite-sized pieces

¼ cup (28 g) oil-packed sun-dried tomatoes, chopped

¼ cup (65 g) prepared pesto

Cook pasta according to package directions. Drain. Heat oil in a large skillet over medium heat. Sauté garlic until tender, then stir in chicken. Cook until chicken is golden and cooked through. In a large bowl, combine pasta, chicken, sun-dried tomatoes, and pesto. Toss to coat evenly.

Yield: 4 servings

Per serving: 462 calories (25% from fat, 20% from protein, 55% from carbohydrate); 23 g protein; 13 g total fat; 3 g saturated fat; 7 g monounsaturated fat; 2 g polyunsaturated fat; 63 g carbohydrate; 3 g fiber; 2 g sugar; 285 mg phosphorus; 139 mg calcium; 3 mg iron; 162 mg sodium; 458 mg potassium; 303 IU vitamin A; 17 mg ATE vitamin E; 9 mg vitamin C; 96 mg cholesterol; 38 g water

Italian Chicken and Mushroom Sauce

This looks like it would be a high-calorie, high-fat meal, but it's not. Add a salad and you have a complete meal.

3 boneless chicken breasts

2 tablespoons (30 ml) olive oil

½ teaspoon (1.5 g) minced garlic

½ pound (225 g) fresh mushrooms, sliced

2 cups (470 ml) skim milk

¼ cup (30 g) flour

2 teaspoons (1.4 g) dried Italian seasoning

Cut chicken into 1-inch (2.5-cm) cubes. Heat olive oil in a skillet over medium-high heat. Sauté garlic, chicken, and mushrooms until chicken is done. Remove from skillet. Shake milk and flour together in a jar with a tight-fitting lid and add to skillet. Stir in Italian seasoning. Cook and stir until thickened and beginning to boil. Stir chicken mixture into sauce. Serve over pasta.

Yield: 6 servings

Per serving: 141 calories (34% from fat, 37% from protein, 28% from carbohydrate); 13 g protein; 5 g total fat; 1 g saturated fat; 3 g monounsaturated fat; 1 g polyunsaturated fat; 10 g carbohydrate; 1 g fiber; 1 g sugar; 201 mg phosphorus; 129 mg calcium; 1 mg iron; 74 mg sodium; 372 mg potassium; 197 IU vitamin A; 52 mg ATE vitamin E; 2 mg vitamin C; 22 mg cholesterol; 136 g water

Lower-Fat Chicken Tetrazzini

This recipe is proof that you can have rich-tasting dishes without the sodium and fat.

1 tablespoon (15 ml) olive oil

1 cup (160 g) onion, chopped

½ cup (35 g) mushrooms, sliced

1 tablespoon (8 g) flour

¼ cup (60 ml) white wine

3 cups (330 g) cooked chicken breast, cubed

12 ounces (340 g) macaroni, cooked

2 cups (470 ml) low sodium chicken broth

Dash nutmeg

4 ounces (115 g) low fat Swiss cheese, diced

2 tablespoons (30 ml) skim milk

Preheat oven to 350°F (180°C, or gas mark 4). In a skillet, heat the oil over low heat. Add onions and cook for 15 minutes, or until golden brown, stirring often. Add mushrooms and cook 5 minutes longer. Stir in flour, blending thoroughly. Stir in remaining ingredients except milk. Transfer to ovenproof casserole dish. Cover and bake for 30 minutes. Stir in milk. Re-cover and bake 5 minutes longer.

Yield: 6 servings

Per serving: 289 calories (19% from fat, 48% from protein, 34% from carbohydrate); 33 g protein; 6 g total fat; 2 g saturated fat; 2 g monounsaturated fat; 1 g polyunsaturated fat; 23 g carbohydrate; 2 g fiber; 2 g sugar; 353 mg phosphorus; 214 mg calcium; 2 mg iron; 130 mg sodium; 369 mg potassium; 54 IU vitamin A; 15 mg ATE vitamin E; 2 mg vitamin C; 66 mg cholesterol; 211 g water

Chicken Breasts Cacciatore

This makes a great-tasting sauce with no extra work. And it's always nice to come home to a meal that's done and has filled the house with such an aroma.

1 cup (160 g) onion, sliced

4 boneless chicken breasts

12 ounces (340 g) no-salt-added tomato paste

¼ teaspoon (0.5 g) black pepper

½ teaspoon (1.5 g) garlic powder

1 teaspoon (1 g) dried oregano

1 teaspoon (0.7 g) dried basil

¼ cup (60 ml) dry white wine

¼ cup (60 ml) water

Place onion in the bottom of a slow cooker. Place chicken on top. Combine remaining ingredients and pour over. Cook on low for 8 to 10 hours.

Yield: 6 servings

Per serving: 119 calories (7% from fat, 46% from protein, 47% from carbohydrate); 14 g protein; 1 g total fat; 0 g saturated fat; 0 g monounsaturated fat; 0 g polyunsaturated fat; 14 g carbohydrate; 3 g fiber; 8 g sugar; 151 mg phosphorus; 39 mg calcium; 2 mg iron; 88 mg sodium; 752 mg potassium; 898 IU vitamin A; 3 mg ATE vitamin E; 15 mg vitamin C; 27 mg cholesterol; 119 g water

Italian Baked Chicken Breasts

A variation on oven-baked chicken recipes, this one with an Italian flavor. Great with pasta and a salad for dinner.

12 low sodium saltines, crushed

1 teaspoon (5 g) brown sugar

½ teaspoon (1.4 g) sesame seeds

1 tablespoon (7 g) wheat germ

½ teaspoon (0.5 g) dried oregano

¼ teaspoon (0.5 g) celery seed

¼ teaspoon (0.8 g) garlic powder

1 teaspoon (3 g) onion, minced

½ teaspoon (0.1 g) dried parsley

1 teaspoon (0.7 g) dried Italian seasoning

4 boneless chicken breasts

¼ cup (60 ml) egg substitute

Preheat oven to 350°F (180°C, or gas mark 4). Combine all ingredients except chicken and egg substitute. Dip the chicken in the egg and then in the crumb mixture, turning to cover on all sides. Place in a 9 × 13-inch (23 × 33-cm) baking dish coated with nonstick vegetable oil spray. Spray chicken with vegetable oil spray until crumbs are moistened. Bake for 30 to 40 minutes, or until done.

Yield: 4 servings

Per serving: 164 calories (11% from fat, 52% from protein, 38% from carbohydrate); 20 g protein; 2 g total fat; 0 g saturated fat; 0 g monounsaturated fat; 1 g polyunsaturated fat; 15 g carbohydrate; 1 g fiber; 1 g sugar; 198 mg phosphorus; 30 mg calcium; 2 mg iron; 170 mg sodium; 283 mg potassium; 112 IU vitamin A; 4 mg ATE vitamin E; 1 mg vitamin C; 41 mg cholesterol; 68 g water

Pasta with Meat Sauce

An updated, healthier version of a typical Hamburger Helper–type meal. This is one that's sure to please young people as well as adults.

8 ounces (255 g) pasta

2 tablespoons (30 ml) olive oil

2 cups (320 g) onion, chopped

1 teaspoon (0.7 g) dried Italian seasoning

½ teaspoon (1.5 g) chopped garlic

1 pound (455 g) extra-lean ground beef (93% lean)

2 cups (360 g) canned no-salt-added crushed tomatoes

½ teaspoon (0.4 g) dried basil

Cook pasta according to package directions, omitting the salt. Drain. Heat olive oil in a large skillet on medium heat. Add the chopped onion and Italian seasoning. Cook for 5 minutes, stirring occasionally, until the onions are softened. Add the garlic. Cook for an additional minute. Remove onion mixture and add meat to pan, breaking it up as you add it. Brown the meat on one side, then turn over to brown the other side. When meat is browned, return the onions to the pan. Add tomatoes and basil. Simmer, uncovered, for 15 minutes. Stir in the cooked pasta. Serve immediately.

Yield: 4 servings

Per serving: 589 calories (29% from fat, 25% from protein, 46% from carbohydrate); 30 g protein; 15 g total fat; 4 g saturated fat; 8 g monounsaturated fat; 1 g polyunsaturated fat; 55 g carbohydrate; 5 g fiber; 8 g sugar; 315 mg phosphorus; 82 mg calcium; 4 mg iron; 97 mg sodium; 800 mg potassium; 167 IU vitamin A; 0 mg ATE vitamin E; 17 mg vitamin C; 78 mg cholesterol; 262 g water

Italian Beef Sauce

A hearty sauce to serve over pasta or rice. This one cooks all day in the slow cooker, so dinner is ready in no time when you get home.

1 pound (455 g) beef round steak, cubed

2 cups (360 g) canned no-salt-added tomatoes

2 tablespoons (30 ml) red wine

¼ teaspoon garlic powder

2 teaspoons (1.4 g) dried Italian seasoning

1 cup (160 g) onion, coarsely chopped

½ cup (35 g) mushrooms, sliced

6 ounces (170 g) no-salt-added tomato paste

Place beef in the bottom of a slow cooker. Stir together remaining ingredients except tomato paste. Pour over beef. Cover and cook on low for 8 to 10 hours. Turn to high. Stir in tomato paste and cook until thickened, 10 to 15 minutes.

Yield: 4 servings

Per serving: 307 calories (18% from fat, 59% from protein, 23% from carbohydrate); 45 g protein; 6 g total fat; 2 g saturated fat; 2 g monounsaturated fat; 0 g polyunsaturated fat; 18 g carbohydrate; 4 g fiber; 10 g sugar; 337 mg phosphorus; 75 mg calcium; 7 mg iron; 111 mg sodium; 1141 mg potassium; 824 IU vitamin A; 0 mg ATE vitamin E; 24 mg vitamin C; 102 mg cholesterol; 261 g water

Risotto

Risotto is a traditional Italian rice dish. It's a little more work than just putting rice to simmer or steam, but the creamy texture and flavor are worth it.

2 cups (470 ml) low sodium chicken broth

4 cups (946 ml) water

2 tablespoons (30 ml) olive oil

½ cup (80 g) onion, chopped

1½ cups (300 g) Arborio rice

¾ cup (180 ml) white wine

1 cup (70 g) mushrooms, sliced

1 cup (134 g) frozen peas, thawed

1 cup (110 g) cooked chicken breast, cubed

Bring broth and water to a simmer in two separate saucepans. Heat the oil in a large skillet or Dutch oven and sauté the onion. Add the rice and sauté until translucent, but not brown. Add the wine and simmer until liquid is almost completely absorbed. Add 1 cup (235 ml) of the broth and simmer until liquid is almost completely absorbed. Alternate adding 1 cup (235 ml) water and then broth, allowing it to cook after each addition until liquid is absorbed and rice is tender. Stir in mushrooms, peas, and chicken with ½ cup (120 ml) of water and simmer until heated through.

Yield: 6 servings

Per serving: 193 calories (32% from fat, 28% from protein, 41% from carbohydrate); 12 g protein; 6 g total fat; 1 g saturated fat; 4 g monounsaturated fat; 1 g polyunsaturated fat; 17 g carbohydrate; 2 g fiber; 2 g sugar; 142 mg phosphorus; 31 mg calcium; 2 mg iron; 136 mg sodium; 275 mg potassium; 565 IU vitamin A; 1 mg ATE vitamin E; 4 mg vitamin C; 20 mg cholesterol; 347 g water

Sun-Dried Tomato Rice

I guess I just get bored easily, but I'm always looking for a way to make things a little different. Don't get me wrong, I love plain rice. I could make a meal of a nice bowlful fresh from the steamer with nothing on it at all. But somehow that seems too plain for a meal. So we added a few Italian things to give you a different side dish. I serve it with a grilled piece of fish that I've marinated in Italian dressing.

2 tablespoons (30 ml) olive oil

¼ cup (40 g) onion, chopped

1 cup (185 g) rice

¼ teaspoon (0.8 g) garlic powder

¼ cup (14 g) sun-dried tomatoes, chopped

2¼ cups (530 ml) water

Heat oil in a large saucepan and sauté onion and rice for 2 minutes or until rice begins to brown. Add remaining ingredients, cover, reduce heat, and simmer for 20 minutes, or until rice is tender.

Yield: 6 servings

Per serving: 85 calories (55% from fat, 5% from protein, 40% from carbohydrate); 1 g protein; 5 g total fat; 1 g saturated fat; 4 g monounsaturated fat; 1 g polyunsaturated fat; 9 g carbohydrate; 1 g fiber; 0 g sugar; 23 mg phosphorus; 11 mg calcium; 1 mg iron; 16 mg sodium; 98 mg potassium; 59 IU vitamin A; 0 mg ATE vitamin E; 5 mg vitamin C; 0 mg cholesterol; 116 g water

Italian Winter Vegetable Soup

When the weather gets cooler, the slow cooker gets more use in my house. This is a different variation on minestrone, with fall or winter vegetables predominating.

1 cup (250 g) dried kidney beans

1 pound (455 g) beef round steak, cut in ½-inch (1.3-cm) cubes

2½ cups (350 g) butternut squash, peeled and cubed

2 medium potatoes, peeled and cubed

2 pounds (905 g) fennel bulbs, cut in 1-inch (2.5-cm) cubes

1 cup (160 g) onion, coarsely chopped

½ teaspoon (1.5 g) minced garlic

4 cups (120 g) spinach, chopped

1 tablespoon (4.5 g) dried Italian seasoning

4 cups (946 ml) low sodium chicken broth

1 cup (235 ml) white wine

Cook beans according to package directions until almost done. In a skillet, brown the beef. Drain. In a large slow cooker, place squash, potatoes, fennel, onion, garlic, and spinach on the bottom. Sprinkle Italian seasoning over top. Add beans and beef. Pour broth and wine over all. Cook on low for 8 to 10 hours.

Yield: 8 servings

Per serving: 346 calories (12% from fat, 38% from protein, 50% from carbohydrate); 32 g protein; 5 g total fat; 1 g saturated fat; 1 g monounsaturated fat; 1 g polyunsaturated fat; 42 g carbohydrate; 11 g fiber; 4 g sugar; 380 mg phosphorus; 255 mg calcium; 7 mg iron; 278 mg sodium; 1756 mg potassium; 16294 IU vitamin A; 0 mg ATE vitamin E; 36 mg vitamin C; 51 mg cholesterol; 489 g water

Vegetarian Minestrone

You can either use canned beans for this or cook your own from dried beans.

½ cup (80 g) onion, chopped

½ cup (65 g) carrot, diced

1 cup (113 g) zucchini, sliced

2 cloves garlic, crushed

2 cups (470 ml) low sodium chicken broth

2 cups (450 g) canned, no-salt-added great northern beans

1 teaspoon (0.7 g) dried basil

1 teaspoon (1 g) dried oregano

2 cups (360 g) canned no-salt-added tomatoes

6 ounces (170 g) fresh spinach

Parmesan cheese (optional)

Sauté onions, carrot, zucchini and garlic until tender. Add to a soup pot with the remaining ingredients and simmer for 1 to 1½ hours. Add additional water if needed. Garnish with Parmesan cheese, if desired.

Yield: 6 servings

Per serving: 149 calories (7% from fat, 26% from protein, 68% from carbohydrate); 10 g protein; 1 g total fat; 0 g saturated fat; 0 g monounsaturated fat; 0 g polyunsaturated fat; 27 g carbohydrate; 7 g fiber; 4 g sugar; 189 mg phosphorus; 133 mg calcium; 3 mg iron; 75 mg sodium; 727 mg potassium; 5370 IU vitamin A; 0 mg ATE vitamin E; 15 mg vitamin C; 0 mg cholesterol; 279 g water

Italian-Style Mixed Vegetables

We originally had this as a side dish with meat loaf. It started out as a toss-together of vegetables we had from the most recent garden harvesting, but it turned out well and has become a regular on our menu.

1 tablespoon (15 ml) olive oil

½ cup (75 g) green bell pepper, chopped

½ cup (80 g) onion, chopped

1 cup (113 g) zucchini, sliced

½ cup (75 g) eggplant, peeled and cubed

1 large potato, cubed

8 ounces (225 g) no-salt-added tomato sauce

1 teaspoon (0.7 g) dried Italian seasoning

¼ teaspoon (0.8 g) minced garlic

Heat oil in a large skillet over medium heat. Sauté green bell pepper, onion, zucchini, and eggplant in oil until just softened. Boil potatoes until soft. Add potatoes to vegetable mixture. Stir in tomato sauce, Italian seasoning, and garlic and heat through.

Yield: 6 servings

Per serving: 92 calories (24% from fat, 10% from protein, 66% from carbohydrate); 2 g protein; 3 g total fat; 0 g saturated fat; 2 g monounsaturated fat; 0 g polyunsaturated fat; 16 g carbohydrate; 2 g fiber; 4 g sugar; 64 mg phosphorus; 21 mg calcium; 1 mg iron; 13 mg sodium; 526 mg potassium; 237 IU vitamin A; 0 mg ATE vitamin E; 26 mg vitamin C; 0 mg cholesterol; 121 g water

Italian Vegetable Bake

A tasty side dish that's almost a meal in itself. Just add a simple piece of meat and you are done.

2 potatoes, sliced ¼-inch (63-mm) thick

12 ounces (340 g) frozen winter vegetable mix, thawed

2 cups (360 g) canned no-salt-added tomatoes, drained

1 teaspoon (0.7 g) dried Italian seasoning

1 teaspoon (0.1 g) dried parsley

1 cup (250 g) low fat ricotta cheese

½ cup (120 ml) egg substitute

Preheat oven to 350°F (180°C, or gas mark 4). Cook potatoes and vegetables until crisp-tender. Drain and combine with tomatoes. Place in an ovenproof casserole. Stir together remaining ingredients until well combined. Pour over vegetables. Bake for 30 minutes, or until mixture is set.

Yield: 6 servings

Per serving: 211 calories (19% from fat, 22% from protein, 60% from carbohydrate); 12 g protein; 5 g total fat; 2 g saturated fat; 1 g monounsaturated fat; 1 g polyunsaturated fat; 33 g carbohydrate; 5 g fiber; 3 g sugar; 224 mg phosphorus; 177 mg calcium; 3 mg iron; 133 mg sodium; 954 mg potassium; 3243 IU vitamin A; 43 mg ATE vitamin E; 24 mg vitamin C; 13 mg cholesterol; 270 g water

Italian Vegetable Casserole

A meatless Italian meal, relatively low in the things most people should be avoiding anyway. Summer would probably be the best time for this, when fresh vegetables are plentiful.

2 cups (300 g) eggplant, sliced

1 cup (150 g) red bell pepper, cut in rings

1 cup (160 g) onion, sliced

16 ounces (455 g) mushrooms, sliced

4 cups (450 g) zucchini, sliced

2 tablespoons (30 ml) olive oil

3 cups (710 ml) low sodium spaghetti sauce

4 ounces (115 g) part-skim mozzarella shredded

Preheat oven to 400°F (200°C, or gas mark 6). Brush eggplant, red bell pepper, onions, mushrooms, and zucchini with olive oil. Grill or pan-fry until soft. Coat a 9 × 13-inch (23 × 33-cm) baking dish with nonstick vegetable oil spray. Spoon enough spaghetti sauce in the bottom to cover. Layer vegetables, adding sauce every couple of layers. Finish with sauce and then top with cheese. Bake for 20 to 25 minutes, or until heated through and cheese is browned.

Yield: 6 servings

Per serving: 278 calories (43% from fat, 15% from protein, 42% from carbohydrate); 11 g protein; 14 g total fat; 3 g saturated fat; 8 g monounsaturated fat; 1 g polyunsaturated fat; 31 g carbohydrate; 7 g fiber; 20 g sugar; 250 mg phosphorus; 208 mg calcium; 2 mg iron; 169 mg sodium; 1107 mg potassium; 1809 IU vitamin A; 23 mg ATE vitamin E; 64 mg vitamin C; 12 mg cholesterol; 324 g water

Pasta with Vegetables

It doesn't get any easier than this when you are looking for a quick, easy dinner. By the time the pasta cooks, everything else will be ready too.

½ pound (225 g) linguine

1 tablespoon (15 ml) olive oil

½ cup (66 g) zucchini, sliced

4 ounces (115 g) mushrooms, sliced

½ cup (75 g) green bell pepper, sliced

½ cup (90 g) tomato, chopped

½ cup (80 g) onion, sliced

½ teaspoon (1.5 g) garlic powder

½ teaspoon (0.5 g) dried oregano

1 teaspoon (0.7 g) dried basil

2 tablespoons (10 g) Parmesan cheese, grated

Cook linguine according to package directions. Heat olive oil in a large skillet over medium-high heat. Sauté zucchini, mushrooms, green bell pepper, tomato, onion, garlic powder, oregano, and basil. Toss with pasta. Sprinkle with cheese.

Yield: 4 servings

Per serving: 287 calories (22% from fat, 15% from protein, 63% from carbohydrate); 11 g protein; 7 g total fat; 2 g saturated fat; 3 g monounsaturated fat; 1 g polyunsaturated fat; 46 g carbohydrate; 3 g fiber; 4 g sugar; 206 mg phosphorus; 72 mg calcium; 2 mg iron; 65 mg sodium; 391 mg potassium; 329 IU vitamin A; 13 mg ATE vitamin E; 22 mg vitamin C; 50 mg cholesterol; 100 g water

Pasta with Portobello Mushrooms

A delicious meatless version of pasta primavera. You can use whatever shape pasta you happen to have on hand.

16 ounces (455 g) pasta

2 tablespoons (30 ml) olive oil

½ teaspoon (1.5 g) minced garlic

½ pound (225 g) Portobello mushroom caps, chopped

¾ cup (113 g) red bell pepper, diced

1 cup (113 g) zucchini, cut into ½-inch (1.3-cm) slices

¼ cup (60 ml) red wine vinegar

2 tablespoons (10 g) Parmesan cheese, grated

In a large pot cook pasta until al dente. Drain. Heat the oil in a large nonstick skillet over medium heat and cook the garlic, mushrooms, red bell pepper, and zucchini for 10 minutes, or until soft, stirring frequently. Stir in red wine vinegar. Toss cooked pasta with mushroom mixture. Top with grated Parmesan cheese. Serve warm.

Yield: 6 servings

Per serving: 359 calories (22% from fat, 14% from protein, 64% from carbohydrate); 13 g protein; 9 g total fat; 2 g saturated fat; 4 g monounsaturated fat; 2 g polyunsaturated fat; 58 g carbohydrate; 4 g fiber; 3 g sugar; 260 mg phosphorus; 58 mg calcium; 2 mg iron; 54 mg sodium; 468 mg potassium; 681 IU vitamin A; 15 mg ATE vitamin E; 27 mg vitamin C; 65 mg cholesterol; 88 g water

Vegetable "Lasagna"

You could use this as a side dish with something like a grilled chicken breast, or just serve it as a vegetarian main dish. I used a George Foreman grill to grill the vegetables, but you could also use a regular grill or roast them in the oven.

4 cups (450 g) zucchini, sliced lengthwise

1 eggplant, sliced

8 ounces (225 g) mushrooms, sliced

1 cup (180 g) onion, sliced

2 cups (470 ml) low sodium spaghetti sauce

8 ounces (225 g) part-skim mozzarella, shredded

Preheat oven to 400°F (200°C, or gas mark 6). Slice zucchini, eggplant, mushrooms, and onion and coat with olive oil spray. Grill until crisp-tender. Place a small amount of spaghetti sauce in an 8 × 12 (20 × 30-cm) baking dish. Layer vegetables and sauce in this order: zucchini, eggplant, sauce, onion, and mushrooms, sauce, eggplant, and zucchini. Top with remaining sauce and sprinkle with cheese. Bake for 15 minutes, or until cheese is melted and starts to brown.

Yield: 6 servings

Per serving: 237 calories (38% from fat, 22% from protein, 40% from carbohydrate); 14 g protein; 10 g total fat; 4 g saturated fat; 4 g monounsaturated fat; 1 g polyunsaturated fat; 25 g carbohydrate; 7 g fiber; 15 g sugar; 296 mg phosphorus; 345 mg calcium; 1 mg iron; 272 mg sodium; 903 mg potassium; 880 IU vitamin A; 47 mg ATE vitamin E; 28 mg vitamin C; 24 mg cholesterol; 291 g water

Portobello Pizzas

Pizza-flavored snacks with Portobello mushroom "crusts." These proved to be an unexpected hit with young people.

5 ounces (140 g) frozen chopped spinach

6 ounces (170 g) part-skim mozzarella, shredded

4 ounces (115 g) turkey pepperoni, coarsely chopped

1 teaspoon (0.7 g) dried basil, crushed

¼ teaspoon (0.5 g) coarsely ground black pepper

12 Portobello mushroom caps, 3- to 4-inches (7.5- to 10-cm) diameter

2 tablespoons (30 ml) olive oil

Fresh basil, for garnish

Preheat oven to 350°F (180°C, or gas mark 4). Thaw spinach; press out liquid; finely chop. Combine spinach, cheese, pepperoni, basil, and pepper. Clean mushrooms; remove stems. Place open side up on lightly greased baking sheet; brush with olive oil. Spoon 2 tablespoons spinach mixture into each. Bake for 12 minutes or broil 4 inches (10 cm) from heat for 3 to 4 minutes. Garnish with fresh basil.

Yield: 12 servings

Per serving: 105 calories (47% from fat, 32% from protein, 20% from carbohydrate); 9 g protein; 6 g total fat; 2 g saturated fat; 3 g monounsaturated fat; 1 g polyunsaturated fat; 6 g carbohydrate; 2 g fiber; 2 g sugar; 180 mg phosphorus; 140 mg calcium; 1 mg iron; 280 mg sodium; 497 mg potassium; 1503 IU vitamin A; 19 mg ATE vitamin E; 0 mg vitamin C; 21 mg cholesterol; 99 g water

French Bread Pizza

Our version of French bread pizza has much less fat and sodium than anything you can get commercially.

1 cup (235 ml) water

2¾ cups (345 g) bread flour

1 tablespoon (13 g) sugar

1½ teaspoons (3.5 g) yeast

1 cup (235 ml) low sodium spaghetti sauce

4 ounces (115 g) part-skim mozzarella, shredded

Place water, flour, sugar, and yeast in bread machine pan in order specified by the manufacturer and process on dough cycle. Remove dough from pan and place in a bowl sprayed with nonstick vegetable oil spray. Turn to coat all sides. Cover and let rise in a warm place until doubled, about 30 minutes. Spray a large baking sheet with nonstick vegetable oil spray. Gently push a fist into the dough to deflate. Roll dough into a 16 × 12-inch (40 × 30-cm) rectangle. Cut in half to form two 8 × 12-inch (20 × 30-cm) rectangles. Fold each 12-inch (30-cm) side of the rectangle over the center. Flatten and place on prepared baking sheet. Cover and let rise until doubled again, about 30 to 40 minutes. Bake at 375°F (190°C, or gas mark 5) for 20 to 25 minutes, or until golden brown. Turn oven up to 400°F (200°C, or gas mark 6). Cut the top half off of each loaf, forming four half-loaves. Spread each with sauce. Add cheese. Bake for 10 to 12 minutes, or until cheese melts and starts to brown.

Yield: 4 servings

Per serving: 497 calories (17% from fat, 16% from protein, 67% from carbohydrate); 20 g protein; 9 g total fat; 4 g saturated fat; 4 g monounsaturated fat; 1 g polyunsaturated fat; 83 g carbohydrate; 4 g fiber; 11 g sugar; 264 mg phosphorus; 256 mg calcium; 5 mg iron; 199 mg sodium; 389 mg potassium; 522 IU vitamin A; 35 mg ATE vitamin E; 7 mg vitamin C; 18 mg cholesterol; 134 g water

Vegetarian Pizza

A good way to use fresh tomatoes—and a very tasty one at that.

½ recipe Whole Wheat Pizza Dough (see recipe page 463)

1 cup (180 g) roma tomatoes, sliced ¼-inch (63-cm) thick

½ cup (75 g) green bell pepper, thinly sliced

½ cup (80 g) onion, thinly sliced

½ cup (66 g) zucchini, thinly sliced

8 ounces (225 g) part-skim mozzarella, shredded

Prepare dough and bake according to directions. Cover with slices of roma tomatoes, then green bell pepper, onion, zucchini, and cheese. Return to oven and bake for 5 minutes, or until vegetables are softened and cheese is melted.

Yield: 6 servings

Per serving: 122 calories (46% from fat, 33% from protein, 21% from carbohydrate); 10 g protein; 6 g total fat; 4 g saturated fat; 2 g monounsaturated fat; 0 g polyunsaturated fat; 7 g carbohydrate; 1 g fiber; 2 g sugar; 191 mg phosphorus; 304 mg calcium; 0 mg iron; 238 mg sodium; 159 mg potassium; 456 IU vitamin A; 47 mg ATE vitamin E; 16 mg vitamin C; 24 mg cholesterol; 79 g water

Deep Dish Pizza

This makes a huge amount of pizza, somewhere around eight or nine meal-size servings. It also makes *good* pizza—my wife, Ginger, says it's the best homemade I've made. The recipe here is for a veggie pizza, so if you add meat you'll need to take that into account when looking at the nutritional values.

1 ⅓ cups (315 ml) water

2 tablespoons (30 ml) olive oil

4 cups (500 g) flour

¼ cup (24 g) nonfat dry milk powder

1 tablespoon (13 g) sugar

2¼ teaspoons (5.3 g) yeast

2 tablespoons (30 ml) olive oil

1 cup (235 ml) low sodium spaghetti sauce

½ cup (80 g) onion, coarsely chopped

½ cup (75 g) green bell pepper, coarsely chopped

1 cup (70 g) mushrooms, sliced

8 ounces (225 g) part-skim mozzarella shredded

TIP *If you don't happen to have 3 round cake pans, as I didn't, you can buy a pack of 3 foil ones for about $1 USD.*

Place first 6 ingredients (through yeast) in bread machine pan in the order specified by the manufacturer. Process on the dough cycle. At the end of the kneading cycle, turn off machine and remove dough. Separate into 3 balls. Put 2 teaspoons (10 ml) of oil in each of three 9-inch (23-cm) round cake pans and rotate pan to coat the entire bottom. Roll each dough ball into a 9-inch (23-cm) circle and place in pan. Spray with nonstick vegetable oil spray, cover, and let rise until doubled, 1 to 1½ hours. Preheat oven to 475°F (240°C, or gas mark 9). Spread ⅓ cup (80 ml) of spaghetti sauce over the dough in each pan. Place onion, green bell pepper, and mushrooms on sauce and cover with cheese. Bake for 20 minutes, or until cheese is bubbly and edges of crust are brown.

Yield: 9 servings

Per serving: 372 calories (29% from fat, 15% from protein, 56% from carbohydrate); 14 g protein; 12 g total fat; 4 g saturated fat; 7 g monounsaturated fat; 1 g polyunsaturated fat; 52 g carbohydrate; 3 g fiber; 7 g sugar; 229 mg phosphorus; 241 mg calcium; 3 mg iron; 178 mg sodium; 292 mg potassium; 367 IU vitamin A; 45 mg ATE vitamin E; 11 mg vitamin C; 16 mg cholesterol; 99 g water

Veggie White Pizza

The cheese is the main ingredient adding fat to pizza (unless you go with the pepperoni lover's variety), so you need to limit it to less than Pizza Hut uses. But that doesn't mean that you can't have a good-tasting treat.

For Dough:
1½ teaspoons (3.5 g) yeast

1¾ cups (220 g) bread flour

¾ cup (180 ml) water

1 tablespoon (15 ml) honey

1 tablespoon (15 ml) olive oil

For Sauce:
1½ cups (355 ml) skim milk

3 tablespoons (24 g) flour

½ teaspoon (1.5 g) garlic powder

½ teaspoon (1.5 g) onion powder

1 teaspoon (0.7 g) dried Italian seasoning

For Toppings:
1 tomato, sliced

½ cup (75 g) green bell pepper, cut in rings

½ cup (80 g) onion, coarsely chopped

1 cup (70 g) broccoli florets

1 cup (115 g) part-skim mozzarella, shredded

¼ cup (25 g) Parmesan cheese, grated

Place dough ingredients in bread machine pan in the order specified by the manufacturer and process on the dough cycle. Turn out the dough onto a floured board. At this point you may form the pizza or refrigerate the dough for several hours, well-wrapped in plastic so it won't dry out. (Although a refrigerator rest is not necessary, it makes the dough easier to handle.) Preheat oven to 400°F (200°C, or gas mark 6). Stretch dough into a 12-inch (30-cm) circle on a pizza pan or baking sheet. Bake for 10 minutes, or until lightly browned around the edges. Shake sauce ingredients together in a jar. Cook in a saucepan over medium heat and stir for 10 to 15 minutes, or until thickened. Spread sauce over crust; arrange toppings on top. Sprinkle cheese over all. Return to oven and bake for 5 to 10 minutes, or until cheese is melted and starting to brown.

Yield: 8 servings

Per serving: 186 calories (16% from fat, 17% from protein, 67% from carbohydrate); 8 g protein; 3 g total fat; 1 g saturated fat; 2 g monounsaturated fat; 0 g polyunsaturated fat; 31 g carbohydrate; 1 g fiber; 3 g sugar; 129 mg phosphorus; 117 mg calcium; 2 mg iron; 80 mg sodium; 203 mg potassium; 418 IU vitamin A; 32 mg ATE vitamin E; 17 mg vitamin C; 4 mg cholesterol; 95 g water

Sun-Dried Tomato Alfredo Sauce

I saw a jar of this on the supermarket shelf and decided to try to get creative and see if I could come up with something similar, but healthier. I was quite happy with the way it turned out. By the way, my ⅓ cup (80 ml) serving size is bigger than the USDA's standard ¼ cup (60 ml) serving of pasta sauce, but I think it seems closer to what people are likely to eat in reality.

2 cups (470 ml) skim milk

2 tablespoons (16 g) cornstarch

½ cup (40 g) Parmesan cheese, shredded

½ cup (55 g) oil-packed sun-dried tomatoes, finely chopped

½ teaspoon (1.5 g) garlic powder

½ teaspoon (0.5 g) dried oregano

Shake milk and cornstarch together in a jar. Place in saucepan. Cook over medium heat and stir for 10 minutes, or until thickened and beginning to boil. Add cheese, tomatoes, garlic powder, and oregano and stir until cheese is melted.

Yield: 6 servings

Per serving: 100 calories (34% from fat, 27% from protein, 38% from carbohydrate); 7 g protein; 4 g total fat; 2 g saturated fat; 2 g monounsaturated fat; 0 g polyunsaturated fat; 10 g carbohydrate; 1 g fiber; 0 g sugar; 167 mg phosphorus; 216 mg calcium; 0 mg iron; 200 mg sodium; 307 mg potassium; 327 IU vitamin A; 60 mg ATE vitamin E; 10 mg vitamin C; 9 mg cholesterol; 80 g water

Tuna Alfredo Sauce

If you're looking for a little something different to put over pasta, this could be just the thing.

2 tablespoons (28 g) margarine

4 ounces (115 g) mushrooms, sliced

2 tablespoons (16 g) flour

1 cup (235 ml) skim milk

1 can (6-ounce, or 170-g) tuna

2 tablespoons (10 g) Parmesan cheese, grated

Melt margarine in a saucepan and sauté mushrooms. Stir in flour, then slowly add milk and tuna, cooking and stirring until thickened and bubbly. Remove from heat and stir in cheese.

Yield: 4 servings

Per serving: 114 calories (20% from fat, 54% from protein, 27% from carbohydrate); 15 g protein; 2 g total fat; 1 g saturated fat; 1 g monounsaturated fat; 1 g polyunsaturated fat; 7 g carbohydrate; 0 g fiber; 1 g sugar; 214 mg phosphorus; 130 mg calcium; 1 mg iron; 107 mg sodium; 312 mg potassium; 147 IU vitamin A; 44 mg ATE vitamin E; 1 mg vitamin C; 22 mg cholesterol; 114 g water

Lower-Fat Pesto Sauce

I really like pesto sauce. It is an easy treat in the summer when the basil is growing in the garden. But while traditional recipes contain a lot of oil, this version is very tasty, and you needn't feel guilty at all!

2 tablespoons (30 ml) low sodium chicken broth

½ teaspoon (1.5 g) minced garlic

1 cup (40 g) fresh basil

⅓ cup (33 g) Parmesan cheese, freshly grated

2 tablespoons (18 g) pine nuts

Combine broth and garlic and heat in the microwave on high for 5 minutes (or heat on the stove). Allow to cool. Chop basil in food processor. Add cooled broth mixture, Parmesan cheese, and pine nuts. Process until everything is finely chopped and blended. Serve over pasta with additional Parmesan cheese, if desired.

Yield: 6 servings

Per serving: 58 calories (53% from fat, 21% from protein, 26% from carbohydrate); 3 g protein; 4 g total fat; 1 g saturated fat; 1 g monounsaturated fat; 1 g polyunsaturated fat; 4 g carbohydrate; 2 g fiber; 0 g sugar; 86 mg phosphorus; 181 mg calcium; 3 mg iron; 88 mg sodium; 221 mg potassium; 550 IU vitamin A; 7 mg ATE vitamin E; 4 mg vitamin C; 5 mg cholesterol; 7 g water

Turkey Italian Sausage

This makes a very nice-flavored sausage, not really hot, but with a little kick. You can vary the amount of red pepper depending on how hot you like your sausage. A serving is 2 ounces (55 g), which may be less than you'd use in a main dish.

2 pounds (905 g) ground turkey

1 tablespoon (5.8 g) fennel seed

2 bay leaves, ground

1 tablespoon (0.4 g) dried parsley

¾ teaspoon (2.3 g) minced garlic

½ teaspoon (1.5 g) onion powder

⅛ teaspoon (0.2 g) red pepper flakes

½ teaspoon (0.5 g) black pepper

¼ cup (60 ml) water

Combine all ingredients and mix well. Pan fry, grill, or broil to desired doneness.

Yield: 16 servings

Per serving: 98 calories (28% from fat, 71% from protein, 2% from carbohydrate); 17 g protein; 3 g total fat; 1 g saturated fat; 1 g monounsaturated fat; 1 g polyunsaturated fat; 0 g carbohydrate; 0 g fiber; 0 g sugar; 123 mg phosphorus; 20 mg calcium; 1 mg iron; 40 mg sodium; 179 mg potassium; 26 IU vitamin A; 0 mg ATE vitamin E; 0 mg vitamin C; 43 mg cholesterol; 41 g water

15

Mexican and Latin American

Ah, Mexican food. A treat for the taste buds, but not for the arteries with its use of shortening and cheese. However, as we've seen in other chapters, there are ways to make unhealthy food healthier by being careful about the ingredients we choose. As with Italian food, choose low fat or fat-free cheese whenever available. Use healthy oils like olive or canola in place of solid fats. Be mindful of the cuts of meat you use. You can make carnitas from pork loin just as easily as from the shoulder or some other higher-fat cut. And let's not forget that there are lots of good Mexican and Latin fish recipes.

Black Bean Burritos

I love Mexican food. And I love it even more when it's good for you. Unlike many burritos, these are low in saturated fat and sodium.

Two 10-inch (25-cm) flour tortillas

1 tablespoon (15 ml) canola oil

1 cup (160 g) onion, chopped

½ cup (75 g) red bell pepper, chopped

1 teaspoon (3 g) minced garlic

1 teaspoon (2.5 g) canned jalapeños

15 ounces (510 g) canned black beans, rinsed and drained

3 ounces (85 g) fat-free cream cheese

2 tablespoons (8 g) chopped fresh cilantro

Preheat oven to 350°F (180°C, or gas mark 4). Wrap tortillas in foil and bake for 15 minutes, or until heated through. Heat oil in a skillet over medium heat. Place onion, bell pepper, garlic, and jalapeños in skillet; cook for 2 minutes, stirring occasionally. Add beans to skillet and cook 3 minutes more, stirring. Cut cream cheese into cubes and add to skillet. Cook for 2 minutes, stirring occasionally. Stir cilantro into mixture. Spoon mixture evenly down the center of warmed tortillas and roll tortillas up.

Yield: 2 servings

Per serving: 481 calories (20% from fat, 18% from protein, 62% from carbohydrate); 23 g protein; 11 g total fat; 1 g saturated fat; 5 g monounsaturated fat; 3 g polyunsaturated fat; 76 g carbohydrate; 22 g fiber; 6 g sugar; 372 mg phosphorus; 122 mg calcium; 6 mg iron; 200 mg sodium; 1019 mg potassium; 1364 IU vitamin A; 0 mg ATE vitamin E; 55 mg vitamin C; 0 mg cholesterol; 259 g water

Chicken Fajitas

Making fajitas out of chicken breast greatly reduces the fat and cholesterol over the beef and shrimp version, with no loss of flavor.

2 tablespoons (30 ml) oil

1 pound (455 g) boneless chicken breasts, thinly sliced

1 cup (160 g) onion, cut in strips

1 cup (150 g) green bell pepper, cut in strips

1 tablespoon (2.6 g) taco seasoning

8 flour tortillas

½ cup (115 g) fat-free sour cream

½ cup (112 g) salsa

Heat oil in a large skillet and sauté chicken, onion, green bell pepper, and taco seasoning for 5 minutes, or until chicken is done. Place tortillas between 2 wet paper towels. Microwave on high for 30 seconds. Place chicken mixture in the center of the tortillas; garnish with sour cream and salsa. Fold in one side, the bottom, and then the other side.

Yield: 4 servings

Per serving: 449 calories (29% from fat, 32% from protein, 39% from carbohydrate); 33 g protein; 13 g total fat; 2 g saturated fat; 5 g monounsaturated fat; 5 g polyunsaturated fat; 40 g carbohydrate; 4 g fiber; 5 g sugar; 355 mg phosphorus; 143 mg calcium; 3 mg iron; 730 mg sodium; 641 mg potassium; 471 IU vitamin A; 37 mg ATE vitamin E; 35 mg vitamin C; 78 mg cholesterol; 227 g water

Baja Chipotle Fish Tacos

Grilled fish and a creamy smoked pepper sauce for that authentic Baja flavor.

1 pound (455 g) boneless fillets of your choice white fish

¼ cup (60 ml) Chipotle Marinade (see recipe page 32)

8 corn tortillas, warmed

2 cups (140 g) cabbage, shredded

¼ cup (60 ml) Chipotle Sauce (see recipe page 33)

Grill fish, turning and brushing with marinade. Heat tortillas in microwave until warm, but not crisp. To serve, divide fish among tortillas. Top with cabbage and drizzle with Chipotle Sauce.

Yield: 4 servings

Per serving: 293 calories (22% from fat, 48% from protein, 29% from carbohydrate); 35 g protein; 7 g total fat; 1 g saturated fat; 1 g monounsaturated fat; 2 g polyunsaturated fat; 21 g carbohydrate; 4 g fiber; 3 g sugar; 472 mg phosphorus; 122 mg calcium; 2 mg iron; 376 mg sodium; 858 mg potassium; 498 IU vitamin A; 61 mg ATE vitamin E; 22 mg vitamin C; 46 mg cholesterol; 162 g water

Chicken Enchiladas

We make this fairly often, sometimes with different meat. In fact, it's one of our favorite uses of leftover Thanksgiving turkey.

½ cup (80 g) onion, sautéed

2 cups (220 g) cooked chicken breast, chopped

1 small jalapeño, chopped

4 ounces (115 g) fat-free cream cheese

6 flour tortillas

½ cup (115 g) fat-free sour cream

½ cup (120 ml) skim milk

¼ cup (30 g) low fat Monterey jack cheese, shredded

Preheat oven to 350°F (180°C, or gas mark 4). Combine the first 4 ingredients (through cream cheese). Roll in tortillas. Place in a 9 × 13-inch (23 × 33-cm) baking dish. Combine the sour cream and milk. Pour over tortillas. Bake for 30 minutes. Sprinkle cheese on top for the last 10 minutes of baking time.

Yield: 6 servings

Per serving: 266 calories (20% from fat, 41% from protein, 38% from carbohydrate); 22 g protein; 5 g total fat; 1 g saturated fat; 2 g monounsaturated fat; 1 g polyunsaturated fat; 20 g carbohydrate; 1 g fiber; 1 g sugar; 245 mg phosphorus; 143 mg calcium; 2 mg iron; 336 mg sodium; 289 mg potassium; 285 IU vitamin A; 73 mg ATE vitamin E; 2 mg vitamin C; 60 mg cholesterol; 104 g water

Tofu Enchiladas

Is this what they call "fusion," a blending of cultures? Bear with me here, this is one of those mad-chemist-type of things that came to me as I was trying to find something for dinner. It's basically a cheese enchilada, but with less fat and sodium and more protein.

12 ounces (340 g) tofu

4 ounces (115 g) fat-free cream cheese

¼ cup (30 g) low fat Monterey jack cheese, shredded

5 flour tortillas

½ teaspoon (0.9 g) Mexican seasoning

1 cup (235 ml) skim milk

½ cup (115 g) fat-free sour cream

Preheat oven to 350°F (180°C, or gas mark 4). Cut tofu into small cubes. Mix with cream cheese and jack cheese. Divide among tortillas. Roll up and place in a 9 × 13-inch (23 × 33-cm) baking dish coated with nonstick vegetable oil spray. Combine Mexican seasoning, milk, and sour cream and pour over rolled tortillas. Bake for 30 minutes.

Yield: 5 servings

Per serving: 248 calories (25% from fat, 26% from protein, 49% from carbohydrate); 12 g protein; 5 g total fat; 1 g saturated fat; 2 g monounsaturated fat; 2 g polyunsaturated fat; 23 g carbohydrate; 1 g fiber; 2 g sugar; 223 mg phosphorus; 208 mg calcium; 2 mg iron; 350 mg sodium; 332 mg potassium; 371 IU vitamin A; 99 mg ATE vitamin E; 1 mg vitamin C; 25 mg cholesterol; 152 g water

Chilis Rellenos Casserole

Canned chili peppers are easy to find and convenient. You can also make this using fresh peppers if you have large mild chilis like ancho or poblano peppers available. If you're using fresh peppers, blanch for 30 to 60 seconds in boiling water before using.

2 cups (240 g) whole chili peppers

1 cup (115 g) low fat cheddar cheese

¼ cup (25 g) scallions, sliced

½ cup (120 ml) egg substitute

½ cup (120 ml) skim milk

¼ cup (32 g) flour

¾ cup (170 g) salsa

1 cup (115 g) part-skim mozzarella

Preheat oven to 325°F (170°C, or gas mark 3). Split chili peppers lengthwise and remove seeds and pith. Spread chilis in a single layer in a 9 × 13-inch (23 × 33-cm) baking dish sprayed with nonstick vegetable oil spray. Sprinkle cheddar cheese and scallions over chilis. In a bowl, beat egg substitute, milk, and flour together until smooth. Pour over chilis and cheese. Bake for 50 minutes, or until a knife inserted in custard comes out clean. Meanwhile, mix salsa with the mozzarella cheese. Sprinkle over casserole and return to oven for 10 minutes or until cheese melts. Let stand for 5 minutes before serving.

Yield: 4 servings

Per serving: 227 calories (33% from fat, 39% from protein, 29% from carbohydrate); 22 g protein; 8 g total fat; 5 g saturated fat; 2 g monounsaturated fat; 1 g polyunsaturated fat; 16 g carbohydrate; 2 g fiber; 4 g sugar; 404 mg phosphorus; 445 mg calcium; 2 mg iron; 483 mg sodium; 505 mg potassium; 860 IU vitamin A; 74 mg ATE vitamin E; 62 mg vitamin C; 26 mg cholesterol; 210 g water

Carne Asada

Most recipes call for skirt or flank steak for this, but any cut of beef will do. The London broil, or round steak, is relatively inexpensive and low in fat.

2 pounds (905 g) beef round steak

¼ cup (60 ml) lime juice

½ teaspoon (1.5 g) minced garlic

2 tablespoons (5.3 g) Mexican seasoning

Place steak in resealable plastic bag with lime juice and garlic. Marinate 2 hours, turning occasionally. Remove from marinade; rub 1 tablespoon (2.6 g) of Mexican seasoning on each side. Grill over medium heat until desired doneness. Slice thinly to serve.

Yield: 6 servings

Per serving: 304 calories (23% from fat, 75% from protein, 1% from carbohydrate); 55 g protein; 8 g total fat; 3 g saturated fat; 3 g monounsaturated fat; 0 g polyunsaturated fat; 1 g carbohydrate; 0 g fiber; 0 g sugar; 343 mg phosphorus; 8 mg calcium; 5 mg iron; 68 mg sodium; 518 mg potassium; 5 IU vitamin A; 0 mg ATE vitamin E; 3 mg vitamin C; 136 mg cholesterol; 98 g water

Low Fat Carnitas

Carnitas are crispy spiced pork that can be used for tacos, burritos, tostadas, or sandwiches.

2 pounds (905 g) pork loin

½ cup (80 g) onion, sliced

½ teaspoon (1.5 g) minced garlic

½ teaspoon (0.5 g) dried oregano

½ teaspoon (1.3 g) cumin

½ teaspoon (1.5 g) garlic powder

In a 3-quart (2.8-L) saucepan combine pork, onion, garlic, oregano, and cumin; add enough water to cover. Bring to a boil, reduce heat, cover, and simmer for 2 hours. Preheat oven to 350°F (180°C, or gas mark 4). Drain meat and place in a baking pan. Sprinkle meat with garlic powder. Bake for 45 minutes. Remove from oven. While meat is still warm, use forks to shred meat.

Yield: 8 servings

Per serving: 151 calories (30% from fat, 67% from protein, 3% from carbohydrate); 24 g protein; 5 g total fat; 2 g saturated fat; 2 g monounsaturated fat; 1 g polyunsaturated fat; 1 g carbohydrate; 0 g fiber; 0 g sugar; 252 mg phosphorus; 20 mg calcium; 1 mg iron; 59 mg sodium; 440 mg potassium; 14 IU vitamin A; 2 mg ATE vitamin E; 2 mg vitamin C; 71 mg cholesterol; 92 g water

Lechón Asado Roast Pork

Lechón asado is a Cuban pork disk. It would typically use sour orange juice, but it can be difficult to find, so I substitute a combination of lime and orange juice here.

3 pounds (1.4 kg) pork loin roast

1 tablespoon (3 g) minced garlic

1 bay leaf, ground

½ teaspoon (0.5 g) dried oregano

½ teaspoon (1.3 g) cumin

1 tablespoon (15 ml) olive oil

½ teaspoon (1 g) freshly ground black pepper

¼ cup (60 ml) orange juice

¼ cup (60 ml) lime juice

¼ cup (60 ml) dry white wine

1½ cups (240 g) onion, sliced

4 medium potatoes, peeled and quartered

Stick pork all over with the tip of a knife. Mash the garlic into a paste, then add the ground bay leaf, oregano, cumin, and olive oil and mix together. Rub spice mixture all over the roast. Place roast in a large glass baking dish , then sprinkle with pepper and pour orange and lime juice and wine over the roast. Scatter the onions over the roast, then wrap the entire roast in plastic and refrigerate. Marinate at least one hour or overnight, turning several times. Preheat oven to 350°F (180°C, or gas mark 4). Put the meat in a roasting pan, save the marinade, and place roast in the oven. Cook for 1 hour. Turn roast over, add marinade and potatoes, and reduce heat to 325°F (170°C, or gas mark 3). Baste frequently with the pan juices and continue cooking until done (30 to 35 minutes per pound, until roast reaches 180°F (82°C) internal temperature). Add water or wine if necessary to keep drippings from burning. Let sit before carving.

Yield: 10 servings

Per serving: 310 calories (22% from fat, 42% from protein, 36% from carbohydrate); 32 g protein; 7 g total fat; 2 g saturated fat; 4 g monounsaturated fat; 1 g polyunsaturated fat; 27 g carbohydrate; 3 g fiber; 3 g sugar; 398 mg phosphorus; 44 mg calcium; 2 mg iron; 80 mg sodium; 1241 mg potassium; 33 IU vitamin A; 3 mg ATE vitamin E; 20 mg vitamin C; 86 mg cholesterol; 258 g water

Latin-Style Pork Roast

Many years ago I had a lunch in a little Cuban restaurant in a multi-ethnic neighborhood in Washington, DC. The main course was an absolutely marvelous roast pork, crispy on the outside, juicy inside, slightly sour and spicy. I've never forgotten it, and I've never had a recipe or even an idea of the name of the dish. This is as close as I've come so far, but my family knows I'll keep trying. I cooked this on the rotisserie, but you could also grill or roast it.

½ cup (120 ml) cider vinegar

1 tablespoon (7 g) cumin

1 teaspoon (3 g) onion powder

½ teaspoon (0.9 g) cayenne pepper

2 pounds (905 g) pork loin

2 tablespoons (30 g) brown sugar

Combine vinegar, cumin, onion powder, and cayenne pepper. Place in a resealable plastic bag with pork roast, turning to coat on all sides. Marinate overnight in refrigerator, turning occasionally. When ready to cook remove roast from marinade, discarding excess. Rub with brown sugar. Prepare grill or preheat oven to 350°F (180°C, or gas mark 4). Roast for 1 hour, or until done.

Yield: 6 servings

Per serving: 221 calories (28% from fat, 61% from protein, 10% from carbohydrate); 32 g protein; 7 g total fat; 2 g saturated fat; 3 g monounsaturated fat; 1 g polyunsaturated fat; 5 g carbohydrate; 0 g fiber; 5 g sugar; 339 mg phosphorus; 36 mg calcium; 2 mg iron; 82 mg sodium; 614 mg potassium; 85 IU vitamin A; 3 mg ATE vitamin E; 2 mg vitamin C; 95 mg cholesterol; 130 g water

Turkey Chorizo

This will give an authentic Mexican flavor to any dish you add it to, without adding a lot of saturated fat that pork sausage contains. I prefer to cook them in the oven and then freeze them as individual pre-cooked patties so I can pull one out and heat it in the microwave for a minute and it's ready to go.

1 pound (455 g) ground turkey

¼ cup (60 ml) cider vinegar

½ teaspoon (1.5 g) garlic powder

2 tablespoons (14 g) cumin

½ teaspoon (0.7 g) cilantro

⅛ teaspoon (0.3 g) cayenne pepper

Combine all ingredients and mix well. Shape into 2-ounce (55-g) patties and cook or freeze for later use as desired.

Yield: 8 servings

Per serving: 104 calories (29% from fat, 68% from protein, 4% from carbohydrate); 17 g protein; 3 g total fat; 1 g saturated fat; 1 g monounsaturated fat; 1 g polyunsaturated fat; 1 g carbohydrate; 0 g fiber; 0 g sugar; 130 mg phosphorus; 29 mg calcium; 2 mg iron; 43 mg sodium; 204 mg potassium; 34 IU vitamin A; 0 mg ATE vitamin E; 0 mg vitamin C; 43 mg cholesterol; 44 g water

Mexican-Style Beans

This recipe gives you beans similar to the canned "Mexi-beans." You can use it in recipes that call for them, as a starter for chili, or the way we had them for lunch, just spooned over rice with a little dollop of salsa on top.

8 ounces (225 g) dried kidney beans

6 cups (1.4 L) water

2 tablespoons (30 ml) vinegar

½ teaspoon (1.5 g) garlic powder

1 teaspoon (3 g) onion powder

1 tablespoon (7.5 g) chili powder

Rinse the beans and place in a large pot with the water. Bring to a boil and cook 2 minutes. Remove from heat and let stand for an hour. Return to heat; add vinegar, garlic powder, onion powder, and chili powder and simmer until beans are tender, 1 to 1½ hours. Add water or low sodium chicken broth if the beans get too dry.

Yield: 4 servings

Per serving: 199 calories (3% from fat, 27% from protein, 70% from carbohydrate); 14 g protein; 1 g total fat; 0 g saturated fat; 0 g monounsaturated fat; 0 g polyunsaturated fat; 36 g carbohydrate; 15 g fiber; 2 g sugar; 240 mg phosphorus; 100 mg calcium; 5 mg iron; 44 mg sodium; 851 mg potassium; 556 IU vitamin A; 0 mg ATE vitamin E; 4 mg vitamin C; 0 mg cholesterol; 368 g water

Mexican Lasagna

Lasagna with a southwestern twist.

¾ pound (340 g) lasagna noodles

½ cup (80 g) onion, chopped

½ cup (75 g) red bell pepper, chopped

½ cup (82 g) frozen corn kernels, thawed

½ teaspoon (1.5 g) chopped garlic

2 cups (450 g) canned black beans, rinsed and drained

2 cups (460 g) refried beans

2¾ cups (645 ml) no-salt-added tomato sauce

½ cup (115 g) salsa

½ cup (30 g) chopped fresh cilantro, divided

1½ cups (340 g) fat-free cottage cheese

1 cup (250 g) low fat ricotta cheese

¼ cup (58 g) fat-free sour cream

1 cup (115 g) low fat Monterey jack cheese, shredded

¼ cup (50 g) black olives, sliced

TIP *This can be frozen unbaked and kept for up to a month. Simply thaw in refrigerator overnight and bake as directed. It tastes even better the second day!*

Preheat oven to 350°F (180°C, or gas mark 4). Bring a large pot of lightly salted water to a boil. Add pasta and cook for 8 to 10 minutes or until al dente. Drain. Coat a large skillet with nonstick vegetable oil spray and place over medium heat. Sauté onion, red bell pepper, corn, and garlic until tender. Stir in black beans, refried beans, tomato sauce, salsa, and ¼ cup (15 g) cilantro. Cook until heated through and slightly thickened; set aside. In a large bowl, combine cottage cheese, ricotta, sour cream, Monterey Jack cheese, and remaining ¼ cup (15 g) chopped cilantro; set aside. Coat a 9 × 13-inch (23 × 33-cm) casserole dish with nonstick vegetable oil spray. Arrange 3 of the cooked lasagna noodles in the bottom of the dish, cutting to fit if necessary. Spread with one-third of the bean mixture, then one-third of the cheese mixture. Repeat layers twice more. Cover and bake for 45 minutes. Garnish with sliced black olives.

Yield: 8 servings

Per serving: 438 calories (13% from fat, 25% from protein, 62% from carbohydrate); 27 g protein; 6 g total fat; 3 g saturated fat; 2 g monounsaturated fat; 1 g polyunsaturated fat; 66 g carbohydrate; 10 g fiber; 7 g sugar; 349 mg phosphorus; 243 mg calcium; 5 mg iron; 638 mg sodium; 914 mg potassium; 1041 IU vitamin A; 53 mg ATE vitamin E; 30 mg vitamin C; 22 mg cholesterol; 270 g water

South-of-the-Border Pie

A slightly different take on Mexican food, you can use this rice and egg casserole either as a side dish or a meatless main dish.

1 tablespoon (15 ml) olive oil

1 cup (160 g) onion, chopped

1 teaspoon (2.6 g) chili powder

1 teaspoon (2.5 g) cumin

½ teaspoon (1.5 g) garlic powder

2 cups (450 g) canned kidney beans, drained

1½ cups cooked brown rice

1 cup low fat cheddar cheese, shredded

¾ cup (180 ml) skim milk

½ cup (120 ml) egg substitute

Chopped green bell pepper and salsa for garnish (optional)

Preheat oven to 350°F (180°C, or gas mark 4). Heat oil in saucepan and cook onion. Stir in chili powder, cumin, and garlic powder and cook for 1 minute. Cool. Stir in beans, rice, cheese, milk, and egg substitute. Spray a 10-inch (25-cm) glass pie plate with nonstick vegetable oil spray. Add rice mixture. Bake uncovered for 30 minutes, or until center is just set. Let stand for 10 minutes. Garnish with chopped green pepper and serve with salsa, if desired.

Yield: 6 servings

Per serving: 477 calories (12% from fat, 23% from protein, 65% from carbohydrate); 28 g protein; 7 g total fat; 2 g saturated fat; 3 g monounsaturated fat; 1 g polyunsaturated fat; 78 g carbohydrate; 18 g fiber; 3 g sugar; 582 mg phosphorus; 255 mg calcium; 7 mg iron; 214 mg sodium; 1160 mg potassium; 312 IU vitamin A; 32 mg ATE vitamin E; 5 mg vitamin C; 5 mg cholesterol; 95 g water

Nacho Chicken Casserole

This is one of those easy throw-together-with-what-you-have-on-hand recipes. But it's the kind of thing that frequently comes up in those "We haven't had that in a while" conversations.

1½ cups (84 g) unsalted tortilla chips, crushed

2 cups (220 g) cooked chicken breast, diced

1 cup (235 ml) low sodium cream of mushroom soup

8 ounces (225 g) fat-free sour cream

½ cup (58 g) low fat cheddar cheese shredded

Preheat oven to 350°F (180°C, or gas mark 4). Line bottom of 1½-quart (1.4-L) casserole dish with crushed tortilla chips. Mix remaining ingredients, except cheese, and cover chips. Top with cheese. Bake for 15 minutes, or until cheese is bubbly.

Yield: 2 servings

Per serving: 602 calories (27% from fat, 49% from protein, 24% from carbohydrate); 58 g protein; 14 g total fat; 4 g saturated fat; 5 g monounsaturated fat; 4 g polyunsaturated fat; 28 g carbohydrate; 2 g fiber; 3 g sugar; 690 mg phosphorus; 326 mg calcium; 3 mg iron; 425 mg sodium; 1038 mg potassium; 544 IU vitamin A; 144 mg ATE vitamin E; 1 mg vitamin C; 174 mg cholesterol; 313 g water

Taco Quiche

A Mexican-flavored quiche. Baking it without a crust reduces the fat content to less than half of what it would be if you bought a pre-made pie crust.

½ pound (225 g) extra-lean ground beef (93% lean)

2 tablespoons (5.3 g) taco seasoning

½ cup (120 ml) water

½ cup (60 g) low fat Monterey jack cheese, shredded

2 ounces (55 g) green chilis, seeded and diced

¾ cup (180 ml) egg substitute

1 cup (235 ml) fat-free evaporated milk

Preheat oven to 375°F (190°C, or gas mark 5). Brown beef in skillet. Drain. Stir in taco seasoning mix and water, cover, and simmer until thickened. Cool 10 minutes. Add cheese and chilis and mix well. Spoon into 9-inch (23-cm) pie pan that has been sprayed with nonstick vegetable oil spray. Combine egg substitute and milk. Mix until smooth. Pour over meat mixture. Bake for 40 to 45 minutes, or until custard is set. Allow pie to stand 5 minutes before serving.

Yield: 6 servings

Per serving: 173 calories (30% from fat, 51% from protein, 19% from carbohydrate); 17 g protein; 4 g total fat; 2 g saturated fat; 2 g monounsaturated fat; 1 g polyunsaturated fat; 6 g carbohydrate; 0 g fiber; 5 g sugar; 229 mg phosphorus; 193 mg calcium; 2 mg iron; 321 mg sodium; 371 mg potassium; 451 IU vitamin A; 57 mg ATE vitamin E; 4 mg vitamin C; 30 mg cholesterol; 119 g water

Mexican Noodles

This was kind of a throw-together that worked well. It makes a nice alternative to rice.

12 ounces (340 g) noodles

¼ cup (24 g) dry cheese sauce mix

1 cup (235 ml) skim milk

½ teaspoon (1.3 g) cumin

½ teaspoon (1.5 g) onion powder

¼ teaspoon (0.8 g) garlic powder

½ cup (115 g) salsa

Cook noodles according to package directions. Combine sauce mix, milk, cumin, onion powder, and garlic powder in a jar with a tight-fitting lid. Shake well until sauce mix is dissolved. Cook and stir until thickened and bubbly. Stir in noodles and salsa.

Yield: 6 servings

Per serving: 116 calories (16% from fat, 15% from protein, 69% from carbohydrate); 5 g protein; 2 g total fat; 1 g saturated fat; 1 g monounsaturated fat; 0 g polyunsaturated fat; 20 g carbohydrate; 3 g fiber; 1 g sugar; 121 mg phosphorus; 99 mg calcium; 0 mg iron; 204 mg sodium; 177 mg potassium; 242 IU vitamin A; 42 mg ATE vitamin E; 1 mg vitamin C; 5 mg cholesterol; 102 g water

Mexican Baked Fish

Depending on the salsa you use, this dish can be either mild or hot.

1½ pounds (680 g) cod fillets

1 cup (225 g) salsa

1 cup (115 g) low fat cheddar cheese, shredded

1 cup (28 g) corn chips, crushed

1 avocado, peeled, pitted, and sliced

¼ cup (58 g) fat-free sour cream

Preheat oven to 400°F (200°C, or gas mark 6). Spray an 8 × 12-inch (20 × 30-cm) baking dish with nonstick vegetable oil spray. Lay fillets side by side in the prepared baking dish. Pour the salsa over the top and sprinkle evenly with the shredded cheese. Top with the crushed corn chips. Bake, uncovered, for 15 minutes, or until fish is opaque and flakes with a fork. Serve topped with sliced avocado and sour cream.

Yield: 6 servings

Per serving: 243 calories (33% from fat, 47% from protein, 20% from carbohydrate); 28 g protein; 9 g total fat; 2 g saturated fat; 4 g monounsaturated fat; 2 g polyunsaturated fat; 11 g carbohydrate; 3 g fiber; 2 g sugar; 387 mg phosphorus; 150 mg calcium; 1 mg iron; 519 mg sodium; 751 mg potassium; 288 IU vitamin A; 37 mg ATE vitamin E; 4 mg vitamin C; 57 mg cholesterol; 169 g water

Mexican Chicken Soup

Southwestern flavor without the heat.

1 pound (455 g) boneless chicken breasts cut in 1-inch (2.5-cm) cubes

1 cup (160 g) onion, chopped

4 cups (720 g) canned no-salt-added tomatoes

2 cups (470 ml) low sodium chicken broth

4 ounces (115 g) chopped chilis

1 teaspoon (1 g) dried oregano

1 teaspoon (2.5 g) cumin

1 cup (165 g) frozen corn, thawed

½ cup (75 g) green bell pepper, chopped

6 corn tortillas, cut in 1-inch (2.5-cm) strips

TIP *For a little added flavor, sprinkle with fresh cilantro.*

Mix first 7 ingredients (through cumin) in a slow cooker. Cover and cook on low for 7 to 8 hours. Turn to high and stir in corn and green peppers. Cook 30 minutes, or until vegetables are tender. Preheat oven to 450°F (180°C, or gas mark 4). Place tortilla strips on baking sheets coated with nonstick vegetable oil spray. Bake for 6 minutes, or until crisp, but not brown. Spoon soup into bowls, top with tortilla strips.

Yield: 6 servings

Per serving: 208 calories (10% from fat, 42% from protein, 48% from carbohydrate); 23 g protein; 2 g total fat; 1 g saturated fat; 1 g monounsaturated fat; 1 g polyunsaturated fat; 26 g carbohydrate; 4 g fiber; 7 g sugar; 297 mg phosphorus; 94 mg calcium; 3 mg iron; 107 mg sodium; 771 mg potassium; 489 IU vitamin A; 5 mg ATE vitamin E; 75 mg vitamin C; 44 mg cholesterol; 366 g water

Mexican Chicken Stew

A stew full of chicken and chunky vegetables, flavored with Mexican spices. Cooked in the slow cooker, it gives the house a nice aroma to come home to.

½ cup (80 g) onion, coarsely chopped

2 boneless chicken breasts cut in 1-inch (2.5-cm) cubes

½ cup (75 g) green bell pepper, coarsely chopped

2 cups (225 g) zucchini, thickly sliced

1½ cups (270 g) plum tomatoes, chopped

½ cup (82 g) frozen corn, thawed

2 cups (470 ml) low sodium chicken broth

1 tablespoon (7.5 g) chili powder

½ tablespoon (3.5 g) cumin

1 tablespoon (3 g) dried oregano

½ teaspoon (1.5 g) garlic powder

TIP *If you want a more substantial meal, you can serve this over rice.*

Place onion in the bottom of a slow cooker. Cover with chicken and then green bell pepper, zucchini, tomatoes, and corn. Combine broth, chili powder, cumin, oregano, and garlic powder and pour over chicken. Cook on low 8 to 10 hours or on high 4 to 5 hours.

Yield: 4 servings

Per serving: 119 calories (14% from fat, 41% from protein, 45% from carbohydrate); 13 g protein; 2 g total fat; 0 g saturated fat; 1 g monounsaturated fat; 1 g polyunsaturated fat; 15 g carbohydrate; 4 g fiber; 5 g sugar; 176 mg phosphorus; 55 mg calcium; 2 mg iron; 91 mg sodium; 646 mg potassium; 1284 IU vitamin A; 2 mg ATE vitamin E; 37 mg vitamin C; 21 mg cholesterol; 305 g water

Three-Bean Chili

Okay, you all have figured out by now that I get bored and start experimenting. Actually, we have been making baked beans with a mixture of beans for a number of years, so a similar chili seemed like a natural extension. Other than the beans, it's a pretty standard recipe.

½ cup (125 g) dried kidney beans

½ cup (125 g) dried black beans

½ cup (125 g) dried white beans

7 cups (1.64 L) water, divided

1 pound (455 g) extra-lean ground beef (93% lean)

1 cup (160 g) onion, chopped

½ cup (75 g) green bell pepper, chopped

4 cups (720 g) canned no-salt-added tomatoes

12 ounces (340 g) no-salt-added tomato sauce

1 cup (235 ml) water

2 tablespoons (15 g) chili powder

½ teaspoon (1.3 g) cumin

½ teaspoon (1.5 g) garlic powder

½ teaspoon (0.5 g) dried oregano

1 tablespoon (15 ml) vinegar

Place beans in 6 cups (1.4 L) water in a large pan. Bring to a boil; boil for 1 minute. Remove from heat and let stand for 1 hour. Return beans to heat and simmer about 30 minutes, or until almost tender. Meanwhile brown beef, onion, and green bell pepper in a skillet. Drain beans. Add beans, beef mixture, and remaining ingredients to a large pot. Simmer for 1 to 1½ hours, or until beans are done and chili is desired consistency. Stir occasionally and add more water if needed.

Yield: 6 servings

Per serving: 374 calories (18% from fat, 33% from protein, 49% from carbohydrate); 26 g protein; 6 g total fat; 2 g saturated fat; 2 g monounsaturated fat; 1 g polyunsaturated fat; 38 g carbohydrate; 12 g fiber; 9 g sugar; 308 mg phosphorus; 155 mg calcium; 7 mg iron; 119 mg sodium; 1415 mg potassium; 1180 IU vitamin A; 0 mg ATE vitamin E; 37 mg vitamin C; 52 mg cholesterol; 576 g water

Tortillas

Newsletter subscriber Carla sent me this easy recipe for making flour tortillas. I have to admit they turned out well, and it wasn't nearly as difficult as I'd anticipated. I was afraid that it would be difficult to roll them thin enough, but it was actually easy to get them the way you find them at restaurants that hand make tortillas.

2 cups (250 g) flour

1 teaspoon (4.6 g) baking powder

1 tablespoon (14 g) unsalted margarine

½ cup (120 ml) warm water

In a mixing bowl stir together flour and baking powder. Cut in margarine until mixture resembles cornmeal. Add warm water and mix until dough can be gathered into a ball, adding more water if needed 1 tablespoon (15 ml) at a time. Let dough rest for 15 minutes. Divide dough into 12 portions; shape into balls. On a lightly floured surface roll each ball to a 7-inch (17.5-cm) round. Trim uneven edges to make a round tortilla. Cook in an ungreased skillet over medium heat (375°F, or 190°C) in an electric skillet) about 1½ minutes per side, or until lightly browned.

Yield: 12 servings

Per serving: 84 calories (12% from fat, 10% from protein, 77% from carbohydrate); 2 g protein; 1 g total fat; 0 g saturated fat; 1 g monounsaturated fat; 0 g polyunsaturated fat; 16 g carbohydrate; 1 g fiber; 0 g sugar; 31 mg phosphorus; 27 mg calcium; 1 mg iron; 52 mg sodium; 24 mg potassium; 50 IU vitamin A; 11 mg ATE vitamin E; 0 mg vitamin C; 0 mg cholesterol; 13 g water

16

Asian

Asian recipes are actually a very good choice for cholesterol-friendly eating. Stir-frying uses very little fat, and lean cuts of meat sliced thinly and cooked quickly can be just as tender as the fattier cuts. There is a wide variety of recipes here for you to try, using chicken, beef, pork, fish, and tofu. There are also some Asian side dishes to add flavor to other meals that feature grilled or broiled meat.

Chicken Stir-Fry

This recipe has a very nice light sauce, without the usual soy sauce. We like it over fried rice.

¼ teaspoon (0.5 g) ground ginger

¼ teaspoon (0.5 g) garlic powder

¼ teaspoon (0.5 g) black pepper

2 tablespoons (30 ml) olive oil, divided

½ cup (75 g) carrot, sliced

½ cup (80 g) onion, chopped

1 cup (70 g) mushrooms, sliced

1 cup (70 g) bok choy, chopped

2 boneless chicken breasts, thinly sliced

1 tablespoon (15 ml) sherry

1 tablespoon (15 ml) hot sauce

1 cup (235 ml) low sodium chicken broth

1 tablespoon (8 g) cornstarch

In a small bowl, combine the ginger, garlic powder, and black pepper; set aside. In a wok heat 1 tablespoon (15 ml) oil. Add the carrots and onion and half the spice mixture and stir-fry for 2 minutes. Add the mushrooms and bok choy and stir-fry 1 minute. Remove vegetables. Add the remaining oil to the wok and heat. Add chicken and remaining spice mixture and stir-fry until chicken is no longer pink. Return the vegetables to the wok. Stir together the sherry, hot sauce, broth, and cornstarch. Add to wok and heat until mixture thickens and begins to bubble.

Yield: 4 servings

Per serving: 151 calories (46% from fat, 28% from protein, 26% from carbohydrate); 11 g protein; 8 g total fat; 1 g saturated fat; 5 g monounsaturated fat; 1 g polyunsaturated fat; 10 g carbohydrate; 1 g fiber; 3 g sugar; 120 mg phosphorus; 27 mg calcium; 1 mg iron; 144 mg sodium; 309 mg potassium; 2773 IU vitamin A; 2 mg ATE vitamin E; 5 mg vitamin C; 21 mg cholesterol; 162 g water

Quick Asian Chicken

About as "real Chinese" as the chow mein you can buy on your grocer's shelves or frozen food case, but it still tastes good.

1 cup (110 g) chicken breast, cubed

12 ounces (340 g) frozen oriental vegetable mix, thawed

4 ounces (115 g) water chestnuts

2 cups (470 ml) low sodium chicken broth

¼ cup (60 ml) Dick's Reduced-Sodium Soy Sauce (see recipe page 30)

2 tablespoons (16 g) cornstarch

Stir-fry chicken in a wok or heavy skillet sprayed with nonstick vegetable oil spray. Remove chicken. Stir-fry vegetables and water chestnuts until crisp-tender. Shake broth, soy sauce, and cornstarch together in a jar with a tight-fitting lid. Add broth mixture to wok and cook until thickened and bubbly. Stir in chicken. Serve over rice.

Yield: 4 servings

Per serving: 161 calories (4% from fat, 12% from protein, 85% from carbohydrate); 16 g protein; 2 g total fat; 1 g saturated fat; 1 g monounsaturated fat; 2 g polyunsaturated fat; 114 g carbohydrate; 4 g fiber; 5 g sugar; 172 mg phosphorus; 40 mg calcium; 1 mg iron; 196 mg sodium; 381 mg potassium; 3651 IU vitamin A; 2 mg ATE vitamin E; 3 mg vitamin C; 30 mg cholesterol; 230 g water

Chicken and Snow Peas

The stir-frying and ingredients give this an Asian feel, although it doesn't use the typical seasonings. It's good over rice, and I would think it would go well with pasta too.

2 tablespoons (30 ml) olive oil, divided

1 pound (455 g) boneless chicken breasts, sliced

(continued on page 348)

¼ cup (60 ml) egg substitute

⅓ cup (43 g) cornstarch

1½ cups (240 g) onions, sliced

½ cup (75 g) green bell pepper, sliced

6 ounces (170 g) snow peas

¼ cup (60 ml) honey

2 tablespoons (16 g) almonds, slivered

Heat 1 tablespoon (15 ml) of the oil in a wok. Dip half the chicken in the egg substitute and dust with cornstarch. Stir-fry for 4 to 5 minutes, or until just cooked. Remove cooked chicken from pan and repeat with remaining chicken. Remove chicken from pan; add the rest of the oil to the wok. Stir fry the onion until it begins to soften. Add the green bell pepper and snow peas and stir-fry for 4 minutes, or until crisp-tender. Add the honey and toss the vegetables in it until well coated. Add the chicken and toss until coated and heated through. Sprinkle the almonds over the top.

Yield: 4 servings

Per serving: 375 calories (27% from fat, 33% from protein, 40% from carbohydrate); 31 g protein; 11 g total fat; 2 g saturated fat; 7 g monounsaturated fat; 2 g polyunsaturated fat; 38 g carbohydrate; 3 g fiber; 22 g sugar; 309 mg phosphorus; 66 mg calcium; 3 mg iron; 109 mg sodium; 589 mg potassium; 613 IU vitamin A; 7 mg ATE vitamin E; 46 mg vitamin C; 66 mg cholesterol; 211 g water

Szechuan Chicken

A spicy Szechuan dish made with diced chicken, peanuts, and chili peppers.

For Marinade:

1½ tablespoons (22 ml) water

1 tablespoon (15 ml) Dick's Reduced-Sodium Soy Sauce (see recipe page 30)

1½ tablespoons (12 g) cornstarch

1 tablespoon (15 ml) rice wine

For Chicken:

1 pound (455 g) boneless chicken breasts

8 dried chili peppers

½ teaspoon (1.5 g) minced garlic

½ cup (75 g) green bell pepper, cut in ½-inch (1.3-cm) pieces

½ cup (75 g) dry-roasted peanuts

For Sauce:

2 tablespoons (30 ml) Dick's Reduced-Sodium Soy Sauce (see recipe page 30)

1 tablespoon (15 ml) sherry

1 tablespoon (13 g) sugar

1 teaspoon (3 g) cornstarch

¼ teaspoon (1 ml) sesame oil

To make the marinade: Mix together marinade ingredients.

To make the chicken: Marinate chicken for at least 20 minutes. Heat wok. When hot, add 2 tablespoons (30 ml) oil. When oil is hot, add dried chili peppers and garlic and stir-fry until brown and fragrant. Add the green pepper cubes. After approximately two minutes, push the peppers up the side of the wok and add the chicken cubes in the middle of the wok. Stir-fry until the chicken cubes are thoroughly cooked.

To make the sauce: Combine sauce ingredients and add into the wok. Stir until thickened. Add peanuts just before removing the chicken mixture from the wok.

Yield: 4 servings

Per serving: 288 calories (17% from fat, 22% from protein, 61% from carbohydrate); 31 g protein; 11 g total fat; 2 g saturated fat; 5 g monounsaturated fat; 5 g polyunsaturated fat; 87 g carbohydrate; 2 g fiber; 7 g sugar; 304 mg phosphorus; 32 mg calcium; 1 mg iron; 156 mg sodium; 499 mg potassium; 383 IU vitamin A; 7 mg ATE vitamin E; 17 mg vitamin C; 66 mg cholesterol; 129 g water

Lemon Chicken

A lemon chicken recipe similar to what you get from your favorite Chinese carryout. This version is pan-fried, rather than deep-fried, to reduce the fat content.

For Chicken:

¼ cup (32 g) cornstarch

⅛ teaspoon black pepper

2 tablespoons (30 ml) water

½ cup (120 ml) egg substitute

4 boneless chicken breasts, cut into bite-sized pieces

2 tablespoons (30 ml) oil

¼ cup (25 g) scallions, sliced

For Lemon Sauce:

¾ cup (180 ml) water

¼ cup (60 ml) lemon juice

2 tablespoons (30 g) brown sugar

1½ tablespoons (12 g) cornstarch

1½ tablespoons (22 ml) honey

1 tablespoon (6 g) low sodium chicken bouillon

¼ teaspoon (0.5 g) ground ginger

To make the chicken: Combine cornstarch and pepper. Blend in water and egg substitute. Dip chicken pieces into cornstarch mixture. Heat oil in a wok or frying pan. Fry chicken in oil for 5 minutes, or until golden. Drain. Sprinkle with scallions.

To make the sauce: Combine all the sauce ingredients in a saucepan. Cook over medium heat, stirring, for 5 minutes, or until sauce boils and thickens. Pour sauce over chicken.

Yield: 4 servings

Per serving: 302 calories (27% from fat, 28% from protein, 45% from carbohydrate); 21 g protein; 9 g total fat; 1 g saturated fat; 2 g monounsaturated fat; 5 g polyunsaturated fat; 34 g carbohydrate; 0 g fiber; 14 g sugar; 42 mg calcium; 2 mg iron; 129 mg sodium; 357 mg potassium; 9 mg vitamin C; 42 mg cholesterol

Chinese Chicken Meatballs

There was a place where I used to get lunch in the pre-diet days that had a Chinese meatball dish that I was quite fond of. I've never been able to duplicate the flavor, but this is my favorite of the ways I've tried. You can use these meatballs in place of the meat in any of the Asian recipes in this cookbook.

1 pound (455 g) ground chicken breast

1 tablespoon (6 g) sodium free beef bouillon

¼ teaspoon (0.5 g) ground ginger

⅛ teaspoon (0.4 g) garlic powder

⅛ teaspoon (0.3 g) black pepper

1 tablespoon (15 ml) sherry

¼ cup (60 ml) egg substitute

Preheat oven to 350°F (180°C, or gas mark 4). Combine all ingredients. Shape into 1-inch (2.5-cm) balls. Place in a roasting pan that has been well coated with nonstick vegetable oil spray. Roast for 30 to 40 minutes, or until done, turning once.

Yield: 4 servings

Per serving: 153 calories (14% from fat, 80% from protein, 6% from carbohydrate); 28 g protein; 2 g total fat; 1 g saturated fat; 1 g monounsaturated fat; 1 g polyunsaturated fat; 2 g carbohydrate; 0 g fiber; 1 g sugar; 245 mg phosphorus; 25 mg calcium; 1 mg iron; 123 mg sodium; 354 mg potassium; 90 IU vitamin A; 7 mg ATE vitamin E; 1 mg vitamin C; 66 mg cholesterol; 100 g water

Sesame Chicken

Just like you get at your local Chinese restaurant, except it's healthy.

¼ cup (32 g) flour

⅛ teaspoon (0.3 g) black pepper

4 boneless chicken breasts, cut into strips

2 tablespoons (30 ml) olive oil

¼ cup (60 ml) Dick's Reduced-Sodium Soy Sauce (see recipe page 30)

¼ cup (50 g) sugar

½ teaspoon (3 ml) sesame oil

2 tablespoons (16 g) sesame seeds, toasted

¼ cup (12 g) chives, chopped

TIP *Don't try to get by without the sesame oil. It should be available in the Asian food section of any large grocery store.*

Combine the flour and pepper in a resealable plastic bag. Add the chicken and shake to coat. Heat the olive oil in a large skillet. Add the chicken and cook until no longer pink. Remove from skillet. Add the soy sauce and sugar to the skillet; cook and stir until the sugar is melted. Toast the sesame seeds by placing them in a dry skillet and cooking over medium heat for 2 to 3 minutes, or until golden brown. Stir and shake the pan frequently to keep them from burning. Stir in the sesame oil and sesame seeds. Add the chicken and chives and stir to coat.

Yield: 4 servings

Per serving: 241 calories (13% from fat, 11% from protein, 75% from carbohydrate); 17 g protein; 9 g total fat; 2 g saturated fat; 6 g monounsaturated fat; 3 g polyunsaturated fat; 117 g carbohydrate; 0 g fiber; 15 g sugar; 141 mg phosphorus; 20 mg calcium; 1 mg iron; 143 mg sodium; 190 mg potassium; 147 IU vitamin A; 3 mg ATE vitamin E; 2 mg vitamin C; 44 mg cholesterol; 58 g water

Sweet-and-Sour Chicken

A simple, quick-to-prepare version that has a very nice sauce.

8½ ounces (240 g) pineapple chunks, undrained

½ cup (120 ml) duck sauce, divided

2 tablespoons (30 g) brown sugar

¼ cup (60 ml) rice vinegar

¼ cup (60 ml) orange juice

1 pound (455 g) boneless chicken breasts, cut in ½-inch (1.3-cm) pieces

1 teaspoon (5 ml) Dick's Reduced-Sodium Soy Sauce (see recipe page 30)

1 pound (455 g) frozen oriental vegetable mix, thawed

¼ teaspoon (0.5 g) ground ginger

2 teaspoons (3 g) cornstarch

1 tablespoon (15 ml) water

Mix juice from pineapple with ¼ cup (60 ml) duck sauce, brown sugar, vinegar, soy sauce, and orange juice. Set aside. In a large skillet with a tight-fitting lid, add chicken and sauté for 5 minutes, or until no longer pink on the outside. Add soy sauce, pineapple chunks, vegetables, and ginger. Cover and simmer until chicken is done and vegetables are crisp-tender. Stir together water and cornstarch. Add to pan with remaining ¼ cup (60 ml) duck sauce. Cook until mixture is thickened and bubbly. Serve over rice.

Yield: 4 servings

Per serving: 330 calories (5% from fat, 34% from protein, 61% from carbohydrate); 30 g protein; 2 g total fat; 0 g saturated fat; 0 g monounsaturated fat; 1 g polyunsaturated fat; 54 g carbohydrate; 6 g fiber; 15 g sugar; 297 mg phosphorus; 64 mg calcium; 3 mg iron; 332 mg sodium; 725 mg potassium; 4926 IU vitamin A; 7 mg ATE vitamin E; 15 mg vitamin C; 66 mg cholesterol; 288 g water

Cashew Chicken

This is Chinese food that doesn't taste like you are watching your diet. It has become one of our favorite Asian meals with plain white or brown rice.

3 boneless chicken breasts

¼ cup (60 ml) Dick's Reduced-Sodium Soy Sauce (see recipe page 30)

2 tablespoons (16 g) cornstarch

½ teaspoon (2 g) sugar

2 tablespoons (30 ml) canola oil, divided

4 ounces (115 g) dry-roasted cashews

½ pound (225 g) snow pea pods, ends and strings removed

1 cup (70 g) mushrooms, sliced

1 cup (235 ml) low sodium chicken broth

2 cups (260 g) bamboo shoots, drained

¼ cup (25 g) scallions, sliced

Slice breasts horizontally into very thin slices and cut into 1-inch (2.5-cm) pieces. Mix soy sauce, cornstarch, and sugar; set aside. Heat 1 tablespoon (15 ml) of the oil in a skillet over moderate heat. Add the cashews and cook for 1 minute, shaking the pan to toast the nuts lightly. Remove cashews and set aside. Pour remaining oil in the pan and fry chicken quickly, turning often until it looks opaque. Add pea pods, mushrooms, and broth. Reduce heat, cover, and cook for 2 minutes. Add soy sauce mixture and bamboo shoots and cook until thickened, stirring constantly. Add scallions and cashews and serve immediately.

Yield: 6 servings

Per serving: 248 calories (25% from fat, 11% from protein, 63% from carbohydrate); 15 g protein; 14 g total fat; 2 g saturated fat; 8 g monounsaturated fat; 4 g polyunsaturated fat; 81 g carbohydrate; 3 g fiber; 6 g sugar; 244 mg phosphorus; 46 mg calcium; 3 mg iron; 112 mg sodium; 650 mg potassium; 474 IU vitamin A; 2 mg ATE vitamin E; 26 mg vitamin C; 21 mg cholesterol; 173 g water

Chinese Pepper Steak

This looks particularly nice if you use a mixture of pepper colors. Using beef round steak helps to keep the fat level down while giving you the traditional flavor.

1½ pounds (680 g) beef round steak, sliced thinly

⅓ cup (80 ml) red wine

2 teaspoons (8 g) sugar

2 tablespoons (30 ml) olive oil, divided

1 tablespoon (10 g) minced garlic

1 cup (160 g) onion, sliced

1 cup (150 g) green bell pepper, sliced

1 cup (150 g) red bell pepper, sliced

1 cup (70 g) mushrooms, sliced

Dash ground ginger

½ cup (120 ml) boiling water

1 teaspoon (2 g) low sodium beef bouillon

2 tablespoons (30 ml) water

1 tablespoon (8 g) cornstarch

In a large bowl combine first 3 ingredients. Cover and marinate overnight, turning beef occasionally. Drain, reserving marinade. In a wok, heat 1 tablespoon (15 ml) of the oil. Add beef and garlic and stir-fry for 2 minutes. Transfer to a platter. In the wok, heat the remaining oil. Add onions, green bell peppers, mushrooms, and ginger. Stir-fry for 2 minutes. In a bowl combine ½ cup (120 ml) boiling water and bouillon and set aside. In second bowl, combine 2 tablespoons (30 ml) water and cornstarch. Set aside. Increase heat under wok. Add beef and bouillon mixture and cook until mixture starts to bubble around the edges. Stir in cornstarch mixture. Cook and stir until sauce thickens.

Yield: 8 servings

Per serving: 235 calories (31% from fat, 57% from protein, 12% from carbohydrate); 32 g protein; 8 g total fat; 2 g saturated fat; 4 g monounsaturated fat; 1 g polyunsaturated fat; 7 g carbohydrate; 1 g fiber; 3 g sugar; 218 mg phosphorus; 15 mg calcium; 3 mg iron; 42 mg sodium; 430 mg potassium; 652 IU vitamin A; 0 mg ATE vitamin E; 41 mg vitamin C; 77 mg cholesterol; 138 g water

Steak and Vegetable Stir-Fry

This Asian dish is similar to pepper steak, but with a greater variety of vegetables.

1½ pounds (680 g) beef round steak

3 tablespoons (45 ml) Dick's Reduced-Sodium Soy Sauce (see recipe page 30)

2 tablespoons (30 ml) olive oil, divided

¼ teaspoon (0.5 g) black pepper

¼ teaspoon (0.8 g) minced garlic

½ teaspoon (0.9 g) ground ginger

1 cup (150 g) green bell pepper, cut in strips

2 cups (140 g) mushrooms, sliced

1 cup (160 g) onion, sliced

½ cup (120 ml) low sodium beef broth

1 tablespoon (8 g) cornstarch

1 cup (180 g) tomatoes, cut in wedges

Partially freeze beef to make it easier to slice. Slice diagonally into ¼ inch (63 cm) slices. In a large bowl combine soy sauce, 1 tablespoon (15 ml) oil, and pepper. Add beef. Toss to coat well and marinate for several hours in the refrigerator. Heat the remaining 1 tablespoon (15 ml) oil in a wok or large skillet and stir-fry the garlic and ginger for 1 minute. Add beef and stir-fry for 4 minutes, or until browned. Remove beef. Add green bell pepper, mushrooms, and onions and stir-fry for 2 minutes, or until crisp-tender. Return beef to wok. Combine remaining marinade, broth, and cornstarch. Pour over beef. Cook and stir until thickened. Add tomatoes and heat through.

Yield: 6 servings

Per serving: 305 calories (19% from fat, 35% from protein, 46% from carbohydrate); 43 g protein; 10 g total fat; 3 g saturated fat; 6 g monounsaturated fat; 2 g polyunsaturated fat; 56 g carbohydrate; 1 g fiber; 3 g sugar; 304 mg phosphorus; 21 mg calcium; 4 mg iron; 120 mg sodium; 624 mg potassium; 251 IU vitamin A; 0 mg ATE vitamin E; 29 mg vitamin C; 102 mg cholesterol; 188 g water

Chinese Pork Stir-Fry

Has anyone out there gotten the impression that I'm fond of Asian food? You would be right. I used to say that I could eat it six nights a week. And if you are careful with the preparation, it doesn't have to be bad for you.

1 pound (455 g) pork loin

¼ cup (60 ml) olive oil

2 cups (140 g) cabbage, shredded

½ cup (65 g) carrots, shredded

1 cup (160 g) onion, cut in strips

½ teaspoon (1 g) oriental seasoning

¼ cup (60 ml) Dick's Reduced-Sodium Soy Sauce (see recipe page 30)

Slice pork thinly, then shred the strips. Heat 2 tablespoons (30 ml) of the oil in a wok or heavy skillet. Stir-fry the pork until cooked through. Remove from wok. Add the remaining 2 tablespoons (30 ml) oil and stir-fry the cabbage, carrots, and onion until crisp-tender. Return the pork to the wok. Add the oriental seasoning and soy sauce. Heat through. Serve over rice.

Yield: 4 servings

Per serving: 251 calories (17% from fat, 16% from protein, 67% from carbohydrate); 25 g protein; 12 g total fat; 3 g saturated fat; 7 g monounsaturated fat; 3 g polyunsaturated fat; 106 g carbohydrate; 2 g fiber; 6 g sugar; 288 mg phosphorus; 55 mg calcium; 1 mg iron; 183 mg sodium; 644 mg potassium; 2748 IU vitamin A; 2 mg ATE vitamin E; 21 mg vitamin C; 71 mg cholesterol; 195 g water

Twice-Cooked Pork

A Szechuan dish in which pork is boiled, then stir-fried with vegetables in a spicy sauce.

¾ pound (340 g) pork loin

2 tablespoons (30 ml) olive oil

1 cup (120 g) leeks, sliced

1 jalapeño pepper, chopped

½ cup (75 g) red bell pepper, cut in ½-inch (1.3-cm) pieces

1 tablespoon (15 g) chili paste

1 tablespoon (15 ml) Dick's Reduced-Sodium Soy Sauce (see recipe page 30)

Cook pork in boiling water for 20 minutes. Remove and let cool. Cut the pork into thin matchbox slices. Heat wok. When hot, add olive oil. Add, one at a time, leeks, jalapeño peppers, and red bell peppers to wok and stir-fry, taking care not to overcook. Add the chili paste and soy sauce, followed by the pork slices. Blend and cook together for 1 to 2 minutes.

Yield: 4 servings

Per serving: 192 calories (33% from fat, 26% from protein, 41% from carbohydrate); 19 g protein; 11 g total fat; 2 g saturated fat; 4 g monounsaturated fat; 5 g polyunsaturated fat; 29 g carbohydrate; 1 g fiber; 2 g sugar; 202 mg phosphorus; 28 mg calcium; 1 mg iron; 96 mg sodium; 411 mg potassium; 1007 IU vitamin A; 2 mg ATE vitamin E; 29 mg vitamin C; 54 mg cholesterol; 110 g water

Sweet-and-Sour Pork

This sweet-and-sour pork recipe is healthier than most, trading the usual breaded, deep-fried pork pieces for lean chunks of pork that still taste great in the zesty sauce.

½ pound (225 g) pork loin

1 tablespoon (15 ml) canola oil

2 teaspoons (10 ml) sesame oil

¼ cup (37 g) carrot, sliced thinly on the diagonal

½ cup (75 g) green bell pepper strips

¼ cup (25 g) scallions, sliced

¼ cup (60 g) brown sugar, packed

2 teaspoons (16 g) cornstarch

2 tablespoons (30 ml) water

2 tablespoons (30 ml) red wine vinegar

1 teaspoon (5 ml) Dick's Reduced-Sodium Soy Sauce (see recipe page 30)

⅛ teaspoon (0.2 g) ground ginger

8 ounces (225 g) pineapple chunks, drained

Partially freeze pork and thinly slice into bite-sized strips. Heat a work or heavy frying pan. Add canola oil and sesame oil to pan. Add the pork. Cook and stir for 2 to 3 minutes, or until pork is no longer pink. Stir in sliced carrot, green bell pepper strips, and scallions. Cook for 2 to 4 minutes more or until the vegetables are crisp-tender. Stir together the brown sugar and cornstarch. Stir in water, red wine vinegar, soy sauce, and ground ginger. Add to pan and cook until thickened and bubbly. Stir in drained pineapple chunks. Cook for about 45 seconds more, or until pineapple is heated through. Serve with rice.

Yield: 2 servings

Per serving: 420 calories (31% from fat, 21% from protein, 49% from carbohydrate); 25 g protein; 17 g total fat; 3 g saturated fat; 8 g monounsaturated fat; 5 g polyunsaturated fat; 59 g carbohydrate; 2 g fiber; 37 g sugar; 279 mg phosphorus; 76 mg calcium; 2 mg iron; 103 mg sodium; 824 mg potassium; 3004 IU vitamin A; 2 mg ATE vitamin E; 43 mg vitamin C; 71 mg cholesterol; 280 g water

Stir-Fried Pork with Vegetables

I like stir-frying for a number of reasons. Not only is it a healthy way to cook, but also it's quick and easy when you are looking for a meal that doesn't take much time and effort to get on the table.

¾ pound (340 g) pork tenderloin

3 tablespoons (45 ml) Dick's Reduced-Sodium Soy Sauce (see recipe page 30)

1 tablespoon (15 ml) dry sherry

2½ teaspoons (7 g) cornstarch

1¼ teaspoons (5 g) sugar

⅛ teaspoon (0.2 g) ground ginger

2 tablespoons (30 ml) canola oil, divided

1 cup (70 g) broccoli, cut into bite-sized pieces

1 cup (70 g) sliced mushrooms

½ cup (65 g) carrot, thinly sliced

½ cup (50 g) scallions, sliced

Cut pork crosswise into ⅛-inch (31-mm) slices. In a medium bowl, mix pork with soy sauce, sherry, cornstarch, sugar, and ginger. Marinate for 30 minutes to 1 hour. Heat 1 tablespoon (15 ml) oil in a skillet or wok over high heat and stir-fry broccoli, mushrooms, carrot, and scallions until vegetables are tender-crisp. Remove vegetables from wok and keep warm. Cook pork in remaining 1 tablespoon (15 ml) oil, stirring constantly, for 3 minutes, or until pork loses its pink color. Return vegetables to wok and stir-fry until heated through. Serve over rice.

Yield: 3 servings

Per serving: 283 calories (18% from fat, 16% from protein, 66% from carbohydrate); 26 g protein; 13 g total fat; 2 g saturated fat; 7 g monounsaturated fat; 5 g polyunsaturated fat; 108 g carbohydrate; 2 g fiber; 6 g sugar; 323 mg phosphorus; 48 mg calcium; 2 mg iron; 190 mg sodium; 743 mg potassium; 3954 IU vitamin A; 2 mg ATE vitamin E; 33 mg vitamin C; 74 mg cholesterol; 191 g water

Teriyaki Salmon

A nice Asian dish with a sweet-and-sour kind of flavor. Serve over plain rice.

¼ cup (60 ml) Dick's Reduced-Sodium Soy Sauce (see recipe page 30)

¼ cup (60 ml) rice wine vinegar

¼ cup (50 g) sugar

¼ teaspoon (0.8 g) garlic powder

½ teaspoon (0.9 g) ground ginger

¼ teaspoon (0.5 g) black pepper

1 pound (455 g) salmon fillets, cubed

½ cup (66 g) zucchini, sliced

½ cup (80 g) onion, quartered

½ cup (75 g) red bell peppers, cubed

1 cup (70 g) mushrooms, sliced in half

2 tablespoons (30 ml) canola oil

2 tablespoons (16 g) cornstarch

Combine soy sauce, vinegar, sugar, garlic powder, ginger, and black pepper. Stir until sugar is dissolved; set aside. Place fish in one resealable plastic bag and zucchini, onion, red bell pepper, and mushrooms in another. Divide soy sauce mixture between the two bags. Seal and marinate in the refrigerator for at least 1 hour, turning occasionally. Drain, reserving marinade. Heat oil in wok, add vegetables, and stir-fry for 5 minutes. Add fish and stir-fry for 1 minute. Stir cornstarch into reserved marinade, add to wok, and cook and stir until thickened.

Yield: 4 servings

Per serving: 374 calories (23% from fat, 13% from protein, 64% from carbohydrate); 24 g protein; 19 g total fat; 3 g saturated fat; 6 g monounsaturated fat; 10 g polyunsaturated fat; 120 g carbohydrate; 2 g fiber; 18 g sugar; 318 mg phosphorus; 34 mg calcium; 1 mg iron; 177 mg sodium; 686 mg potassium; 1494 IU vitamin A; 17 mg ATE vitamin E; 66 mg vitamin C; 67 mg cholesterol; 202 g water

Sweet-and-Sour Fish

This recipe produces a great tasting sweet-and-sour dish, with the health benefits of fish. Serve over plain brown rice to add even more healthy food to the menu.

1 pound (455 g) catfish fillets

2 tablespoons (30 ml) olive oil

¾ cup (113 g) green bell pepper, chopped

½ cup (65 g) carrot, sliced

¼ teaspoon (0.8 g) minced garlic

1½ cups (355 ml) low sodium chicken broth

¾ cup (150 g) sugar

½ cup (120 ml) red wine vinegar

1 tablespoon (15 ml) Dick's Reduced-Sodium Soy Sauce (see recipe page 30)

3 tablespoons (24 g) cornstarch

¼ cup (60 ml) water

Preheat oven to 350°F (180°C, or gas mark 4). Place fish fillets in a glass baking dish that has been coated with nonstick vegetable oil spray. Bake for 12 minutes, or until done. Meanwhile, heat oil in a large saucepan over medium-high heat and sauté green bell peppers, carrots, and garlic until tender. Add broth, sugar, vinegar, and soy sauce. Bring to a boil and cook for 1 minute. Stir cornstarch into cold water until dissolved. Stir into hot mixture. Cook and stir until thickened. Cut fish into bite-sized pieces. Stir into sauce.

Yield: 6 servings

Per serving: 278 calories (28% from fat, 16% from protein, 56% from carbohydrate); 13 g protein; 11 g total fat; 2 g saturated fat; 6 g monounsaturated fat; 2 g polyunsaturated fat; 48 g carbohydrate; 1 g fiber; 27 g sugar; 182 mg phosphorus; 18 mg calcium; 1 mg iron; 86 mg sodium; 360 mg potassium; 1901 IU vitamin A; 11 mg ATE vitamin E; 16 mg vitamin C; 36 mg cholesterol; 174 g water

Asian Tuna Steaks

Tuna steaks are better if they marinate before cooking to help keep them moist. The marinade gives them a new Asian flavor.

2 tablespoons (30 ml) orange juice

1 tablespoon (15 ml) sesame oil

1 tablespoon (8 g) sesame seeds

2 tablespoons (30 ml) Dick's Reduced-Sodium Soy Sauce

2 teaspoons (5.4 g) fresh ginger, grated, or 1¼ teaspoons (2.3 g) ground ginger

¼ cup (25 g) scallions, chopped

1 pound (455 g) tuna steaks

In a resealable plastic bag, combine first 6 ingredients (through scallions). Add the tuna and let marinate for 20 minutes. Broil or grill the tuna 6 inches (15 cm) from the heat source for 4 to 5 minutes per side. Cook until done as desired.

Yield: 4 servings

Per serving: 208 calories (21% from fat, 27% from protein, 52% from carbohydrate); 27 g protein; 9 g total fat; 2 g saturated fat; 3 g monounsaturated fat; 4 g polyunsaturated fat; 51 g carbohydrate; 0 g fiber; 1 g sugar; 299 mg phosphorus; 19 mg calcium; 1 mg iron; 98 mg sodium; 349 mg potassium; 2548 IU vitamin A; 743 mg ATE vitamin E; 4 mg vitamin C; 43 mg cholesterol; 100 g water

Chicken Egg Foo Young

This can also be made meatless or, as I like to do, with some leftover chicken.

For Sauce:

2 tablespoons (30 ml) Dick's Reduced-Sodium Soy Sauce (see recipe page 30)

½ cup (120 ml) low sodium chicken broth

1 teaspoon (4 g) sugar

1 teaspoon (5 ml) rice vinegar

1 teaspoon (3 g) cornstarch

For Chicken:

1½ cups (355 ml) egg substitute

2 cups Chinese mixed vegetables

1 cup (110 g) cooked chicken breast, diced

2 tablespoons (30 ml) canola oil

To make the sauce: In a jar with a tight-fitting lid, shake together the sauce ingredients until cornstarch is dissolved. Pour into a saucepan and heat until just boiling. Simmer 5 minutes. Set aside.

To make the chicken: Mix the egg substitute, mixed vegetables, and chicken. Heat the oil in a heavy skillet. Spoon the egg mixture into the skillet to form small patties. Turn, browning both sides. Serve with sauce.

Yield: 4 servings

Per serving: 274 calories (23% from fat, 22% from protein, 55% from carbohydrate); 25 g protein; 11 g total fat; 2 g saturated fat; 3 g monounsaturated fat; 7 g polyunsaturated fat; 64 g carbohydrate; 4 g fiber; 6 g sugar; 255 mg phosphorus; 83 mg calcium; 3 mg iron; 285 mg sodium; 600 mg potassium; 4241 IU vitamin A; 2 mg ATE vitamin E; 3 mg vitamin C; 31 mg cholesterol; 216 g water

Spinach and Mushroom Stir-Fry

A vegetable stir-fry, this makes an excellent accompaniment to one of the Asian-flavored fish recipes.

2 tablespoons (30 ml) olive oil

½ teaspoon (1.5 g) minced garlic

1 teaspoon (2 g) fresh ginger, minced

¼ teaspoon (0.3 g) red pepper flakes

1 cup (150 g) red bell pepper, cut in 1-inch (2.5 cm) pieces

½ cup (35 g) mushrooms, sliced

10 ounces (280 g) fresh spinach, washed, stemmed, and coarsely chopped

Heat wok over high heat 1 minute or until hot. Drizzle oil into wok; heat 30 seconds. Add garlic, ginger, and red pepper flakes; stir-fry for 30 seconds. Add red bell pepper and mushrooms; stir-fry for 2 minutes. Add spinach; stir-fry for 1 to 2 minutes or until spinach is wilted.

Yield: 4 servings

Per serving: 96 calories (62% from fat, 13% from protein, 25% from carbohydrate); 4 g protein; 7 g total fat; 1 g saturated fat; 5 g monounsaturated fat; 1 g polyunsaturated fat; 7 g carbohydrate; 4 g fiber; 2 g sugar; 54 mg phosphorus; 113 mg calcium; 2 mg iron; 71 mg sodium; 330 mg potassium; 9761 IU vitamin A; 0 mg ATE vitamin E; 50 mg vitamin C; 0 mg cholesterol; 106 g water

Fried Rice

This is similar to the fried rice flavor of Rice-a-Roni. I don't know if any of you have been missing that kind of boxed convenience or not, but this is very nearly as easy to make (there's just a little extra measuring) and a whole lot better for you.

1 tablespoon (15 ml) olive oil

1 cup (185 g) long-grain rice

½ cup (90 g) orzo, or other small pasta

3½ cups (825 ml) water

½ teaspoon (1.5 g) onion powder

¼ teaspoon (0.5 g) garlic powder

1 teaspoon (0.1 g) dried parsley

1 tablespoon (6 g) oriental seasoning

¼ cup (60 ml) Dick's Reduced-Sodium Soy Sauce
(see recipe page 30)

TIP *If water is not all absorbed (it will depend on the kind of pasta you use), you may need to remove the lid for the last 5 minutes of cooking time.*

Heat oil in a skillet over medium-high heat and sauté rice and pasta for 2 minutes, or until pasta is golden brown. Add remaining ingredients, cover, reduce heat, and simmer for 20 minutes or until rice is tender.

Yield: 6 servings

Per serving: 213 calories (5% from fat, 4% from protein, 91% from carbohydrate); 5 g protein; 3 g total fat; 0 g saturated fat; 2 g monounsaturated fat; 2 g polyunsaturated fat; 105 g carbohydrate; 1 g fiber; 2 g sugar; 81 mg phosphorus; 24 mg calcium; 2 mg iron; 77 mg sodium; 112 mg potassium; 22 IU vitamin A; 0 mg ATE vitamin E; 0 mg vitamin C; 0 mg cholesterol; 159 g water

Lo Mein

Who says you can't have healthy Chinese food? This version is vegetarian, but you could add a little shredded chicken breast or leftover pork loin without blowing the fat content. Tofu would work well too. I find that something like that makes a great lunch for those days you are home, because it's quick to prepare and very healthy.

1 tablespoon (15 ml) canola oil

¼ cup (40 g) onion, chopped

¼ cup (38 g) green bell pepper, chopped

½ cup (65 g) carrots, sliced

12 ounces (340 g) spaghetti, cooked and drained

¼ cup (60 ml) Dick's Reduced-Sodium Soy Sauce (see recipe page 30)

1 teaspoon (2 g) oriental seasoning

Heat oil in a wok or large skillet. Stir fry onion, green bell pepper, and carrots until crisp-tender. Add spaghetti and soy sauce. Mix together and continue cooking until heated through. Sprinkle with oriental seasoning.

Yield: 6 servings

Per serving: 126 calories (7% from fat, 4% from protein, 90% from carbohydrate); 4 g protein; 3 g total fat; 0 g saturated fat; 1 g monounsaturated fat; 3 g polyunsaturated fat; 85 g carbohydrate; 2 g fiber; 3 g sugar; 48 mg phosphorus; 15 mg calcium; 1 mg iron; 78 mg sodium; 106 mg potassium; 1820 IU vitamin A; 0 mg ATE vitamin E; 6 mg vitamin C; 0 mg cholesterol; 71 g water

Pan-Fried Noodles

This lets you get that Chinese flavor while still staying heart-healthy. The sesame oil adds a nice flavor if you have it.

6 ounces (170 g) ramen noodles, without the seasoning

2 tablespoons (30 ml) sesame oil, divided

2 tablespoons (30 ml) Dick's Reduced-Sodium Teriyaki Sauce (see recipe page 31)

Cook the noodles according to package directions. Heat a wok or large nonstick frying pan over high heat until hot. Add 1 tablespoon (15 ml) of the sesame oil and swirl it around to cover the bottom. Spread the noodles over the oil. Sprinkle the teriyaki sauce over the noodles. Cook until the noodles start to get crisp on the bottom. Turn over all in one piece. Sprinkle the remaining 1 tablespoon (15 ml) sesame oil over the top and cook until that side crisps. Remove from heat and cut in wedges to serve.

TIP *Let the noodles cook without stirring until the teriyaki sauce caramelizes and the noodles start to get crisp.*

Yield: 4 servings

Per serving: 260 calories (48% from fat, 7% from protein, 45% from carbohydrate); 4 g protein; 14 g total fat; 4 g saturated fat; 5 g monounsaturated fat; 3 g polyunsaturated fat; 29 g carbohydrate; 0 g fiber; 1 g sugar; 14 mg phosphorus; 2 mg calcium; 2 mg iron; 27 mg sodium; 20 mg potassium; 0 IU vitamin A; 0 mg ATE vitamin E; 0 mg vitamin C; 0 mg cholesterol; 8 g water

Japanese-Style Eggplant

Asian eggplant is usually long and thin, but I had an abundance of the more traditional American round ones from the garden, so that's what I used for this Japanese-flavored recipe.

1 eggplant

1 tablespoon (15 g) brown sugar

3 tablespoons (45 ml) Dick's Reduced-Sodium Soy Sauce (see recipe page 30)

1 tablespoon (5.5 g) ground ginger

1 tablespoon (15 ml) rice vinegar

½ teaspoon (2.5 ml) sesame oil

½ teaspoon (1.5 g) minced garlic

Peel and cut eggplant into ½-inch (1.3-cm) cubes. Coat a skillet with nonstick vegetable oil spray. Sauté eggplant in skillet until it starts to soften. Mix together remaining ingredients. Stir into eggplant. Cook and stir until eggplant is soft and evenly coated with sauce.

Yield: 4 servings

Per serving: 60 calories (2% from fat, 1% from protein, 96% from carbohydrate); 1 g protein; 1 g total fat; 0 g saturated fat; 0 g monounsaturated fat; 2 g polyunsaturated fat; 84 g carbohydrate; 4 g fiber; 8 g sugar; 41 mg phosphorus; 22 mg calcium; 1 mg iron; 82 mg sodium; 326 mg potassium; 37 IU vitamin A; 0 mg ATE vitamin E; 3 mg vitamin C; 0 mg cholesterol; 125 g water

17

Cajun and Creole

For those of you like me who love the taste of Cajun and Creole cooking, the good news is that it is generally pretty healthy from a cholesterol standpoint. It gets its flavor from spices (and the holy trinity of onions, bell peppers, and celery) and doesn't have to rely on fat. You do, as always, need to be careful about the cut of meat you use. Many of these recipes use boneless chicken breasts, which has become a mainstay of low fat cooking for me. But there are also two recipes for making your own low fat Cajun and Creole turkey sausage to spice things up just a little bit more.

Creole Chicken

This is a typical Creole recipe, with chicken cooked in a tomato-based sauce.
It's good over rice or pasta.

½ cup (80 g) onion, chopped

1 cup (150 g) green bell pepper, chopped

2 cups (360 g) tomatoes, chopped

½ teaspoon (1.5 g) garlic powder

1 teaspoon (1 g) dried thyme

2 bay leaves

2 tablespoons (0.8 g) dried parsley

¼ teaspoon (0.5 g) black pepper

⅛ teaspoon (0.3 g) cayenne pepper

2 boneless chicken breasts, cubed

In a heavy saucepan over high heat, cook the onion and green bell pepper, stirring, until they begin to color. Add the remaining ingredients. Cover and simmer for 10 to 15 minutes, or until chicken is cooked through.

Yield: 4 servings

Per serving: 73 calories (10% from fat, 50% from protein, 40% from carbohydrate); 10 g protein; 1 g total fat; 0 g saturated fat; 0 g monounsaturated fat; 0 g polyunsaturated fat; 8 g carbohydrate; 2 g fiber; 2 g sugar; 104 mg phosphorus; 24 mg calcium; 1 mg iron; 33 mg sodium; 369 mg potassium; 801 IU vitamin A; 2 mg ATE vitamin E; 54 mg vitamin C; 21 mg cholesterol; 151 g water

Chicken Creole with Mango

This recipe is a little more work than some, but it produces a very flavorful chicken. The fruit gives it that island character.

4 boneless chicken breasts

½ cup (120 ml) orange juice

¼ cup (60 ml) lemon juice

1 teaspoon (3 g) minced garlic

¼ teaspoon (0.5 g) black pepper

4 cups (946 ml) water

1 cup (150 g) green bell pepper, chopped

½ cup (65 g) carrots, sliced

1 cup (150 g) red bell pepper, chopped

1 cup (160 g) onion, cut in ½-inch (1.3-cm) slices

3 tablespoons (45 ml) cider vinegar

2 tablespoons (32 g) no-salt-added tomato paste

2 tablespoons (30 g) sugar

2 tablespoons (16 g) cornstarch

2 tablespoons (30 ml) water

2 mangoes, peeled, pitted and cut into ½-inch (1.3-cm) pieces

Combine chicken, orange juice, lemon juice, garlic, and black pepper in large bowl. Cover and let stand, turning occasionally, for 1 hour. Transfer chicken mixture to large saucepan; add water and green bell pepper. Heat to a boil, then reduce heat and simmer, covered, for 20 minutes, or until chicken is almost tender; remove chicken and pat dry. Meanwhile, skim grease from cooking liquid; add carrots, red bell pepper, onion, vinegar, tomato paste, and sugar. Dissolve cornstarch in water and stir into cooking liquid. Heat until mixture thickens and bubbles for 2 minutes; reduce heat. Add mangoes. Transfer chicken to platter. Spoon sauce over chicken.

Yield: 4 servings

Per serving: 283 calories (15% from fat, 26% from protein, 59% from carbohydrate); 19 g protein; 5 g total fat; 1 g saturated fat; 1 g monounsaturated fat; 2 g polyunsaturated fat; 43 g carbohydrate; 5 g fiber; 28 g sugar; 199 mg phosphorus; 56 mg calcium; 1 mg iron; 80 mg sodium; 772 mg potassium; 4954 IU vitamin A; 4 mg ATE vitamin E; 130 mg vitamin C; 41 mg cholesterol; 559 g water

Chicken Étouffée

Another of the classic Cajun dishes, along with gumbo and jambalaya. Étouffée is meat served in a brown, tomato-flavored sauce. It's typically served over rice.

2 tablespoons (28 g) unsalted margarine

1 cup (160 g) onion, chopped

1 tablespoon (8 g) flour

1 pound (455 g) boneless chicken breasts

¾ cup (180 ml) water

2 tablespoons (30 ml) lemon juice

2 tablespoons (32 g) no-salt-added tomato paste

¼ teaspoon (0.5 g) cayenne pepper

2 tablespoons (13 g) scallions, sliced

1 tablespoon (0.4 g) dried parsley

In a saucepan with a tight-fitting lid, melt margarine, add onion, and cook over medium heat until tender. Stir in the flour, blend well. Add chicken, water, lemon, tomato paste, and cayenne pepper. Cook over low heat for 15 minutes, adding more water if necessary. Add scallions and parsley. Serve over steamed rice.

Yield: 4 servings

Per serving: 208 calories (31% from fat, 53% from protein, 15% from carbohydrate); 27 g protein; 7 g total fat; 2 g saturated fat; 4 g monounsaturated fat; 1 g polyunsaturated fat; 8 g carbohydrate; 1 g fiber; 3 g sugar; 249 mg phosphorus; 35 mg calcium; 1 mg iron; 147 mg sodium; 465 mg potassium; 607 IU vitamin A; 75 mg ATE vitamin E; 12 mg vitamin C; 66 mg cholesterol; 183 g water

Chicken Gumbo

Gumbo is *the* classic Cajun recipe, and this is one of my favorite recipes. Despite being low in sodium and fat, it has an excellent flavor that brings back memories of little restaurants just off Bourbon Street. Filé powder, or powdered sassafras leaves, is frequently used in Cajun cooking and acts as a flavoring and thickening agent.

2 pounds (905 g) boneless chicken breast

2 tablespoons (6 g) minced garlic

¼ cup (60 ml) olive oil

1 cup (150 g) red bell peppers, chopped

1 cup (160 g) onion, chopped

⅓ cup (40 g) flour

2 cups (360 g) canned no-salt-added tomatoes

½ cup (90 g) frozen okra, thawed

¼ teaspoon (1.3 ml) hot pepper sauce

1 tablespoon filé powder

Cook chicken with 5 cups (1.2 L) water and garlic until tender. Cut chicken into bite-sized pieces. Skim any fat off cooking liquid. Heat the oil in a skillet over medium heat and brown the red bell pepper and onions. Add the flour and brown. Gradually stir in some of the cooking liquid to make a roux (to desired thickness). Add tomatoes, cover and simmer for 30 minutes, adding more cooking liquid if needed. Add chicken and okra. Simmer for a few minutes. Season with hot pepper sauce. Add gumbo filé powder and stir until blended (it has a tendency to lump).

Yield: 8 servings

Per serving: 232 calories (33% from fat, 49% from protein, 18% from carbohydrate); 28 g protein; 8 g total fat; 1 g saturated fat; 5 g monounsaturated fat; 1 g polyunsaturated fat; 11 g carbohydrate; 2 g fiber; 3 g sugar; 257 mg phosphorus; 47 mg calcium; 2 mg iron; 85 mg sodium; 504 mg potassium; 703 IU vitamin A; 7 mg ATE vitamin E; 34 mg vitamin C; 66 mg cholesterol; 184 g water

Cajun Chicken Kabobs

The yogurt, while not traditionally a Cajun ingredient, helps to keep the chicken moist and limit the spiciness.

1 pound (455 g) boneless chicken breast halves, cubed

5½ ounces (155 g) plain fat-free yogurt

1 tablespoon (9.6 g) Cajun seasoning

2 teaspoons (4 g) ground coriander

½ teaspoon (2.5 ml) lemon juice

1 cup (150 g) red bell pepper, diced

8 ounces (225 g) pineapple chunks

TIP *We usually serve this over rice, but it's also good as part of a main dish salad.*

Preheat grill or broiler. Place the chicken in a bowl. Mix the yogurt, Cajun seasoning, coriander, and lemon juice together and stir into the chicken. Refrigerate for 10 to 15 minutes. Thread onto 4 large skewers, alternating with the red bell pepper and pineapple pieces. Place on the grill or under the broiler and cook for 10 to 15 minutes, turning occasionally, basting with any remaining marinade.

Yield: 4 servings

Per serving: 176 calories (9% from fat, 67% from protein, 24% from carbohydrate); 29 g protein; 2 g total fat; 0 g saturated fat; 0 g monounsaturated fat; 0 g polyunsaturated fat; 10 g carbohydrate; 1 g fiber; 9 g sugar; 297 mg phosphorus; 105 mg calcium; 1 mg iron; 106 mg sodium; 557 mg potassium; 1233 IU vitamin A; 8 mg ATE vitamin E; 57 mg vitamin C; 67 mg cholesterol; 207 g water

Creole Chicken Spaghetti

This is a creamy, spicy dish that is typical of Creole cooking, which relies more heavily on the French influence than Cajun cooking does.

2 quarts (1.9 L) water

1 cup (160 g) onion, chopped, divided

1 cup (150 g) green bell pepper, chopped, divided

½ cup (50 g) celery, sliced, divided

½ teaspoon (1 g) black pepper

½ teaspoon (0.9 g) cayenne pepper

1 teaspoon (2.4 g) Cajun seasoning

1 pound (455 g) boneless chicken breast

2 tablespoons (30 ml) olive oil

1 cup (70 g) mushrooms, sliced

10.5-ounce (295-g) can low sodium cream of mushroom soup

½ cup (60 g) low fat Monterey jack cheese, shredded

12 ounces (340 g) angel hair pasta

Bring water to a boil. Add ½ cup (80 g) onion, ½ cup (75 g) green pepper, and ¼ cup (25 g) celery. Stir in black pepper, cayenne pepper, and Cajun seasoning. Add boneless chicken breast and boil for 30 minutes, or until chicken is done. Strain and save cooking liquid. While chicken is cooking, heat olive oil in a skillet and sauté remaining bell pepper, onion, and celery until soft. When vegetables are almost done, add mushrooms and sauté until tender. Add cream of mushroom soup. Add cheese to vegetable mixture and stir until melted. Add 1 cup (235 ml) of reserved cooking liquid. Season vegetable mixture to taste with additional cayenne pepper and Cajun seasoning, if desired. Cut chicken into 1-inch (2.5-cm) cubes and add to mixture. Boil angel hair pasta in remaining cooking liquid according to package directions. Combine pasta with chicken sauce.

Yield: 4 servings

Per serving: 390 calories (30% from fat, 35% from protein, 35% from carbohydrate); 35 g protein; 13 g total fat; 3 g saturated fat; 6 g monounsaturated fat; 3 g polyunsaturated fat; 34 g carbohydrate; 6 g fiber; 5 g sugar; 420 mg phosphorus; 130 mg calcium; 2 mg iron; 218 mg sodium; 582 mg potassium; 413 IU vitamin A; 22 mg ATE vitamin E; 36 mg vitamin C; 70 mg cholesterol; 792 g water

Chicken with Okra

This makes a gumbo-like dish, almost a soup. It's best served over rice.

1 tablespoon (15 ml) olive oil

1 pound (455 g) boneless chicken breasts

1 cup (160 g) onion, coarsely chopped

1 cup (150 g) green bell peppers, coarsely chopped

½ cup (60 g) celery, sliced

½ teaspoon (1.5 g) minced garlic

⅔ pounds (305 g) okra, sliced

2 cups (360 g) tomatoes, chopped

¼ cup (15 g) fresh parsley, chopped

½ teaspoon (1.3 g) paprika

1 bay leaf

½ cup (120 ml) low sodium chicken broth

¼ cup (60 ml) white wine

¼ teaspoon (1 ml) hot pepper sauce

Heat oil in a nonstick Dutch oven over medium heat. Add chicken and cook, stirring occasionally, for 10 minutes, or until brown on all sides. Remove chicken from pan. Add onion, green bell pepper, celery, and garlic; stir and cook for 5 minutes. Add okra and cook, stirring, for 5 minutes more. Stir in tomatoes, parsley, paprika, and bay leaf. Return chicken to Dutch oven and spoon vegetable mixture over top. In a small bowl, mix together chicken broth, wine and hot pepper sauce, pour over all. Cover, reduce heat to low, and cook for 30 minutes, or until chicken is done.

Yield: 4 servings

Per serving: 236 calories (21% from fat, 52% from protein, 27% from carbohydrate); 30 g protein; 5 g total fat; 1 g saturated fat; 3 g monounsaturated fat; 1 g polyunsaturated fat; 16 g carbohydrate; 5 g fiber; 4 g sugar; 322 mg phosphorus; 106 mg calcium; 2 mg iron; 174 mg sodium; 905 mg potassium; 1439 IU vitamin A; 7 mg ATE vitamin E; 75 mg vitamin C; 66 mg cholesterol; 351 g water

Slow-Cooker Chicken Jambalaya

I'm a big fan of jambalaya and similar rice dishes. This is an easy way to make it, simple in preparation. And there's something very nice about coming home to a house that smells of Cajun cooking.

1 pound (455 g) boneless chicken breast

½ pound (225 g) Mild Cajun Turkey Sausage (see recipe page 387)

4 cups (720 g) canned no-salt-added tomatoes

½ cup (80 g) onion, chopped

½ cup (75 g) green pepper, chopped

1 cup (235 ml) low sodium chicken broth

½ cup (120 ml) white wine

2 teaspoons (2 g) dried oregano

2 teaspoons (0.2 g) dried parsley

2 teaspoons (5 g) Cajun seasoning

1 teaspoon (1.8 g) cayenne pepper

2 cups (330 g) cooked rice

Cut up chicken and crumble sausage. Add to slow cooker along with onion and green pepper. Add remaining ingredients, except rice. Cook on low for 6 to 8 hours. Half an hour before eating, add cooked rice; heat through.

Yield: 6 servings

Per serving: 202 calories (8% from fat, 45% from protein, 47% from carbohydrate); 21 g protein; 2 g total fat; 0 g saturated fat; 0 g monounsaturated fat; 0 g polyunsaturated fat; 22 g carbohydrate; 3 g fiber; 4 g sugar; 227 mg phosphorus; 79 mg calcium; 3 mg iron; 85 mg sodium; 607 mg potassium; 430 IU vitamin A; 5 mg ATE vitamin E; 27 mg vitamin C; 44 mg cholesterol; 312 g water

Chicken Jambalaya

I love a good Jambalaya. This dish takes a little more effort, but it's worth it in my opinion.

1 pound (455 g) boneless chicken breast

4 cups (946 ml) water

2 cups (320 g) onion, chopped

½ cup (60 g) celery

3 tablespoons (30 g) garlic, minced

1 tablespoon (15 ml) olive oil

½ pound (225 g) Mild Cajun Turkey Sausage (see recipe page 387)

½ cup (75 g) green bell peppers

¼ cup (25 g) scallions

2 cups (360 g) canned no-salt-added tomatoes, undrained

2 tablespoons (30 ml) Worcestershire sauce

¼ teaspoon (0.3 g) dried thyme

¼ teaspoon (0.5 g) cayenne pepper

2 cups (370 g) long-grain rice

In a large saucepan, combine the chicken breasts, the water, half the chopped onion, half the chopped celery, and one-third of the garlic. Bring to a simmer over medium-high heat. Reduce the heat to medium-low and cook, partially covered, for 20 to 25 minutes, or until the chicken juices run clear when pierced with a fork. Remove the chicken breasts from the cooking liquid. In a sieve set over a large bowl, drain and reserve the cooking liquid, discarding the solids. You should have about 4 cups (946 ml) of liquid; add water, if necessary. Chop the breast meat coarsely and set it aside. Heat the oil in a 5-quart (4.7-L) Dutch oven. Add the sausage and cook over medium heat, stirring often, for 5 minutes, or until lightly browned. Then stir in the reserved cooking liquid; the remaining, onion, celery, and garlic; the green bell peppers; scallions; tomatoes with their juice; Worcestershire sauce; thyme; and cayenne pepper. Bring to a simmer, breaking up the tomatoes with a spoon. Stir in the rice and return to a simmer. Cook over medium-low heat, tightly covered, until the rice has absorbed all the liquid, about 25 minutes. Remove the Dutch oven from the heat, stir in the reserved chicken, cover, and let stand for 5 minutes.

Yield: 6 servings

(continued on page 380)

Per serving: 439 calories (15% from fat, 27% from protein, 58% from carbohydrate); 29 g protein; 7 g total fat; 2 g saturated fat; 3 g monounsaturated fat; 1 g polyunsaturated fat; 63 g carbohydrate; 3 g fiber; 6 g sugar; 338 mg phosphorus; 92 mg calcium; 8 mg iron; 235 mg sodium; 682 mg potassium; 328 IU vitamin A; 21 mg ATE vitamin E; 45 mg vitamin C; 64 mg cholesterol; 397 g water

Cajun Red Beans and Rice

I've always been a fan of red beans and rice, although most of the packaged ones leave a lot to be desired from a healthy cooking standpoint. So I began experimenting. This is my favorite so far, producing a nice "gravy" with just enough heat, without being overpowering, and just slightly sweet. Feel free to vary the amount of spices to suit your idea of how hot they should be.

1 pound (455 g) dried kidney beans

6 cups (1.4 L) water

2 teaspoons (10 ml) hot pepper sauce

½ teaspoon (3 ml) Worcestershire sauce

2 tablespoons (30 ml) oil

¾ cup (112 g) green bell pepper, chopped

1 cup (100 g) scallions, chopped

1 cup (160 g) onions, chopped

½ teaspoon (1.5 g) minced garlic

2 teaspoons (10 g) brown sugar

¼ cup (30 g) flour

½ teaspoon (1 g) black pepper

½ teaspoon (1.2 g) Cajun seasoning

Place beans in a large pot and cover with water. Add hot pepper sauce and Worcestershire and allow to soak overnight. Heat oil in a large skillet over medium-high heat and sauté the green bell pepper, scallions, and onions until onions are soft. Add garlic, brown sugar, and flour. Stir constantly over medium heat for 5 to 6 minutes, or until browned. Add to pot with beans. Cook over low heat for 2 to 3 hours, or until beans are soft and mixture is thickened. Stir occasionally, adding water as needed. Add pepper and Cajun seasoning to suit your taste. Serve with rice.

Yield: 8 servings

Per serving: 136 calories (24% from fat, 17% from protein, 59% from carbohydrate); 6 g protein; 4 g total fat; 1 g saturated fat; 1 g monounsaturated fat; 2 g polyunsaturated fat; 21 g carbohydrate; 5 g fiber; 3 g sugar; 99 mg phosphorus; 39 mg calcium; 2 mg iron; 155 mg sodium; 333 mg potassium; 197 IU vitamin A; 0 mg ATE vitamin E; 16 mg vitamin C; 0 mg cholesterol; 259 g water

Cajun Rice

Just a little spicy, enough to give you that Cajun flavor. If you like more heat, add a little more hot pepper sauce. This makes quite a lot, which is good for me because I take the leftovers to work for lunch. You could halve the quantities if you want less.

2 tablespoons (30 ml) olive oil

½ cup (80 g) onion, chopped

½ cup (75 g) green bell pepper, chopped

½ cup (50 g) scallions, chopped

½ teaspoon (1.5 g) garlic, crushed

1 cup (70 g) mushrooms, sliced

2 cups (360 g) canned no-salt-added tomatoes

¼ cup (35 g) chopped green chilis

1 teaspoon (2.4 g) Cajun seasoning

¼ cup (15 g) chopped fresh cilantro

⅛ teaspoon hot pepper sauce

4 cups (660 g) cooked brown rice

Heat oil in a large skillet over medium-high heat and sauté the onion, green bell pepper, scallions, garlic, and mushrooms for 5 10 minutes, or until soft. Add the remaining ingredients except rice and mix well. Stir in the cooked rice, heat through, and serve.

Yield: 8 servings

Per serving: 394 calories (14% from fat, 9% from protein, 77% from carbohydrate); 8 g protein; 6 g total fat; 1 g saturated fat; 3 g monounsaturated fat; 1 g polyunsaturated fat; 76 g carbohydrate; 5 g fiber; 3 g sugar; 336 mg phosphorus; 51 mg calcium; 2 mg iron; 35 mg sodium; 408 mg potassium; 262 IU vitamin A; 0 mg ATE vitamin E; 17 mg vitamin C; 0 mg cholesterol; 103 g water

Okra Pilaf

A Cajun version of rice pilaf, with okra and tomatoes added. This makes a great side dish with blackened fish.

2 cups (200 g) okra, thinly sliced

2 slices low sodium bacon, diced

1 cup (150 g) green bell pepper, chopped

1 cup (160 g) onion, chopped

1 cup (195 g) uncooked rice

2 cups(470 ml) low sodium chicken broth

2 cups (360 g) canned no-salt-added tomatoes

In a large skillet, sauté okra and bacon until lightly browned. Add green bell peppers and onions; continue cooking until vegetables are crisp-tender. Add rice and chicken broth. Bring to a boil, stir once, cover, reduce heat and simmer for 20 minutes, or until rice is tender and liquid is absorbed. Add tomatoes; heat through and fluff with a fork.

Yield: 4 servings

Per serving: 149 calories (16% from fat, 19% from protein, 64% from carbohydrate); 8 g protein; 3 g total fat; 1 g saturated fat; 1 g monounsaturated fat; 0 g polyunsaturated fat; 26 g carbohydrate; 4 g fiber; 6 g sugar; 152 mg phosphorus; 103 mg calcium; 3 mg iron; 100 mg sodium; 649 mg potassium; 468 IU vitamin A; 0 mg ATE vitamin E; 55 mg vitamin C; 4 mg cholesterol; 372 g water

Hopping John Soup

This soup has a flavor of the Hopping John, which is usually made as a skillet dish. The greens add an additional layer of flavor. This would make a good New Year's Day lunch, since you are supposed to eat black-eyed peas then for good luck.

½ cup (125 g) dried black-eyed peas

1 cup (235 ml) water

3 cups (710 ml) low sodium chicken broth

¼ teaspoon (0.3 g) red pepper flakes

½ teaspoon (1.5 g) minced garlic

¼ cup (50 g) uncooked rice

½ cup (80 g) onion, chopped

½ cup (75 g) green bell pepper, chopped

¼ teaspoon (0.5 g) black pepper

1 teaspoon (2 g) celery seed

1 cup (235 ml) low sodium vegetable juice, such as V8

2 cubes low sodium chicken bouillon

2 cups (72 g) collard greens, chopped

Bring black-eyed peas, water, and broth to a boil in a large saucepan or Dutch oven. Boil uncovered for 2 minutes; remove from heat. Cover and let stand for 1 hour. Do not drain. Stir in red pepper flakes and garlic. Heat to a boil, then reduce heat, cover, and simmer for 1 to 1½ hours, or until black-eyed peas are tender. (Do not boil or peas will burst.) Stir in rice, onions, green bell pepper, black pepper, celery seed, vegetable juice, and bouillon cubes. Cover and simmer for 25 minutes, stirring occasionally. Cut stems out of the center of the collard green leaves. Slice and chop in small strips. Stir in collard greens and simmer until heated through.

Yield: 4 servings

Per serving: 109 calories (14% from fat, 25% from protein, 61% from carbohydrate); 7 g protein; 2 g total fat; 0 g saturated fat; 1 g monounsaturated fat; 0 g polyunsaturated fat; 18 g carbohydrate; 3 g fiber; 5 g sugar; 114 mg phosphorus; 69 mg calcium; 2 mg iron; 152 mg sodium; 466 mg potassium; 2244 IU vitamin A; 0 mg ATE vitamin E; 41 mg vitamin C; 0 mg cholesterol; 362 g water

Cajun Snapper

Somewhat spicy grilled snapper fillets. We prefer this with plain brown rice to help balance the more intense flavor of the fish.

2 pounds (910 g) snapper fillet

1 teaspoon (5 ml) Hot pepper sauce

2 tablespoons (6 g) dried dill

¼ cup (25 g) scallions, chopped

¼ cup (38 g) green bell pepper, chopped

¼ cup (38 g) red bell pepper, chopped

1 teaspoon (2.6 g) filé powder

1 cup (235 ml) Sauterne wine

Lay snapper fillets in a pan that you have sprayed liberally with nonstick vegetable oil spray. Mix remaining ingredients together and pour over the fish. Cover the pan and marinate for 2 to 6 hours. Broil fish in oven or grill to desired doneness.

Yield: 6 servings

Per serving: 191 calories (12% from fat, 81% from protein, 7% from carbohydrate); 31 g protein; 2 g total fat; 0 g saturated fat; 0 g monounsaturated fat; 1 g polyunsaturated fat; 3 g carbohydrate; 0 g fiber; 1 g sugar; 317 mg phosphorus; 74 mg calcium; 1 mg iron; 107 mg sodium; 729 mg potassium; 483 IU vitamin A; 45 mg ATE vitamin E; 17 mg vitamin C; 56 mg cholesterol; 166 g water

Creole Sauce

This is perfect served with grilled chicken breasts or fish.

1 tablespoon (15 ml) olive oil

2 cups (320 g) onion, chopped

1 cup (150 g) yellow bell pepper, chopped

½ cup (60 g) celery, chopped

1 teaspoon (3 g) garlic, minced

4 cups (720 g) canned no-salt-added tomatoes, drained

1 cup (235 ml) low sodium chicken broth

1 teaspoon (0.8 g) fresh thyme

TIP *Sauce may be prepared 1 day ahead and kept chilled and covered, then reheated for serving.*

Heat oil in a heavy saucepan and cook onions, bell pepper, celery, and garlic over moderately low heat, stirring occasionally, until celery is softened. Add tomatoes, broth, and thyme and simmer sauce for 25 minutes, or until most of the liquid is evaporated.

Yield: 12 servings

Per serving: 43 calories (27% from fat, 13% from protein, 60% from carbohydrate); 2 g protein; 1 g total fat; 0 g saturated fat; 1 g monounsaturated fat; 0 g polyunsaturated fat; 7 g carbohydrate; 1 g fiber; 3 g sugar; 34 mg phosphorus; 36 mg calcium; 1 mg iron; 21 mg sodium; 252 mg potassium; 147 IU vitamin A; 0 mg ATE vitamin E; 38 mg vitamin C; 0 mg cholesterol; 137 g water

Hot Creole Turkey Sausage

These are moderately spicy sausages. You can vary the heat by adjusting the amount of cayenne pepper.

1 jalapeño, stems and seed removed, chopped

½ teaspoon (0.9 g) cayenne pepper

1½ pounds (680 g) ground turkey

½ cup (80 g) onion, finely chopped

½ teaspoon (1.5 g) minced garlic

½ teaspoon (1 g) freshly ground black pepper

1 tablespoon (4 g) fresh parsley, minced

¼ teaspoon (1.5 g) salt

¼ teaspoon (0.3 g) dried thyme

1 bay leaf, crumbled

⅛ teaspoon allspice

⅛ teaspoon mace

TIP *These are good for breakfast as well as a dinner meat and are a great addition to classic Cajun recipes like jambalaya and gumbo.*

Combine all ingredients and mix well (running the mixture through a grinder helps to ensure thorough mixing). Stuff casings and form into links or make into patties as desired. Refrigerate up to 3 days for flavors to blend. Sausages may be grilled, pan-fried, or oven-cooked.

Yield: 8 servings

Per serving: 151 calories (27% from fat, 70% from protein, 4% from carbohydrate); 25 g protein; 4 g total fat; 1 g saturated fat; 1 g monounsaturated fat; 1 g polyunsaturated fat; 1 g carbohydrate; 0 g fiber; 1 g sugar; 186 mg phosphorus; 26 mg calcium; 2 mg iron; 134 mg sodium; 280 mg potassium; 102 IU vitamin A; 0 mg ATE vitamin E; 2 mg vitamin C; 65 mg cholesterol; 66 g water

Mild Cajun Turkey Sausage

This is a recipe for an andouille-type sausage. Not as hot as some Cajun sausages, this lower-fat version can be browned and crumbled into various dishes to give them that little extra bit of Cajun flavor.

1 pound (455 g) ground turkey

2 teaspoons (6 g) minced garlic

¼ teaspoon (0.5 g) black pepper

¼ teaspoon (0.5 g) cayenne pepper

1 teaspoon (5 ml) liquid smoke

¼ teaspoon (0.6 g) paprika

⅛ teaspoon dried thyme

⅛ teaspoon dried sage

Mix spices thoroughly into turkey and grill, pan-fry, or bake as desired.

Yield: 8 servings

Per serving: 98 calories (27% from fat, 71% from protein, 2% from carbohydrate); 17 g protein; 3 g total fat; 1 g saturated fat; 1 g monounsaturated fat; 1 g polyunsaturated fat; 0 g carbohydrate; 0 g fiber; 0 g sugar; 122 mg phosphorus; 16 mg calcium; 1 mg iron; 40 mg sodium; 176 mg potassium; 62 IU vitamin A; 0 mg ATE vitamin E; 0 mg vitamin C; 43 mg cholesterol; 37 g water

18

The Wonders of Oat Bran (and Other Soluble Fiber)

As mentioned in the Introduction and Chapter 1 there have been a number of studies that have shown that soluble fiber can reduce the amount of LDL cholesterol (the bad kind). Oatmeal and oat bran have gotten a lot of the attention here and have even been allowed to make medical claims about cholesterol reduction on their packaging. However, there are other good sources of soluble fiber too. Dried peas and beans are one. Grains like barley are another. This chapter contains a variety of recipes that make use of these products. Most of them could have fit easily in another chapter, from breakfast to soup to Mexican and Cajun. But I felt that learning to increase the soluble fiber in your diet was important enough to pull these recipes all together here and give you a quick look at some of the things that you can do on a daily basis.

Multi-Bean Soup

Most large markets carry a bean mixture in their dried bean section. The one I found had 16 varieties. This is a meatless soup, but very filling. It could be made vegetarian by leaving out the chicken bouillon.

1 pound (455 g) mixed dried beans

½ cup (80 g) onion, chopped

½ cup (60 g) celery, sliced

½ cup (65 g) carrot, sliced

1 tablespoon (6 g) low sodium chicken bouillon

2 cups (360 g) canned no-salt-added tomatoes

½ teaspoon (1 g) black pepper

6 cups (1.4 L) water

Soak and drain beans. In a large saucepan or Dutch oven combine all ingredients. Bring to a boil. Reduce heat, cover, and simmer until beans are tender, about 1½ hours.

Yield: 8 servings

Per serving: 215 calories (4% from fat, 22% from protein, 74% from carbohydrate); 12 g protein; 1 g total fat; 0 g saturated fat; 0 g monounsaturated fat; 1 g polyunsaturated fat; 41 g carbohydrate; 10 g fiber; 5 g sugar; 251 mg phosphorus; 117 mg calcium; 4 mg iron; 37 mg sodium; 848 mg potassium; 1449 IU vitamin A; 0 mg ATE vitamin E; 9 mg vitamin C; 0 mg cholesterol; 263 g water

Beef Mushroom Soup with Barley

We have several recipes for beef vegetable soup that we make regularly, but this one is definitely a favorite. It just seems to be the kind of thing you want on a cold day.

1 pound (455 g) beef round steak, coarsely chopped

1 cup (160 g) onion, chopped

1½ cups (105 g) mushrooms, sliced

2 cups (470 ml) reduced-sodium beef broth

4 cups (946 ml) water

1 cup (200 g) pearl barley

½ teaspoon (1.5 g) garlic powder

2 teaspoons (10 ml) Worcestershire sauce

½ teaspoon (0.5 g) dried thyme

1 cup (130 g) carrots, shredded

½ cup (60 g) celery, sliced

½ teaspoon (1 g) black pepper

Brown beef and onion. When beef is almost done add mushrooms and cook a few minutes more. Transfer to a slow cooker, add remaining ingredients, and cook on low for 8 to 10 hours.

Yield: 6 servings

Per serving: 306 calories (14% from fat, 47% from protein, 39% from carbohydrate); 36 g protein; 5 g total fat; 1 g saturated fat; 2 g monounsaturated fat; 1 g polyunsaturated fat; 30 g carbohydrate; 7 g fiber; 3 g sugar; 309 mg phosphorus; 43 mg calcium; 4 mg iron; 176 mg sodium; 699 mg potassium; 3637 IU vitamin A; 0 mg ATE vitamin E; 8 mg vitamin C; 68 mg cholesterol; 348 g water

Black Bean Soup

A flavorful Latin-style soup that's low in fat.

1½ cups (375 g) dried black beans

4 cups (946 ml) water

1 tablespoon (15 ml) olive oil

1 cup (160 g) onion, finely chopped

½ cup (75 g) green bell pepper, finely chopped

½ teaspoon (1.5 g) garlic, minced

½ cup (65 g) carrot, finely chopped

½ cup (60 g) celery, finely chopped

1 teaspoon (2.5 g) cumin

¼ teaspoon (0.5 g) cayenne pepper

1 tablespoon (15 ml) lime juice

¼ cup (56 g) salsa

Soak beans in water overnight. Heat oil in a large Dutch oven over medium-high heat and sauté onion, green bell pepper, garlic, carrots, and celery until almost soft. Add cumin and cayenne pepper and sauté a few minutes more. Add beans, soaking water, lime juice, and salsa and simmer for 1½ to 2 hours, or until beans are beginning to fall apart.

Yield: 6 servings

Per serving: 101 calories (23% from fat, 18% from protein, 60% from carbohydrate); 5 g protein; 3 g total fat; 0 g saturated fat; 2 g monounsaturated fat; 0 g polyunsaturated fat; 16 g carbohydrate; 5 g fiber; 2 g sugar; 82 mg phosphorus; 38 mg calcium; 1 mg iron; 86 mg sodium; 314 mg potassium; 1948 IU vitamin A; 0 mg ATE vitamin E; 14 mg vitamin C; 0 mg cholesterol; 251 g water

Lentil Soup

This is a hearty soup, full of flavor. A dark multi-grain bread would go well with it.

1 tablespoon (15 ml) olive oil

1 cup (160 g) onion, diced

1 tablespoon (10 g) minced garlic

2 cups (360 g) canned no-salt-added tomatoes

1 cup (130 g) carrots, sliced

¼ cup (30 g) celery, sliced

6 cups (1.4 L) water

2 cups (450 g) lentils

Heat oil in a Dutch oven over medium-high heat and sauté onion and garlic until onion starts to soften. Add tomatoes and sauté for 1 minute more. Add remaining ingredients. Bring to a boil, reduce heat to medium-low, and simmer for 1 hour or until lentils are soft.

Yield: 8 servings

Per serving: 99 calories (17% from fat, 21% from protein, 62% from carbohydrate); 5 g protein; 2 g total fat; 0 g saturated fat; 1 g monounsaturated fat; 0 g polyunsaturated fat; 16 g carbohydrate; 5 g fiber; 4 g sugar; 114 mg phosphorus; 46 mg calcium; 2 mg iron; 29 mg sodium; 390 mg potassium; 2779 IU vitamin A; 0 mg ATE vitamin E; 9 mg vitamin C; 0 mg cholesterol; 304 g water

Split Pea Soup

This soup has great flavor, even without the traditional ham, which adds more sodium than I can have. It also has a large helping of soluble fiber to help clean out your blood vessels.

1 cup (160 g) onion, chopped

½ cup (60 g) celery, chopped

½ cup (65 g) carrot, sliced

2 tablespoons (30 ml) olive oil

1½ cups (295 g) split peas

6 cups (1.4 L) low sodium chicken broth

½ teaspoon (0.5 g) dried thyme

½ teaspoon (0.4 g) dried basil

1 teaspoon (2 g) black pepper

TIP *If you prefer a smoother soup, process in batches in a blender or food processor until smooth.*

Heat oil in a large Dutch oven over medium-high heat and sauté onion, celery, and carrot until onion is soft. Add remaining ingredients. Bring to a boil, then reduce heat and simmer for 1 hour, or until peas are very soft. Mash peas with a spoon against the side of the pot until you reach the desired consistency.

Yield: 8 servings

Per serving: 115 calories (34% from fat, 23% from protein, 43% from carbohydrate); 7 g protein; 5 g total fat; 1 g saturated fat; 3 g monounsaturated fat; 1 g polyunsaturated fat; 13 g carbohydrate; 4 g fiber; 3 g sugar; 101 mg phosphorus; 25 mg calcium; 1 mg iron; 66 mg sodium; 365 mg potassium; 1384 IU vitamin A; 0 mg ATE vitamin E; 2 mg vitamin C; 0 mg cholesterol; 229 g water

Mexican Bean Soup

I created this recipe one weekend when I was looking for a fairly large pot of some kind of soup to use for lunches during the week. My original idea was chili, but I had lots of navy beans and no kidney or pinto ones, so this is what we came up with. This is a vegetarian version, but you could add some chicken to it if you're the kind who *has* to have meat. Chipotle peppers are dried, smoked jalapeños. In this recipe, I left the pepper whole so I could take it out at the end. If you can't find them in large markets near you, you could use fresh jalapeños. This makes a moderately spicy soup, but you can also adjust the heat to your desire by using more or less chipotle pepper.

1½ cups (375 g) dried navy beans

6 cups (1.4 L) water

½ chipotle pepper

½ cup (80 g) onion, chopped

½ teaspoon (1.5 g) garlic powder

1½ teaspoons (3.8 g) cumin

2 cups (360 g) canned no-salt-added tomatoes

6 ounces (170 g) frozen corn, thawed

8 ounces (225 g) orzo, or other small pasta

Soak beans in water overnight or bring to boil, boil for 1 minute ,and let stand 1 hour. Add chipotle pepper, onion, garlic powder, and cumin and simmer for 1 to 1½ hours, or until beans are almost tender. Add tomatoes, corn, and pasta and cook until pasta and beans are done. Remove chipotle pepper before serving.

Yield: 8 servings

Per serving: 197 calories (4% from fat, 17% from protein, 78% from carbohydrate); 9 g protein; 1 g total fat; 0 g saturated fat; 0 g monounsaturated fat; 0 g polyunsaturated fat; 40 g carbohydrate; 5 g fiber; 3 g sugar; 151 mg phosphorus; 60 mg calcium; 3 mg iron; 237 mg sodium; 399 mg potassium; 293 IU vitamin A; 0 mg ATE vitamin E; 7 mg vitamin C; 0 mg cholesterol; 297 g water

Black-Eyed Pea Gumbo

Looking for a chili alternative? This could fit the bill. It has great flavor and is a lot lower in fat.

1 pound (455 g) black-eyed peas

1 tablespoon (15 ml) olive oil

1 cup (160 g) onion, chopped

½ cup (75 g) green bell pepper, chopped

½ cup (60 g) celery, chopped

2 cups (470 ml) low sodium chicken broth

1 cup (190 g) brown rice

2 cups (360 g) canned no-salt-added tomatoes

4 ounces (112 g) canned jalapeño, diced

½ teaspoon (1.5 g) minced garlic

Cook black-eyed peas according to package directions. Drain. Heat the olive oil in a large saucepan over medium heat and cook the onion, green bell pepper, and celery until tender. Add the chicken broth, rice, cooked black-eyed peas, tomatoes, jalapeño, and garlic. Bring to a boil, reduce heat to low, and simmer 45 minutes, or until rice is tender. Add water if soup is too thick.

Yield: 8 servings

Per serving: 210 calories (14% from fat, 16% from protein, 70% from carbohydrate); 9 g protein; 3 g total fat; 1 g saturated fat; 2 g monounsaturated fat; 1 g polyunsaturated fat; 38 g carbohydrate; 6 g fiber; 6 g sugar; 188 mg phosphorus; 51 mg calcium; 3 mg iron; 273 mg sodium; 519 mg potassium; 417 IU vitamin A; 0 mg ATE vitamin E; 18 mg vitamin C; 0 mg cholesterol; 199 g water

Turkey Chili

This makes a rather mild chili, but you can easily add more chili powder or some red pepper flakes to spice it up if that's the way you like your chili.

1 pound (455 g) ground turkey

1 tablespoon (15 ml) olive oil

½ cup (80 g) onion, chopped

½ cup (75 g) green bell pepper, seeded and chopped

½ teaspoon (1.5 g) minced garlic

4 cups (900 g) canned black beans, rinsed and drained

2 cups (360 g) canned no-salt-added tomatoes

8 ounces (225 g) no-salt-added tomato sauce

1 cup (235 ml) dark beer

1 tablespoon (7.5 g) chili powder

1 tablespoon (7 g) cumin

1 teaspoon (6 g) coriander

1 teaspoon (1 g) dried oregano

Heat a large, heavy saucepan or Dutch oven over medium-high heat. Brown the turkey until done. Drain and set aside. In the pan, add the oil and bring to medium heat. Add the onion, green bell pepper, and garlic and cook for 5 to 6 minutes, or until vegetables are tender. Return turkey to pan. Add remaining ingredients. Bring chili to a boil; then reduce heat and simmer for 30 to 45 minutes, or until thickened, stirring occasionally. Adjust seasonings to taste.

Yield: 6 servings

Per serving: 361 calories (19% from fat, 39% from protein, 43% from carbohydrate); 34 g protein; 7 g total fat; 2 g saturated fat; 3 g monounsaturated fat; 2 g polyunsaturated fat; 38 g carbohydrate; 12 g fiber; 4 g sugar; 371 mg phosphorus; 103 mg calcium; 6 mg iron; 86 mg sodium; 1025 mg potassium; 679 IU vitamin A; 0 mg ATE vitamin E; 25 mg vitamin C; 57 mg cholesterol; 294 g water

Chicken Chili

This is not like any chili you've had before. I suppose it's a stretch to call it chili at all. But the flavor is great, even if a bit unexpected, and it tastes like chili, so . . .

1 tablespoon (15 ml) olive oil

1 cup (160 g) onion, chopped

½ teaspoon (1.5 g) minced garlic

2 cups (470 ml) water

¾ cup (140 g) quick-cooking barley

4 cups (720 g) canned no-salt-added tomatoes

2 cups (470 ml) low sodium chicken broth

6 ounces (170 g) frozen corn, thawed

6-ounce (170-g) can jalapeños, chopped

1 tablespoon (7.5 g) chili powder

½ teaspoon (1.3 g) cumin

3 cups (330 g) cooked chicken breast, cubed

Heat oil in a Dutch oven and cook onion and garlic until onion is tender. Add remaining ingredients except chicken. Bring to a boil. Reduce heat, cover, and simmer for 10 minutes, stirring occasionally. Add chicken and continue simmering an additional 5 to 10 minutes, or until chicken is heated through and barley is tender.

Yield: 9 servings

Per serving: 143 calories (24% from fat, 47% from protein, 30% from carbohydrate); 17 g protein; 4 g total fat; 1 g saturated fat; 2 g monounsaturated fat; 1 g polyunsaturated fat; 11 g carbohydrate; 2 g fiber; 4 g sugar; 162 mg phosphorus; 52 mg calcium; 2 mg iron; 76 mg sodium; 442 mg potassium; 396 IU vitamin A; 3 mg ATE vitamin E; 13 mg vitamin C; 40 mg cholesterol; 267 g water

White Chili

A delicious, mildly spicy chili with white beans and chicken. You could also use leftover turkey breast.

1 pound (455 g) dried large white beans

6 cups (1.4 L) low sodium chicken broth

½ teaspoon (1.5 g) minced garlic

1 cup (160 g) chopped onion, divided

1 tablespoon (15 ml) olive oil

8 ounces (225 g) canned chili peppers

2 teaspoons (5 g) ground cumin

1½ teaspoons (1.5 g) dried oregano

¼ teaspoon (0.5 g) cayenne pepper

4 cups (440 g) cooked chicken breast, diced

1½ cups (170 g) low fat Monterey jack cheese, grated

Soak beans overnight in water. Drain. Combine beans, chicken broth, garlic, and ½ cup (80 g) onions in a large soup pot and bring to a boil. Reduce heat and simmer for at least 3 hours, or until beans are very soft. Add additional water if necessary. Heat oil in a skillet over medium-high heat and sauté remaining ½ cup (80 g) onions until tender. Add chilis, cumin, oregano, and cayenne pepper and mix thoroughly. Add to bean mixture. Add chicken and continue to simmer for 1 hour. Serve topped with grated cheese.

Yield: 8 servings

Per serving: 407 calories (17% from fat, 44% from protein, 39% from carbohydrate); 45 g protein; 8 g total fat; 3 g saturated fat; 3 g monounsaturated fat; 1 g polyunsaturated fat; 40 g carbohydrate; 10 g fiber; 3 g sugar; 519 mg phosphorus; 272 mg calcium; 8 mg iron; 269 mg sodium; 1461 mg potassium; 213 IU vitamin A; 19 mg ATE vitamin E; 25 mg vitamin C; 65 mg cholesterol; 285 g water

Baked Beans

A picnic's not a picnic without baked beans. These also freeze well, so you might want to make a double batch while you're at it.

½ pound (225 g) dried navy beans

4 cups (946 ml) water

1 cup (235 ml) chili sauce

¾ cup (120 g) onion, chopped

2 tablespoons (30 ml) molasses

2 tablespoons (30 g) brown sugar

1½ teaspoons (4.5 g) dry mustard

¼ teaspoon (0.8 g) garlic powder

1 cup (235 ml) water

Place beans and 4 cups (946 ml) water in a large saucepan. Bring to a boil and cook for 1 minute. Remove from heat and let stand for 1 hour, then return to heat and simmer for 1 hour, or until almost done. Drain. Mix beans with remaining ingredients. Place in a 1½ quart (1.4 L) baking dish. Cover and bake for 4 hours. Add water if needed during cooking.

Yield: 6 servings

Per serving: 107 calories (4% from fat, 13% from protein, 83% from carbohydrate); 4 g protein; 0 g total fat; 0 g saturated fat; 0 g monounsaturated fat; 0 g polyunsaturated fat; 23 g carbohydrate; 3 g fiber; 12 g sugar; 60 mg phosphorus; 56 mg calcium; 1 mg iron; 454 mg sodium; 262 mg potassium; 670 IU vitamin A; 0 mg ATE vitamin E; 9 mg vitamin C; 0 mg cholesterol; 280 g water

Black Beans

These beans are best served over rice. Feel free to increase the pepper sauce if you like things spicy—the lunch I had with the leftovers when I added more hot sauce and cumin was even better than the original meal.

1 cup (250 g) dried black beans

4 cups (946 ml) water

1 tablespoon (15 ml) olive oil

1 cup (160 g) onion, chopped

1 tablespoon (10 g) minced garlic

½ cup (75 g) red bell pepper, diced

¼ cup (60 ml) vinegar

⅛ teaspoon (0.6 ml) hot pepper sauce

1 teaspoon (2.5 g) cumin

¼ cup (15 g) fresh cilantro, chopped

Soak beans in water overnight. Cook over medium heat for 1½ hours, or until tender. Heat the oil in a large skillet and sauté the onion until tender. Add the garlic and red bell pepper and sauté an additional 2 minutes. Add the drained beans, vinegar, hot pepper sauce, and cumin. Bring to a boil and simmer 5 minutes. Stir in the cilantro. Serve over rice.

Yield: 4 servings

Per serving: 114 calories (29% from fat, 16% from protein, 55% from carbohydrate); 5 g protein; 4 g total fat; 1 g saturated fat; 2 g monounsaturated fat; 0 g polyunsaturated fat; 16 g carbohydrate; 5 g fiber; 3 g sugar; 83 mg phosphorus; 36 mg calcium; 1 mg iron; 14 mg sodium; 287 mg potassium; 765 IU vitamin A; 0 mg ATE vitamin E; 28 mg vitamin C; 0 mg cholesterol; 335 g water

Peas and Rice

Black-eyed peas are a southern tradition for New Year's Day. The more you eat on that day, the more prosperous you will be in the coming year. This pea recipe is easy to make and makes a hearty vegetarian meal or a great side dish with pork.

1 cup (250 g) dried black-eyed peas

4 cups (946 ml) water

3 teaspoons (6 g) low sodium chicken bouillon

½ teaspoon (1.5 g) crushed garlic

1 tablespoon (4 g) cilantro

1 tablespoon (4 g) fresh parsley

½ teaspoon (1 g) black pepper

½ cup (80 g) onion, chopped

2 cups (360 g) canned no-salt-added tomatoes

1 cup (195 g) uncooked rice

Combine black-eyed peas and water in large saucepan; add bouillon and garlic. Bring black-eyed pea mixture to a boil; reduce heat and stir in cilantro, parsley, and pepper. Cover and simmer for 15 minutes. Stir in onion and tomatoes. Cover and simmer for 15 minutes, or until black-eyed peas are almost soft. Stir in rice; cover. Cook for 20 minutes, or until rice and black-eyed peas are tender. Remove from heat and let stand.

Yield: 4 servings

Per serving: 231 calories (6% from fat, 21% from protein, 73% from carbohydrate); 13 g protein; 1 g total fat; 0 g saturated fat; 0 g monounsaturated fat; 1 g polyunsaturated fat; 44 g carbohydrate; 6 g fiber; 4 g sugar; 238 mg phosphorus; 99 mg calcium; 6 mg iron; 70 mg sodium; 873 mg potassium; 288 IU vitamin A; 0 mg ATE vitamin E; 15 mg vitamin C; 0 mg cholesterol; 401 g water

Curried Chickpeas

This makes a great side dish with grilled chicken (try the Indian Chicken recipe on page 143).

1 tablespoon (15 ml) olive oil

1 tablespoon (11 g) mustard seeds

dash red pepper flakes

½ cup (80 g) shallot, minced

4 cups (960 g) cooked garbanzo beans

½ teaspoon (1.1 g) turmeric

½ teaspoon (1.3 g) cumin

¼ teaspoon (0.5 g) ground ginger

¼ cup (15 g) fresh cilantro

Heat oil in a large saucepan and fry mustard seeds until they begin to pop. Add red pepper flakes and shallots and sauté until shallots are soft. Add garbanzo beans, turmeric, cumin, ginger, and enough water to prevent sticking. Simmer for 15 minutes, then sprinkle with cilantro.

Yield: 6 servings

Per serving: 220 calories (23% from fat, 19% from protein, 59% from carbohydrate); 11 g protein; 6 g total fat; 1 g saturated fat; 3 g monounsaturated fat; 2 g polyunsaturated fat; 33 g carbohydrate; 9 g fiber; 5 g sugar; 210 mg phosphorus; 72 mg calcium; 4 mg iron; 11 mg sodium; 394 mg potassium; 309 IU vitamin A; 0 mg ATE vitamin E; 3 mg vitamin C; 0 mg cholesterol; 78 g water

Lentils

This recipe can be used as a side dish or as the center of a meatless meal. And it provides a large serving of fiber while being low in fat.

1 cup (192 g) dried lentils
1 tablespoon (15 ml) olive oil
½ cup (80 g) onion, chopped
3 cups (710 ml) water

Soak the lentils using the traditional overnight method or the quick soak method on the bag. Heat oil in a skillet and sauté onions until just soft. Combine lentils, onions, and water in a pan and bring to a boil over high heat. Reduce to low heat, cover, and cook for 30 minutes. Drain and serve.

Yield: 2 servings

Per serving: 191 calories (33% from fat, 19% from protein, 48% from carbohydrate); 9 g protein; 7 g total fat; 1 g saturated fat; 5 g monounsaturated fat; 1 g polyunsaturated fat; 24 g carbohydrate; 9 g fiber; 3 g sugar; 190 mg phosphorus; 39 mg calcium; 3 mg iron; 14 mg sodium; 427 mg potassium; 9 IU vitamin A; 0 mg ATE vitamin E; 4 mg vitamin C; 0 mg cholesterol; 459 g water

Black-Eyed Pea Salad

This recipe comes to us from the South, with roots back to Africa.

1½ cups (250 g) dried black-eyed peas, cooked and drained

1 cup (160 g) onion, minced

½ cup (75 g) green bell pepper, chopped

½ cup (75 g) red bell pepper, chopped

1 teaspoon (3 g) minced garlic

3 tablespoons (45 ml) red wine vinegar

2 tablespoons (30 ml) olive oil

½ teaspoon (0.5 g) dried thyme

Pour the drained black-eyed peas into a medium bowl and add the onion, green and red bell peppers, and garlic. In another bowl, combine the vinegar, olive oil, and thyme to form the marinade. Pour the marinade over the black-eyed pea mixture, cover with plastic wrap, and refrigerate overnight so that the flavors blend, stirring occasionally.

Yield: 4 servings

Per serving: 172 calories (37% from fat, 14% from protein, 48% from carbohydrate); 6 g protein; 7 g total fat; 1 g saturated fat; 5 g monounsaturated fat; 1 g polyunsaturated fat; 21 g carbohydrate; 6 g fiber; 6 g sugar; 100 mg phosphorus; 31 mg calcium; 2 mg iron; 7 mg sodium; 378 mg potassium; 705 IU vitamin A; 0 mg ATE vitamin E; 44 mg vitamin C; 0 mg cholesterol; 123 g water

Cranberry Orange Oat Bran Cereal

If you are looking for a little different taste for breakfast, this could be it. This works with regular oatmeal just as well too. Dried fruits are a favorite of mine. They make great snacks when you want something sweet.

½ cup (120 ml) water

½ cup (120 ml) orange juice

⅓ cup (33 g) oat bran

¼ cup (38 g) dried cranberries

Combine ingredients in a microwave-safe bowl and cook according to oat bran package microwave directions.

Yield: 1 serving

Per serving: 205 calories (6% from fat, 5% from protein, 89% from carbohydrate); 3 g protein; 2 g total fat; 0 g saturated fat; 0 g monounsaturated fat; 1 g polyunsaturated fat; 49 g carbohydrate; 3 g fiber; 22 g sugar; 95 mg phosphorus; 48 mg calcium; 5 mg iron; 61 mg sodium; 316 mg potassium; 244 IU vitamin A; 44 mg ATE vitamin E; 43 mg vitamin C; 0 mg cholesterol; 234 g water

Apple Oat Bran Cereal

How about a nice easy-to-fix hot breakfast?

½ cup (50 g) oat bran

½ cup (120 ml) apple juice

¾ cup (180 ml) water

¼ cup (35 g) raisins

½ teaspoon (1.2 g) cinnamon

Combine ingredients in a microwave-safe bowl. Microwave on high power for 2½ to 3 minutes. Serve with skim milk and honey.

Yield: 1 serving

Per serving: 182 calories (2% from fat, 3% from protein, 95% from carbohydrate); 1 g protein; 0 g total fat; 0 g saturated fat; 0 g monounsaturated fat; 0 g polyunsaturated fat; 47 g carbohydrate; 2 g fiber; 38 g sugar; 51 mg phosphorus; 47 mg calcium; 2 mg iron; 19 mg sodium; 467 mg potassium; 3 IU vitamin A; 0 mg ATE vitamin E; 2 mg vitamin C; 0 mg cholesterol; 289 g water

Oat Bran Waffles

If you have a waffle iron, you might want give these a try. They make a crunchy waffle that's great for a dinner meal when topped with something like chicken à la king.

½ cup (60 g) flour

½ cup (40 g) quick-cooking oats

½ cup (50 g) oat bran

1 teaspoon (4.6 g) baking powder

¼ cup (60 ml) egg substitute

¾ cup (180 ml) skim milk

1 tablespoon (15 ml) honey

2 tablespoons (28 g) unsalted margarine, melted

Mix together first 4 ingredients. Combine egg substitute, milk, honey, and margarine. Add to dry ingredients, mixing until just blended. Cook according to waffle iron instructions.

Yield: 3 servings

Per serving: 288 calories (30% from fat, 14% from protein, 56% from carbohydrate); 10 g protein; 10 g total fat; 2 g saturated fat; 4 g monounsaturated fat; 3 g polyunsaturated fat; 40 g carbohydrate; 3 g fiber; 7 g sugar; 255 mg phosphorus; 216 mg calcium; 4 mg iron; 265 mg sodium; 290 mg potassium; 610 IU vitamin A; 132 mg ATE vitamin E; 2 mg vitamin C; 1 mg cholesterol; 79 g water

Oat Bran Raisin Muffins

A healthy and tasty muffin treat, loaded with artery-cleaning oat bran cereal.

2¼ cups (225 g) oat bran

½ cup (75 g) raisins

1 tablespoon (14 g) baking powder

¼ cup (60 g) packed brown sugar

1¼ cups (285 ml) skim milk

½ cup (120 ml) egg substitute

3 tablespoons (45 ml) canola oil

Preheat oven to 425°F (220°C, or gas mark 7). In a large bowl, combine oat bran, raisins, baking powder, and brown sugar. Combine milk, egg substitute, and oil. Stir into dry ingredients until just moistened. Coat 12 muffin cups with nonstick vegetable oil spray or line with paper liners. Spoon batter into prepared pan and bake for 15 minutes, or until done.

Yield: 12 servings

Per serving: 120 calories (31% from fat, 11% from protein, 57% from carbohydrate); 4 g protein; 4 g total fat; 0 g saturated fat; 2 g monounsaturated fat; 1 g polyunsaturated fat; 18 g carbohydrate; 1 g fiber; 10 g sugar; 119 mg phosphorus; 133 mg calcium; 3 mg iron; 189 mg sodium; 186 mg potassium; 172 IU vitamin A; 40 mg ATE vitamin E; 1 mg vitamin C; 1 mg cholesterol; 33 g water

Oat Bran Apple Muffins

I've always been fond of apple muffins, and the extra cholesterol-fighting benefit of oat bran in these makes them even more appealing.

¾ cup (90 g) flour

¾ cup (90 g) whole wheat flour

1½ teaspoons (3.5 g) cinnamon

1 teaspoon (4.6 g) baking powder

½ teaspoon (2.3 g) baking soda

1 cup (235 ml) buttermilk

½ cup (50 g) oat bran

¼ cup (60 g) packed brown sugar

2 tablespoons (30 ml) canola oil

¼ cup (60 ml) egg substitute

1½ cups (225 g) apple, peeled, cored, and chopped

Preheat oven to 400°F (200°C, or gas mark 6). Coat 12 muffin cups with nonstick vegetable oil spray or line with paper liners. In a large bowl, combine flours, cinnamon, baking powder, and baking soda. In a medium bowl, beat buttermilk, oat bran, brown sugar, oil, and egg substitute until blended. Stir buttermilk mixture into flour mixture just until combined. Fold in apples. Divide batter among muffin cups. Bake 18 to 20 minutes or until wooden pick inserted in centers comes out clean.

Yield: 12 servings

Per serving: 119 calories (22% from fat, 11% from protein, 67% from carbohydrate); 3 g protein; 3 g total fat; 0 g saturated fat; 2 g monounsaturated fat; 1 g polyunsaturated fat; 20 g carbohydrate; 2 g fiber; 7 g sugar; 80 mg phosphorus; 64 mg calcium; 2 mg iron; 133 mg sodium; 125 mg potassium; 49 IU vitamin A; 7 mg ATE vitamin E; 1 mg vitamin C; 1 mg cholesterol; 37 g water

Bran Muffins

Those who think bran muffins have to be dry, tasteless creations should try this recipe. While still providing a fiber boost, these muffins are moist and delicious.

1¼ cups (150 g) whole wheat flour

1 cup (100 g) wheat bran

¼ cup (50 g) sugar

2 teaspoons (9.2 g) baking powder

1 cup (235 ml) skim milk

1 tablespoon (15 ml) canola oil

¼ cup (60 ml) molasses

¼ cup (60 ml) egg substitute

½ teaspoon (1.2 g) cinnamon

¼ teaspoon (0.6 g) nutmeg

1 tablespoon (5 g) orange zest

½ cup (65 g) carrot, grated

Preheat oven to 350°F (180°C, or gas mark 4). Coat 12 muffin cups with nonstick vegetable oil spray or line with paper liners. Mix first 4 ingredients. In a second bowl, mix remaining ingredients. Combine until just moistened. Spoon batter into prepared pan and bake for 20 to 22 minutes.

Yield: 12 servings

Per serving: 116 calories (13% from fat, 12% from protein, 74% from carbohydrate); 4 g protein; 2 g total fat; 0 g saturated fat; 1 g monounsaturated fat; 1 g polyunsaturated fat; 24 g carbohydrate; 4 g fiber; 8 g sugar; 143 mg phosphorus; 103 mg calcium; 2 mg iron; 110 mg sodium; 284 mg potassium; 961 IU vitamin A; 13 mg ATE vitamin E; 1 mg vitamin C; 0 mg cholesterol; 31 g water

Oat Bran Pancakes

Why should breakfast be boring or unhealthy? Try these pancakes and you will not be bored.

1 cup (100 g) oat bran

½ cup (60 g) flour

2 teaspoons (9 g) sugar

2 teaspoons (9.2 g) baking powder

1 cup (235 ml) skim milk

1 tablespoon (15 ml) canola oil

2 tablespoons (30 ml) egg substitute

Heat griddle over medium-high heat. Spray lightly with nonstick vegetable oil spray. Stir first 4 ingredients together. Combine remaining ingredients, add to the oat bran mixture, and mix well. Spoon batter onto griddle and cook until bubbles form on the tops. Turn over and cook until done.

Yield: 4 servings

Per serving: 171 calories (24% from fat, 15% from protein, 61% from carbohydrate); 6 g protein; 5 g total fat; 1 g saturated fat; 2 g monounsaturated fat; 1 g polyunsaturated fat; 27 g carbohydrate; 2 g fiber; 4 g sugar; 205 mg phosphorus; 251 mg calcium; 5 mg iron; 336 mg sodium; 205 mg potassium; 263 IU vitamin A; 71 mg ATE vitamin E; 2 mg vitamin C; 1 mg cholesterol; 64 g water

Oat Bran Peanut Cookies

Another old favorite updated to include oat bran. Just one more tasty way to get your daily helping (and not feel guilty about eating a little something sweet).

½ cup (120 ml) canola oil

1 cup (260 g) reduced-sodium peanut butter

½ cup (120 ml) egg substitute

½ cup (115 g) packed brown sugar

½ cup (100 g) sugar

2 cups (200 g) oat bran

1 cup (125 g) flour

1 teaspoon (4.6 g) baking powder

1 teaspoon (4.6 g) baking soda

Preheat oven to 350°F (180°C, or gas mark 4). In a large bowl combine the oil, peanut butter, and egg substitute until well blended. Mix in the brown sugar, then the remaining ingredients. Refrigerate overnight. Form into 1-inch (2.5-cm) balls and place on an ungreased baking sheet. Press down on the tops of the cookies with a fork to form the typical crisscross pattern. Bake for 15 minutes, or until lightly browned.

Yield: 24 servings

Per serving: 180 calories (51% from fat, 9% from protein, 39% from carbohydrate); 4 g protein; 10 g total fat; 1 g saturated fat; 5 g monounsaturated fat; 3 g polyunsaturated fat; 18 g carbohydrate; 1 g fiber; 10 g sugar; 71 mg phosphorus; 30 mg calcium; 2 mg iron; 119 mg sodium; 135 mg potassium; 55 IU vitamin A; 11 mg ATE vitamin E; 0 mg vitamin C; 0 mg cholesterol; 5 g water

Oat Bran Cookies

The old favorite oatmeal raisin cookies updated to be even healthier with the addition of oat bran.

1 cup (235 ml) canola oil

1 teaspoon (5 ml) vanilla

½ cup (120 ml) egg substitute

1½ cups (340 g) packed brown sugar

2 cups (160 g) quick-cooking or rolled oats

2 cups (200 g) oat bran

1 cup (125 g) flour

½ teaspoon (2.3 g) baking soda

1 cup (165 g) raisins

Preheat oven to 350°F (180°C, or gas mark 4). Mix oil, vanilla, egg substitute, and sugar together in a large bowl. Combine remaining ingredients and stir into sugar mixture. Stir in raisins. Drop onto a baking sheet coated with nonstick vegetable oil spray. Bake for 15 minutes, or until lightly browned.

Yield: 48 servings

Per serving: 122 calories (39% from fat, 6% from protein, 55% from carbohydrate); 2 g protein; 5 g total fat; 0 g saturated fat; 3 g monounsaturated fat; 2 g polyunsaturated fat; 17 g carbohydrate; 1 g fiber; 9 g sugar; 55 mg phosphorus; 16 mg calcium; 1 mg iron; 28 mg sodium; 97 mg potassium; 28 IU vitamin A; 6 mg ATE vitamin E; 0 mg vitamin C; 0 mg cholesterol; 4 g water

Oat Bran Ginger Cookies

Similar to gingersnaps, these cookies still offer the health effects of oat bran.

¾ cup (170 g) packed brown sugar

½ cup (120 ml) light corn syrup

8 tablespoons (112 g) unsalted margarine, softened

¼ cup (60 ml) egg substitute

3 cups (300 g) oat bran

¾ cup (90 g) flour

2 teaspoons (3.6 g) ground ginger

1 teaspoon (2.3 g) cinnamon

1 teaspoon (4.6 g) baking soda

¼ cup (50 g) sugar

Preheat oven to 350°F (180°C, or gas mark 4). Beat brown sugar, corn syrup, and margarine until light and fluffy. Add egg substitute and beat until well blended. In a large bowl combine the oat bran, flour, ginger, cinnamon, and baking soda. Gradually add the oat bran mixture to the brown sugar mixture. Mix well. Shape into 1-inch (2.5-cm) balls. Roll in sugar. Place 2 inches (5 cm) apart on ungreased baking sheet. Flatten to 2-inch (5-cm) diameter. Bake for 12 minutes, or until light golden brown.

Yield: 42 servings

Per serving: 72 calories (29% from fat, 4% from protein, 66% from carbohydrate); 1 g protein; 2 g total fat; 0 g saturated fat; 1 g monounsaturated fat; 1 g polyunsaturated fat; 12 g carbohydrate; 0 g fiber; 7 g sugar; 22 mg phosphorus; 12 mg calcium; 1 mg iron; 49 mg sodium; 37 mg potassium; 133 IU vitamin A; 30 mg ATE vitamin E; 0 mg vitamin C; 0 mg cholesterol; 3 g water

19

Low Fat Baking

Baked goods tend to be high in fat. Sometimes it's the good kind of fat like canola oil, but more often it's the undesirable kind like solid shortening. However, there are ways to improve that situation. Many of the muffins and other baked goods here are fat-free. One key trick is to replace the oil in recipes with applesauce or strained baby fruit. This gives you baked goods with the same texture as their higher-fat cousins. Depending on the other ingredients, you may not be able to taste the difference at all. In some cases, like the apple and peach muffins, the fruit actually complements and adds to the flavor. There also are some reduced-fat versions here of baked goods that usually contain significant amounts of solid shortening, such as biscuits and cornbread.

Apple Muffins

The weekends are a good time to do a little breakfast baking. Not only do you have the time, but if your family is like mine, there are likely to be more people around to enjoy it. And the leftovers make a good grab-and-go breakfast for the first few days of the work week. These muffins are fat-free, owing to the substitution of applesauce for the usual oil.

1½ cups (185 g) flour

¼ cup (50 g) plus 2 teaspoons (25 g) sugar, divided

2½ teaspoons (11.5 g) baking powder

1 teaspoon (2.3 g) cinnamon, divided

¾ cup (180 ml) skim milk

¼ cup (60 ml) egg substitute

⅓ cup (80 ml) applesauce

1 cup (150 g) apple, peeled and chopped

Preheat oven to 400°F (200°C, or gas mark 6). In a large bowl, stir together flour, ¼ cup (50 g) sugar, baking powder, and ½ teaspoon (1.2 g) cinnamon. Make a well in the center. Stir together milk, egg substitute, applesauce, and apple. Add all at once to dry ingredients. Stir until just moistened. Spoon into greased or paper-lined muffin pans. Mix together remaining ½ teaspoon (1.2 g) cinnamon and 2 teaspoons (25 g) sugar. Sprinkle over the tops of the muffins. Bake for 20 minutes.

Yield: 12 servings

Per serving: 95 calories (4% from fat, 12% from protein, 84% from carbohydrate); 3 g protein; 0 g total fat; 0 g saturated fat; 0 g monounsaturated fat; 0 g polyunsaturated fat; 20 g carbohydrate; 1 g fiber; 7 g sugar; 63 mg phosphorus; 86 mg calcium; 1 mg iron; 120 mg sodium; 77 mg potassium; 56 IU vitamin A; 9 mg ATE vitamin E; 1 mg vitamin C; 0 mg cholesterol; 34 g water

Apple Butter Muffins

Sweet enough to eat without adding any toppings.

2 cups (250 g) flour

1 tablespoon (13.8 g) baking powder

2 tablespoons (25 g) sugar

5 tablespoons (70 g) unsalted margarine

¼ cup (60 ml) egg substitute

½ cup (120 ml) skim milk

6 tablespoons (90 ml) apple butter, divided

2 tablespoons (30 g) brown sugar

1 tablespoon (8 g) flour

¼ teaspoon (0.6 g) cinnamon

Preheat oven to 400°F (200°C, or gas mark 6). Combine flour, baking powder, and sugar in a mixing bowl. Cut in margarine until mixture resembles coarse crumbs. Combine egg substitute, milk, and 2 tablespoons (30 ml) of the apple butter. Stir until just moistened. Spoon into 12 paper-lined or greased muffin cups. Top each with 1 teaspoon (5 ml) of the apple butter. Combine brown sugar, flour, and cinnamon and sprinkle over the top. Bake for 20 to 25 minutes.

Yield: 12 servings

Per serving: 161 calories (29% from fat, 8% from protein, 63% from carbohydrate); 3 g protein; 5 g total fat; 1 g saturated fat; 2 g monounsaturated fat; 2 g polyunsaturated fat; 25 g carbohydrate; 1 g fiber; 8 g sugar; 68 mg phosphorus; 93 mg calcium; 1 mg iron; 140 mg sodium; 77 mg potassium; 251 IU vitamin A; 51 mg ATE vitamin E; 0 mg vitamin C; 0 mg cholesterol; 22 g water

Apple Raisin Muffins

You could cook some apples to use for these muffins, but I happened to have a can of unsweetened apple pie filling on hand when I made them, and that is a lot easier.

½ cup (120 ml) water

½ cup (75 g) raisins

1½ cups (180 g) flour

¼ cup (50 g) sugar

2½ teaspoons (11.5 g) baking powder

½ teaspoon (1.2 g) cinnamon

1 cup (260 g) unsweetened apple pie filling

¼ cup (60 ml) egg substitute

¼ cup (60 ml) skim milk

Preheat oven to 400°F (200°C, or gas mark 6). Place raisins in water. Heat in microwave for 2 minutes. Allow to cool for 10 minutes. Stir together flour, sugar, baking powder, and cinnamon. Make a well in the center. Cut up the apples in the filling. Stir together apples, egg substitute, milk, and cooled raisin mixture. Add all at once to dry ingredients. Stir until just moistened. Spoon into greased or paper-lined muffin pans. Bake for 20 minutes.

Yield: 12 servings

Per serving: 112 calories (4% from fat, 9% from protein, 87% from carbohydrate); 3 g protein; 0 g total fat; 0 g saturated fat; 0 g monounsaturated fat; 0 g polyunsaturated fat; 25 g carbohydrate; 1 g fiber; 11 g sugar; 58 mg phosphorus; 74 mg calcium; 1 mg iron; 116 mg sodium; 107 mg potassium; 38 IU vitamin A; 3 mg ATE vitamin E; 0 mg vitamin C; 0 mg cholesterol; 36 g water

Banana Strawberry Wheat Muffins

These are a seasonal sort of thing, good with fresh strawberries.

1 cup (125 g) flour

½ cup (60 g) whole wheat flour

¼ cup (50 g) sugar

¼ cup (28 g) wheat germ

2½ teaspoons (11.5 g) baking powder

½ teaspoon (2.3 g) baking soda

¼ cup (60 ml) egg substitute

¾ cup (180 ml) skim milk

⅓ cup (80 ml) canola oil

½ cup (110 g) banana, mashed

½ cup (85 g) strawberries, chopped

Preheat oven to 350°F (180°C, or gas mark 4). Stir together the first 6 ingredients (through baking soda). Mix together the rest of the ingredients and stir into the dry ingredients, stirring until just moistened. Spoon into greased or paper-lined muffin tins. Bake for 20 to 25 minutes, or until done.

Yield: 12 servings

Per serving: 157 calories (39% from fat, 10% from protein, 52% from carbohydrate); 4 g protein; 7 g total fat; 1 g saturated fat; 4 g monounsaturated fat; 2 g polyunsaturated fat; 21 g carbohydrate; 2 g fiber; 6 g sugar; 104 mg phosphorus; 87 mg calcium; 1 mg iron; 173 mg sodium; 142 mg potassium; 60 IU vitamin A; 9 mg ATE vitamin E; 5 mg vitamin C; 0 mg cholesterol; 33 g water

Strawberry Muffins

A muffin with a flavor like strawberry shortcake. Less sweet than most muffins, with just enough cream cheese to give it a little flavor surprise. Baby food replaces the oil in this recipe, adding flavor and removing fat.

1¾ cups (215 g) flour

2 tablespoons (25 g) sugar

3 teaspoons (13.8 g) baking powder

¼ cup (60 ml) egg substitute

¾ cup (180 ml) skim milk

⅓ cup (80 g) baby food bananas

6 ounces (170 g) frozen strawberries, thawed and drained

6 tablespoons (90 g) fat-free cream cheese

Preheat oven to 400°F (200°C, or gas mark 6). Stir together flour, sugar, and baking powder. Combine egg substitute, milk, and baby food bananas. Stir into dry ingredients, mixing until just moistened. Stir in strawberries. Spoon two-thirds of the batter into the bottom of paper-lined or greased muffin cups. Place ½ tablespoon (7.5 g) cream cheese in each cup. Divide remaining batter evenly among muffin cups. Bake for 20 to 25 minutes, or until done.

Yield: 12 servings

Per serving: 112 calories (5% from fat, 16% from protein, 79% from carbohydrate); 4 g protein; 1 g total fat; 0 g saturated fat; 0 g monounsaturated fat; 0 g polyunsaturated fat; 20 g carbohydrate; 1 g fiber; 3 g sugar; 83 mg phosphorus; 106 mg calcium; 1 mg iron; 164 mg sodium; 106 mg potassium; 106 IU vitamin A; 23 mg ATE vitamin E; 10 mg vitamin C; 5 mg cholesterol; 43 g water

Fresh Berry Muffins

Sweet muffins with a real berry flavor.

2 cups (250 g) flour

2 teaspoons (9.6 g) baking powder

2 tablespoons (25 g) sugar

¼ cup (60 ml) egg substitute

2 tablespoons (28 g) unsalted margarine, melted

1 cup (235 ml) skim milk

½ cup (85 g) strawberries, sliced

Preheat oven to 350°F (180°C, or gas mark 4). Stir together the flour, baking powder, and sugar. In a bowl, mix together the remaining ingredients and stir into the dry ingredients until just moistened. Spoon into greased or paper-lined muffin cups. Bake for 20 to 25 minutes, or until done.

Yield: 12 servings

Per serving: 116 calories (18% from fat, 13% from protein, 69% from carbohydrate); 4 g protein; 2 g total fat; 0 g saturated fat; 1 g monounsaturated fat; 1 g polyunsaturated fat; 20 g carbohydrate; 1 g fiber; 2 g sugar; 70 mg phosphorus; 82 mg calcium; 1 mg iron; 103 mg sodium; 87 mg potassium; 145 IU vitamin A; 31 mg ATE vitamin E; 4 mg vitamin C; 0 mg cholesterol; 31 g water

Blueberry Muffins

These are a real breakfast treat. And you won't even notice that they are fat-free.

1½ cups (180 g) flour

6 tablespoons (75 g) sugar, divided

2½ teaspoons (11.5 g) baking powder

1 teaspoon (2.3 g) cinnamon, divided

¼ cup (60 ml) egg substitute

¾ cup (180 ml) skim milk

(continued on page 422)

⅓ cup (80 ml) applesauce

½ cup (73 g) blueberries

Preheat oven to 400°F (200°C, or gas mark 6). Stir together flour, 4 tablespoons (50 g) sugar, baking powder, and ½ teaspoon (1.2 g) cinnamon. Make a well in the center. Stir together milk, egg substitute, and applesauce. Add all at once to dry ingredients. Stir until just moistened. Stir in blueberries. Spoon into greased or paper-lined muffin cups. Mix together remaining cinnamon and sugar. Sprinkle over the tops of the muffins. Bake for 20 minutes.

Yield: 12 servings

Per serving: 99 calories (4% from fat, 12% from protein, 85% from carbohydrate); 3 g protein; 0 g total fat; 0 g saturated fat; 0 g monounsaturated fat; 0 g polyunsaturated fat; 21 g carbohydrate; 1 g fiber; 8 g sugar; 63 mg phosphorus; 86 mg calcium; 1 mg iron; 120 mg sodium; 73 mg potassium; 56 IU vitamin A; 9 mg ATE vitamin E; 1 mg vitamin C; 0 mg cholesterol; 31 g water

Cranberry Orange Muffins

Easy to make and a good, healthy way to start the day.

1¾ cups (215 g) flour

¼ cup (50 g) sugar

2½ tablespoons (7 g) baking powder

¼ cup (60 ml) egg substitute

¼ cup (60 ml) orange juice

2 tablespoons (30 ml) canola oil

¼ cup (60 ml) applesauce

½ cup (75 g) dried cranberries

Preheat oven to 400°F (200°C, or gas mark 6). Stir together flour, sugar, and baking powder. Combine egg substitute, orange juice, oil, and applesauce. Add all at once to dry ingredients. Stir until just mixed. Fold in cranberries. Fill 12 greased or paper-lined muffin cups. Bake for 20 to 25 minutes.

Yield: 12 servings

Per serving: 129 calories (19% from fat, 8% from protein, 73% from carbohydrate); 3 g protein; 3 g total fat; 0 g saturated fat; 1 g monounsaturated fat; 1 g polyunsaturated fat; 24 g carbohydrate; 1 g fiber; 8 g sugar; 90 mg phosphorus; 176 mg calcium; 1 mg iron; 315 mg sodium; 53 mg potassium; 24 IU vitamin A; 0 mg ATE vitamin E; 2 mg vitamin C; 0 mg cholesterol; 17 g water

Cranberry Sauce Muffins

A good use for leftover cranberry sauce, and great-tasting too.

1½ cups (180 g) flour

½ cup (100 g) sugar

2 teaspoons (9.2 g) baking powder

½ teaspoon (1.2 g) cinnamon

½ teaspoon (0.9 g) ground ginger

½ cup (120 ml) applesauce

¼ cup (60 ml) egg substitute

½ cup (140 g) whole berry cranberry sauce

½ cup (120 ml) orange juice

Preheat oven to 400°F (200°C, or gas mark 6). Stir together flour, sugar, baking powder, cinnamon, and ginger. Combine applesauce, egg substitute, cranberry sauce, and orange juice. Add to dry ingredients and stir until just mixed. Spoon into greased or paper-lined muffin cups. Bake for 19 to 20 minutes.

Yield: 12 servings

Per serving: 121 calories (3% from fat, 8% from protein, 89% from carbohydrate); 2 g protein; 0 g total fat; 0 g saturated fat; 0 g monounsaturated fat; 0 g polyunsaturated fat; 27 g carbohydrate; 1 g fiber; 14 g sugar; 43 mg phosphorus; 53 mg calcium; 1 mg iron; 95 mg sodium; 66 mg potassium; 35 IU vitamin A; 0 mg ATE vitamin E; 4 mg vitamin C; 0 mg cholesterol; 31 g water

Peach Muffins

A good way to start a cold Saturday morning … or a warm one. This recipe uses a trick I read somewhere for reducing fat in baked goods. Instead of the usual suggestion to replace the oil with applesauce, here we use peach baby food, which adds to the peach flavor of the muffins.

For muffins:

1 cup (125 g) flour

½ cup (40 g) oatmeal

¼ cup (50 g) sugar

2½ teaspoons (11.5 g) baking powder

¼ cup (60 ml) egg substitute

¾ cup (180 ml) skim milk

⅓ cup (80 g) baby food peaches

½ cup (100 g) peaches, diced

½ teaspoon (2.5 ml) almond extract

For topping:

2 tablespoons (25 g) sugar

½ teaspoon (1.2 g) cinnamon

To make the muffins: Preheat oven to 400°F (200°C, or gas mark 6). Stir together the flour, oatmeal, sugar, and baking powder. Make a well in the center. Stir together egg substitute, milk, and baby food. Add all at once to dry ingredients. Stir until just moistened. Stir in peaches and almond extract. Spoon into greased or paper-lined muffin cups.

To make the topping: Mix together sugar and cinnamon. Sprinkle over the tops of the muffins. Bake for 20 minutes.

Yield: 12 servings

Per serving: 106 calories (7% from fat, 13% from protein, 80% from carbohydrate); 3 g protein; 1 g total fat; 0 g saturated fat; 0 g monounsaturated fat; 0 g polyunsaturated fat; 21 g carbohydrate; 1 g fiber; 8 g sugar; 92 mg phosphorus; 88 mg calcium; 1 mg iron; 121 mg sodium; 109 mg potassium; 83 IU vitamin A; 9 mg ATE vitamin E; 3 mg vitamin C; 0 mg cholesterol; 32 g water

Tropical Muffins

For those mornings when you are trying to escape the last cold, wet days of winter, these muffins make it a little easier to picture Hawaii.

1¾ cups (215 g) flour

¼ cup (60 g) brown sugar

2½ teaspoons (11.5 g) baking powder

¼ cup (60 ml) egg substitute

¾ cup (180 ml) skim milk

⅓ cup (80 ml) applesauce

6 ounces (170 g) crushed pineapple with syrup, drained

¼ cup (18 g) flaked dried coconut

Preheat oven to 400°F (200°C, or gas mark 6). In a medium bowl, stir together flour, brown sugar, and baking powder. Combine egg substitute, milk, and applesauce and add to dry ingredients. Stir until just mixed. Stir in pineapple and coconut. Spoon into muffin cups lined with paper or coated with nonstick vegetable oil spray. Bake for 20 to 25 minutes.

Yield: 12 servings

Per serving: 112 calories (7% from fat, 11% from protein, 81% from carbohydrate); 3 g protein; 1 g total fat; 1 g saturated fat; 0 g monounsaturated fat; 0 g polyunsaturated fat; 23 g carbohydrate; 1 g fiber; 7 g sugar; 68 mg phosphorus; 90 mg calcium; 1 mg iron; 123 mg sodium; 106 mg potassium; 57 IU vitamin A; 9 mg ATE vitamin E; 1 mg vitamin C; 0 mg cholesterol; 39 g water

Whole Wheat Banana Muffins

Another fresh muffin idea, this time with a way to get rid of those overripe bananas.

¼ cup (60 ml) egg substitute

¾ cup (180 ml) skim milk

⅓ cup (80 ml) applesauce

½ cup (115 g) banana, mashed

1 cup (125 g) flour

½ cup (60 g) whole wheat flour

¼ cup (28 g) wheat germ

2½ teaspoons (11.5 g) baking powder

¼ teaspoon (0.6 g) cinnamon

Preheat oven to 375°F (190°C, or gas mark 5). Combine egg, milk, applesauce, and banana. Stir together remaining ingredients. Add milk mixture and stir until just combined. Spoon into 12 lined or greased muffin cups. Bake for 20 to 25 minutes.

Yield: 12 servings

Per serving: 86 calories (7% from fat, 17% from protein, 76% from carbohydrate); 4 g protein; 1 g total fat; 0 g saturated fat; 0 g monounsaturated fat; 0 g polyunsaturated fat; 17 g carbohydrate; 2 g fiber; 2 g sugar; 103 mg phosphorus; 87 mg calcium; 1 mg iron; 121 mg sodium; 138 mg potassium; 61 IU vitamin A; 9 mg ATE vitamin E; 1 mg vitamin C; 0 mg cholesterol; 33 g water

Date Muffins

I've always been fond of muffins for breakfast. And the good news is that there are lots of nice, healthy recipes for them. Like these whole wheat date muffins, for example.

1 cup (125 g) whole wheat flour

1 cup (125 g) flour

2 tablespoons (25 g) sugar

4 teaspoons (18.4 g) baking powder

¼ cup (60 ml) egg substitute

1 cup (235 ml) skim milk

2 tablespoons (30 ml) canola oil

½ cup (55 g) dates, chopped

Preheat oven to 400°F (200°C, or gas mark 6). Combine flours, sugar, and baking powder. Combine egg substitute, milk, and oil; mix well and add dates. Add to dry ingredients, stirring only until flour mixture is moistened. Fill greased muffin pans and bake for 20 to 25 minutes, or until a wooden pick inserted in the center comes out clean.

Yield: 12 servings

Per serving: 135 calories (18% from fat, 12% from protein, 70% from carbohydrate); 4 g protein; 3 g total fat; 0 g saturated fat; 1 g monounsaturated fat; 1 g polyunsaturated fat; 24 g carbohydrate; 2 g fiber; 7 g sugar; 113 mg phosphorus; 130 mg calcium; 1 mg iron; 185 mg sodium; 155 mg potassium; 62 IU vitamin A; 13 mg ATE vitamin E; 0 mg vitamin C; 0 mg cholesterol; 27 g water

Graham Cracker Muffins

The graham crackers give these muffins flavor as well as whole-grain goodness.

2 cups (168 g) graham crackers, crushed

¼ cup (50 g) sugar

2 teaspoons (9.2 g) baking powder

1 cup (235 ml) skim milk

¼ cup (60 ml) egg substitute, slightly beaten

2 tablespoons (30 ml) honey

Preheat oven to 400°F (200°C, or gas mark 6). Grease 12 muffin cups or line with paper muffin liners. In a large bowl, combine cracker crumbs, sugar, and baking powder. Stir in milk, egg substitute, and honey; mixing just until moistened. Spoon batter into prepared muffin cups. Bake for 15 to 18 minutes, or until a wooden pick inserted in the center comes out clean. Let stand for 5 minutes.

Yield: 12 servings

(continued on page 428)

Per serving: 99 calories (15% from fat, 10% from protein, 76% from carbohydrate); 2 g protein; 2 g total fat; 0 g saturated fat; 1 g monounsaturated fat; 1 g polyunsaturated fat; 19 g carbohydrate; 0 g fiber; 11 g sugar; 61 mg phosphorus; 81 mg calcium; 1 mg iron; 187 mg sodium; 76 mg potassium; 61 IU vitamin A; 13 mg ATE vitamin E; 0 mg vitamin C; 0 mg cholesterol; 24 g water

Chocolate Muffins

Something for those days when you're looking for a sweeter breakfast.

2 cups (250 g) flour

¾ cup (150 g) sugar

2½ teaspoons (11.5 g) baking powder

2 tablespoons (11 g) instant coffee granules

1 cup (235 ml) warm skim milk

½ cup (120 ml) applesauce

¼ cup (60 ml) egg substitute

1 teaspoon (5 ml) vanilla

¾ cup (170 g) miniature chocolate chips

Preheat oven to 375°F (190°C, or gas mark 5). In a bowl, combine flour, sugar, and baking powder. In another bowl, stir coffee into milk until dissolved. Add applesauce, egg substitute, and vanilla and mix well. Stir into dry ingredients until just moistened. Stir in chocolate chips. Fill greased or paper-lined muffin pans two-thirds full. Bake for 17 to 20 minutes, or until muffins are done.

Yield: 12 servings

Per serving: 201 calories (16% from fat, 9% from protein, 75% from carbohydrate); 4 g protein; 4 g total fat; 2 g saturated fat; 1 g monounsaturated fat; 0 g polyunsaturated fat; 38 g carbohydrate; 1 g fiber; 19 g sugar; 97 mg phosphorus; 112 mg calcium; 1 mg iron; 132 mg sodium; 140 mg potassium; 82 IU vitamin A; 18 mg ATE vitamin E; 0 mg vitamin C; 3 mg cholesterol; 35 g water

Streusel Muffins

These muffins are relatively low fat as well as low sodium, and they taste like old-fashioned coffee cake.

For Streusel:
½ cup (115 g) brown sugar

2 tablespoons (16 g) flour

2 teaspoons (4.6 g) cinnamon

For Muffins:
1½ cups (188 g) flour

½ cup (100 g) sugar

2 teaspoons (9.6 g) baking powder

¼ cup (56 g) unsalted margarine

½ cup (120 ml) skim milk

¼ cup (60 ml) egg substitute

To make the streusel: Stir together brown sugar, flour, and cinnamon. Set aside.

To make the muffins: Preheat oven to 375°F (190°C, or gas mark 5). Stir together flour, sugar, and baking powder. Cut in margarine until mixture resembles coarse crumbs. Combine milk and egg substitute. Add to dry ingredients and stir until just mixed. Divide half the batter evenly among 12 greased or paper-lined muffin cups. Sprinkle with half the streusel topping. Top with remaining batter and then remaining streusel topping. Bake for 20 to 25 minutes.

Yield: 12 servings

Per serving: 172 calories (21% from fat, 7% from protein, 72% from carbohydrate); 3 g protein; 4 g total fat; 1 g saturated fat; 2 g monounsaturated fat; 1 g polyunsaturated fat; 31 g carbohydrate; 1 g fiber; 17 g sugar; 58 mg phosphorus; 81 mg calcium; 1 mg iron; 142 mg sodium; 92 mg potassium; 241 IU vitamin A; 52 mg ATE vitamin E; 0 mg vitamin C; 0 mg cholesterol; 16 g water

Good-for-You Muffins

These are my all-time favorite muffins, just packed with things that are good for you, as well as good-tasting.

½ cup (80 g) raisins

2 cups (250 g) flour

1 cup (200 g) sugar

2 teaspoons (9.2 g) baking soda

2 teaspoons (4.6 g) cinnamon

¾ cup (98 g) carrot, grated

1 green apple, grated

½ cup (60 g) sliced almonds

½ cup (35 g) shredded coconut

¾ cup (180 ml) egg substitute

⅔ cup (160 ml) applesauce

2 teaspoons (10 ml) vanilla

Soak raisins in enough hot water to cover for 30 minutes; drain thoroughly. Preheat oven to 350°F (180°C, or gas mark 4). Mix flour, sugar, baking soda, and cinnamon in bowl. Stir in raisins, carrots, apple, almonds, and coconut. Beat egg substitute with applesauce and vanilla to blend. Stir into flour mixture until just combined. Divide batter evenly among 12 greased or paper-lined muffin cups. Bake for 20 to 22 minutes, or until golden brown and a wooden pick inserted in the center comes out clean. Cool 5 minutes before removing from pan.

Yield: 12 servings

Per serving: 241 calories (18% from fat, 9% from protein, 73% from carbohydrate); 6 g protein; 5 g total fat; 1 g saturated fat; 2 g monounsaturated fat; 1 g polyunsaturated fat; 45 g carbohydrate; 2 g fiber; 24 g sugar; 86 mg phosphorus; 37 mg calcium; 2 mg iron; 247 mg sodium; 226 mg potassium; 1411 IU vitamin A; 0 mg ATE vitamin E; 1 mg vitamin C; 0 mg cholesterol; 46 g water

Banana Bread

Another good recipe for using up bananas. This makes a great breakfast or snack.

1¾ cups (215 g) flour

1¼ teaspoons (5.8 g) baking powder

1 teaspoon (4.6 g) baking soda

2/3 cup (133 g) sugar

¼ cup (56 g) unsalted margarine

½ cup (120 ml) egg substitute

¼ cup (60 ml) skim milk

1 cup (225 g) mashed banana

¼ cup (30 g) chopped pecans

Preheat oven to 350°F (180°C, or gas mark 4). Stir together flour, baking powder, and baking soda. In a mixing bowl, cream sugar and margarine with an electric mixer until light and fluffy. Add egg substitute and milk, beating until smooth. Add dry ingredients and banana alternately, beating until smooth after each addition. Stir in pecans. Pour batter into lightly greased 9 × 4 × 2-inch (23 × 10 × 5-cm) loaf pan. Bake for 60 to 65 minutes, or until a knife inserted near the center comes out clean. Cool 10 minutes before removing from pan.

Yield: 12 servings

Per serving: 187 calories (28% from fat, 8% from protein, 64% from carbohydrate); 4 g protein; 6 g total fat; 1 g saturated fat; 3 g monounsaturated fat; 1 g polyunsaturated fat; 30 g carbohydrate; 1 g fiber; 14 g sugar; 61 mg phosphorus; 49 mg calcium; 1 mg iron; 219 mg sodium; 145 mg potassium; 261 IU vitamin A; 49 mg ATE vitamin E; 2 mg vitamin C; 0 mg cholesterol; 30 g water

Cranberry Bread

Reader Miguel sent me this recipe that gets rid of your leftover cranberry sauce. I don't know about you, but that is the one thing that never seems to be completely finished here after Thanksgiving, so I was really grateful. The flavor is excellent. I used the jellied cranberry sauce, but I don't see any reason why the whole berry sauce wouldn't work just as well.

½ cup (120 ml) applesauce

1 cup (200 g) sugar

½ cup (120 ml) egg substitute

1 teaspoon (5 ml) vanilla

2 cups (250 g) flour

1 teaspoon (4.6 g) baking soda

⅓ cup (80 g) orange juice

1 cup (150 g) apples, peeled and chopped

1 cup (277 g) cranberry sauce

1 cup (125 g) chopped walnuts

Preheat oven to 350°F (180°C, or gas mark 4). Cream together the applesauce and sugar until light and fluffy. Beat in egg substitute and vanilla. Combine flour and baking soda. Add dry ingredients alternately with orange juice to egg mixture, beating just until blended. Fold in apples, cranberry sauce, and walnuts. Lightly coat two 7½ × 3¾ × 2¼-inch (18.8 × 9.4 × 5.6-cm) loaf pans with nonstick vegetable oil spray. Pour batter into prepared pans and bake for 50 minutes, or until a wooden pick inserted in the center comes out clean.

Yield: 24 servings

Per serving: 133 calories (22% from fat, 9% from protein, 69% from carbohydrate); 3 g protein; 3 g total fat; 0 g saturated fat; 1 g monounsaturated fat; 2 g polyunsaturated fat; 23 g carbohydrate; 1 g fiber; 14 g sugar; 46 mg phosphorus; 9 mg calcium; 1 mg iron; 66 mg sodium; 73 mg potassium; 31 IU vitamin A; 0 mg ATE vitamin E; 2 mg vitamin C; 0 mg cholesterol; 24 g water

Whole Wheat Pineapple Zucchini Bread

The pineapple adds flavor and moistness to a great breakfast bread.

¾ cup (180 ml) egg substitute

1 cup (235 ml) applesauce

2 cups (400 g) sugar

2 teaspoons (10 ml) vanilla

2 cups (250 g) shredded zucchini

8 ounces (225 g) crushed pineapple, drained

2 cups (250 g) flour

1 cup (125 g) whole wheat flour

2 teaspoons (9.2 g) baking soda

½ teaspoon (2.3 g) baking powder

1½ teaspoons (3.5 g) cinnamon

¾ teaspoon (1.7 g) nutmeg

Preheat oven to 350°F (180°C, or gas mark 4). Grease two 9 × 5-inch (12.5 × 23-cm) loaf pans. Combine egg substitute, applesauce, sugar, and vanilla in a large bowl. Mix well. Add zucchini and pineapple and mix well. Combine flours, baking soda, baking powder, cinnamon, and nutmeg. Stir into zucchini mixture until just moistened. Pour into prepared loaf pans. Bake for 1 hour, or until knife inserted near center comes out clean.

Yield: 24 servings

Per serving: 139 calories (3% from fat, 8% from protein, 89% from carbohydrate); 3 g protein; 1 g total fat; 0 g saturated fat; 0 g monounsaturated fat; 0 g polyunsaturated fat; 31 g carbohydrate; 1 g fiber; 19 g sugar; 46 mg phosphorus; 18 mg calcium; 1 mg iron; 131 mg sodium; 104 mg potassium; 56 IU vitamin A; 0 mg ATE vitamin E; 3 mg vitamin C; 0 mg cholesterol; 35 g water

Pumpkin Bread

If you have some leftover pumpkin when you make pumpkin pie, you can make it into pumpkin bread. This makes a great breakfast without even needing to put any toppings on it.

3 cups (600 g) sugar

1 cup (235 ml) applesauce

1 cup (235 ml) egg substitute

16 ounces canned or cooked fresh pumpkin

3½ cups (438 g) flour

4 teaspoons (18.4 g) baking soda

1 teaspoon (4.6 g) baking powder

2 teaspoons (4.6 g) cinnamon

1 teaspoon (1.8 g) ground ginger

⅔ cup (160 ml) water

Preheat oven to 350°F (180°C, or gas mark 4). Cream sugar and applesauce. Add egg substitute and pumpkin; mix well. Sift together flour, baking soda, baking powder, cinnamon, and ginger. Add to pumpkin mixture alternately with water. Mix well after each addition. Divide batter evenly between two well-greased and floured glass 9 × 5-inch (23 × 12.5-cm) loaf pans. Bake for 1½ hours, or until knife inserted near center comes out clean. Let stand for 10 minutes. Remove from pans to cool.

Yield: 24 servings

Per serving: 184 calories (3% from fat, 7% from protein, 90% from carbohydrate); 3 g protein; 1 g total fat; 0 g saturated fat; 0 g monounsaturated fat; 0 g polyunsaturated fat; 42 g carbohydrate; 1 g fiber; 27 g sugar; 44 mg phosphorus; 28 mg calcium; 1 mg iron; 250 mg sodium; 103 mg potassium; 2983 IU vitamin A; 0 mg ATE vitamin E; 1 mg vitamin C; 0 mg cholesterol; 43 g water

Apple Pinwheels

These little apple rolls are another good weekend breakfast—sweet, but low in fat.

2 cups (250 g) sifted flour

4 teaspoons (18.4 g) baking powder

4 tablespoons (56 g) unsalted margarine, divided

¾ cup (180 ml) skim milk

4 cups (600 g) apple, peeled and sliced

1 teaspoon (2.3 g) cinnamon

1¼ cups (285 g) brown sugar, divided

Preheat oven to 425°F (220°C, or gas mark 7). Sift flour with baking powder. Using two spatulas or a party blender, cut in 2 tablespoons (28 g) margarine. Add milk, mixing quickly and lightly. Turn onto a lightly floured surface. Roll into an oblong sheet ¼-inch (0.6-cm) thick. Melt remaining 2 tablespoons (28 g) margarine and brush over dough. Cover with apples. Mix together cinnamon and 1 cup (225 g) of the brown sugar and sprinkle over the apple. Roll up like a jelly roll. Cut into 12 slices. Sprinkle remaining ¼ cup (60 g) brown sugar over baking sheet sprayed with nonstick vegetable oil spray. Place rolls, cut sides down, on pan. Bake for 25 minutes.

Yield: 12 servings

Per serving: 221 calories (16% from fat, 5% from protein, 79% from carbohydrate); 3 g protein; 4 g total fat; 1 g saturated fat; 2 g monounsaturated fat; 1 g polyunsaturated fat; 44 g carbohydrate; 1 g fiber; 26 g sugar; 83 mg phosphorus; 140 mg calcium; 2 mg iron; 181 mg sodium; 165 mg potassium; 214 IU vitamin A; 45 mg ATE vitamin E; 2 mg vitamin C; 0 mg cholesterol; 49 g water

Banana Sticky Buns

Am I the only one that seems to always have bananas at that use-or-throw-away stage? I hate throwing things away, so I went looking for a different recipe to use bananas and found this one.

¾ cup (75 g) unsalted pecans

¼ cup (56 g) unsalted margarine

⅓ cup (75 g) plus ¼ cup (60 g) brown sugar, divided

2 cups (250 g) flour

1 tablespoon (13.8 g) baking powder

6 tablespoons (90 ml) applesauce

⅔ cup (150 g) mashed bananas

Preheat oven to 375°F (190°C, or gas mark 5). Divide pecans, margarine, and ⅓ cup (75 g) brown sugar between 12 muffin cups. Bake for 5 minutes, or until margarine is melted. Combine flour and baking powder. Stir in applesauce and banana until mixture forms a soft dough. On a lightly floured surface, knead dough a few times until it holds together. Roll or press dough into a 9 × 12-inch (23 × 30-cm) rectangle. Spread remaining ¼ cup (60 g) brown sugar over dough. Roll up from long side. Slice into 12 rolls. Place each in a muffin cup. Bake for 12 to 15 minutes, or until golden. Allow to cool 1 minute before inverting onto a serving platter.

Yield: 12 servings

Per serving: 212 calories (37% from fat, 6% from protein, 58% from carbohydrate); 3 g protein; 9 g total fat; 1 g saturated fat; 5 g monounsaturated fat; 2 g polyunsaturated fat; 31 g carbohydrate; 2 g fiber; 13 g sugar; 75 mg phosphorus; 89 mg calcium; 2 mg iron; 168 mg sodium; 142 mg potassium; 214 IU vitamin A; 46 mg ATE vitamin E; 1 mg vitamin C; 0 mg cholesterol; 20 g water

Reduced-Fat Biscuits

This is a basic biscuit recipe, to which you could add other herbs and spices, a little low fat cheese, or whatever strikes your fancy. They can be made as drop biscuits as well as the rolled and cut version described below.

2 cups (250 g) flour

4 teaspoons (18.4 g) baking powder

2 teaspoons (8 g) sugar

½ teaspoon (1.5 g) cream of tartar

¼ cup (56 g) unsalted margarine

⅔ cup (160 ml) skim milk

TIP *If you don't have a biscuit cutter, you can use a drinking glass or just cut the dough into squares with a knife.*

Preheat oven to 450°F (230°C, or gas mark 8). Stir together flour, baking powder, sugar, and cream of tartar. Cut in margarine until mixture resembles coarse crumbs. Add milk. Stir until just mixed. Knead gently on a floured surface a few times. Press to ½-inch (1.3-cm) thickness. Cut out with a 2½-inch (6.3-cm) biscuit cutter. Transfer to an ungreased baking sheet. Bake for 10 to 12 minutes, or until golden brown.

Yield: 10 servings

Per serving: 142 calories (30% from fat, 9% from protein, 60% from carbohydrate); 3 g protein; 5 g total fat; 1 g saturated fat; 3 g monounsaturated fat; 1 g polyunsaturated fat; 21 g carbohydrate; 1 g fiber; 1 g sugar; 89 mg phosphorus; 139 mg calcium; 1 mg iron; 255 mg sodium; 87 mg potassium; 273 IU vitamin A; 65 mg ATE vitamin E; 0 mg vitamin C; 0 mg cholesterol; 19 g water

Whole Wheat Biscuits

A small variation of the standard biscuit recipe. I sometimes add a little dill to them. If you don't have a biscuit cutter, you can use a drinking glass or just cut it into squares with a knife.

1½ cups (188 g) flour

½ cup (60 g) whole wheat flour

2 teaspoons (8 g) sugar

1 tablespoons (13.8 g) baking powder

¼ cup (56 g) unsalted margarine

⅔ cup (160 ml) skim milk

Preheat oven to 450°F (230°C, or gas mark 8). Stir together flours, sugar, and baking powder. Cut in margarine until mixture resembles coarse crumbs. Add milk. Stir until just mixed. Knead gently on a floured surface a few times. Press to ½-inch (1.3-cm) thickness. Cut out with a 2½-inch (6.3-cm) biscuit cutter. Transfer to an ungreased baking sheet. Bake for 10 to 12 minutes, or until golden brown.

Yield: 10 servings

Per serving: 141 calories (30% from fat, 10% from protein, 60% from carbohydrate); 4 g protein; 5 g total fat; 1 g saturated fat; 3 g monounsaturated fat; 1 g polyunsaturated fat; 22 g carbohydrate; 1 g fiber; 1 g sugar; 153 mg phosphorus; 275 mg calcium; 2 mg iron; 498 mg sodium; 80 mg potassium; 274 IU vitamin A; 65 mg ATE vitamin E; 0 mg vitamin C; 0 mg cholesterol; 19 g water

Lower-Fat Restaurant-Style Biscuits

This recipe has the flakiness and the buttery flavor typical of biscuits served at fast-food chicken restaurants, but without the fat and sodium.

2 cups (250 g) flour

1 tablespoon (13.8 g) baking powder

4 tablespoons (56 g) unsalted margarine, divided

2 ounces (55 g) fat-free sour cream

½ cup (120 ml) club soda, at room temperature

Preheat oven to 375°F (190°C, or gas mark 5). Stir flour and baking powder together. Cut in 2 tablespoons (28 g) margarine with a pastry blender or two knives until mixture resembles coarse crumbs. Mix sour cream and club soda into flour mixture. Turn out onto a lightly floured surface and knead lightly. Roll or pat to ½-inch (1.3-cm) thickness. Cut into 6 biscuits with a biscuit cutter or sharp knife. Place biscuits in an 8 × 8-inch (20 × 20-cm) baking dish sprayed with nonstick vegetable oil spray. Melt remaining margarine and pour over the top. Bake for 20 to 25 minutes, or until golden brown.

Yield: 6 servings

Per serving: 232 calories (32% from fat, 9% from protein, 59% from carbohydrate); 5 g protein; 8 g total fat; 2 g saturated fat; 4 g monounsaturated fat; 1 g polyunsaturated fat; 33 g carbohydrate; 1 g fiber; 0 g sugar; 109 mg phosphorus; 158 mg calcium; 2 mg iron; 335 mg sodium; 66 mg potassium; 435 IU vitamin A; 101 mg ATE vitamin E; 0 mg vitamin C; 4 mg cholesterol; 34 g water

Lower-Fat Cornbread

Cornbread goes well with a lot of things. I've found here, like with a lot of recipes, that reducing the amount of fat called for doesn't really affect the end product at all.

1 cup (140 g) cornmeal

1 cup (125 g) flour

¼ cup (50 g) sugar

1 tablespoon (13.8 g) baking powder

2 tablespoons (28 g) unsalted margarine

1 cup (235 ml) skim milk

¼ cup (60 ml) egg substitute

Preheat oven to 425°F (220°C, or gas mark 7). Mix together cornmeal, flour, sugar, and baking powder. Cut in margarine until mixture resembles coarse crumbs. Stir milk and egg substitute together and add to dry ingredients, stirring until just mixed. Place in a 9-inch (23-cm) square pan sprayed with nonstick vegetable oil spray and bake for 20 to 25 minutes.

Yield: 12 servings

(continued on page 440)

Per serving: 133 calories (17% from fat, 11% from protein, 73% from carbohydrate); 4 g protein; 2 g total fat; 1 g saturated fat; 1 g monounsaturated fat; 0 g polyunsaturated fat; 24 g carbohydrate; 1 g fiber; 4 g sugar; 81 mg phosphorus; 103 mg calcium; 1 mg iron; 165 mg sodium; 88 mg potassium; 189 IU vitamin A; 35 mg ATE vitamin E; 0 mg vitamin C; 0 mg cholesterol; 26 g water

Oatmeal Pancakes

A nice change for Sunday morning breakfast.

1¼ cups (285 ml) skim milk

1 cup (80 g) quick-cooking oats

½ cup (120 ml) egg substitute

½ cup (60 g) whole wheat flour

1 tablespoon (15 g) brown sugar

1 teaspoon (2.3 g) cinnamon

1 tablespoon (13.8 g) baking powder

Combine milk and oats in a bowl and let stand 5 minutes. Add egg substitute and mix well. Add remaining ingredients and stir until just blended. Cook on a hot griddle, turning when bubbles form on the tops of the pancakes and burst. Flip pancakes and finish cooking on the other side.

Yield: 6 servings

Per serving: 135 calories (12% from fat, 23% from protein, 65% from carbohydrate); 8 g protein; 2 g total fat; 0 g saturated fat; 1 g monounsaturated fat; 1 g polyunsaturated fat; 22 g carbohydrate; 3 g fiber; 3 g sugar; 232 mg phosphorus; 237 mg calcium; 2 mg iron; 313 mg sodium; 260 mg potassium; 181 IU vitamin A; 31 mg ATE vitamin E; 1 mg vitamin C; 1 mg cholesterol; 66 g water

20

Multigrain Yeast Breads

I f you have a bread machine, here's another easy way to increase the whole grains and fiber in your diet. This chapter contains 27 recipes for yeast breads containing whole grain flour or grains. It includes everything from light, simple wheat breads to dense, dark breads, as well as rolls and whole wheat versions of things like bagels and pizza dough. I first started using my bread machine regularly as a way to reduce the sodium in the bread I ate, but now I can't imagine not making at least one loaf of homemade bread a week. There is just nothing like the aroma and taste of freshly baked bread.

100% Whole Wheat Bread

This recipe is based on one that came with my bread machine. I've reduced the fat and sodium content, but it still makes a very tasty loaf.

1¼ cups (285 ml) water

2 tablespoons (28 g) unsalted margarine

3 cups (375 g) whole wheat flour

¼ cup (60 g) brown sugar

1¾ teaspoons (7 g) yeast

Place all ingredients in the bread machine pan in the order specified by the manufacturer. Process on the whole wheat cycle.

Yield: 12 servings

Per serving: 137 calories (15% from fat, 12% from protein, 73% from carbohydrate); 4 g protein; 2 g total fat; 1 g saturated fat; 1 g monounsaturated fat; 0 g polyunsaturated fat; 26 g carbohydrate; 4 g fiber; 5 g sugar; 114 mg phosphorus; 17 mg calcium; 1 mg iron; 25 mg sodium; 151 mg potassium; 103 IU vitamin A; 23 mg ATE vitamin E; 0 mg vitamin C; 0 mg cholesterol; 28 g water

Crunchy Honey Wheat Bread

This makes a nice bread with soup or for sandwiches. It has a lot of flavor, and the nuts add texture.

1¼ cups (285 ml) water

3 tablespoons (45 ml) honey

2 tablespoons (28 g) unsalted margarine

2 cups (250 g) whole wheat flour

1½ cups (185 g) bread flour

½ cup (60 g) sliced almonds, toasted

1¼ teaspoons (5 g) yeast

Place all ingredients in the bread machine pan in the order specified by the manufacturer. Process on the whole wheat cycle.

Yield: 12 servings

Per serving: 199 calories (24% from fat, 12% from protein, 63% from carbohydrate); 6 g protein; 6 g total fat; 1 g saturated fat; 3 g monounsaturated fat; 1 g polyunsaturated fat; 33 g carbohydrate; 4 g fiber; 5 g sugar; 122 mg phosphorus; 25 mg calcium; 2 mg iron; 25 mg sodium; 153 mg potassium; 103 IU vitamin A; 23 mg ATE vitamin E; 0 mg vitamin C; 0 mg cholesterol; 31 g water

Wheat Bread

This recipe is lighter than a lot of homemade breads and just sweet enough. I can't help but wonder if the lower-than-usual amount of yeast had anything to do with that. I'd been experimenting by reducing the yeast in some recipes, but not usually this low. Time for some more experimentation—I may be on to something here!

1 cup (235 ml) plus 1 tablespoon (15 ml) water

1½ tablespoons (21 g) unsalted margarine

¼ cup (60 ml) honey

1½ cups (185 g) bread flour

1½ cups (185 g) whole wheat flour

1 tablespoon (7.5 g) nonfat dry milk powder

1 teaspoon (4 g) yeast

Place all ingredients in the bread machine pan in the order specified by the manufacturer. Process on the whole wheat cycle.

Yield: 12 servings

Per serving: 149 calories (12% from fat, 12% from protein, 77% from carbohydrate); 4 g protein; 2 g total fat; 0 g saturated fat; 1 g monounsaturated fat; 0 g polyunsaturated fat; 29 g carbohydrate; 2 g fiber; 6 g sugar; 77 mg phosphorus; 14 mg calcium; 1 mg iron; 19 mg sodium; 96 mg potassium; 85 IU vitamin A; 20 mg ATE vitamin E; 0 mg vitamin C; 0 mg cholesterol; 26 g water

Sesame Wheat Bread

A good sandwich bread, with a little crunch and the flavor of sesame seeds.

1½ cups (355 ml) water

2 tablespoons (28 g) unsalted margarine

1½ cups (185 g) bread flour

1½ cups (185 g) whole wheat flour

1 cup (187 g) uncooked multigrain cereal

¼ cup (30 g) sesame seeds

3 tablespoons (45 g) brown sugar

1½ teaspoons (6 g) yeast

Place all ingredients in the bread machine pan in the order specified by the manufacturer. Process on the whole wheat cycle.

Yield: 12 servings

Per serving: 211 calories (15% from fat, 12% from protein, 73% from carbohydrate); 6 g protein; 4 g total fat; 1 g saturated fat; 2 g monounsaturated fat; 1 g polyunsaturated fat; 39 g carbohydrate; 3 g fiber; 3 g sugar; 105 mg phosphorus; 39 mg calcium; 2 mg iron; 25 mg sodium; 127 mg potassium; 102 IU vitamin A; 23 mg ATE vitamin E; 0 mg vitamin C; 0 mg cholesterol; 35 g water

Buttermilk Wheat Bread

Another great bread with a nice hot bowl of soup or stew for dinner. The buttermilk gives it an almost sourdough flavor. It's also good toasted.

1 cup (235 ml) buttermilk

¼ cup (60 ml) water

1 tablespoon (14 g) unsalted margarine

1½ cups (185 g) whole wheat flour

1½ cups (185 g) bread flour

1 tablespoon (13 g) sugar

1 teaspoon (4 g) yeast

Place all ingredients in the bread machine in the order specified by the manufacturer.
Process on the whole wheat cycle.

Yield: 12 servings

Per serving: 134 calories (11% from fat, 14% from protein, 74% from carbohydrate); 5 g protein; 2 g total
fat; 0 g saturated fat; 1 g monounsaturated fat; 0 g polyunsaturated fat; 25 g carbohydrate; 2 g fiber; 2 g
sugar; 92 mg phosphorus; 32 mg calcium; 1 mg iron; 33 mg sodium; 117 mg potassium; 57 IU vitamin A;
13 mg ATE vitamin E; 0 mg vitamin C; 1 mg cholesterol; 27 g water

Debbie's Multigrain Bread

This recipe was sent to me by newsletter subscriber Debbie. Unlike most of our recipes, this is a
hand-mixed and kneaded bread, rather than a bread machine one. I tried it that way, and it's got
a great flavor.

1 cup (235 ml) lukewarm water

4½ teaspoons (10.5 g) yeast (2 packages)

¼ cup (60 ml) molasses

5 cups (625 g) whole wheat flour, divided

¼ cup (56 g) unsalted margarine

½ cup wheat germ

½ cup flaxseed

½ cup oat bran

¼ cup brown sugar

1 cup (235 ml) boiling water,

Preheat oven to 375°F (190°C, or gas mark 5). Dissolve the yeast in the lukewarm water, add the
molasses, and let stand for 5 minutes. Beat in 2 cups (250 g) of the whole wheat flour, cover, and
let rise for 30 to 60 minutes. This will create a "sponge."

(continued on page 446)

Meanwhile, in a large bowl, combine the remaining ingredients, except the 3 cups (375 g) of whole wheat flour. Let stand 30 to 60 minutes. Add the risen sponge to the oat bran mixture and then stir in the remaining 3 cups (375 g) of whole wheat flour. Knead to make an elastic dough. Cover and let rise until doubled in bulk (1 to 1½ hours). Divide dough in 2 pieces and shape into loaves. Place in greased loaf pans and let rise for 1 hour. Bake for 25 to 30 minutes, or until crust is as brown as you prefer.

Yield: 24 servings

Per serving: 154 calories (23% from fat, 13% from protein, 64% from carbohydrate); 5 g protein; 4 g total fat; 1 g saturated fat; 1 g monounsaturated fat; 2 g polyunsaturated fat; 26 g carbohydrate; 5 g fiber; 5 g sugar; 153 mg phosphorus; 32 mg calcium; 2 mg iron; 30 mg sodium; 233 mg potassium; 114 IU vitamin A; 26 mg ATE vitamin E; 0 mg vitamin C; 0 mg cholesterol; 24 g water

15-Grain Bread

This makes a fairly heavy loaf, good for sandwiches or with a soup and salad–type meal.

1 cup (235 ml) plus 2 tablespoons (30 ml) water

2 tablespoons (28 g) unsalted margarine

1⅓ cups (166 g) bread flour

1 cup (125 g) whole wheat flour

¼ cup (29 g) 15-grain cereal

3 tablespoons (45 g) brown sugar

2¼ teaspoons (5.3 g) yeast

Place all ingredients in the bread machine in the order specified by the manufacturer. Process on the whole wheat cycle.

Yield: 12 servings

Per serving: 131 calories (16% from fat, 12% from protein, 72% from carbohydrate); 4 g protein; 2 g total fat; 0 g saturated fat; 1 g monounsaturated fat; 1 g polyunsaturated fat; 24 g carbohydrate; 2 g fiber; 3 g sugar; 71 mg phosphorus; 11 mg calcium; 1 mg iron; 4 mg sodium; 98 mg potassium; 86 IU vitamin A; 18 mg ATE vitamin E; 0 mg vitamin C; 0 mg cholesterol; 26 g water

Seven-Grain Bread

You should be able to find seven-grain cereal in most large grocery stores. This makes a good sandwich bread and also toasts well.

1⅓ cups (315 ml) water

1½ tablespoons (21 g) unsalted margarine

1¼ cups (155 g) bread flour

1 cup (125 g) whole wheat flour

2 tablespoons (26 g) sugar

¾ cup (87 g) seven-grain cereal

1½ tablespoons (11.3 g) nonfat dry milk powder

1½ teaspoons (6 g) yeast

Add all ingredients to the bread machine pan in the order suggested by the manufacturer. Process on the white bread cycle.

Yield: 12 servings

Per serving: 150 calories (11% from fat, 12% from protein, 76% from carbohydrate); 5 g protein; 2 g total fat; 0 g saturated fat; 1 g monounsaturated fat; 0 g polyunsaturated fat; 29 g carbohydrate; 2 g fiber; 2 g sugar; 71 mg phosphorus; 16 mg calcium; 2 mg iron; 20 mg sodium; 86 mg potassium; 89 IU vitamin A; 21 mg ATE vitamin E; 0 mg vitamin C; 0 mg cholesterol; 31 g water

Crunchy Oatmeal Bread

This has a lovely, crunchy texture. It is one of my favorite breads for toast and is great with apple butter for breakfast.

1 cup (235 ml) water

¼ cup (60 ml) honey

2 tablespoons (28 g) unsalted margarine

3 cups (375 g) bread flour

½ cup (40 g) quick-cooking oats

2 tablespoons (15 g) nonfat dry milk powder

2 teaspoons (8 g) yeast

½ cup (160 g) unsalted sunflower seeds

Place all ingredients except sunflower seeds in the bread machine pan in the order specified by the manufacturer. Process on the large white loaf cycle. Add the sunflower seeds at the beep, or 5 minutes before the end of kneading.

Yield: 12 servings

Per serving: 210 calories (23% from fat, 12% from protein, 66% from carbohydrate); 6 g protein; 5 g total fat; 1 g saturated fat; 2 g monounsaturated fat; 2 g polyunsaturated fat; 35 g carbohydrate; 2 g fiber; 6 g sugar; 128 mg phosphorus; 22 mg calcium; 2 mg iron; 27 mg sodium; 123 mg potassium; 118 IU vitamin A; 28 mg ATE vitamin E; 0 mg vitamin C; 0 mg cholesterol; 26 g water

Old-Fashioned Oatmeal Bread

The molasses gives this bread a nice, sweet flavor, perfect for sandwiches with simple meats like sliced chicken or turkey.

1 cup (235 ml) water

¼ cup (60 ml) molasses

2 tablespoons (28 g) unsalted margarine

3 cups (375 g) bread flour

½ cup (40 g) quick-cooking oats

2 tablespoons (15 g) nonfat dry milk powder

2 teaspoons (8 g) yeast

Place all ingredients in the bread machine pan in the order specified by the manufacturer. Process on the white bread cycle.

Yield: 12 servings

Per serving: 178 calories (14% from fat, 12% from protein, 75% from carbohydrate); 5 g protein; 3 g total fat; 1 g saturated fat; 1 g monounsaturated fat; 1 g polyunsaturated fat; 33 g carbohydrate; 1 g fiber; 4 g sugar; 68 mg phosphorus; 33 mg calcium; 2 mg iron; 29 mg sodium; 177 mg potassium; 117 IU vitamin A; 28 mg ATE vitamin E; 0 mg vitamin C; 0 mg cholesterol; 27 g water

Hearty Oatmeal Bread

This has a wonderful, slightly sweet flavor that is great toasted for breakfast or for sandwiches.

1 cup (80 g) quick-cooking oats

2/3 cup (160 ml) skim milk

1/3 cup (80 ml) water

1 tablespoon (14 g) unsalted margarine

2½ cups (310 g) bread flour

3 tablespoons (45 g) brown sugar

1 teaspoon (4 g) yeast

Preheat oven to 350°F (180°C, or gas mark 4). Spread the oats in a baking pan and toast in the oven for 15 minutes, or until lightly browned, stirring occasionally. Place all ingredients in the bread machine pan in the order specified by the manufacturer. Process on the whole-grain cycle.

Yield: 12 servings

Per serving: 157 calories (11% from fat, 13% from protein, 76% from carbohydrate); 5 g protein; 2 g total fat; 0 g saturated fat; 1 g monounsaturated fat; 0 g polyunsaturated fat; 29 g carbohydrate; 1 g fiber; 3 g sugar; 81 mg phosphorus; 31 mg calcium; 2 mg iron; 21 mg sodium; 97 mg potassium; 78 IU vitamin A; 20 mg ATE vitamin E; 0 mg vitamin C; 0 mg cholesterol; 23 g water

Brown Bread

A hearty bread, great with full-flavored soups or chili. It also makes great toast.

¼ cup (60 ml) egg substitute

1 cup (235 ml) water

2 tablespoons (28 g) unsalted margarine

2 tablespoons (30 ml) molasses

1 tablespoon (15 g) brown sugar

1½ cups (185 g) bread flour

1 cup (125 g) whole wheat flour

½ cup (40 g) oats, rolled or quick-cooking

⅓ cup (47 g) cornmeal

1½ teaspoons (6 g) yeast

Place all ingredients in the bread machine pan in the order specified by the manufacturer. Process on the whole wheat cycle.

Yield: 12 servings

Per serving: 174 calories (16% from fat, 13% from protein, 71% from carbohydrate); 6 g protein; 3 g total fat; 1 g saturated fat; 1 g monounsaturated fat; 1 g polyunsaturated fat; 31 g carbohydrate; 3 g fiber; 3 g sugar; 105 mg phosphorus; 23 mg calcium; 2 mg iron; 34 mg sodium; 177 mg potassium; 130 IU vitamin A; 23 mg ATE vitamin E; 0 mg vitamin C; 0 mg cholesterol; 30 g water

Russian Black Bread

This is almost purely a sandwich bread. It's perfect with mild-flavored fillings like chicken or turkey.

1 cup (235 ml) water

¼ cup (60 ml) molasses

1 tablespoon (14 g) unsalted margarine

2 cups (250 g) bread flour

1¼ cups (155 g) rye flour

2 tablespoons (10.8 g) cocoa

1½ teaspoons (6 g) yeast

Place all ingredients in the bread machine pan in the order specified by the manufacturer. Process on the whole wheat cycle.

Yield: 12 servings

Per serving: 154 calories (9% from fat, 10% from protein, 80% from carbohydrate); 4 g protein; 2 g total fat; 0 g saturated fat; 1 g monounsaturated fat; 0 g polyunsaturated fat; 31 g carbohydrate; 3 g fiber; 4 g sugar; 59 mg phosphorus; 23 mg calcium; 2 mg iron; 15 mg sodium; 175 mg potassium; 50 IU vitamin A; 11 mg ATE vitamin E; 0 mg vitamin C; 0 mg cholesterol; 25 g water

Rustic Italian Bread

This is a recipe that we've been using for a while, and it's our favorite for Italian bread. I use the bread machine to make my dough and then bake it in the oven to get that traditional look.

1 cup (235 ml) water

2 tablespoons (30 ml) olive oil

3 cups (375 g) bread flour

2 teaspoons (8 g) sugar

2 teaspoons (8 g) active dry yeast

2 tablespoons (18 g) cornmeal, for baking sheet

1 egg white, slightly beaten

(continued on page 452)

Add water, oil, flour, sugar, and yeast to your bread machine pan according to the manufacturer's instructions. Set on the dough setting. When the cycle is done, remove dough from the machine. Sprinkle cornmeal onto a baking sheet. Punch dough down and form into a long or oval loaf. Cover and let rise for 25 more minutes, or until doubled again. Preheat oven to 375°F (190°C, or gas mark 5). Uncover dough and slash the top with a sharp knife or razor. Brush all over with the beaten egg white. Bake for 25 to 35 minutes, or until it sounds hollow when tapped on the bottom.

Yield: 12 servings

Per serving: 156 calories (17% from fat, 12% from protein, 71% from carbohydrate); 5 g protein; 3 g total fat; 0 g saturated fat; 2 g monounsaturated fat; 0 g polyunsaturated fat; 27 g carbohydrate; 1 g fiber; 1 g sugar; 44 mg phosphorus; 6 mg calcium; 2 mg iron; 6 mg sodium; 55 mg potassium; 4 IU vitamin A; 0 mg ATE vitamin E; 0 mg vitamin C; 0 mg cholesterol; 27 g water

Cornmeal Bread

An alternative to cornbread, this is a great accompaniment to a soup or chili meal.

1 cup (235 ml) water

¼ cup (60 ml) olive oil

¼ cup (60 ml) egg substitute

2 tablespoons (26 g) sugar

1 cup (140 g) cornmeal

2 cups (250 g) bread flour

1½ teaspoons (6 g) yeast

Place all ingredients in the bread machine pan in the order specified by the manufacturer. Process on the white bread cycle.

Yield: 12 servings

Per serving: 185 calories (26% from fat, 10% from protein, 64% from carbohydrate); 5 g protein; 5 g total fat; 1 g saturated fat; 3 g monounsaturated fat; 1 g polyunsaturated fat; 29 g carbohydrate; 1 g fiber; 2 g sugar; 49 mg phosphorus; 8 mg calcium; 2 mg iron; 12 mg sodium; 70 mg potassium; 48 IU vitamin A; 0 mg ATE vitamin E; 0 mg vitamin C; 0 mg cholesterol; 29 g water

Whole Wheat French Bread

This is particularly good with soup or a bean dish.

¾ teaspoon (3 g) yeast

1 tablespoon (15 ml) honey

1 cup (235 ml) water

2 cups (250 g) whole wheat flour

1½ cups (185 g) bread flour

Place all ingredients in the bread machine pan in the order specified by the manufacturer. Process on the dough cycle. Remove the dough from the machine. Shape into a tapered loaf. Place on a greased baking sheet, cover with a towel, and let rise until doubled, about 30 minutes. Preheat oven to 400°F (200°C, or gas mark 6). Cut diagonal slices about ¼ inch (0.4 cm) long across the top of the loaf with a sharp knife. Brush with cold water. Bake for 15 to 20 minutes, or until done.

Yield: 12 servings

Per serving: 136 calories (4% from fat, 14% from protein, 82% from carbohydrate); 5 g protein; 1 g total fat; 0 g saturated fat; 0 g monounsaturated fat; 0 g polyunsaturated fat; 28 g carbohydrate; 3 g fiber; 2 g sugar; 89 mg phosphorus; 10 mg calcium; 2 mg iron; 2 mg sodium; 104 mg potassium; 2 IU vitamin A; 0 mg ATE vitamin E; 0 mg vitamin C; 0 mg cholesterol; 24 g water

Tomato Sandwich Bread

The perfect bread for tomato sandwiches.

1 tablespoon (15 ml) water

3 cups (375 g) bread flour

¼ teaspoon (0.8 g) garlic powder

2 tablespoons (26 g) sugar

1½ teaspoons (1 g) dried basil

2 teaspoons (8 g) yeast

⅓ cup (37 g) oil-packed sun-dried tomatoes

(continued on page 454)

Place all ingredients except tomatoes in the bread machine pan in the order specified by the manufacturer. Process on the white bread cycle. Add the tomatoes at the beep, or 5 minutes before the end of the kneading cycle.

Yield: 12 servings

Per serving: 141 calories (7% from fat, 13% from protein, 80% from carbohydrate); 5 g protein; 1 g total fat; 0 g saturated fat; 0 g monounsaturated fat; 0 g polyunsaturated fat; 28 g carbohydrate; 1 g fiber; 2 g sugar; 47 mg phosphorus; 9 mg calcium; 2 mg iron; 9 mg sodium; 99 mg potassium; 48 IU vitamin A; 0 mg ATE vitamin E; 3 mg vitamin C; 0 mg cholesterol; 8 g water

Italian Wheat Bread

This great bread recipe came from subscriber Pat. This could also be taken out of the machine at the end of the dough cycle and shaped into a more traditional Italian loaf.

3 tablespoons (45 ml) olive oil

1 cup (235 ml) warm water

1½ cups (185 g) whole wheat flour

1½ cups (185 g) bread flour

1½ teaspoons (6 g) yeast

Place all ingredients in the bread machine pan in the order specified by the manufacturer. Process on the white or French bread cycle.

Yield: 12 servings

Per serving: 144 calories (24% from fat, 12% from protein, 64% from carbohydrate); 4 g protein; 4 g total fat; 1 g saturated fat; 3 g monounsaturated fat; 1 g polyunsaturated fat; 23 g carbohydrate; 2 g fiber; 0 g sugar; 75 mg phosphorus; 9 mg calcium; 1 mg iron; 2 mg sodium; 88 mg potassium; 2 IU vitamin A; 0 mg ATE vitamin E; 0 mg vitamin C; 0 mg cholesterol; 24 g water

Whole Wheat Zucchini Bread

Most zucchini bread is the sweet, quick bread variety. This one is a hearty yeast loaf that goes very well with soup for dinner.

1 cup (235 ml) warm water

2 teaspoons (10 ml) honey

1 tablespoon (15 ml) canola oil

¾ cup (95 g) shredded zucchini

¾ cup (90 g) whole wheat flour

2 cups (250 g) bread flour

½ teaspoon (0.4 g) dried basil

2 teaspoons (5.4 g) sesame seeds

1½ teaspoons (6 g) yeast

Place all ingredients in the bread machine in the order specified by the manufacturer. Process on the wheat or whole-grain cycle.

Yield: 12 servings

Per serving: 124 calories (12% from fat, 13% from protein, 75% from carbohydrate); 4 g protein; 2 g total fat; 0 g saturated fat; 0 g monounsaturated fat; 1 g polyunsaturated fat; 23 g carbohydrate; 2 g fiber; 1 g sugar; 58 mg phosphorus; 9 mg calcium; 1 mg iron; 3 mg sodium; 85 mg potassium; 19 IU vitamin A; 0 mg ATE vitamin E; 1 mg vitamin C; 0 mg cholesterol; 31 g water;

Caramel Apple Bread

A good breakfast bread. Also great for French toast.

1 cup (235 ml) water

2 tablespoons (28 g) unsalted margarine

3 cups (375 g) bread flour

¼ cup (60 g) brown sugar

¾ teaspoon (1.7 g) cinnamon

2 teaspoons (8 g) yeast

⅓ cup (40 g) pecans, chopped and toasted

½ cup (75 g) apple, coarsely chopped

Place all ingredients except apple and pecans in the bread machine pan in the order specified by the manufacturer. Process on the sweet bread or white bread cycle. Add pecans and apple at the beep or after the first kneading.

Yield: 12 servings

Per serving: 183 calories (23% from fat, 10% from protein, 67% from carbohydrate); 5 g protein; 5 g total fat; 1 g saturated fat; 2 g monounsaturated fat; 1 g polyunsaturated fat; 31 g carbohydrate; 1 g fiber; 5 g sugar; 53 mg phosphorus; 16 mg calcium; 2 mg iron; 24 mg sodium; 83 mg potassium; 105 IU vitamin A; 23 mg ATE vitamin E; 0 mg vitamin C; 0 mg cholesterol; 29 g water

Three-Apple Bread

This makes a nice breakfast bread—just sweet enough without jelly.

½ cup (120 ml) apple juice

½ cup (120 ml) unsweetened applesauce

3 cups (375 g) bread flour

1½ tablespoons (21 g) unsalted margarine

½ cup (75 g) apple, peeled and chopped

½ teaspoon (1.2 g) cinnamon

¼ teaspoon (0.6 g) nutmeg

1½ teaspoons (6 g) yeast

Place all the ingredients in the bread machine pan in the order specified by the manufacturer. Process on the light crust setting. Allow to cool 1 hour before slicing.

Yield: 12 servings

Per serving: 149 calories (12% from fat, 12% from protein, 76% from carbohydrate); 4 g protein; 2 g total fat; 0 g saturated fat; 1 g monounsaturated fat; 0 g polyunsaturated fat; 28 g carbohydrate; 1 g fiber; 2 g sugar; 43 mg phosphorus; 9 mg calcium; 2 mg iron; 17 mg sodium; 71 mg potassium; 81 IU vitamin A; 17 mg ATE vitamin E; 2 mg vitamin C; 0 mg cholesterol; 27 g water

TIP *Use apple cider instead of juice for an even deeper flavor.*

Whole Wheat Hamburger Buns

Slightly sweet and quite light for homemade bread, these are my favorite sandwich rolls.

1 cup (235 ml) water

2 tablespoons (28 g) unsalted margarine

¼ cup (60 ml) egg substitute

2 cups (250 g) bread flour

1¼ cups (155 g) whole wheat flour

¼ cup (50 g) sugar

1 tablespoon (12 g) yeast

Place all the ingredients in the bread machine pan in the order specified by the manufacturer. Process on the dough cycle. At the end of the cycle, remove dough to a floured board. Pull into 10 pieces. Shape each into a rounded, flattened roll and place on greased baking sheet. Cover and let rise until doubled, about 30 minutes. Preheat oven to 375°F (190°C, or gas mark 5) and bake for 12 to 15 minutes, or until golden brown.

Yield: 10 servings

Per serving: 198 calories (15% from fat, 13% from protein, 72% from carbohydrate); 7 g protein; 3 g total fat; 1 g saturated fat; 1 g monounsaturated fat; 1 g polyunsaturated fat; 36 g carbohydrate; 3 g fiber; 5 g sugar; 103 mg phosphorus; 16 mg calcium; 2 mg iron; 38 mg sodium; 136 mg potassium; 144 IU vitamin A; 27 mg ATE vitamin E; 0 mg vitamin C; 0 mg cholesterol; 35 g water

Whole Wheat Onion Rolls

If you are looking for a roll with flavor to use for sandwiches with things like roast beef or meat loaf, you might want to give these a try. I used an envelope of Goodman's low sodium onion soup mix for the flavoring (available in the kosher section of the international aisle in my local Safeway), but you could get much the same taste with 4 tablespoons (24 g) low sodium beef bouillon, 1 teaspoon (3 g) of onion powder, and 2 tablespoons of dried minced onion.

¾ cup (180 ml) flat beer

½ cup (120 ml) water

1 tablespoon (14 g) unsalted margarine

4 ounces (115 g) low sodium onion soup mix

2 cups (250 g) bread flour

1¼ cups (155 g) whole wheat flour

4 teaspoons (16 g) sugar

1¾ teaspoons (7 g) yeast

Place all the ingredients in the bread machine pan in the order specified by the manufacturer. Process on the dough cycle. Remove the dough from the machine and separate into 10 balls. Shape each into a round, flattened roll. Place on a baking sheet sprayed with nonstick vegetable oil spray. Cover and let rise until doubled, about 30 minutes. Preheat oven to 375°F (190°C, or gas mark 5) and bake for 12 to 15 minutes, or until lightly browned.

Yield: 10 servings

Per serving: 183 calories (10% from fat, 13% from protein, 77% from carbohydrate); 6 g protein; 2 g total fat; 0 g saturated fat; 1 g monounsaturated fat; 0 g polyunsaturated fat; 35 g carbohydrate; 3 g fiber; 2 g sugar; 91 mg phosphorus; 17 mg calcium; 2 mg iron; 95 mg sodium; 108 mg potassium; 62 IU vitamin A; 14 mg ATE vitamin E; 0 mg vitamin C; 0 mg cholesterol; 34 g water

Seven-Grain Sesame Seed Rolls

These are a nice, crunchy, chewy sort of roll, perfect for mild-flavored fillings like turkey or chicken salad.

1¼ cups (285 ml) water

3 tablespoons (23 g) nonfat dry milk powder

1½ tablespoons (22 ml) canola oil

3 tablespoons (45 ml) molasses

2½ cups (310 g) bread flour

1 cup (116 g) seven-grain cereal

2 teaspoons (8 g) yeast

3 tablespoons (24 g) sesame seeds

Add all ingredients to the bread machine pan in the order specified by the manufacturer. Process on the dough cycle. Remove dough from the bread machine at the end of the cycle, form into rolls, cover, and let rise until doubled. Preheat oven to 375°F (190°C, or gas mark 5) and bake for 15 minutes, or until golden brown.

Yield: 10 servings

Per serving: 218 calories (13% from fat, 12% from protein, 75% from carbohydrate); 7 g protein; 3 g total fat; 0 g saturated fat; 1 g monounsaturated fat; 1 g polyunsaturated fat; 41 g carbohydrate; 3 g fiber; 5 g sugar; 112 mg phosphorus; 39 mg calcium; 2 mg iron; 13 mg sodium; 234 mg potassium; 34 IU vitamin A; 9 mg ATE vitamin E; 0 mg vitamin C; 0 mg cholesterol; 37 g water

Sun-Dried Tomato Wheat Rolls

These have a great flavor for sandwiches. We made them originally for sliced pork subs, but they would also be good with something simple like the chicken salad or a burger. The leftover ones became breakfast sandwiches for me several days one week. You can add the tomatoes right at the beginning, rather than at the beep—the fact that they get chopped up and mixed into the dough more won't hurt them at all.

1 cup (235 ml) skim milk

¼ cup (60 g) fat-free sour cream

1 tablespoon (13 g) sugar

2 cups (250 g) bread flour

1 cup (125 g) whole wheat flour

¼ cup oil-packed sun-dried tomatoes, chopped

2½ teaspoons (10 g) yeast

Place all ingredients in the bread machine pan in the order specified by the manufacturer. Process on the dough cycle. At the end of the cycle, remove dough to a floured board. Pull into 10 pieces (or less if making sub rolls). Shape each into a rounded, flattened roll and place on a greased baking sheet. Cover and let rise until doubled, about 1 hour. Preheat oven to 350°F (180°C, or gas mark 4) and bake for 20 to 25 minutes, or until golden brown.

Yield: 10 servings

Per serving: 172 calories (6% from fat, 16% from protein, 78% from carbohydrate); 7 g protein; 1 g total fat; 0 g saturated fat; 0 g monounsaturated fat; 0 g polyunsaturated fat; 32 g carbohydrate; 2 g fiber; 1 g sugar; 118 mg phosphorus; 52 mg calcium; 2 mg iron; 26 mg sodium; 192 mg potassium; 109 IU vitamin A; 21 mg ATE vitamin E; 3 mg vitamin C; 3 mg cholesterol; 33 g water

Whole Wheat Bagels

Bagels really aren't as difficult to make as they sound. This recipe produces big, soft bagels that are crispy on the outside and just a little chewy on the inside, like what is typically called New York–style. They are good cold for sandwiches, toasted, or warm right out of the oven.

1½ cups (355 ml) warm water

2 tablespoons (30 ml) honey

1 tablespoon (15 ml) vinegar

2 cups (250 g) whole wheat flour

1¼ cups (155 g) bread flour

1½ tablespoons (22 ml) olive oil

2 teaspoons (8 g) yeast

Place all ingredients in the bread machine pan in the order specified by the manufacturer. Process on the dough cycle. At the end of the cycle, separate dough into 8 pieces. Shape each into a flattened ball, then use your thumbs to pull a hole in the center of each and stretch into a doughnut shape. Place on a greased baking sheet, cover, and let rise until doubled, about 30 minutes. While dough is rising, bring about 2 inches (5 cm) of water to boil in a large pan and preheat oven to 350°F (180°C, or gas mark 4). Drop bagels a few at a time into boiling water and boil for 1 minute, turning once. Remove with a slotted spoon or pancake turner and return to baking sheet. When all bagels have been boiled, bake for 20 to 25 minutes, or until golden brown.

Yield: 8 servings

Per serving: 221 calories (14% from fat, 12% from protein, 74% from carbohydrate); 7 g protein; 3 g total fat; 1 g saturated fat; 2 g monounsaturated fat; 1 g polyunsaturated fat; 42 g carbohydrate; 4 g fiber; 5 g sugar; 138 mg phosphorus; 16 mg calcium; 2 mg iron; 4 mg sodium; 167 mg potassium; 3 IU vitamin A; 0 mg ATE vitamin E; 0 mg vitamin C; 0 mg cholesterol; 53 g water

Whole Wheat Pizza Dough

We used this dough to make a pizza full of fresh vegetables from the garden, but you could use it with any toppings you desire.

2 teaspoons (8 g) active dry yeast

2 cups (250 g) bread flour

1½ cups (185 g) whole wheat flour

1 tablespoon (13 g) sugar

2 tablespoons (30 ml) olive oil

1½ cups (355 ml) water

Place all ingredients in the bread machine pan in the order specified by the manufacturer and process on the dough cycle. Turn out the dough onto a floured board. At this point you may form the pizzas or refrigerate the dough for several hours, well wrapped in plastic so it won't dry out. Makes enough dough for two 12-inch (30-cm) pizzas, or two 10-inch (25-cm) thick-crust pizzas. Preheat oven to 400°F (200°C, or gas mark 6). Bake for 15 minutes, or until lightly browned around the edges. Top as desired and return to oven for 5 to 10 minutes, or until cheese is melted and crust is browned.

Yield: 16 servings

Per serving: 119 calories (16% from fat, 12% from protein, 71% from carbohydrate); 4 g protein; 2 g total fat; 0 g saturated fat; 1 g monounsaturated fat; 0 g polyunsaturated fat; 22 g carbohydrate; 2 g fiber; 1 g sugar; 62 mg phosphorus; 7 mg calcium; 1 mg iron; 2 mg sodium; 73 mg potassium; 1 IU vitamin A; 0 mg ATE vitamin E; 0 mg vitamin C; 0 mg cholesterol; 26 g water

21

Desserts and Sweets

The story of most desserts is similar to the one for quick breads: They often contain more fat than they need to. In this chapter you'll find a number of healthier options to satisfy your sweet tooth. It includes not just lower-fat versions of cakes and cookies, but also some naturally healthy things that you may not normally consider, like cobblers and fruit desserts.

Low Fat Apple Cake

This recipe originally came from my mother. It was one of my favorites for years. I reduced the fat by replacing the oil in the original recipe with applesauce.

1 cup (235 ml) applesauce

2 cups (400 g) sugar

¾ cup (180 ml) egg substitute

2½ cups (310 g) flour

2 teaspoons (9.2 g) baking powder

1 teaspoon (4.6 g) baking soda

½ teaspoon (1.2 g) cinnamon

½ teaspoon (1.1 g) nutmeg

1 teaspoon (5 ml) vanilla

3 cups (450 g) apples, peeled and chopped

Preheat oven to 350°F (180°C, or gas mark 4). Mix applesauce and sugar together, add egg substitute. Sift together flour, baking powder, baking soda, cinnamon, and nutmeg; add to sugar mixture. Stir in vanilla; fold in apples. Pour into 9 × 13-inch (23 × 33-cm) pan. Bake for 1 to 1½ hours, or until knife inserted in center comes out clean. Dust top with powdered sugar, if desired.

Yield: 24 servings

Per serving: 131 calories (3% from fat, 7% from protein, 90% from carbohydrate); 2 g protein; 0 g total fat; 0 g saturated fat; 0 g monounsaturated fat; 0 g polyunsaturated fat; 30 g carbohydrate; 1 g fiber; 19 g sugar; 34 mg phosphorus; 30 mg calcium; 1 mg iron; 107 mg sodium; 61 mg potassium; 37 IU vitamin A; 0 mg ATE vitamin E; 1 mg vitamin C; 0 mg cholesterol; 29 g water

Low Fat Cranberry Cake

When I first came across a version of this recipe it sounded so good that I had to try it. Of course, the original was full of fat and sodium, but we've solved that problem with no loss of taste.

2 cups (220 g) cranberries

1¾ cups (350 g) sugar, divided

½ cup (120 ml) water

1 cup (125 g) flour

1½ teaspoons (7 g) baking powder

½ cup (120 ml) applesauce

¼ cup (60 ml) egg substitute

¼ cup (60 ml) skim milk

¼ cup (60 ml) orange juice

1 teaspoon (1.7 g) orange peel, grated

½ teaspoon (3 ml) vanilla

Preheat oven to 375°F (190°C, or gas mark 5). Spray bottom and sides of a 9-inch (23-cm) round baking pan with nonstick vegetable oil spray. Combine cranberries, 1 cup (200 g) sugar, and water in a large saucepan. Bring to a boil. Reduce heat and simmer for 10 minutes, or until slightly thickened to a syrupy consistency. Pour into prepared pan. Cool to room temperature. Sift together flour, remaining ¾ cup (150 g) sugar, and baking powder into a large bowl. In another bowl, stir applesauce, egg substitute, milk, orange juice, orange peel, and vanilla until blended. Stir into dry ingredients just until blended. Pour over cranberry mixture. Bake for 25 to 30 minutes, or until a wooden pick inserted in the center comes out clean. Let cake cool in pan about 5 minutes. Loosen cake around edges of pan. Place inverted serving platter over cake and turn both upside down. Shake gently, then remove pan. Serve warm.

Yield: 12 servings

Per serving: 232 calories (2% from fat, 3% from protein, 94% from carbohydrate); 2 g protein; 1 g total fat; 0 g saturated fat; 0 g monounsaturated fat; 0 g polyunsaturated fat; 57 g carbohydrate; 2 g fiber; 44 g sugar; 39 mg phosphorus; 49 mg calcium; 1 mg iron; 75 mg sodium; 64 mg potassium; 35 IU vitamin A; 3 mg ATE vitamin E; 2 mg vitamin C; 0 mg cholesterol; 37 g water

Low Fat Devil's Food Cake

This makes a fairly heavy, very moist cake, almost like brownies or bars.

2 cups (250 g) flour

1¾ cups (350 g) sugar

½ cup (43 g) unsweetened cocoa powder

1 tablespoon (13.8 g) baking soda

⅔ cup (160 ml) applesauce

⅓ cup (80 ml) buttermilk

2 tablespoons (30 ml) canola oil

1 cup (235 ml) coffee

Preheat oven to 350°F (180°C, or gas mark 4). Spray a 9 × 13-inch (23 × 33-cm) pan with nonstick vegetable oil spray and then dust with flour, shaking out the excess. In a large bowl, mix together flour, sugar, cocoa, and baking soda. Stir in applesauce, buttermilk, and oil. Heat coffee to boiling and stir into batter. Batter will be thin. Pour into prepared pan. Bake for 35 to 40 minutes, or until a wooden pick inserted in the center comes out clean.

Yield: 24 servings

Per serving: 116 calories (12% from fat, 5% from protein, 83% from carbohydrate); 2 g protein; 2 g total fat; 0 g saturated fat; 1 g monounsaturated fat; 0 g polyunsaturated fat; 25 g carbohydrate; 1 g fiber; 16 g sugar; 28 mg phosphorus; 8 mg calcium; 1 mg iron; 162 mg sodium; 55 mg potassium; 2 IU vitamin A; 0 mg ATE vitamin E; 0 mg vitamin C; 0 mg cholesterol; 20 g water

Lower-Fat Carrot Cake

This is lighter than most carrot cakes, but the flavor is very close to the traditional one.

¼ cup (60 ml) canola oil

¾ cup (180 ml) applesauce

½ cup (120 ml) skim milk

1½ cups (300 g) sugar

¾ cup (180 ml) egg substitute

2 cups (250 g) flour

4 teaspoons (18.4 g) baking soda

2½ teaspoons (5.8 g) cinnamon

½ teaspoon (1.1 g) nutmeg

½ teaspoon (1.2 g) ground cloves

1½ teaspoons (8 ml) vanilla

2 cups (260 g) shredded carrot

½ cup (60 g) chopped walnuts

½ cup (80 g) raisins

8 ounces (225 g) crushed pineapple, undrained

Preheat oven to 350°F (180°C, or gas mark 4). Coat a rectangular 9 × 13-inch (23 × 33-cm) cake pan with nonstick vegetable oil spray. In one bowl, beat together oil, applesauce, milk, sugar, and egg substitute. In another bowl, stir together flour, baking soda, cinnamon, nutmeg, and cloves. Combine both sets of ingredients and beat, mixing in vanilla. Add carrots, walnuts, raisins, and pineapple, mixing well after each addition. Bake for 1 hour, or until done. Cool and remove from pan.

Yield: 16 servings

Per serving: 239 calories (24% from fat, 8% from protein, 68% from carbohydrate); 5 g protein; 7 g total fat; 1 g saturated fat; 3 g monounsaturated fat; 3 g polyunsaturated fat; 42 g carbohydrate; 2 g fiber; 27 g sugar; 73 mg phosphorus; 37 mg calcium; 1 mg iron; 353 mg sodium; 206 mg potassium; 2757 IU vitamin A; 5 mg ATE vitamin E; 3 mg vitamin C; 0 mg cholesterol; 55 g water

Apple Crunch

An easy-to-put-together apple dessert that satisfies without having too much fat.

For Apples:

4 apples, peeled, cored, and chopped

½ cup (100 g) sugar

1 teaspoon (2.3 g) cinnamon

1 tablespoon (14 g) unsalted margarine

For Topping:

½ cup (60 g) flour

½ cup (100 g) sugar

1 teaspoon (4.6 g) baking powder

¼ cup (60 ml) egg substitute

½ cup (100 g) sugar

1 tablespoon (14 g) unsalted margarine

To make the apples: Preheat oven to 350°F (180°C, or gas mark 4). Mix apples, sugar, and cinnamon; pour into a greased 8 × 8-inch (20 × 20-cm) baking dish. Dot with margarine.

To make the topping: Mix topping ingredients and pour over apples. Bake for 30 to 35 minutes.

Yield: 6 servings

Per serving: 317 calories (12% from fat, 3% from protein, 85% from carbohydrate); 3 g protein; 4 g total fat; 1 g saturated fat; 2 g monounsaturated fat; 1 g polyunsaturated fat; 70 g carbohydrate; 2 g fiber; 59 g sugar; 53 mg phosphorus; 65 mg calcium; 1 mg iron; 141 mg sodium; 130 mg potassium; 271 IU vitamin A; 46 mg ATE vitamin E; 4 mg vitamin C; 0 mg cholesterol; 85 g water

Berry Cobbler

You could use any kind of berry that happens to be available for this dessert. I prefer either blackberries or raspberries, but blueberries or strawberries would work too.

2 tablespoons (16 g) cornstarch

½ cup (120 ml) water, divided

1½ cups (300 g) sugar, divided

1 tablespoon (15 ml) lemon juice

4 cups (580 g) blackberries

1 cup (125 g) flour

1 teaspoon (4.6 g) baking powder

3 tablespoons (42 g) unsalted margarine

Preheat oven to 400°F (200°C, or gas mark 6). In a saucepan, stir together the cornstarch and ¼ cup (60 ml) cold water until cornstarch is completely dissolved. Add 1 cup (200 g) sugar, lemon juice, and blackberries; combine gently. In a bowl, combine the flour, remaining sugar, and baking powder. Blend in the margarine until the mixture resembles coarse meal. Boil the remaining ¼ cup (60 ml) water and stir into the flour mixture until it just forms a dough. Transfer the blackberry mixture to a 1½-quart (1.4-L) baking dish. Drop spoonfuls of the dough carefully onto the berries, and bake the cobbler on a baking sheet in the middle of the oven for 20 to 25 minutes, or until the topping is golden.

Yield: 8 servings

Per serving: 280 calories (15% from fat, 4% from protein, 82% from carbohydrate); 3 g protein; 5 g total fat; 1 g saturated fat; 2 g monounsaturated fat; 1 g polyunsaturated fat; 59 g carbohydrate; 4 g fiber; 41 g sugar; 48 mg phosphorus; 61 mg calcium; 1 mg iron; 109 mg sodium; 142 mg potassium; 379 IU vitamin A; 52 mg ATE vitamin E; 16 mg vitamin C; 0 mg cholesterol; 83 g water

Crumb-Topped Cherry Cobbler

A quick and easy cobbler recipe, low in fat.

21-ounce (595-g) can cherry pie filling

2 tablespoons (28 g) unsalted margarine

½ cup (40 g) quick-cooking oats

¼ cup (30 g) flour

½ cup (100 g) sugar

2 tablespoons (16 g) chopped pecans

Preheat oven to 350°F (180°C, or gas mark 4). Spray a 2-quart (1.9-L) casserole dish with nonstick vegetable oil spray. Pour cherry pie filling into prepared dish. Mix margarine, oats, flour, sugar, and pecans. Crumble over cherry pie filling. Bake for 20 to 25 minutes.

Yield: 8 servings

Per serving: 205 calories (19% from fat, 3% from protein, 77% from carbohydrate); 2 g protein; 4 g total fat; 1 g saturated fat; 2 g monounsaturated fat; 1 g polyunsaturated fat; 40 g carbohydrate; 1 g fiber; 13 g sugar; 46 mg phosphorus; 15 mg calcium; 1 mg iron; 44 mg sodium; 111 mg potassium; 303 IU vitamin A; 34 mg ATE vitamin E; 3 mg vitamin C; 0 mg cholesterol; 55 g water

Red and Blue Berry Cobbler

With a little vanilla ice cream or whipped topping, you can have a quick red, white, and blue American dessert.

2 cups strawberries, halved

2 cups (290 g) blueberries

½ cup (120 ml) raspberry jam

2 tablespoons (8 g) cornstarch

1 cup (125 g) flour

2 tablespoons (26 g) plus ½ teaspoon (2 g) sugar, divided

2 teaspoons (9.2 g) baking powder

2 tablespoons (28 g) unsalted margarine

2 tablespoons (30 ml) skim milk

¼ cup (60 ml) egg substitute

Preheat oven to 425°F (220°C, or gas mark 7). Grease 1½-quart baking dish. In large bowl, combine berries, jam, and cornstarch. Mix gently. Spread in prepared baking dish. Bake for 15 to 20 minutes, or until berries begin to bubble. Meanwhile, in a large bowl, combine flour, 2 tablespoons (26 g) sugar, and baking powder. Mix well. With a pastry blender or two forks, cut in margarine until crumbly. In a small bowl, combine milk and egg substitute; beat well. Stir into flour mixture until stiff dough forms, adding additional milk if necessary. On a lightly floured surface, roll out dough to ½-inch (1.3-cm) thickness. With a cookie cutter, cut out stars or other shapes. Stir hot fruit mixture; top with dough cutouts. Sprinkle cutouts with remaining ½ teaspoon (2 g) sugar. Bake for 10 to 20 minutes, or until fruit bubbles around edges and biscuits are light golden brown

Yield: 8 servings

Per serving: 208 calories (15% from fat, 7% from protein, 78% from carbohydrate); 4 g protein; 4 g total fat; 1 g saturated fat; 2 g monounsaturated fat; 1 g polyunsaturated fat; 41 g carbohydrate; 2 g fiber; 19 g sugar; 87 mg phosphorus; 95 mg calcium; 1 mg iron; 215 mg sodium; 160 mg potassium; 211 IU vitamin A; 37 mg ATE vitamin E; 28 mg vitamin C; 0 mg cholesterol; 85 g water

Easy Apple Dessert

The microwave preparation makes this especially quick and easy.

½ cup (42 g) graham crackers, crushed

5 apples, cored and peeled

½ teaspoon (1.2 g) cinnamon

¼ teaspoon (0.5 g) allspice

¼ cup (40 g) raisins

⅓ cup (80 ml) apple juice

Spray a microwave-safe pie plate with nonstick vegetable oil spray. Spread the cracker crumbs in the plate. Cover with apple slices. Sprinkle with cinnamon and allspice. Spread raisins over the top. Pour juice over. Cover and microwave for 15 minutes.

Yield: 6 servings

Per serving: 108 calories (7% from fat, 3% from protein, 90% from carbohydrate); 1 g protein; 1 g total fat; 0 g saturated fat; 0 g monounsaturated fat; 0 g polyunsaturated fat; 26 g carbohydrate; 2 g fiber; 18 g sugar; 27 mg phosphorus; 14 mg calcium; 1 mg iron; 44 mg sodium; 175 mg potassium; 42 IU vitamin A; 0 mg ATE vitamin E; 5 mg vitamin C; 0 mg cholesterol; 106 g water

Apple Tapioca

My wife has been looking for the apple tapioca recipe that used to be on the Minute brand tapioca box for years. This is the closest one we've found so far, even though it's a slow cooker one rather than the original stovetop recipe.

4 cups (600 g) apples, peeled and sliced

½ cup (115 g) brown sugar

¾ teaspoon (1.7 g) cinnamon

2 tablespoons (1 g) tapioca

2 tablespoons (30 ml) lemon juice

1 cup (235 ml) boiling water

(continued on page 474)

In a medium bowl, toss apples with brown sugar, cinnamon, and tapioca until evenly coated. Place apples in a slow cooker. Pour lemon juice over the top. Pour in boiling water. Cook on high for 3 to 4 hours.

Yield: 4 servings

Per serving: 176 calories (1% from fat, 1% from protein, 98% from carbohydrate); 0 g protein; 0 g total fat; 0 g saturated fat; 0 g monounsaturated fat; 0 g polyunsaturated fat; 46 g carbohydrate; 2 g fiber; 38 g sugar; 19 mg phosphorus; 37 mg calcium; 1 mg iron; 13 mg sodium; 207 mg potassium; 44 IU vitamin A; 0 mg ATE vitamin E; 8 mg vitamin C; 0 mg cholesterol; 162 g water

Sweet Potato Pudding

Coconut milk gives this pudding its unique flavor. You should be able to find it in the baking aisle of many large supermarkets.

4 cups (1.3 kg) cooked and mashed sweet potatoes

¾ cup (150 g) sugar

½ cup (120 ml) egg substitute

½ cup (120 ml) coconut milk

1 tablespoon (15 ml) lime juice

¼ cup (60 ml) rum

½ teaspoon (2.3 g) baking powder

½ teaspoon (1.2 g) cinnamon

¼ cup (40 g) raisins

Preheat oven to 350°F (180°C, or gas mark 4). To mashed potatoes, alternate adding sugar and egg substitute, mixing well after each addition. Add coconut milk. Blend well. Mix in lime juice and rum. Mix well. Combine baking powder and cinnamon and add to potato mixture, along with raisins. Mix well. Pour mixture into a greased tube cake or Bundt pan and bake for 50 minutes, or until done.

Yield: 8 servings

Per serving: 271 calories (13% from fat, 7% from protein, 80% from carbohydrate); 5 g protein; 4 g total fat; 3 g saturated fat; 0 g monounsaturated fat; 0 g polyunsaturated fat; 53 g carbohydrate; 4 g fiber; 31 g sugar; 97 mg phosphorus; 77 mg calcium; 2 mg iron; 105 mg sodium; 502 mg potassium; 25871 IU vitamin A; 0 mg ATE vitamin E; 22 mg vitamin C; 0 mg cholesterol; 162 g water

Baked Apples

A simple dessert, but one that is sure to please. Serve with a little milk or low fat ice cream, if you desire.

6 apples

¼ cup (60 g) brown sugar

½ cup (80 g) raisins

½ teaspoon (1.2 g) cinnamon

¼ teaspoon (0.6 g) nutmeg

1 tablespoon (14 g) unsalted margarine

Preheat oven to 350°F (180°C, or gas mark 4). Wash and core apples; place in a shallow baking dish. Combine brown sugar, raisins, cinnamon, and nutmeg in a small bowl. Fill the center of each apple with brown sugar mixture and dot with ½ teaspoon (2 g) of the margarine. Add just enough water to the baking dish to cover the bottom; bake, uncovered, for 30 minutes, or until apples are tender, basting with juices occasionally.

Yield: 6 servings

Per serving: 155 calories (11% from fat, 2% from protein, 87% from carbohydrate); 1 g protein; 2 g total fat; 1 g saturated fat; 1 g monounsaturated fat; 0 g polyunsaturated fat; 36 g carbohydrate; 2 g fiber; 30 g sugar; 31 mg phosphorus; 25 mg calcium; 1 mg iron; 26 mg sodium; 253 mg potassium; 149 IU vitamin A; 23 mg ATE vitamin E; 6 mg vitamin C; 0 mg cholesterol; 114 g water

Honey Grilled Apples

A great finish to your grilled meal. And the best part is that it cooks while you're eating the rest of the meal.

4 apples

1 tablespoon (15 ml) honey

2 tablespoons (30 ml) lemon juice

1 tablespoon (14 g) unsalted margarine

Core apples and cut slices through the skin to make each apple resemble orange sections. Mix together the honey, lemon juice, and margarine. Spoon mixture into apple cores. Wrap apples in greased heavy-duty aluminum foil, fold up, and seal. Grill until tender, about 20 minutes.

Yield: 4 servings

Per serving: 104 calories (23% from fat, 2% from protein, 75% from carbohydrate); 0 g protein; 3 g total fat; 1 g saturated fat; 2 g monounsaturated fat; 0 g polyunsaturated fat; 21 g carbohydrate; 2 g fiber; 17 g sugar; 17 mg phosphorus; 10 mg calcium; 0 mg iron; 31 mg sodium; 131 mg potassium; 200 IU vitamin A; 34 mg ATE vitamin E; 9 mg vitamin C; 0 mg cholesterol; 119 g water

Apple Tart

This makes a nice apple pie–like dessert without the extra work and fat of the crust.

4 apples, peeled and sliced

1 teaspoon (2.3 g) cinnamon

½ cup (100 g) plus 1 tablespoon (13 g) sugar, divided

¼ cup (60 ml) egg substitute

¼ cup (56 g) unsalted margarine, melted

½ teaspoon (2.3 g) baking powder

1 cup (125 g) flour

Preheat oven to 350°F (180°C, or gas mark 4). Place the apples in a bowl. Add cinnamon and 1 tablespoon (13 g) sugar and mix well. Pour into a 10-inch (25-cm) glass pie plate coated with nonstick vegetable oil spray. In the same bowl beat the egg substitute. Add melted margarine, the remaining ½ cup (100 g) sugar, baking powder, and flour. Pour over apples. Bake for 40 to 45 minutes, or until golden brown and a wooden pick inserted in the center comes out clean.

Yield: 8 servings

Per serving: 200 calories (27% from fat, 5% from protein, 68% from carbohydrate); 3 g protein; 6 g total fat; 1 g saturated fat; 3 g monounsaturated fat; 2 g polyunsaturated fat; 35 g carbohydrate; 1 g fiber; 21 g sugar; 41 mg phosphorus; 31 mg calcium; 1 mg iron; 45 mg sodium; 104 mg potassium; 306 IU vitamin A; 54 mg ATE vitamin E; 3 mg vitamin C; 0 mg cholesterol; 65 g water

Reduced-Fat Pie Crust

This pie crust replaces the usual unhealthy fat of margarine or other solid shortening with oil. I actually find this pie crust easier to work with, and it seems to stay flaky through more handling.

⅓ cup (80 ml) canola oil

1⅓ cups (160 g) flour

2 tablespoons (30 ml) cold water

Add oil to flour and mix well with a fork. Sprinkle water over and mix well. With your hands, press dough into a ball and flatten. Roll between two pieces of waxed paper. Remove the top piece of waxed paper, invert over pie plate, and remove the other piece of waxed paper. Press into place. For pies that do not require a baked filling, bake at 400°F (200°C, or gas mark 6) for 12 to 15 minutes, or until lightly browned.

Yield: 8 servings

Per serving: 158 calories (54% from fat, 5% from protein, 40% from carbohydrate); 2 g protein; 10 g total fat; 1 g saturated fat; 6 g monounsaturated fat; 3 g polyunsaturated fat; 16 g carbohydrate; 1 g fiber; 0 g sugar; 23 mg phosphorus; 3 mg calcium; 1 mg iron; 1 mg sodium; 22 mg potassium; 0 IU vitamin A; 0 mg ATE vitamin E; 0 mg vitamin C; 0 mg cholesterol; 6 g water

Strawberry Pie Filling

This comes from my mother, who sent it to me when she heard we'd been berry picking.

3 cups (510 g) strawberries, sliced

one prepared pie crust

1 cup (235 ml) water

2 tablespoons (16 g) cornstarch

½ cup (100 g) sugar

one 3-ounce (85 g) box sugar-free strawberry gelatin

TIP *The sugar-free gelatin has quite a bit less sodium than the regular kind.*

Put sliced berries in pie crust. Combine water, cornstarch, and sugar. Heat until sugar is melted and mixture is clear. Stir in gelatin and pour over berries. Chill until set.

Yield: 8 servings

Per serving: 79 calories (2% from fat, 5% from protein, 93% from carbohydrate); 1 g protein; 0 g total fat; 0 g saturated fat; 0 g monounsaturated fat; 0 g polyunsaturated fat; 19 g carbohydrate; 1 g fiber; 15 g sugar; 30 mg phosphorus; 10 mg calcium; 0 mg iron; 4 mg sodium; 88 mg potassium; 7 IU vitamin A; 0 mg ATE vitamin E; 34 mg vitamin C; 0 mg cholesterol; 82 g water

Sweet Potato Pie

You'll be hard pressed to tell the difference between this and pumpkin pie.

For Crust:

⅓ cup (80 ml) canola oil

1⅓ cups (165 g) flour

2 tablespoons (30 ml) cold water

For Filling:

2 cups (650 g) cooked and mashed sweet potatoes

¾ cup (150 g) sugar

½ teaspoon (0.9 g) ground ginger

½ teaspoon (1.1 g) nutmeg

½ teaspoon (1.2 g) cinnamon

½ cup (120 ml) egg substitute

1½ cups (355 ml) fat-free evaporated milk

1 teaspoon (5 ml) vanilla

Preheat oven to 400°F (200°C, or gas mark 6).

To make the crust: Add oil to flour and mix well with a fork. Sprinkle water over and mix well. With your hands, press dough into a ball and flatten. Roll between two pieces of waxed paper. Remove the top piece of waxed paper, invert over pie plate, and remove the other piece of waxed paper. Press into place.

To make the filling: Combine sweet potatoes, sugar, ginger, nutmeg, and cinnamon in a mixing bowl. Add egg substitute and mix well. Add milk and vanilla and combine. Pour into pie shell. Bake for 45 to 50 minutes, or until knife inserted near the center comes out clean.

Yield: 8 servings

Per serving: 345 calories (26% from fat, 10% from protein, 64% from carbohydrate); 9 g protein; 10 g total fat; 1 g saturated fat; 3 g monounsaturated fat; 5 g polyunsaturated fat; 55 g carbohydrate; 3 g fiber; 29 g sugar; 162 mg phosphorus; 175 mg calcium; 2 mg iron; 106 mg sodium; 426 mg potassium; 13153 IU vitamin A; 57 mg ATE vitamin E; 11 mg vitamin C; 2 mg cholesterol; 123 g water

Meringue Cookies

These might just be the ultimate in fat-free cookies. They are such crunchy, sweet little nuggets that you won't even miss the fat.

3 egg whites

¼ teaspoon (0.8 g) cream of tartar

¾ cup (150 g) superfine sugar

TIP *If you can't find superfine sugar, process regular sugar in a blender or food processor until it is powdery.*

Preheat oven to 225°F (110°C). Beat egg whites with an electric mixer on medium speed until foamy. Add cream of tartar and continue beating egg whites until soft peaks form. Gradually add sugar, beating well after each addition. Mix until all the sugar has been added and the egg whites are stiff and glossy. Drop by the tablespoon onto a baking sheet. Bake for 1 hour. Switch off oven and leave cookies in the oven for 2 to 3 hours.

Yield: 24 servings

Per serving: 17 calories (1% from fat, 11% from protein, 89% from carbohydrate); 0 g protein; 0 g total fat; 0 g saturated fat; 0 g monounsaturated fat; 0 g polyunsaturated fat; 4 g carbohydrate; 0 g fiber; 4 g sugar; 1 mg phosphorus; 0 mg calcium; 0 mg iron; 7 mg sodium; 12 mg potassium; 0 IU vitamin A; 0 mg ATE vitamin E; 0 mg vitamin C; 0 mg cholesterol; 4 g water

Thumbprint Cookies

These are wonderful cookies that no one will ever know are low in fat.

¼ cup (56 g) unsalted margarine, softened

½ cup (115 g) packed brown sugar

¼ cup (60 ml) egg substitute

1 teaspoon (5 ml) vanilla

1½ cups (185 g) flour

6 tablespoons (90 ml) raspberry jam

Preheat oven to 350°F (180°C, or gas mark 4). In a large bowl, cream margarine and brown sugar together using an electric mixer. Add egg substitute and vanilla, and mix until blended. Gradually add flour and mix, forming a large ball. Form 1-inch (2.5-cm) balls and place them 1 inch (2.5-cm) apart on a baking sheet, making a deep thumbprint in the center of each. Bake for 10 minutes. Remove from oven. After 1 minute, place on a wire rack to cool. Place 1 teaspoon (5 ml) of raspberry jam in the center of each cookie.

Yield: 24 servings

Per serving: 79 calories (23% from fat, 6% from protein, 71% from carbohydrate); 1 g protein; 2 g total fat; 0 g saturated fat; 1 g monounsaturated fat; 1 g polyunsaturated fat; 14 g carbohydrate; 0 g fiber; 7 g sugar; 14 mg phosphorus; 8 mg calcium; 1 mg iron; 8 mg sodium; 38 mg potassium; 93 IU vitamin A; 18 mg ATE vitamin E; 0 mg vitamin C; 0 mg cholesterol; 5 g water

Chocolate Chip Cookies

These are lighter than most chocolate chip cookies, owing to the beaten egg white. But the taste will satisfy any cookie lover.

2¼ cups (280 g) flour

1 teaspoon (4.6 g) baking powder

¾ cup (170 g) brown sugar, packed

2 tablespoons (28 g) unsalted margarine

1 teaspoon (5 ml) vanilla extract

4 large egg whites, room temperature

½ cup (100 g) sugar

⅓ cup (80 ml) light corn syrup

1¼ cups (220 g) semisweet chocolate chips

Preheat oven to 375°F (190°C, or gas mark 5). Lightly spoon flour into dry measuring cups and level with a knife. Combine flour and baking powder. Beat brown sugar, margarine, and vanilla extract with an electric mixer on medium speed for 5 minutes, or until well-blended. Beat egg whites until foamy using clean, dry beaters. Gradually add sugar, 1 tablespoon at a time; beat until soft peaks form. Add corn syrup; beat until stiff peaks form. Fold brown sugar mixture into egg white mixture. Add flour mixture and stir to combine. Drop dough by level tablespoons 1 inch (2.5 cm) apart onto baking sheets coated with nonstick vegetable oil spray. Bake for 10 minutes, or until golden. Remove from the oven and let stand 5 minutes. Remove cookies from pans, and cool on wire racks. Store loosely covered.

Yield: 48 servings

Per serving: 76 calories (21% from fat, 6% from protein, 73% from carbohydrate); 1 g protein; 2 g total fat; 1 g saturated fat; 1 g monounsaturated fat; 0 g polyunsaturated fat; 15 g carbohydrate; 0 g fiber; 8 g sugar; 16 mg phosphorus; 12 mg calcium; 0 mg iron; 23 mg sodium; 39 mg potassium; 25 IU vitamin A; 6 mg ATE vitamin E; 0 mg vitamin C; 0 mg cholesterol; 4 g water

Low Fat Pumpkin Cookies

These cookies sometimes end up being eaten for breakfast around our house. They are almost like muffins, only smaller.

2 cups (250 g) flour

1 teaspoon (4.6 g) baking powder

½ teaspoon (2.3 g) baking soda

1 teaspoon (2.3 g) cinnamon

½ teaspoon (0.9 g) ground ginger

1 teaspoon (1.9 g) ground allspice

¼ cup (60 ml) canola oil

1 cup (225 g) packed brown sugar

6 tablespoons (90 ml) egg substitute

1 cup (225 g) canned or cooked fresh pumpkin

1 teaspoon (5 ml) vanilla

Preheat oven to 350°F (180°C, or gas mark 4). In a medium bowl, combine flour, baking powder, baking soda, cinnamon, ginger, and allspice. In a large bowl beat oil, brown sugar, egg substitute, pumpkin, and vanilla. Stir flour mixture into wet ingredients until just combined. Drop spoonfuls of dough about 1 inch (2.5 cm) apart on an ungreased baking sheet. Bake for 12 to 14 minutes.

Yield: 30 servings

Per serving: 81 calories (23% from fat, 7% from protein, 70% from carbohydrate); 1 g protein; 2 g total fat; 0 g saturated fat; 1 g monounsaturated fat; 1 g polyunsaturated fat; 14 g carbohydrate; 1 g fiber; 7 g sugar; 21 mg phosphorus; 22 mg calcium; 1 mg iron; 46 mg sodium; 63 mg potassium; 1283 IU vitamin A; 0 mg ATE vitamin E; 0 mg vitamin C; 0 mg cholesterol; 11 g water

Dessert Pizza

We've made this several times for kids' parties, and it is always one of the most popular items. By the way, grown-ups seem to like it too.

½ cup (112 g) unsalted margarine

¾ cup (170 g) brown sugar

1 egg yolk

1 teaspoon (5 ml) vanilla

1½ cups (185 g) flour

1¼ cups (220 g) chocolate chips

1½ cups (75 g) miniature marshmallows

½ cup (75 g) dry-roasted peanuts, chopped

Preheat oven to 350°F (180°C, or gas mark 4). Beat the margarine in a large mixing bowl with an electric mixer on medium-high speed for 30 seconds. Add brown sugar and beat until combined. Beat in egg yolk and vanilla until combined. Beat in as much of the flour as you can with the mixer. Stir in any remaining flour with a wooden spoon. Spread dough in a lightly greased 12-inch (30-cm) pizza pan. Bake for 25 minutes, or until golden. Sprinkle hot crust with the chocolate chips. Let stand for 1 to 2 minutes to soften. Spread chocolate over crust. Sprinkle with marshmallows and nuts. Bake for 3 minutes more or until marshmallows are puffed and beginning to brown. Cool in pan on a wire rack.

Yield: 16 servings

Per serving: 247 calories (44% from fat, 6% from protein, 50% from carbohydrate); 4 g protein; 12 g total fat; 4 g saturated fat; 6 g monounsaturated fat; 2 g polyunsaturated fat; 32 g carbohydrate; 1 g fiber; 20 g sugar; 67 mg phosphorus; 44 mg calcium; 1 mg iron; 81 mg sodium; 135 mg potassium; 338 IU vitamin A; 79 mg ATE vitamin E; 0 mg vitamin C; 16 mg cholesterol; 4 g water

Lemon Biscotti

These make a nice snack or a quick breakfast with whatever your favorite breakfast beverage is. The double baking gives them the traditional crunchiness.

2½ cups (310 g) flour

1 teaspoon (4.6 g) baking powder

1 teaspoon (4.6 g) baking soda

1 cup (235 ml) egg substitute

¾ cup (150 g) sugar

1 tablespoon (5 g) lemon zest

1½ teaspoons (8 ml) lemon juice

TIP *If you're not into dunking and want a softer cookie, reduce the second baking time to 10 minutes.*

Preheat oven to 325°F (170°C, or gas mark 3). Sift together flour, baking powder, and baking soda. In another bowl, beat egg substitute and sugar together, then beat in lemon zest and lemon juice. Add flour mixture to egg mixture and stir until well mixed. On a floured surface, knead dough for 2 minutes. Divide dough in half and shape into 2 logs, about 1 inch (2.5 cm) high and 4 inches (10 cm) wide. Bake for 30 minutes, or until golden brown. Remove from oven and cool. Reduce oven temperature to 300°F (150°C, or gas mark 2). Slice logs diagonally into ½-inch (1.3-cm) thick slices and put slices back on baking sheet, cut side down. Bake for another 20 minutes.

Yield: 24 servings

Per serving: 81 calories (5% from fat, 13% from protein, 82% from carbohydrate); 3 g protein; 0 g total fat; 0 g saturated fat; 0 g monounsaturated fat; 0 g polyunsaturated fat; 16 g carbohydrate; 0 g fiber; 6 g sugar; 31 mg phosphorus; 19 mg calcium; 1 mg iron; 92 mg sodium; 49 mg potassium; 38 IU vitamin A; 0 mg ATE vitamin E; 0 mg vitamin C; 0 mg cholesterol; 11 g water

22

Cooking Terms, Weights and Measurements, and Gadgets

Cooking Terms

Confused about a term I used in one of the recipes? Take a look at the list here and see if there might be an explanation. I've tried to include anything that I thought might raise a question.

Al dente

"To the tooth," in Italian. The pasta is cooked just enough to maintain a firm, chewy texture.

Bake

To cook in the oven. Food is cooked slowly with gentle heat, concentrating the flavor.

Baste

To brush or spoon liquid, fat, or juices over meat during roasting to add flavor and to prevent it from drying out.

Beat

To smoothen a mixture by briskly whipping or stirring it with a spoon, fork, wire whisk, rotary beater, or electric mixer.

Blend

To mix or fold two or more ingredients together to obtain equal distribution throughout the mixture.

Boil

To cook food in heated water or other liquid that is bubbling vigorously.

Braise

A cooking technique that requires browning meat in oil or other fat and then cooking slowly in liquid. The effect of braising is to tenderize the meat.

Bread

To coat the food with crumbs (usually with soft or dry bread crumbs), sometimes seasoned.

Broil

To cook food directly under the heat source.

Broth or Stock

A flavorful liquid made by gently cooking meat, seafood, or vegetables (and/or their by-products, such as bones and trimming), often with herbs and vegetables, in liquid (usually water).

Brown

A quick sautéing, pan/oven broiling, or grilling done either at the beginning or end of meal preparation, often to enhance flavor, texture, or visual appeal.

Brush

Using a pastry brush, to coat a food such as meat or bread with melted butter, glaze, or other liquid.

Chop

To cut into irregular pieces.

Coat

To evenly cover food with flour, crumbs, or a batter.

Combine

To blend two or more ingredients into a single mixture.

Core

To remove the inedible center of fruits such as pineapples.

Cream

To beat butter or margarine, with or without sugar, until light and fluffy. This process traps in air bubbles, later used to create height in cookies and cakes.

Cut In

To work margarine or butter into dry ingredients.

Dash

A measure approximately equal to $1/16$ teaspoon.

Deep Fry

To completely submerge the food in hot oil. A quick way to cook some food and, as a result, this method often seems to seal in the flavors of food better than any other technique.

Dice

To cut into cubes.

Direct Heat

Heat waves radiate from a source and travel directly to the item being heated with no conductor between them. Examples are grilling, broiling, and toasting.

Dough

Used primarily for cookies and breads. Dough is a mixture of shortening, flour, liquid, and other ingredients that maintains its shape when placed on a flat surface, although it will change shape once baked through the leavening process.

Dredge

To coat lightly and evenly with sugar or flour.

Dumpling

A batter or soft dough, which is formed into small mounds that are then steamed, poached, or simmered.

Dust

To sprinkle food lightly with spices, sugar, or flour for a light coating.

Fold

To cut and mix lightly with a spoon to keep as much air in the mixture as possible.

Fritter

Sweet or savory foods coated or mixed into batter, then deep-fried.

Fry

To cook food in hot oil, usually until a crisp brown crust forms.

Glaze

A liquid that gives an item a shiny surface. Examples are heated fruit jams or thinned chocolate.

Grease

To coat a pan or skillet with a thin layer of oil.

Grill

To cook over a heat source (traditionally over wood coals, although gas grills are becoming more popular) in the open air.

Grind

To mechanically cut a food into small pieces.

Hull

To remove the leafy parts of soft fruits such as strawberries or blackberries.

Knead

To work dough with the heels of your hands in a pressing and folding motion until it becomes smooth and elastic.

Marinate

To combine food with aromatic ingredients to add flavor.

Mince

To chop food into tiny, irregular pieces.

Mix

To beat or stir two or more foods together until they are thoroughly combined.

Pan-fry

To cook in a hot pan with small amount of hot oil, butter, or other fat, turning the food over once or twice.

Poach

Simmering in a liquid.

Pot Roast

A large piece of meat, usually browned in fat, cooked in a covered pan.

Purée

Food that has been mashed or sieved.

Reduce

To cook liquids down so that some of the water they contain evaporates.

Roast

To cook uncovered in the oven.

Sauté

To cook with a small amount of hot oil, butter, or other fat, tossing the food around over high heat.

Sear

To brown a food quickly on all sides using high heat to seal in the juices.

Shred

To cut into fine strips.

Simmer

To cook slowly in a liquid over low heat.

Skim

To remove the surface layer (of impurities, scum, or fat) from liquids such as stocks and jams while cooking. This is usually done with a flat, slotted spoon.

Smoke

To expose foods to wood smoke to enhance their flavor and help preserve and/or evenly cook them.

Steam

To cook in steam by suspending foods over boiling water in a steamer or covered pot.

Stew

To cook food in liquid for a long time until tender, usually in a covered pot.

Stir

To mix ingredients with a utensil.

Stir-fry

To cook quickly over high heat with a small amount of oil by constantly stirring. This technique often employs a wok.

Toss

To mix ingredients lightly by lifting and dropping them using two utensils.

Whip

To beat an item to incorporate air, augment volume, and add substance.

Zest

The thin, brightly colored outer part of the rind of citrus fruits. It contains volatile oils and is used as a flavoring.

Weights and Measurements

First of all, here's a quick refresher on U.S. measurements.

3 teaspoons = 1 tablespoon

2 tablespoons = 1 fluid ounce

4 tablespoons = 2 fluid ounces = ¼ cup

5⅓ tablespoons = 16 teaspoons = ⅓ cup

8 tablespoons = 4 fluid ounces = ½ cup

16 tablespoons = 8 fluid ounces = 1 cup

2 cups = 1 pint

4 cups = 2 pints = 1 quart

16 cups = 8 pints = 4 quarts = 1 gallon

Metric Conversions

One of the questions that my newsletter readers have raised is whether I could also publish recipes with metric measurements. This would certainly be a good idea, since most of the world uses the metric system. Unfortunately, the software I use doesn't have a way to automatically convert from U.S. to metric measurements. There are some measurements for which I can give you an easy conversion formula, such as Fahrenheit to Celsius oven temperatures. Other things are not so easy. The information below is intended to be helpful to those readers who use the metric system of weights and measures.

Measurements of Liquid Volume

The following measures are approximate but close enough for most, if not all, of the recipes in this book.

1 quart = 1 liter
1 cup = 235 milliliters
¾ cup = 180 milliliters
½ cup = 120 milliliters
⅓ cup = 80 milliliters
¼ cup = 60 milliliters
1 fluid ounce = 28 milliliters
1 tablespoon = 15 milliliters
1 teaspoon = 5 milliliters

Measurements of Weight

Much of the world measures dry ingredients by weight, rather than volume, as is done in the United States. There is no easy conversion for this, since each item is different. However, the following conversions may be useful.

1 ounce = 28 grams
1 pound = 455 grams (about half a kilo)

Oven Temperatures

Finally, we come to one that is relatively straightforward: the Fahrenheit to Celsius conversion.

100°F = 38°C	350°F = 180°C
150°F = 66°C	375°F = 190°C
200°F = 95°C	400°F = 200°C
225°F = 110°C	425°F = 220°C
250°F = 120°C	450°F = 230°C
275°F = 140°C	475°F = 240°C
300°F = 150°C	500°F = 250°C
325°F = 170°C	

Gadgets

The following are some of the tools that I use in cooking. Some are used very often and some very seldom, but all help make things a little easier or quicker. Why are some things listed here and others not? No reason except that most of these are things I considered a little less standard than a stove, oven, grill, and mixer.

Blender

Okay, so everyone has a blender. And it's a handy little tool for blending and puréeing things. I don't really think I need to say any more about that.

Bread Machine

When I went on a low sodium diet, I discovered that one of the biggest single changes that you can make to reduce your sodium intake is to make your own bread. Most commercial bread has well over 100 mg per slice. Many rolls and specialty breads are in the 300 to 400 mg range. A bread machine can reduce the amount of effort required to make your own bread to a manageable level. It takes, at most, 10 minutes to load it and turn it on. You can even set it on a timer to have your house filled with the aroma of fresh bread when you come home. Even if you're not watching your sodium, there is nothing like the smell of bread baking and the taste right out of the "oven."

Canning Kettle

If you are planning on making batches of things like pickles and salsa in volume so you don't have to go through the process every couple of weeks, then you are going to need a way to preserve things. Most items can be frozen, of course, if that is your preference. But some things just seem to me to work better in jars. What you need is a kettle big enough to make sure the jars can be covered by water when being processed in a boiling water bath. There are also racks to sit the jars in and special tongs to make lifting them in and out of the water easier. I've had a porcelain covered kettle I use for this purpose for many years, and it also doubled as a stockpot before I got the one I describe below. It's better for canning than for soup because the relatively thin walls allow the water to heat faster (and the soup to burn).

Deep Fryer

Obviously, if you are watching your fat intake, this should not be one of your most often-used appliances. I don't use it nearly as often as I used to, but it still occupies a place in the appliance garage in the corner of the kitchen counter. It's a Fry Daddy, big enough to cook a batch of fries or fish for 3 to 4 people at a time.

Food Processor

I'm a real latecomer to the food processor world. It always seemed like a nice thing to have, but something I could easily do without. We bought one to help shred meat and other things for my wife's mother, who was having some difficulty swallowing large chunks of food. I use it now all the time to grind bread into crumbs or chop the peppers and onions that seem to go into at least three meals a week. It's a low-end model that doesn't have the power to grind meat or perform some of the heavier tasks, but I've discovered it's a real time-saver for a number of things.

Contact Grill

The George Foreman models are the most popular example of this item. My son's girlfriend gave me this for Christmas a few years ago. (And he didn't have the good sense to hang onto her . . . but that's a different story.) I use it fairly often. When we built our house, we included a cooktop with a built-in grill, and for years we used that regularly. We still use it for some things—I much prefer the way it does burgers or steak when it's too cold to grill them outside—but it's difficult to clean and doesn't do nearly as nice a job as the contact grill with foods like grilled vegetables and fish. And the design allows the fat to drain away, giving you a healthier, lower-fat meal.

Grinder

Many years ago we bought a multifunction appliance that included a stand mixer, blender (the one we still use), food chopper, and a grinder attachment. The grinder was never a big deal that got any use until I started experimenting with sausage recipes. Since then I've discovered that grinding your own meat can save you both money and fat. Buying a beef or pork roast on sale, trimming it of most of the fat, and grinding it yourself can give you hamburger or sausage meat that is well over 90% lean and still less expensive than the fattier stuff you buy at the store. So now the grinder gets fairly regular use.

Hand Chopper

My daughter got this gem in North Carolina while she was in school there. It was from one of those guys with the podium and the auctioneer's delivery and the extra free gifts if you buy it within the next 10 minutes. Neither of us has ever seen one like it since. The food processor has taken over some of its work, but it still does a great job chopping things like onions as fine as you could want without liquefying them.

Pasta Maker

I bought this toy after seeing it on a Sunday morning TV infomercial. It's a genuine "As Seen on TV" special, but try not to hold that against it. Unlike the pasta cutters that merely slice rolled dough into flat noodles, this one mixes the whole mess then extrudes it through dies with various shaped holes in them. The recipes say you can use any kind of flour, but I've found that buying the semolina flour that is traditionally used for pasta gives you dough that's easier to work with, as well as better texture and flavor. The characterization of it as a "toy" is pretty accurate. There aren't really any nutritional advantages over store-bought pasta. If you buy the semolina, the cost is probably about the same as some of the more expensive imported pasta. But it's fun to play with, makes a great conversation piece, and the pasta tastes good.

Salad Shooter

We seem to end up with a lot of these gadgets, don't we? This is another one that's been around for a while, but it's still my favorite implement for shredding potatoes for hash browns or cabbage for coleslaw.

Sausage Stuffer

This is really an addition to the grinder that was part of the multifunction appliance I described above. I found it at an online appliance repair site. It is really just a series of different sized tubes that fit on the end of the grinder to stuff your ground meat into casings. I do this occasionally to make link sausage, but most of the time I just make patties or bulk sausage.

Slicer

This was a close-out floor model that I bought years ago. Before going on the low sodium diet I used to buy deli meat in bulk and slice it myself. Now I most often use it to slice a roast or smoked piece of meat for sandwiches.

Slow Cooker

No kitchen should be without one.

Smoker

This was another pre-diet purchase that has been used even more since. I started with one that originally used charcoal. Then I bought an add-on electric heat source for it that works a lot better in cold weather. Last year the family gave me a fancy electric one that seals like an oven and has a thermostat to hold the temperature. Not only do I like the way it does ribs and other traditional smoked foods, but we also use it fairly regularly to smoke a beef or pork roast or turkey breast to use for sandwiches.

Springform Pan

A round, straight-sided pan. The sides are formed into a hoop that can be unclasped and detached from its base.

Steamer (Rice Cooker)

I use this primarily for cooking rice, but it really does a great job steaming vegetables too. It does make excellent rice, perfect every time. So I guess the bottom line is that those of you who have trouble making rice, like me (probably because, like me, you can't follow the instructions not to peek under the lid while the rice is cooking), should consider getting one of these.

Stockpot

The key here is to spend the extra money to get a heavy-gauge one (another thing I eventually learned from personal experience). The lighter-weight ones not only will dent and not sit level on the stove, but they will burn just about everything you put in them. Mine also has a heavy glass lid that seals the moisture in well.

Turbocooker

Another infomercial sale. It is a large dome-lidded fry pan with racks that fit inside it. You can buy them at many stores too, but mine is the "plus" model that has two steamer racks and a timer. It really will cook a whole dinner quickly, "steam frying" the main course and steaming one or two more items. The only bad news is most of the recipes involve additions and changes every few minutes, so even if you only take 30 minutes to make dinner, you spend that whole time at the stove.

Waffle maker

We don't use this often, but it makes a nice change of pace for breakfast or dinner.

Wok

A round-bottomed pan popular in Asian cooking.

Acknowledgments

Putting together a book like this requires a lot of help. It would be impossible to list everyone by name, but I'd like to recognize a few special people.

My wife Ginger and children Tori, Ted, and Ben have spent the last nine years "testing" these and many other recipes. Over this time they've learned that healthy food can taste good, but they've also shared in the failures. Often it takes several tries to get a recipe that you are happy with. Some of the early versions are less of a pleasure to eat, but eat them they did.

All of the people in the Quayside Publishing Group at Fair Winds Press have been great. Their expertise at editing and producing great books shows in the final product. I'd like to mention specifically Sr. Acquisitions Editor Jill Alexander, who first approached me about doing this book and has shepherded it through the process of creation and publication.

The subscribers of my own LowSodiumCooking.com newsletter have inspired me to keep doing this for more than eight years, many silently by continuing to subscribe, but many others in a more active manner. Their comments, recipe submissions, and the heartwarming stories about how the recipes have made a difference in their lives are what continue to make it worth doing.

About the Author

After being diagnosed with congestive heart failure, Dick Logue threw himself into the process of creating healthy versions of his favorite recipes. A cook since the age of twelve, Logue grows his own vegetables, bakes his own bread, and cans a variety of foods. He currently has a website, www.lowsodiumcooking.com, and his weekly online newsletter, complete with the latest recipes and tips, is read by more than 17,000 people. He lives on a little farm in the woods of southern Maryland with his wife, Ginger, two of their three children, and an assortment of animals.

Index

soluble fiber, 13, 15, 19, 21, 388–414

soups, 100, 131–132, 181, 186, 208–218, 220, 223, 226, 306–307, 341, 383, 389–394. *See also* chili; stews

sour cream, 16, 53

Southern Pork Chops, 193–194

Southern-Style Greens, 289

South-of-the-Border Pie, 336

soy, 13, 18, 19. *See also* soy sauce; tofu

soybeans, 19

soy oil, 18

soy sauce, 30–31, 122

spaghetti, 89–90, 149, 287, 367, 376

spaghetti squash, 287

Spaghetti with Fish, 125

Spaghetti with Italian Vegetables, 89–90

spice blends, 22, 36, 37, 38, 160

spices, 143. *See also* curries; spice blends; *specific spices*

Spicy Baked French Fries, 263

Spicy Snack Mix, 60

Spicy Sweet Potatoes, 295

spinach, 52, 90–91, 93–94, 220, 248, 267, 288, 314, 365

Spinach and Artichoke Dip, 52

Spinach and Mushroom Stir-Fry, 365

Spinach Salad, 248

Spinach-Stuffed Tomatoes, 93–94

split peas, 393

Split Pea Soup, 393

spreads, 51, 55. *See also* dips

squash, 86, 137, 232, 284, 287, 294–295, 306. *See also* pumpkin; zucchini
butternut, 294–295, 306
yellow, 137, 284

Squash and Rice Bake, 86

Steak and Vegetable Stir-Fry, 356

Steak Bites, 45

Steak Cacciatore, 176–177

Steak Chili, 231

stews, 100, 129–130, 182–183, 185, 203, 208, 215–216, 219, 221–222, 224–225, 227, 342

sticky buns, 436

Stir-Fried Pork and Cabbage, 197

Stir-Fried Pork with Vegetables, 360

stir-fries, 98, 197, 346, 347–348, 356, 357, 360, 365

stratas, 107

strawberries, 78, 79, 80, 419, 420, 421, 478

Strawberry Muffins, 420

Strawberry Pie Filling, 478

Strawberry Smoothie, 79

Streusel Muffins, 429

Stuffed Banana Peppers, 172

Stuffed Pork Chops, 190–191

Stuffed Pork Roast, 199–200

subs, 101

Sun-Dried Tomato Alfredo Sauce, 319

sun-dried tomatoes, 40–41, 237, 270, 297, 305, 319, 453–454, 461

Sun-Dried Tomato Rice, 305

Sun-Dried Tomato Vinaigrette, 237

Sun-Dried Tomato Wheat Rolls, 461

sunflower-seed oil, 18

Swedish Salmon Stew, 129

Sweet-and-Sour Chicken, 353

Sweet-and-Sour Fish, 362

Sweet-and-Sour Pork, 359

sweet peppers. *See* banana peppers; *specific bell peppers*

Sweet Potatoes, 264

sweet potatoes, 294–295, 474–475, 479

Sweet Potatoes, Squash, and Apples, 294–295

Sweet Potato Fries, 264

Sweet Potato Pie, 479

Sweet Potato Pudding, 474–475

sweets, 464–485

Sweet Spiced Nuts, 62

Swiss cheese, 101, 299

swordfish, 109, 123

Szechuan Chicken, 348–349

T

Taco Chicken Wings, 44

Taco Quiche, 338

tacos, 325, 338

tapioca, 473–474

tarts, 476–477

Terikayi Fish, 122

Teriyaki Salmon, 361

teriyaki sauce, 31–32

Texas Caviar, 47

Y

Z